THE TWO TRUTHS DEBATE

THE TWO TRUTHS DEBATE

Tsongkhapa and Gorampa on the Middle Way

Sonam Thakchoe

Foreword by Jay L. Garfield

Wisdom Publications • Boston

Wisdom Publications, Inc.
199 Elm Street
Somerville MA 02144 USA
www.wisdompubs.org

Library of Congress Cataloging-in-Publication Data
Thakchoe, Sonam.
The two truths debate : Tsongkhapa and Gorampa on the middle way / Sonam Thakchoe ; foreword by Jay L. Garfield.
p. cm.
Includes bibliographical references.
ISBN 0-86171-501-2 (pbk. : alk. paper)
1. Truth—Religious aspects—Buddhism. 2. Tson-kha-pa Blo-bzan-grags-pa, 1357-1419. 3. Go-rams-pa Bsod-nams-sen-ge, 1429-1489. 4. Madhyamika (Buddhism) 5. Buddhism—China—Tibet—Doctrines. I. Title.
BQ4255.T47 2007
294.3'420423—dc22
2007035443

ISBN 0-86171-501-2
11 10 09 08 07
5 4 3 2 1

Cover design by Gina Phelan and Dan Tesser
Cover images of Tsongkhapa and Gorampa come from the collection of the Rubin Museum of Art. Our many thanks to them.
Interior design by Gopa & Ted2, Inc. Set in Diacritical Garamond 10.5/13 pt.

Wisdom Publications' books are printed on acid-free paper and meet the guidelines for permanence and durability of the Committee for Production Guidelines for Book Longevity of the Council on Library Resources.

Printed in the United States of America.

This book was produced with Environmental Mindfulness. We have elected to print this title on 50% PCW recycled paper. As a result, we have saved the following resources: 23 trees, 16 million BTUs of energy, 2,060 lbs. of greenhouse gases, 8,549 gallons of water, and 1,098 lbs. of solid waste. For more information, please visit our website, www.wisdompubs.org

Contents

Publisher's Acknowledgement

The publisher gratefully acknowledges the generous help of the Hershey Family Foundation in sponsoring the printing of this book.

Foreword

The tendency of many students and even scholars of Buddhist philosophy to fasten onto a single philosopher or school of thought when approaching Tibetan philosophy leads to the misapprehension that Tibetan philosophy is uniform, that there is a single Tibetan view about, or approach to, every problem in Buddhist philosophy. Nothing could be further from the truth. The Tibetan scholastic adage, "where you find agreement, there you find fools," reflects the diversity of this tradition and its commitment to the prosecution of philosophical debates and the juxtaposition of alternative viewpoints. There is no more dramatic instance of this diversity than the debate presented in this volume.

Among Tibetan philosophers there is near unanimity that Madhyamaka, the Middle Way philosophy that originates in the work of Nāgārjuna, represents the apex of Indian Buddhist philosophical thought. Two of Tibet's greatest Madhyamaka exegetes are Tsongkhapa (1357–1419), founder of the Gelug order, and Gorampa (1429–89), a major figure in the Sakya order. While Tsongkhapa and Gorampa agree that Nāgārjuna's philosophical outlook is the highest expression of Buddhist insight, and that Candrakārti is his definitive Indian commentator, their agreement ends there.

Central to Nāgārjuna's philosophical system is his distinction between the two truths—conventional and ultimate—and his complex account of their relationship. Dr. Sonam Thakchoe is correct to focus on this disagreement as an entrée into the divergent outlooks of these two enormously influential and subtle philosophers. The heart of Madhyamaka philosophy is the doctrine of the two truths, and to disagree about this doctrine is to disagree about the very nature of the philosophical theory.

Dr. Thakchoe is also correct to focus on the views of Gorampa and Tsongkhapa for his entrée into the complex Tibetan debates about the interpretation of Madhyamaka. Tsongkhapa develops the most radical defense of the importance and robust reality of the conventional as one can find in Tibetan philosophy, and does so with great ingenuity, scholarship, and subtlety. Gorampa is a match for Tsongkhapa in scholarship and acumen, and develops a radical critique of the reality and importance of the conventional.

The dispute is both ontological and epistemological. Tsongkhapa argues for the ontological identity of the two truths, despite their conceptual distinctness. Gorampa defends the view that ontologically the two truths are entirely distinct—one real, the other unreal. Tsongkhapa defends the view that there are standards of correctness for cognitive engagement with the conventional; Gorampa that all engagement with the conventional is delusive, and that there can be no sense in which cognitive engagement with the conventional can be described as correct. Dr. Thakchoe patiently takes the reader through these complex issues as well as the considerations that drive Tsongkhapa and Gorampa in such different directions from such similar starting points.

Dr. Thakchoe's exploration of Nāgārjuna's philosophy and its development through the Indian and Tibetan commentarial tradition is exceptionally clear and precise. He demonstrates to us that it is both genuinely difficult to work out the details and ramifications of the doctrine of the two truths and genuinely rewarding to do so. He shows that Buddhist philosophical inquiry, as prosecuted in India and in Tibet, can be prosecuted in English today with great profit.

Dr. Thakchoe is eminently qualified for this task. He has a sound traditional Tibetan education, with undergraduate and postgraduate degrees from the Central Institute of Higher Tibetan Studies in India, where he was taught by some of the finest Tibetan scholars of Madhyamaka. He holds the Ph.D. from the University of Tasmania, where he received a fine training in Western philosophy. He is a native speaker of Tibetan with an excellent sense of philosophical English. This volume reflects this remarkable range of training and competence, replete with analyses grounded in extraordinary textual scholarship and nuanced familiarity with Tibetan interpretative traditions, powerfully argued, and containing elegant and felicitous translations and commentary on translation practice.

Dr. Thakchoe demonstrates that the tradition of philosophical debate brought from India to Tibet is alive and well in the West. *The Two Truths Debate* is an invaluable resource for the Buddhist Studies community and for all those interested in Indian and Tibetan Buddhist philosophy.

Jay L. Garfield

Acknowledgments

I DEDICATE THIS BOOK to my beloved parents, my late father, Changrawa Sonam Tashi, and my mother, Changrawa Youdon. Their unfailing love and vision has been the source of inspiration behind the work.

This book had its origins in a dissertation I submitted to fulfill my doctoral degree at the University of Tasmania in 2002. The manuscript has undergone significant changes, both in content and style, as a result of feedback from the examiners and the reviewers, though the substance of my thesis remains. I am thankful to Wisdom Publications for publishing this book, with special thanks to David Kittelstrom, Senior Editor, for his guidance and for his commitment to this work.

This book is a product of cumulative efforts by many individuals, and I gratefully acknowledge the contributions each has made toward its successful completion. I owe my greatest gratitude to my teachers and mentors at the Central Institute of Higher Tibetan Studies (CIHTS): the Ven. Prof. Samdhong Rinpoche (current Prime Minister of the Tibetan Government-in-Exile), the Ven. Prof. Geshe Yeshe Thabkhay, Prof. Sempa Dorjee, the Ven. Prof. Geshe Jigme Dawa (former abbot of the Gelugpa Students' Welfare Committee), the Ven. Prof. Geshe Losang Gyatso (current abbot of the Drepung Loselling Monastic University, South India), Prof. Geshe Ngawang Samten (current director and Vice Chancellor of CIHTS), Prof. Phuntsok Dhondup, Prof. Wangchuk Dorjee Negi, Prof. Acharya Lobsang Norbu Shastri (Head of the Translation Unit), the Ven. Sherab Gyatso (former abbot of the Sakya Students' Welfare Committee), and the Ven. Dorje Tsering (former abbot of the Nyingmapa Students' Welfare Committee)—they truly opened my eyes and awakened my interest in the field of Buddhist philosophy during my nine years of intensive studies at CIHTS. I also owe boundless gratitude to Ācārya S.N. Goenka, a vipassanā yogi and teacher, who helped me understand the practical, psychological, and ethical dimensions of the Buddhadharma.

Among those directly involved in making this project a success, I am most indebted to my two distinguished academic mentors: Professor Jay. L. Garfield, Smith College, and Professor Jeffrey Malpas, University of Tasmania. Professor Garfield introduced me to Western philosophy, spending countless hours reading my drafts, providing detailed and invaluable criticisms and comments, and immeasurable guidance on philosophical, stylistic, syntactic, and grammatical matters. I am deeply grateful to Professor Malpas for his comments and guidance on structural and grammatical issues and, in particular, for his time and energy in editing my penultimate draft. The fluency and coherence of the book are largely due to Prof. Malpas' help. I also gratefully acknowledge very useful comments from Professor Guy Newland, Central Michigan University, and Professor Gareth Sparham, University of Michigan—two examiners of my Ph.D. dissertation. I also express my sincere gratitude to Professor Tom Tillemans, University of Lausanne, and Professor José Cabezón, University of California–Santa Barbara, whose invaluable comments and criticisms improved the final presentation.

My sincere thanks also go to Janet Counsell, the coordinator of ELSIS, English Language Centre, University of Tasmania, for her enormous patience and goodwill in editing my eccentric Indo-Tibetan English. Her contributions to this project have been crucial. I am also deeply thankful to Toni Byers, Dr. Angela Rosier, Dr. Pauline Enright, and Tessa Saunders for their careful proofreading, pointing out many typographical and punctuation errors. Thanks to Dr. Angela Rosier, Dr. Cynthia Townley, Dr. Pauline Enright, Dr. Mitch Parsell, Eliza Goddard, Matthew Piscioneri, Elidh St. John, Bruce Wilson, Tessa Saunders, Paul Cutler, Paul McNamara, Graham Wood, and other graduate students and staff of the School of Philosophy for their highly useful feedback.

I also owe an enormous debt to my friends at the Central Institute of Higher Tibetan Studies. I appreciate the valuable assistance I received from the CIHTS library staff, particularly from Sonam Tsewang-la and Penpa Tsering-la, both of whom made a large corpus of relevant materials available for my project. I am also thankful to my good friends, Tenzin Sangmo-la, Tsewang Dorjee-la, Sangay Dolma-la, and my cousin Kalsang Norbu-la, who were particularly helpful in finding relevant works from the CIHTS library and shipping them to me in Tasmania. Without their support, my research in Tasmania would have been severely hampered. I am also grateful to Karma and Roselin Phuntsok for allowing me to use their collections.

In terms of financial contributions I received to undertake this research,

I gratefully acknowledge the crucial support from the University of Tasmania for granting me a University of Tasmania International Scholarship under the Tasmania-Tibet Partnership Program. I am also grateful to Jane Franklin Hall, especially to its principal, Dr. David Daintree, for his enormous generosity and hospitality. My thanks also goes to Master Wang Xin-De, the Patriarch Master of the Holy Tantra Jin-Gang-Dhyana Buddhism, for his generous financial support.

I am also profoundly thankful to my Tasmanian friends, in particular David Chambers, and Tania Chambers, Toni, and Jacki. David and Tania supported me in many ways, and extended an open invitation to their home, making me feel part of their family. I thank them from the depths of my heart. I am also deeply thankful to Jennifer Dunbabin, Sandra Kellet, Irene Sawford, Eliza Goddard, Diane Smith, Glen Barwick, David McGregor, Nigel Curtain Smith, and Dr. Anna Alomes for their invaluable logistical, technical, and other support.

Technical Notes

SINCE THE RELEVANT materials on Tsongkhapa and Gorampa are largely available in Tibetan only, most representations of their writings here are my own translations. Except in a few instances where the Tibetan texts are too long to be cited, the Tibetan text appears in the notes.

Throughout this book Sanskrit words are transliterated, while Tibetan proper names use phonetic spellings with transliteration given only at their first occurrence. The first and not the root letter is capitalized in transliterated proper names and texts (e.g., *Rgyal mtshan* not *rGyal mtshan*). Tibetan text titles are translated in parentheses at their first appearance and subsequently appear only in Tibetan. Tibetan convention commonly addresses works by simplified titles, and these abbreviated forms are used here. Complete titles for Tibetan works can be found in the list of abbreviations and at their first reference in the notes.

For referencing Pāli sources, I have mostly followed the convention of the Access to Insight website: www.accesstoinsight.org/abbrev.html.

Introduction

The buddhas' teachings of the Dharma is based on two truths:
a truth of worldly conventions and an ultimate truth.
—Nāgārjuna, *Mūlamadhyamakakārikā* 24:8

The Objectives and Scope of this Book

THE PRIMARY OBJECTIVE of this book is to interrogate the age-old controversy over the two truths doctrine (Tib. *bden pa gnyis;* Skt. *satyadvaya*) and to demonstrate that the Tibetan Prāsaṅgika Madhyamaka tradition offers at least two radically distinct epistemological, ontological, and soteriological approaches concerning the doctrine, with a view to explaining the nature of the distinction between those accounts.[1] Given the widespread tendency to construe the Tibetan Prāsaṅgika as a single homogeneous system, the book not only has implications for the understanding of the two figures that are the focus of discussion, but also for the broader understanding of Tibetan philosophy in general.[2]

The two approaches at issue here are those associated with the Tibetan Mādhyamikas[3] Tsongkhapa Lobsang Dragpa (Tsong kha pa Blo bzang grags pa, 1357–1419) and Gorampa Sönam Sengé (Go rams pa Bsod nams seng ge, 1429–89). The book is a comparative analysis of their conceptions of the two truths—their respective understandings of the definitions of the two truths, the relationship between the two truths, the ontological status of the two truths, the epistemic resources for accessing the two truths, the problems concerning the limits of language and thought as these relate to the notion of ultimate truth, the different ways of realizing ultimate truth, and, finally, the nature and possibility of knowledge of the two truths and the implications of such knowledge for the attainment of enlightenment. Through a comparative analysis of Tsongkhapa and Gorampa on these issues, the manuscript demonstrates where, why, and how the two Tibetan readings of the original Indian sources exhibit distinct and independent characters.

I have not set out to adjudicate which of the two readings gets the Indian sources right, but I do often juxtapose the two readings against some of the more obvious assertions made by the founding fathers of the tradition—such as the Buddha,[4] Nāgārjuna (ca. 150–250 C.E.),[5] Āryadeva (ca. 170–270 C.E.),[6] and Candrakīrti (ca. 570–650 C.E.),[7] giving readers the opportunity to draw their own conclusions.

Chapter 1 of this book compares Tsongkhapa's and Gorampa's responses to three principal questions: What is divided into the two truths? How are they related? Are there two actual truths or just one truth? Examining his works in light of these questions reveals Tsongkhapa as a pluralist. For him the two truths are actual truths. Conventional truth and ultimate truth are mutually interlocking, with no hierarchical relation between them. Both truths are equal in their ontological, epistemological, and even soteriological importance. Gorampa, on the other hand, is a monist. Conventional truth, according to him, is not actual truth. Ultimate truth alone is the truth. Thus the two truths are distinct, hierarchically ordered, and mutually exclusive. Ultimate truth precedes conventional truth in its ontological, epistemological, and soteriological importance.

Chapter 2 compares the two Prāsaṅgika Mādhyamikas' interpretations of how the two truths are defined. For Tsongkhapa, definitions of the two truths are based on the two natures that are verified by, respectively, empirically valid and ultimately valid cognition. Tsongkhapa, however, does not simply reduce the two truths to these two modes of cognition; ultimate truth in particular, he says, cannot be metaphysically unconditioned—reducible to an independent and *ultimate* mode of cognition—even though it may be unconditioned epistemologically. For Gorampa, ignorance and wisdom respectively determine the character, and therefore the definition, of each of the two truths. The two truths are thus underlaid by, and reducible to, two conflicting modes of cognition. Ultimate truth is therefore unconditioned metaphysically—it is defined by an independent and *ultimate* mode of cognition.

Chapter 3 compares Tsongkhapa's and Gorampa's positions on the limits of language and conceptual thought. For Tsongkhapa ultimate truth is, to a certain extent, both effable and conceptually knowable, while for Gorampa it is ineffable and conceptually unknowable. Tsongkhapa argues for the possibility of valid conceptual cognition, therefore, and Gorampa argues against it.

Chapter 4 compares Tsongkhapa and Gorampa on the three principal modes of knowing ultimate truth: by way of not seeing it; by way of transcending conceptual elaborations; and by way of ascending to nonduality. Tsongkhapa mobilizes all three of these modes of knowing ultimate truth to establish that empirically given phenomena (those accessible to the senses) are without essence and thus dependently arisen.[8] He then proceeds to argue that transcendent knowledge is equivalent to knowledge of empirical phenomena in being dependently arisen. Gorampa, on the other hand, mobilizes the three modes of knowing ultimate truth as epistemological scaffolding that allows one to ascend to a metaphysical nonduality. Transcendent knowledge, he argues, is utterly distinct from conventional knowledge. Thus the knowledge of empirically given phenomena as dependently arisen and the knowledge of transcendent ultimate truth as nondual must be distinct and contradictory.

The fifth chapter looks at the unique features of enlightened knowledge—the way a buddha's mind works in relation to the two truths. This is where the disagreement between Tsongkhapa and Gorampa reaches its climax. Tsongkhapa argues that enlightenment is the perfection of knowledge of empirically given phenomena from both empirical and ultimate standpoints. Thus the two truths—and their two modes of knowing—are united in a perfect equilibrium. For Gorampa enlightenment represents a breach between the two truths, for with enlightenment the conventional world and conventional knowledge disappear, and one is conscious only of a transcendent absolute.

The sixth and final chapter concludes the book with a discussion of the four main philosophical themes: soteriology, ontology, epistemology, and ethics.

Why Compare Tsongkhapa and Gorampa?

Tsongkhapa and Gorampa are two of the most widely read and respected figures within Tibetan philosophy. Their scholarship is respected not only within the schools to which each belonged but also among the larger philosophical community. In addition, their philosophical works are gaining increasing attention from contemporary interpreters. Both Tsongkhapa and Gorampa systematically formulated a complete Buddhist epistemological, ontological, and soteriological agenda based on their understandings of Indian Madhyamaka. Both rank the Prāsaṅgika Madhyamaka as the most profound of all Buddhist philosophical schools. And, most importantly, despite both claiming that their views are Prāsaṅgika Madhyamaka, their views are philosophically and hermeneutically distinct.

Tsongkhapa is the founder of the Gelug (Dge lugs) order of Tibetan Buddhism.[9] He wrote extensively on Madhyamaka philosophy. His *Lam rim chen mo (Great Stages of the Path)*[10] and *Legs bshad snying po (Essence of Eloquent Teachings)*[11] are widely recognized as his two most illustrious works. His *Dgongs pa rab gsal (Illumination of the Middle Way),* a commentary on the *Madhyamakāvatāra* of Candrakīrti, and his *Rtsa she ṭīk chen (Ocean of Reasoning),* a commentary on the *Mūlamadhyamakakārikā* of Nāgārjuna, are the most celebrated of his commentarial works.[12]

Gorampa is a pillar of the Sakya (Sa skya) school.[13] Although not the founder of the Sakya order, his writings receive more attention than almost all other scholars of this tradition. In academic institutions affiliated with the Sakya school, Gorampa's writings are compulsory textbooks. His most highly regarded writings include the two independent works, the *Lta ba'i shan 'byed (Distinguishing Views)*[14] and the *Nges don rab gsal (Window on the Definitive Meaning).* Among his commentaries are the *Lta ba'i 'od zer (Illuminating the View),* his commentary on Nāgārjuna's *Mūlamadhyamakakārikā,* and the *Lta ba ngan sel (Eliminating the Erroneous View),* his commentary on Candrakīrti's *Madhyamakāvatāra.*

In their respective schools of thought, Tsongkhapa and Gorampa are recognized as impeccable interpreters of Nāgārjuna's philosophy as transmitted through Buddhapālita and Candrakīrti. However, from the perspective of the other's school, the position of each is viewed as thoroughly problematic. A succession of Tibetan scholars—Rongtön Shakya Gyaltsen (Rong ston Śākya rgyal tshan, 1367–1449), the translator Taktsang Lotsawa (Stag tsang Lo tsā ba, 1405–?), Gorampa (1429–89), Shakya Chogden (Śākya Mchog ldan, 1428–1509), the Eighth Karmapa Mikyö Dorje (Kar ma pa Mi skyod rdo rje, 1504-57), Mipham Rinpoche (Mi pham Rin po che, 1846–1912), Gendün Chöpel (Dge 'dun chos 'phel, 1903–51), and others—have raised serious and fierce objections against Tsongkhapa's position on the doctrine of the two truths. Likewise, Gyaltsab Jé (Rgyal tshab Rje, 1364–1432), Khedrub Jé (Mkhas grub Rje, 1385–1438), Gendün Drub (Dge 'dun grub, 1391–1474), Sera Jetsün Chökyi Gyaltsen (Se ra Rje tsun Chos kyi rgyal tshan, 1469–1544), Panchen Sönam Dragpa (Paṇ chen Bsod nams grags pa,1478–1554), Panchen Lobsang Chökyi Gyaltsen (Paṇ chen Blo bzang chos kyi rgyal tshan, 1567–1662), Jamyang Shepai Dorje ('Jam dbyangs Bzhad ba'i Rdo rje, 1648–1722), Changkya Rölpai Dorje (Lcang skya Rol pa'i rdo rje, 1717–86), Könchog Jigmé Wangpo (Kon mchog 'jigs med dbang po, 1728–91), and others have vehemently defended Tsongkhapa's interpretation while rejecting that of Gorampa.[15]

This book attempts neither to reconcile Tsongkhapa and Gorampa nor to create any unnecessary division between the two. I have striven to present their philosophical approaches as accurately as I can, and there has been no deliberate intention on my part to adjudicate one view over the other. That said, readers should be aware, and may discern, that I personally found Tsongkhapa's arguments more convincing. I like to think that my attraction to Tsongkhapa's view is due to its intrinsic virtues and not due to my own past training as a monk in the Gelug tradition. Readers will have to decide for themselves whether this preference is due more to my conditioning or to the merits of the arguments at hand.

1. The Relationship Between the Two Truths

Introduction

THIS CHAPTER examines the relationship between the two truths. It has three sections. The first section analyzes how the two truths are divided. The second section looks at how the two truths interact with one another. And the third section asks whether there are actually two truths.

Technically speaking, the first section explores the *basis of the division (dbye gzhi, jñeya)* into two truths. The precise identification of the basis of the division is critical for both Tsongkhapa and Gorampa. For the former, it relates to his effort to maintain a compatibility between the two truths, while for the latter, it relates to his effort to maintain an irreducible difference between them. As we will see, Tsongkhapa argues that "objects of knowledge" *(shes bya)* constitute the basis of the division, and he therefore grounds his exposition on the dual nature of empirically given phenomena. Gorampa argues that "mere mind" *(blo tsam)* constitutes the basis of the division, and he grounds his exposition on two opposing perspectives.

The second section concerns the way in which the two truths are related. For Tsongkhapa, the two truths constitute a "single ontological identity" *(ngo bo gcig)* with "different conceptual identities" *(ldog pa tha dad),* whereas Gorampa argues that the truths are separate in a way that is "incompatible with their unity" *(gcig pa bkag pa'i tha dad)* or identity.

Here two rather technical phrases provide the context for our examination. The Tibetan phrase *ngo bo gcig* used in Tsongkhapa's philosophy, particularly in the context of the relationship between the two truths, is often translated in English as "one entity."[16] Although *entity* has some connotations of *being,* as pointed out in *The Oxford Companion to Philosophy,* it usually refers to a *thing.*[17] In Tsongkhapa's sense, despite an underlying assumption that the two truths constitute *one entity* or *one thing* or *one phenomenon,* the *ngo bo* does not as such directly refer to a *thing.* Even in ordinary Tibetan discourses, *ngo bo* does not have any *explicit* reference to things. There is however an *implicit* reference to things, since *ngo bo* always refers to the identity, nature, or the property of that thing.

The *Great Tibetan-Chinese Dictionary* defines *ngo bo* as *rang bzhin,* meaning "nature," or *gnas lugs,* meaning "mode of being."[18] It also explains *ngo bo gcig pa* as meaning "having natures that are not distinct, like [the two states of] being a jar and being impermanent."[19] Making it even clearer, the dictionary states that *rang bzhin gcig pa,* meaning "single nature," and *bdag nyid gcig pa,* meaning "identical character," are synonyms for *ngo bo gcig pa,* meaning "single ontological identity."[20] Thus, instead of "entity," we will translate *ngo bo* as "ontological identity" and *ngo bo gcig* as "single ontological identity" or as "nature"[21] interchangeably, depending on context. As we will see, the analysis of the relationship between the two truths for Tsongkhapa amounts to analyzing the relationship between the two natures.

The second Tibetan phrase is *ldog pa tha dad.* This phrase is often translated in English as "isolate,"[22] or less frequently as "opposite"[23] or "distinguisher."[24] However, *ldog pa* is explained in the *Great Tibetan-Chinese Dictionary* as "a phenomenon that appears to the conceptual mind as being different categories...or it is that which appears not being different. For instance, the *ldog pa* of a jar is the aspect that is merely not being of the non-jar, like the form that appears to the conceptual mind."[25] Dreyfus, who translates *ldog pa* as "distinguisher," clarifies that the *ldog pa* of a phenomenon "is its conceptual identity. It is the property of a phenomenon being not what it is not. For example, a jar is distinct from everything else [that is not jar]. This is explained by the Collected Topics to be its distinguisher. Since such a distinguisher is a distinction made by thought, it is conceptual."[26] Similarly, Dreyfus explains "when we think that the Vedic language is impermanent, we apply the distinguisher, that is, the concept of impermanence, to the Vedic language."[27]

As these explanations reveal, *ldog pa* has more to do with conceptual identification than with the thing itself. To be closer to the meaning at issue here, although the translation is less literal, I tentatively use the term *conceptual identity* for the Tibetan phrase *ldog pa. Ngo bo gcig la ldog pa tha dad* is therefore tentatively rendered as "single ontological identity with different conceptual identities." These two Tibetan phrases are conjunctly explained in the *Great Tibetan-Chinese Dictionary* as follows: "despite not having distinct natures, exist as separate conceptual identities. For example, [it is like the conceptual relationships between] a jar and an object of knowledge; being impermanent and things; people and their causal conditions, the five aggregates; and the like."[28]

The final issue to be taken up in this chapter is the question of whether there really are two truths. By applying the principle of "single ontological identity" with "different conceptual identities," Tsongkhapa argues that there are two truths and that this is coherent. While declaring that the two truths are distinct and incompatible, Gorampa proposes that there is in fact only one truth.

What Is Divided into the Two Truths?

Jamyang Shepai Dorje (1648–1722) notes six different bases of the division asserted by non-Gelug scholars.[29] They include (1) "mere appearance" *(snang tsam),* (2) "entities ranging from material form to omniscience" *(gzugs nas rnam mkhyen bar gyi ngo bo),* (3) "nonreified objects" *(sgro ma btags pa'i yul),* (4) "unanalyzed objects" *(ma rtags ma dpyad pa'i yul),* (5) "truth" *(bden pa),* and (6) "unspecified basis." Newland notes as many as seven different ways of positing the basis of the two truths among non-Gelug Mādhyamikas:[30] (1) truths, (2) all entities from form to omniscient consciousness, (3) mere appearances, (4) unanalyzed knowables, (5) phenomena, (6) perspectives, and (7) mere minds. These lists indicate that there is no unanimity among Tibetan Mādhyamikas regarding the basis of the divisions of the two truths. Let us first turn to Tsongkhapa's account.

The Objects of Knowledge as the Basis of the Division

Although Tsongkhapa is aware of the views of his predecessors, he maintains that "objects of knowledge" *(shes bya)* are the basis for dividing the two truths.[31] For him, this means that the two truths relate to two different objects of knowledge. This view, according to Helmut Tauscher, is also held by Chapa Chökyi Senge (Phya pa chos kyi seng ge, 1109–69). Chapa lays great emphasis on determining the two realities as "identical in nature and different with regard to the characteristic distinction."[32] Tauscher also recognizes: "Equally, in Tsongkhapa's Madhyamaka exegesis, the same determination is of utmost importance."[33] Tsongkhapa however makes no reference to Chapa. Instead he heavily relies on the following statement of the Buddha from the *Pitāputrasamāgama Sūtra:*

> ...The Tathāgata understands both the empirical *(kun rdzob)*[34] and the ultimate *(don dam),* for the objects of knowledge exhaustively comprise conventional and ultimate truths. Besides, the Bhagavān perfectly sees, perfectly understands, and thoroughly actualizes emptiness. Because of this, he is described as omniscient.[35]

It also says:

> The knower of the universe taught these two truths without hearing from others. There is the empirical and likewise the ultimate. There can never be a third truth.[36]

An *object of knowledge* is defined as "an object that is cognizable *(blo'i yul du bya rung ba).* Whether a pillar, a jar, or any other phenomenon, it must be an object of cognition in general, [cognitions] ranging from those of [ordinary] sentient beings through to those of enlightened beings."[37] This definition, Tsongkhapa agrees, attempts to capture any thing knowable in the broadest possible sense. Since the Buddha maintains knowledge of the two truths to be necessary for enlightenment, the understanding of the two truths must constitute an exhaustive understanding of all objects of knowledge.

Tsongkhapa agrees with Gorampa that the doctrine of the two truths is pedagogically important in conveying the Buddha's message. Yet Tsongkhapa firmly believes that the Buddha's distinction between the two truths is not merely pedagogical. For Tsongkhapa, the most important reason for the division is to reveal that every empirically *(tha snyad)* or conventionally *(kun rdzob)* given phenomenon possesses dual natures: namely, the *empirical nature* (or conventional nature) and the *ultimate nature.* Yet one is putatively described as false and deceptive while the other is described as true and nondeceptive. "The division of two truths," as Hopkins puts it, "emphasizes two types of objects of consciousness, truths and falsities. Both, however, are falsely existent or falsely established because neither is independent; each depends on its imputing consciousness and on the other."[38]

Since both realities pertain to every phenomenon, the division of the two truths means the division of each phenomenon into two natures. Thus the division of the two truths, according to Tsongkhapa, "reveals that it makes sense to divide even the nature of a single entity, like a sprout, into dual natures—its empirical and its ultimate natures."[39] He adds: "It does not however show that the one nature of the sprout is itself divided into two truths in relation to ordinary beings *(so skye)* and to *āryas.*"[40]

The division of the nature of each phenomenon into two, Tsongkhapa argues, does not contradict his own claim that the two truths constitute a single ontological identity with different conceptual identities. For Tsongkhapa, these two ideas are, in fact, interdependent and mutually supporting. Without the twofold nature, there could not be a single ontological identity with different conceptual identities. Likewise, without the notion of a single ontological identity with distinct conceptual identities, a single phenomenon could not have multiple natures.

How can the single ontological identity of a phenomenon be bifurcated into two distinct conceptual identities? It comes down to the way the single ontological identity appears to a cognizing consciousness—deceptively and nondeceptively. The two natures correspond to these deceptive or nondeceptive modes of appearance. While they both belong to the same ontological identity, they are epistemologically or conceptually mutually exclusive.[41] Take a sprout for instance. If it exists, it necessarily exhibits a dual nature, and yet those two natures cannot be ontologically distinct. The ultimate nature of the sprout cannot be separate from its conventional nature—its color, texture, shape, extension, and so on. As an object of knowledge, the sprout retains its single ontological identity, but it is known through its two natures. These two natures exclude one another so far as knowledge is concerned. The mind that verifies the deceptive empirical nature of the sprout thus does not have direct access to its nondeceptive ultimate nature. Similarly, the mind that verifies the nondeceptive ultimate nature of the sprout does not have direct access to its deceptive empirical nature. Newland explains:

> A table and its emptiness are a single entity. When an ordinary conventional mind takes a table as its object of observation, it sees a table. When a mind of ultimate analysis searches for the table, it finds the emptiness of the table. Hence, the two truths are posited in relation to a single entity by way of the perspectives of the observing consciousness. This is as close as Ge-luk-bas will come to defining the two truths as perspectives.[42]

It is important to recognize that, for Tsongkhapa, the two types of verifying consciousness do not imply two different individuals. A single cognitive agent is potentially capable of verifying both the truths. If the two verifying consciousnesses belonged to two different individuals or types of individuals—empirically valid consciousness for an ordinary being and ultimately valid consciousness for an ārya (as Gorampa would argue)—then the two verifying consciousnesses would conflict with each other. The former would constitute ignorance, while the latter would constitute wisdom. Recognizing this, Newland also writes:

> These distinctions are critical to the Ge-luk-ba philosophical project, the preservation of non-paradoxical compatibility between the two truths. The conventional mind that finds a table is not discredited by the ultimate mind that finds the emptiness of the table. The first is valid because the table (a conventional truth) does exist; the second is also valid because the table's real nature is an emptiness of inherent existence (an ultimate truth).[43]

For Tsongkhapa, the two verifying consciousnesses stand on an equal footing; neither is superior to the other. Moreover, they may both belong to the same cognitive agent. In spite of their different roles, they are mutually entailing. You must realize their mutuality in order to realize both truths.

Mere Mind as the Basis of the Division

Let us now turn to Gorampa's account of the basis of the division of the two truths. Gorampa outlines four bases of the division. They are:

- mere mind *(blo tsam)*
- mere interdependence *(rten 'brel tsam)*
- mere objects of knowledge *(shes bya tsam)*
- mere subjects of the Buddha's discourses *(gsung rab gyi brjod bya tsam)*[44]

In emphasizing the first basis of the division, *mere mind,* Gorampa rules out the possibility that the division has an objective basis. The distinctions between the two truths are purely subjective—a matter of mere mind. Closely connected to mere mind is the second possible basis, mere interdependence. *Mere interdependence,* in Gorampa's usage, implies simply that the division of the two truths is dependent on two minds, ignorance and wisdom. In other words, were there no ignorance and wisdom, not only the distinction between the two truths, but also the two truths themselves, would not exist. Gorampa's third basis is *mere objects of knowledge.* For him, all objects of knowledge except ultimate truth are thought constructs, reifications of ignorance. Ultimate truth is none other than the transcendent wisdom itself. By suggesting that the basis of the division of the two truths is mere objects of knowledge, Gorampa avoids contradicting his earlier claim that the basis of the division of the two truths is mere mind. He claims that the Buddha taught conventional truth for purely pedagogical purposes. Hence, *mere subjects of the Buddha's discourses* is the fourth basis for the division of the two truths.

Since all four options equally emphasize the subjective nature of the distinction between the two truths, so, in Gorampa's view, all four bases for the division are mutually compatible. "There is no conflict at all in positing either mere mind...[or] mere interdependence...[or] mere objects of knowledge...[or] mere subjects of the Buddha's discourses to all be the basis of the division," says Gorampa.[45] Nevertheless, Gorampa emphasizes mere mind and mere subjects of the Buddha's discourses. Of the former, he states: "Although there are not two truths in terms of the object's mode of existence *(gnas tshul),* the truths are divided into two in terms of [the contrasting perspectives of] the mind that sees the mode of existence and the mind that does not see the mode of existence...This makes perfect sense."[46] The point here is to stress the subjective nature of the division. The division of the two truths cannot be grounded ontologically, for there is only one reality. The two truths are divided only according to the cognitive experiences of individuals. He who sees only phenomena, according to Gorampa, is ignorant, and he who sees reality, rather than the phenomena, is wise. This is because he who sees phenomena is caught within the web of conceptual elaboration, and he who sees reality has transcended conceptual elaboration.

Gorampa emphasizes the pedagogical necessity of the two truths. In discussing *mere subjects of the Buddha's discourses* as one basis for the division of the two truths, he says:

> [Besides, reality] cannot be revealed through linguistic expressions *(sgra)* in the context of the Madhyamaka literature. Yet it is nominally expressed through terms. The two truths, although indivisible, are presented to disciples as distinct. In this way, looking at the consistency of the whole [philosophical system], from the beginning until the end, I think [the subjects of the Buddha's discourses provide] a perfectly plausible [basis of the division].[47]

Although all phenomena are entirely false and deceptive, with no grounding in reality, Gorampa asserts that the Buddha posited empirically given phenomena as empirical truths for pedagogical reasons. Since ordinary beings are obsessed with empirical phenomena, the Buddha saw the practical application of positing empirical truth. He recognized its ultimate falsity, and yet saw its provisional utility as an instructional device to coax his disciples beyond the phenomenal realm.

> In terms of the way things exist *(gnas tsul),* one cannot distinguish between characteristic and characterized, the basis of division and the divided, and the like. However, when empirical truth is fabricated *(sgro brtags pa)* as an instructional device for disciples, it is important to consider the basis of division like the divided components.[48]

As far as Gorampa is concerned, the Buddha teaches about empirical truth simply as a means to lead ordinary beings into the ultimate realm from the delusional worldly realm. The empirical world, according to this view, provides purely instrumental rather than actual truth. This interpretation of the two truths is common among contemporary academics as well. "A relative or conventional truth *(saṃvṛtisatya),*" as Lindtner puts it, "serves as the means for obtaining the absolute or ultimate truth *(paramārthasatya).*"[49] He explicitly echoes Gorampa's view by stating "the theory of *satyadvaya* is above all a pedagogical device."[50]

In discussing the pedagogical necessity of the two truths, Gorampa paraphrases his earlier statement regarding mere mind as the basis of the division. He writes that "based on the subjective consciousness *(yul can gyi blo),* truth is twofold: empirical truth and ultimate truth."[51] Although this reinforces his preference for the subjective *(yul can)* division of the two truths over the objective *(yul),* it does not expressly reject an objective reference for the division. But then Gorampa writes: "Here in the Madhyamaka literature, it is not coherent to divide the object *per se* into the two truths."[52] In his commentary on the *Madhyamakāvatāra,* he writes, "A basis *per se* is separated in terms of its modes of appearance. Otherwise—in terms of the object—there is no division."[53] Since empirical phenomena are entirely false and deceptive, the division between the two truths cannot apply to empirical phenomena themselves—what is false and deceptive cannot be divided into the deceptive and the nondeceptive. Gorampa forcefully summarizes his view:

> Here in the Madhyamaka system, the object itself cannot be divided into two truths. Empirical truth and ultimate truth are

> divided in terms of the modes of apprehension *(mthong tshul)*—in terms of the subject apprehending falsehood and the subject apprehending truth; or mistaken and unmistaken apprehensions *('khrul ma 'khrul);* or deluded or undeluded apprehensions *(rmongs ma rmongs);* or erroneous or nonerroneous apprehensions *(phyin ci log ma log);* or valid or invalid cognitions *(tshad ma yin min).*[54]

And he adds:

> Because two truths are posited in terms of the subjective consciousness depending on whether it is deluded *(rmongs)* or nondeluded *(ma rmongs),* a perception of falsity *(brdzun pa thong ba)* or a perception of reality *(yang dag mthong ba),* and mistaken *(khrul)* or unmistaken *(ma khrul),* the position of [the truths] in terms of the subjective consciousness is unanimously accepted by all Prāsaṅgikas and Svātantrikas of India.[55]

It is worth underlining the two points at issue here. Since the minds of ordinary beings are always deluded, mistaken, and erroneous, they falsely experience conventional truth. Conventional truth is thus posited only in relation to the perspective of ordinary beings. Ordinary beings always assume the sensory experiences of empirical entities as veridical, despite the fact that they are utterly false. However, since the wisdom of āryas' meditative equipoise and enlightened minds is never mistaken, always nondeluded, and nonerroneous, āryas flawlessly experience ultimate truth. Ultimate truth is thus posited strictly in relation to an ārya's or a buddha's perspective.

Other Tibetans who maintain Gorampa's line of argument on the basis of the division of the two truths are Longchen Rabjam (1308–63),[56] Sakya Paṇḍita (1182–1251),[57] Mipham Rinpoche,[58] Rongtön Shakya Gyaltsen,[59] Taktsang Lotsawa,[60] Shakya Chogden,[61] and Mikyö Dorje.[62] They all agree with Gorampa that the distinctions between the two truths are merely subjective. Generally speaking, they all argue that the two truths are reducible to the two conflicting perspectives, namely, ignorance and wisdom. Modern scholars, including T.R.V. Murti,[63] La Vallée Poussin,[64] Jaideva Singh,[65] Christian Lindtner, and C.W. Huntington,[66] also endorse a similar interpretation. Guy Newland confirms that "Many Western scholars hold that the two truths are not two types of object, but rather two viewpoints, perspectives, or types of consciousnesses" and goes on to give several examples from the writing of Frederick Streng.[67]

As we have already seen, according to Tsongkhapa, the object of knowledge as that which can be known by means of two different modes of cognition, each of which may be verified by the same cognizing agent, is the basis of the division of the two truths. The key point of Tsongkhapa's argument is that every empirically given object of knowledge consists of *dual natures*—conventional and ultimate—that form the objective basis of the two truths. Despite the fact that the different cognitions corresponding to the two natures engage with the same phenomenon, it is this objective basis that differentiates Tsongkhapa's view from the subjective division of the two truths advanced by Gorampa. Therefore, as Hopkins puts it, "there are standards and criteria for valid establishment, and in this sense both suchness and the phenomena qualified by it are objective."[68]

While Tsongkhapa thus distances himself from the subjective division of the two truths, Gorampa attempts to demonstrate the validity of his view by arguing that mere mind provides the primary basis for the division of the two truths. Unlike Tsongkhapa, Gorampa holds that the two truths do not have any objective basis. Instead they are entirely reducible to the experiences of the deluded minds of ordinary beings and the experiences of the wisdom of āryas.

There is one last crucial point to be emphasized before we move to the next section. According to Tsongkhapa, the agent who cognizes the two truths may be one and the same individual. Each agent has all the requisite cognitive resources that are potentially capable of accessing both truths. Ordinary beings have only conceptual access to ultimate truth, while āryas, who are in the process of learning, have direct, but intermittent, access. Enlightened beings, however, invariably have simultaneous access to both truths. The view held by Gorampa argues for separate cognitive agents corresponding to each of the two truths. Ordinary beings have direct access to conventional truth, but are utterly incapable of accessing ultimate truth. The āryas in training have direct access to both ultimate and conventional truths. Buddhas, on the other hand, only have access to ultimate truth. They have no access to conventional truth whatsoever from the enlightened perspective. (See chapter 5 for a detailed treatment of the issue.)

How Are the Two Truths Related?

Two important background issues should be borne in mind at this stage. Central to Tsongkhapa's account of the relationship between the two truths is his emphasis on the relationship between the "two natures of a single entity." He thus implicitly suggests that the two truths constitute one and the same phenomenon (or entity or thing)—they do not, in any way, represent two ontologically distinct identities. Tsongkhapa's primary aim is therefore to establish the mutually compatible relationship between two modes of cognition that relate to the *two* natures of a *single* phenomenon or entity. In other words, for Tsongkhapa the two modes of cognition and the two natures corresponding to the two truths are underlaid by one phenomenon. Gorampa, however, views the relationship between the two truths as one between *two distinct and incompatible modes of cognition,* of which only the ultimate refers to a real phenomenon.

The Two Truths Are Ontologically Identical but Conceptually Distinct

The principle of single ontological identity with distinct conceptual identities, mentioned earlier, is founded on the concept of the two natures. This concept not only serves as the basic reference point for Tsongkhapa in his exposition of the basis of the division of the two truths, their meanings and definitions, but also serves as the basic ontological reference for his account of the relationship between the two truths.

Tsongkhapa traces the notion of the two natures back to Candrakīrti. "[The Buddha] said that all things have two natures—those found by perceivers of reality and of falsities," says Candrakīrti in the *Madhyamakāvatāra.*[69] While glossing the statement in the *Madhyamakāvatārabhāṣya,* Candrakīrti also writes: "All phenomena—interior and exterior—such as conditioned phenomena and the sprout, have two natures."[70] Khedrub Jé (1385–1438) rephrases it this way: "As both the root texts of the *[Madhyamakāvatāra]* and its commentary maintain...all conventional and ultimate phenomena possess natures, and if their natures exist they must be either one or different. For if [two natures] exist they must be either the same or different."[71] Since the dual natures are ontologically locked together within the framework of each phenomenon, it is obvious that the two truths constitute the same phenomenon. Therefore the question concerning the relationship between the two truths is the same as that concerning the relationship between the two natures. To establish the relationship between the two truths is thus equivalent to examining the precise relationship between the two natures.

So, how are the two natures related? Are they identical or distinct?[72] For Tsongkhapa the short answer is that the two natures are neither identical nor distinct in any unqualified sense. They are related in terms of a single ontological identity with distinct conceptual identities—thus they are both the same and different. Since the two natures are the basis of the relationship between the two truths, the relationship between the two truths will reflect the relationship between the two natures. Ultimate truth and conventional truth thus possess the same ontological status. As the two natures are of the same ontological structure, so the two truths relate to the same ontological structure also.

Tsongkhapa likens the relationship between the two truths and the two natures to the relationship between being conditioned and being impermanent.[73] He borrows this point from Nāgārjuna's *Bodhicittavivaraṇa,* which states: "Reality is not perceived as separate from conventionality. The conventionality is explained to be empty. Empty alone is the conventionality," and therefore, for Nāgārjuna, "if one of them does not exist, neither will the other, like being conditioned and being impermanent."[74] Commenting on this passage from the *Bodhicittavivaraṇa,* Tsongkhapa writes:

> The first four lines show that things as they really are, are not ontologically distinct from that of the conventionality. The latter two lines establish their relationship such that if one did not exist, neither could the other *(med na mi 'bung ba'i 'brel ba).* This, in fact, is equivalent to their being constituted by a single-property relationship *(bdag cig pa'i 'brel ba).* Therefore, like the case of being conditioned and being impermanent, [the relation between the two truths] is demonstrated as one of a single ontological identity.[75]

The way in which the two truths are related is thus analogous to the relationship between being conditioned and being impermanent. Insofar as the character of being conditioned and being impermanent is concerned, they are ontologically identical and mutually entailing. Whatever is impermanent is also conditioned, likewise whatever is conditioned is also impermanent. If impermanence did not exist, conditioned phenomena would not exist, and vice versa. Just as a conditioned state is not a result of impermanence, so emptiness is not a result of form or the destruction of form—hence in the *Vimalakīrtinirdeśa Sūtra* it is stated: "Matter itself is void. Voidness does not result from the destruction of matter, but the nature of matter is itself voidness."[76] The same principle applies in the case of consciousness and the emptiness of consciousness, as well as to the rest of the five psychophysical aggregates—the aggregate and its emptiness are not causally related. For the causal relationship would imply either the aggregate is the cause, therefore its emptiness is the result, or the aggregate is the result, and its emptiness the cause. This would imply either the aggregate or the emptiness is temporally prior to its counterpart, thus leading to the conclusion that the aggregate and its emptiness exist independently of each other. Such a view is completely unacceptable to Tsongkhapa.

The ontological identity between being conditioned and being impermanent does not imply identity in *all* and *every* respect. Insofar as their mode of appearance is concerned, conditioned and impermanent phenomena are distinct and contrasting. Impermanence always presents itself to the cognizing mind as impermanent, but not as conditioned. Similarly, being conditioned always presents itself to its cognizing mind as conditioned, but not as impermanent. Thus it does not necessarily follow that the two truths are identical in every respect just because they share a common ontological identity. Where the modes of appearance are concerned, ultimate nature and conventional nature are distinct. The mode of appearance of ultimate nature is nondeceptive and consistent with its mode of existence, while that of conventional nature is deceptive and inconsistent with its mode of existence.

Conventional nature is uncritically verified by empirical valid cognition, whereas ultimate nature is critically verified by ultimately valid cognition. Hence, just as ultimate nature is inaccessible to the empirically valid cognition for its uncritical mode of engagement, so, too, is conventional nature inaccessible to ultimately valid cognition for its critical mode of engagement. This is how, in Tsongkhapa's view, the truths differ conceptually despite sharing a common ontological identity.

In summarizing Tsongkhapa's points, Khedrub Jé writes: "The two truths are therefore of the same nature, but different conceptual identities. They have a single-nature relationship such that, if one did not exist, neither could the other, just like being conditioned and impermanent."[77] In commenting on Gelug thought, Newland also upholds the same point:

> That the two truths are different isolates means, for example, that a table and its emptiness can be distinguished in terms of

> how they are understood by a conceptual consciousness. To say that two things are different isolates is to make only the most minimal distinction between them. Since conceptual consciousnesses often operate under the sway of language, things are different isolates as soon as they are given different names—even if those names refer to the same object.[78]

Since the meaning of *distinct conceptual identities (ldog pa tha dad),* in Tsongkhapa's view, is rooted in the two natures, the conceptual distinction between the two truths must *not* be understood as a pure epistemological distinction. This distinction, according to Tsongkhapa, is not reducible to two different perspectives, or even to two different linguistic practices. Since both truths have their own objective references, namely, the two natures, they are not reducible to subjective viewpoints, nor are they reducible to merely a difference of language. José Cabezón is one commentator who does hold the distinction between the two truths as entirely linguistic, writing that the two truths, "although having the same referent... have different names, different designations, being the opposites of different entities *qua* names."[79] Both Newland and Cabezón are correct in pointing out that distinct conceptual identities in Tsongkhapa's sense are distinctions drawn by the conceptual consciousness, and so clearly have a linguistic component. They are also correct in pointing out, as I have above, that the two truths have only one entity or one phenomenon as their referent. Yet to then say that the differences between the two truths are purely linguistic in nature is to ignore Tsongkhapa's own emphasis on the role of the two natures corresponding to the two truths. The distinction between those two natures is not merely linguistic.

Although the two truths presuppose, according to Tsongkhapa, a single phenomenon or entity as their common referent, this does not mean that they share exactly the same *objective* referent. Ultimate truth has the ultimate nature of the phenomenon as its referent, while conventional truth has the conventional nature of the same phenomenon as its referent. Thus, while engaging with the same phenomenon, both verifying consciousnesses have their own distinctive referents according to their *modus operandi*—one critically, the other uncritically. This is a central thesis of Tsongkhapa, allowing him to ground both the identity and difference that stem from the relationship between the two truths on the single ontological identity and different conceptual natures of a single phenomenon. In doing this, he effectively dismisses the idea of treating the difference between the truths as merely one of contradictory perspectives or different linguistic practices. Thus he accords equal significance to both the epistemological and ontological issues involved in the relationship between the two truths. To say that they share a single ontological identity with different conceptual identities does not mean, therefore, that the distinctions at issue are purely epistemological. This is consistent with his position that the two truths have equal status and do not constitute an ontological or epistemological hierarchy.

The Two Truths Are Distinct and Incompatible

Let us now examine how Gorampa formulates the relationship between the two truths. From his perspective, the position advanced by Tsongkhapa is utterly unacceptable. To say that the two truths are ontologically identical is similar to equating ignorance with wisdom. Jay Garfield precisely anticipates Gorampa's general approach to the doctrine of the two truths when he writes:

> By distinguishing the conventional from the ultimate, it is tempting to disparage the former in contrast to the latter, developing a sort of theory of one truth and one falsehood. This is done if one reifies the entities associated with the ultimate, such as emptiness or impermanence or the Four Noble Truths, or the Buddha. Then one treats these as real, intrinsically existent phenomena. The conventional then become the world of illusion.[80]

As we saw above, the main point of reference in Gorampa's exposition of the basis of the two truths is what he calls "mere mind," since this is what underpins the view that the distinction between the two truths is purely subjective. Moreover, because Gorampa denies that there is any ontological unity that underlies the distinction between the two truths—that the distinction is one of mere mind, such that the two truths cannot both have an objective referent—the two truths must constitute conflicting and incompatible perspectives. According to this view, then, the relationship between the two truths is equivalent to the relationship between the two conflicting perspectives—namely, ignorance and wisdom. The question now arises: How is ignorance related to wisdom? Or conversely, how does wisdom relate to ignorance? In answer, Gorampa suggests four possible sets of relationships between the two truths. He derives them from Sakya Paṇḍita:

> Generally the twofold division is analyzed in order to determine (1) whether its members are substantially distinct *(rdzas tha dad),* like a mattress and a jar, (2) or [to determine whether they are] a single identity with distinct conceptual identities, like being conditioned and impermanent, (3) or co-referential but different in meaning *(rnams grangs pa'i tha dad),* like "moon" and "that which has a cooling effect" *(bsil zer byed pa),* (4) or distinct in the sense that is incompatible with oneness, like entity and without entity. This [relationship] between the two truths also has to be analyzed in this way.[81]

Among these four sets of relations, Gorampa ignores the first—substantially distinct—and the third—co-referential, but different in meaning. The second type of relationship—single ontological identity with distinct conceptual identities—is the one advocated by Tsongkhapa, and Gorampa rejects it (we will turn to his objections shortly). His own account is based on the fourth type of relation—that the two truths are distinct in the sense that they are incompatible with unity, like entity and without entity.

For Gorampa the relationship between the two truths is quite straightforward. In the ultimate sense, he argues, the two truths transcend identity and difference.[82] "The transcendence of identity and difference from the ultimate standpoint is synonymous with the transcendence of identity and difference from the purview of the ārya's meditative equipoise."[83] However, from the empirical standpoint, he claims that the two truths are distinct in the sense that they are incompatible with their unity. He likens this relationship to the one between entity and without entity.[84]

Gorampa's claim that the two truths are distinct and incompatible encompasses both ontological and epistemological distinctions. Since what is divided into the two truths is mere mind, it is obvious that there is no single phenomenon that could serve as the objective referent for both. This also means that the two truths must be construed as corresponding to distinct spheres belonging to distinct modes of consciousness: conventional truth corresponds to ignorance and ultimate truth to wisdom. It is thus inappropriate to describe the relationship between the two truths, and their corresponding modes of consciousness, in terms of two ways of perceiving the *same* entity. Although the two truths can be thought of as two ways of *perceiving,* one based on ignorance and the other on wisdom, there is no *same* entity perceived by both. There is nothing common between the two truths, and if they are both ways of perceiving, then they do not perceive the same thing.

Gorampa's formulation of the distinct and incompatible relationship between the two truths is also reinforced by his objections launched against the notion that the two truths share a common ontological identity. One of these objections states that:[85]

> If the two truths were identical in their natures, then metaphorically speaking, the hairs seen through blurred vision and the nonexistence of hairs seen through correct vision would absurdly become identical. This would follow from the two truths being identical in their natures. [86]

According to this view, the relationship between conventional truth and ultimate truth is analogous to the relationship between the appearance of falling hairs when vision is impaired by cataracts and the absence of such hairs when vision is unimpaired. Although this is a metaphor, it has a direct application to determining the relationship between the two truths. Conventional truth is like seeing falling hairs as a result of cataracts: both conventional truth and such false seeing are illusory, in the ontological sense that there is nothing to which each corresponds, and in the epistemological sense that there is no true knowledge in either case. Ultimate truth is therefore analogous, ontologically and epistemologically, to the true seeing unimpaired by cataracts and free of the appearance of falling hairs. Just as cataracts give rise to illusory appearances, so ignorance, according to Gorampa, gives rise to all conventional truths; wisdom, on the other hand, gives rise to ultimate truth. As each is the result of a different state, there is no common link between them in terms of either an ontological identity or an epistemological or conceptual identity.

For Gorampa the idea that the two truths refer to one ontological identity with different conceptual identities is highly problematic. It is equivalent to claiming that there is an ontological identity between the falling hairs seen as a result of cataracts and their absence when no cataracts are present. The same reasoning applies to any claim that the two truths share an epistemological link. Gorampa further rejects the identity of the two truths by relying on the *Saṃdhinirmocana Sūtra.* This sūtra, according to him, exposes four absurdities in claiming that the two truths are ontologically identical.[87] If the two truths were identical, then:

> [1] Just as the childish directly perceive conventional things such as form and sound, they would absurdly directly perceive ultimate truth. [2] Just as conventional [truth] comprises many

> divisions of categories, such as form and sound, even so, ultimate [truth] would absurdly comprise many divisions. [3] Just as conventional [truth] by definition has the nature of deluded ignorance, ultimate truth would [absurdly] be the same. [4] Just as conventional meaning is not sought apart from what is seen by the childish, ultimate truth would absurdly be the same.[88]

By reading the *Saṃdhinirmocana Sūtra* as presenting the relationship between the two truths as distinct and incompatible, Gorampa does not mean to suggest that the two truths constitute *two* distinct entities. Nor does he propose that the two truths are *one* entity seen under two conflicting aspects. There are two grounds for this: First, the basis of the divisions of the two truths is mere mind, and it is not coherent to divide mind into two distinct entities. Second, all entities are classified as belonging to conventional truth, while ultimate truth is purely "without entity."

If the two truths were really two distinct entities, then, Gorampa argues, they would give rise to a second set of absurdities, also four in number, as set out in the *Saṃdhinirmocana Sūtra:*

> ...if the two truths were distinct [entities], then: [1] Āryas, while directly realizing ultimate [truth], absurdly would remain unreleased *(mi grol ba)* from the conventional bondage *(kun rdzob kyi 'ching ba).* [2] Reality—that is, ultimate [truth]—would not be conventional phenomena's universal characteristic *(spyi tshan nyid, sāmānya-lakṣaṇa).* [3] Either conditioned phenomena *('du byed),* i.e., conventionalities, would remain unestablished, or selflessness would absurdly not be the ultimate truth. [4] The continuum of each person would absurdly accommodate both afflictive characteristics and liberating qualities.[89]

This second quartet of absurd consequences shows, according to Gorampa, that the two truths are not utterly *distinct* entities even though they they are distinct and incompatible *perspectives*—perspectives that are in no way convergent.

While Tsongkhapa himself does not explicitly cite the *Saṃdhinirmocana Sūtra,* his view is diametrically opposed to Gorampa's interpretation of the passage. In Tsongkhapa's view, the first four absurdities do not support the position that treats the two truths as equivalent—i.e., as identical in every respect. Instead, these absurdities expose the problems inherent in any such identification. Many later Gelug scholars do refer to the passage and, just as Gorampa did, harnass the four absurdities to settle the issue of whether the two truths are equivalent. Consider the example of Khensur Pema Gyaltsen (Mkhan zur Pad ma rgyal mtshan), who writes:

> If the two truths [not only have a single ontological identity but] a single conceptual identity, then [1] common beings would directly realize the ultimate reality; [2] the awareness of that reality would generate delusions such as attachment; [3] that [reality] would be comprised of colors, shapes, and so forth, and [4] a yogi's efforts to meditate on reality would absurdly be pointless. This would follow because a jar and its ultimate reality would fall under a single conceptual identity.[90]

On the issue of whether the two truths are distinct, both Tsongkhapa and Gorampa differ from their predecessor, Dölpopa Sherab Gyaltsen (Dol po pa Shes rab rgyal tshan, 1292–1361), the founder of the Jonang school,[91] who argues in favor of a marked distinction. According to Kapstein, Dölpopa's view represents perhaps the most radical division between the two truths in the Tibetan tradition. Kapstein considers the following remarks from Dölpopa's *Bden gyis gsal ba'i nyi ma:*

> The defining characteristic of relative truth is that it is an object of consciousness that in its fundamental nature is itself essentially empty of veridical being, while the defining characteristic of absolute truth is that it is an object of authentic, sublime gnosis that in its fundamental nature is itself essentially not empty of veridical being...
>
> Because the relative does not exist in fact, it is intrisically empty, and appears to consciousness but not to gnosis. Because the absolute exists in fact, it is not intrinsically empty, but is extrinsically empty, and appears to gnosis but never at all to consciousness...
>
> Thus, to those who are childish, according to their own dispositions, only inauthentical characteristics appear, but not the authentic suchness, and in the same way, to the bodhisattvas, according to their own dispositions, only the authentic appears, but not what is inauthentic.[92]

Kapstein argues that in Dölpopa's view, "the nature of absolute is such that relative reality is in some sense wholly other with respect to it."[93] Dölpopa argues that the two truths are fundamentally separate and therefore incompatible with their unity *(gcig pa bkag pa'i tha dad)*.

Neither Tsongkhapa nor Gorampa agree with such a marked ontological separation. Such a view of the two truths, "far from revealing to us a soteriologically valuable dialectic," Kapstein points out, "leaves us with the unedifying vision of two mutually exclusive, but somehow compresent, orders of being, in which our discovery of a higher truth does nothing to overcome our previous unknowing."[94] Furthermore, Khedrub Jé concludes, "If the two truths are ontologically distinct, they must be distinct unrelated things, because ontologically distinct things cannot have a single-character relationship."[95] But such a single-character relationship is essential for the unity of the two truths. Here, too, later Gelug scholars turn to the *Saṃdhinirmocana Sūtra*[96] to reinforce their position. For example, Khensur Pema Gyaltsen further expounds on the four absurdities that would follow were the two truths entirely distinct:

> [1] A jar's emptiness of true existence would not be the jar's mode of existence; [2] the realization of a jar's emptiness of true existence would not eradicate the reification through the conception of true existence; [3] it would make no sense to say that a jar is the basis of the repudiation of the true existence of the jar and so forth; and [4] the fact that an ārya buddha's continuum does not simultaneously accommodate both—the wisdom realizing the emptiness and the grasping at true existence of a jar—would become absurd. This would follow if the jar and the jar's emptiness of true existence are distinct.[97]

The assumption here is that the radical dualism proposed by Dölpopa, as Kapstein remarks, "effectively underwrites the metaphysical equivalence, while undermining the identity, of the two truths."[98]

Although these four absurdities are here employed to argue against the view that takes the two truths to be utterly distinct, this is not an argument that directly concerns Gorampa. He is not interested in demonstrating such a radical division of the two truths; rather he seeks to prove that they constitute two distinct perspectives. Tsongkhapa and the other Gelug scholars, however, by drawing attention to these absurdities, are aiming implicitly at establishing the mutual interdependence of the two truths.

Other Tibetan scholars, including Longchen Rabjam,[99] Rongtön Shakya Gyaltsen,[100] Mipham Rinpoche,[101] and Gendün Chöpel, come closer to Gorampa's view the way the two truths are distinct. Gendün Chöpel, for example,[102] in criticizing Tsongkhapa for holding that there is a noncontradictory relationship between the two truths, writes:

> The so-called mutually compatible relationship between the two truths might be possible if there were ever a time whereby the āryas' wisdom and the conception of ordinary beings become mutually compatible without contradiction. Otherwise, such [a relationship] is utterly impossible...There is indeed no opportunity to attain liberation for those who hold conventional and ultimate [truths] as noncontradictory. [This also holds true] in terms of the modes of analysis of both the truths.[103]

He also states:

> This implies the acceptance of the mutually compatible and the noncontradictory relationship between the mental states of the naïve ordinary beings—the lowest foolishness—and the enlightened knowledge—the highest erudition. If by accepting this, it did [justice to the enlightened wisdom], then there should be no problem even in accepting the mutually compatible relationship between the objects of ignorance and reasoning consciousness (i.e., an āryas' wisdom), [would there?]...In short, the view that holds the two truths as noncontradictory is a philosophical system that accepts all categories of mental states from buddhas down to sentient beings as noncontradictory.[104]

Still others such as Sakya Paṇḍita,[105] Rendawa (Red mda' ba, 1349–1412),[106] Shakya Chogden,[107] and Karmapa Mikyö Dorjé[108] argue that the relationship between the two truths is essentially inexpressible. They claim that ultimately the two truths transcend the notion of identity and difference *(gcig dang tha dad spros pa dang bral ba),* and, conventionally, their relationship is not expressible as either identical or distinct *(de nyid dang gzhan du brjod du med).*[109]

In short, the two accounts we are considering here differ markedly in their views regarding the relationship between the two truths. Tsongkhapa insists that the two truths constitute a single ontological structure and that they share a common ontological identity, while denying that the two truths are identical in every respect. They are different in their mode of appearance and their mode of existence. The appearance of conventional truth does not cohere with its mode of existence (its appearance belying its contingency), whereas the appearance of ultimate truth is coherent with its mode of existence (its noncontingency being apparent). Conventional and ultimate truth differ, then, in terms of the two natures upon which they are founded, and therefore also to their respective cognizing consciousnesses.

The identity and difference of the two truths must, according to Tsongkhapa, be both ontologically and epistemologically grounded in the two natures. This renders the reduction of the two truths to a mere subjective distinction impossible, since the two natures do not constiutute a merely subjective distinction. In contrast, Gorampa's account of the relationship between the two truths takes them to be reducible to two conflicting perspectives. The cognitive experiences of ordinary beings and the cognitive experiences of buddhas are distinct in every possible sense. There is nothing in common between these two conflicting perspectives, including any common ontological identity or epistemological link.

The divergence in Tsongkhapa and Gorampa's views regarding the relationship between the two truths will become more apparent as we delve further into the topic. In the following section, we will compare their views in relation to the authority of the two truths: are there really two truths or is there just one?

Two Truths or One Truth?

For Tsongkhapa the truth is always twofold while for Gorampa it is always single. The disagreement between Tsongkhapa and Gorampa regarding the basis of the division between the two truths is fundamental to this debate. For Tsongkhapa, since the two natures of every empirically given phenomenon provide the ontological and epistemological foundation for each of the truths, the division of truth into two is entirely appropriate. Both the conventional and the ultimate are actual truths, and since the two natures are mutually interlocking, neither of the two truths has primacy over the other—both have equal status, ontologically, epistemologically, and even soteriologically. For Gorampa, however, truth *per se* is not divisible into two. Since mere mind provides the basis of the division of the two truths wherein ultimate truth—namely, wisdom—alone is seen as convincingly satisfying the criterion of truth, so conventional truth—namely, ignorance—cannot properly be taken as truth. Wisdom and ignorance are invariably contradictory, and thus the two truths cannot coexist. Gorampa argues, in fact, that conventional truth must be eliminated in the ascent to ultimate truth. Given wisdom's primacy over ignorance, in the final analysis it is ultimate truth alone that must prevail without its merely conventional counterpart. Ultimate truth is therefore infinitely more significant than conventional truth in all respects—ontologically, epistemologically, and soteriologically.

How Is Conventional Truth "Truth" at All?

Given his stance on conventional truth as actual truth and his argument for the equal status of the two truths, Tsongkhapa must now address the question: How can conventional truth, which is described as false and deceptive, be truth at all? In other words, how can the two truths be of equal status if conventional truth is false? Since Tsongkhapa grounds both truths in the dual nature of a single phenomenon, then "just as the ultimate reality of the sprout [for instance] is taken as characteristic of the sprout, hence it is described as the sprout's nature, so, too," argues Tsongkhapa, "are the sprout's color, shape, etc., the sprout's characteristics. Therefore they too are its nature."[110] Since the two natures are ontologically mutually entailing, the sprout's ultimate truth cannot exist without its conventional truth, and vice versa. In other words, neither truth could exist without the other.

In the interests of preserving a compatible relationship between the two truths, it is crucial for Tsongkhapa to demonstrate their equal footing. To this end, he appropriates Nāgārjuna's arguments establishing the unity between the two truths. In the *Mūlamadhyamakakārikā,* particularly in chapter 24, Nāgārjuna offers his most explicit statements on the unity of the two truths by advancing two separate arguments, one emphasizing their epistemological link, and the other emphasizing their ontological unity. Both these lines of argument draw upon an understanding of the connection between conventional truth and dependent arising on the one hand, and between ultimate truth and emptiness on the other.

Firstly, in order to articulate the epistemological link between the two truths, Nāgārjuna states: "Without relying upon empirical [truth], the meaning of the ultimate cannot be explained. Without understanding the meaning of the ultimate, nirvāṇa is not attained."[111] Similarly, "To whomsoever emptiness makes sense, everything [the four noble truths] makes sense. To whomsoever emptiness makes no sense, everything makes no sense."[112] In the *Vigrahavyāvartanī,* Nāgārjuna phrases this point slightly differently: "Wherever emptiness is possible, there every function is possible. Wherever emptiness is not possible, there every function is not possible."[113] Secondly, in order to demonstrate the ontological unity between the two truths, in the *Mūlamadhyamakakārikā* Nāgārjuna writes: "Whatever is dependently arisen, is itself explained to be empty. That being dependently designated, is itself the middle path."[114] In the *Vigrahavyāvartanī* Nāgārjuna attributes this same point to the Buddha: "I pay homage to this peerless Buddha, who perfectly explained that the identity of meaning of emptiness and dependent arising constitutes the middle path."[115] More explicitly, he argues that "There is no thing that is not dependently arisen; therefore, there is no thing that is not empty."[116]

In the *Madhyamakāvatāra,* Candrakīrti reinforces the unity between the two truths by emphasizing the causal efficacy of empty phenomena. "It is not a secret that empty entities like reflections and so forth depend on aggregation (of causes and conditions), and a consciousness may arise in the form of an image of such an empty reflection."[117] Moreover, he argues that "All entities are, in the similar characteristics, not only empty [as effects], but they are produced out of empty [causal conditions]."[118] This must follow "because there is no essence whatsoever from the standpoints of both truths"; hence all entities, according to Candrakīrti, "are neither permanent nor subject to annihilation."[119]

Tsongkhapa supports this view of Nāgārjuna and Candrakīrti that empty phenomena and dependently arisen phenomena are synonymous. The concept of emptiness is incoherent unless it is applied to dependently arisen phenomena, and equally the concept of dependent arising is incoherent unless it is applied to empty phenomena. In the *Rten 'brel stod pa (In Praise of Dependent Arising),* Tsongkhapa mobilizes his arguments to reinforce the unity between the two truths:

> According to you [i.e., the Buddha], since emptiness means dependent arising, the emptiness of essence and the efficacy of action and its agent are not contradictory. If emptiness, however, is seen as contradictory with [dependent arising], there would be neither action in empty [phenomena], nor empty [phenomena] in action. This way, you accept that one falls in a precipice of despair.[120]
>
> ... Since there is no phenomenon other than what is depend-

> ently arisen, there is no phenomenon other than what is empty of essence.[121]...The "utter nonexistence of essence" and making sense of everything in the light of the principle "this arises depending on this"—there is indeed no need to say that they are noncontradictory.[122]...Therefore, despite the fact that whatever is dependently arisen is primordially devoid of essence, it nonetheless appears. [Phenomena] all are thus proclaimed as illusion-like.[123]

In the *Lam gtso rnam gsum (The Three Principal Pathways),* Tsongkhapa varies his argument slightly to establish this unity. "Appearance avoids the extreme of existence, and empty [phenomena] avoids the extreme of nonexistence. Hence by understanding that the empty [phenomenon] itself is the bearer of cause and effect, one is not robbed by the extreme view."[124] As indicated in Nāgārjuna and Candrakīrti's arguments, the efficacy of empty phenomena, the bearers of cause and effect, is particularly significant to this view. The idea of empty phenomena acting as the basis of cause and effect is crucial in understanding Tsongkhapa's view of the inextricable relationship between ultimate truth and conventional truth.

Since empty and dependently arisen phenomena are *ontologically* united, the knowledge of empty phenomena is *epistomologically* interlinked with that of dependently arisen phenomena—the latter is, in fact, founded on the former. To the extent that empty phenomena are understood in terms of relational and dependently arisen phenomena, empty phenomena are always functional and causally effective. The phrase "empty phenomena," although expressed negatively, is not negative in a metaphysical sense—it is not equivalent to no-thingness. Although the empty phenomenon appears to its cognizing consciousness negatively and without any positive affirmation, it is nonetheless equivalent to a relational and dependently arisen phenomenon seen in a different light. Since seeing phenomena as empty does not violate the inevitable epistemic link with the understanding of phenomena as dependently arisen, and the converse also applies, so the unity between the two truths—understanding things both as empty and as dependently arisen—is made clear.

Tsongkhapa also argues, moreover, that the realization of phenomena as dependently arisen is a necessary condition for the realization of both truths; one can't realize phenomena as empty unless one sees them as dependently arisen. "So long as the understanding pertaining to empirically consistent appearances—dependently arisen—and the understanding pertaining to the empty [phenomena]—free from all claims—are seen as mutually exclusive," Tsongkhapa avers, "the purport of the Buddha is not yet understood."[125] Thus for Tsongkhapa the philosophical inquiry is not complete until one achieves simultaneous realizations of the two truths.

> However, the process of philosophical analysis is complete whenever these [two realizations] operate simultaneously, not in turn, and consequently all conceived objects [blindfolding] the discerning wisdom are eschewed merely by seeing empirically consistent dependently arisen phenomena.[126]

The unity between the two truths, according to Tsongkhapa, does not apply merely to ontological and epistemological issues; it applies equally to soteriology—the practical means to Buddhist liberation, the freedom from suffering. As Jamyang Shepai Dorje, one of the central commentators on Tsongkhapa's works, notes:

> Undermining either of the two truths would result in a similar downfall—a similar eventual ruin. If, however, they are not undermined, they are alike insofar as the accomplishment of the two accumulations and the attainment of the two kāyas,[127] and so forth, are concerned. If one undermined conventional [truth] by denying it, one would succumb to the extreme of nihilism, which robs the root of virtue, and consequently migrate to the realm of unfortunates. It would also undermine the fruit and the means by which rūpakāya is accomplished. It is therefore not sensible to approach the two truths with bias...Since this relation continues [as a means to avoid] falling into extremes and being ruined thereby, and also to accomplish the two accumulations and attain the two kāyas, it is imperative that the two truths be understood as mutually interrelated.[128]

The ultimate soteriological goal for Tsongkhapa is to attain perfect enlightenment, and this attainment, as the above passages explain, depends on the accomplishment of a buddha's rūpakāya (form body) and dharmakāya (truth body). The accomplishment of the two kāyas in turn depends on properly comprehending the unity of the two truths. The rūpakāya is accomplished as a result of the exhaustive accumulation of virtues, while the dharmakāya results from the exhaustive accumulation of penetrative wisdom. The former emphasizes an engagement with the wisdom of dependent arising, while the latter emphasizes an engagement with the wisdom of emptiness.

Accomplishing the virtues requires a practical orientation and a conventional engagement with the world, activities such as practicing the first five of the so-called six perfections—generosity, morality, forbearance, effort, and meditative stability. All these engagements are undertaken in conformity with worldly conventions and the wisdom of dependent arising. The accumulation of penetrative wisdom, the sixth perfection, emphasizes the direct experience of ultimate truth, including the direct experience of impermanent, selfless, and empty phenomena. This requires the transcendence of worldly conventions on the basis of meditative equipoise. The accomplishment of both accumulations, however, culminates in the purification of defilements and the simultaneous realization of both emptiness and dependent arising, the two truths.

Bearing in mind the soteriological unity of the two truths, and therefore of empty and dependently arisen phenomena, Nāgārjuna thus remarks: "By virtue of this meritorious deed, may all people accumulate merit and wisdom, and attain the two noble fruits [i.e., rūpakāya and dharmakāya] that arise from merit and wisdom."[129] The Buddha himself implies how the two truths are soteriologically intertwined in this invocation of the well-known four noble truths: "Bhikkhus, he who sees suffering sees also the origin of suffering, sees also the cessation of suffering, sees also the way leading to the cessation of suffering."[130] As Kapstein notes, "...the two truths scheme is no longer essentially a hermeneutical device used to interpret the four noble truths discourse, nor is it merely an alternative classificatory scheme; rather, the two truths embrace and include the four noble truths themselves."[131] Since the four noble truths are divisions within the two truths,[132] and since the four noble truths are soteriologically intertwined, the Buddha clearly points out that the two truths are united even in soteriological terms. In Gyaltsab Jé's words:

> Since the two kāyas—the *jñānadharmakāya* and *saṃbhogakāya* —depend on the appropriation of the same actual conditions, they are related. They are also consummated simultaneously... Therefore logically it follows that the phenomenal basis consists of a unity between the two truths, the soteriology consists of a unity between the two accumulations, and the result consists of a unity between dharmakāya and rūpakāya.[133]

Kalupahana puts it similarly: "*Artha* as well as *paramārtha* are truths *(satya)*. The former [conventional truth] is not presented as an un-truth *(a-satya)* in relation to the latter [ultimate truth], as it would be in an absolutistic tradition. Neither is the former sublated by the latter." And further: "There is no indication whatsoever that these are two truths with different standing as higher and lower."[134] Neither truth is higher nor lower than the other, neither more true nor less true, and neither more significant nor less significant.[135] Therefore Candrakīrti states: "The doctrines taught by the Buddha are based on the two truths."[136] He stresses this point by saying, "Were there any other truth whatsoever [apart from the four noble truths], that too would certainly be contained within the categories of the two truths."[137] Tsongkhapa agrees.

Why Is Conventional Truth False and Deceptive?

If the two natures are ontologically identical, why is conventional truth described as deceptive and false, while ultimate truth is described as nondeceptive and true? "Nondeceptive," Tsongkhapa argues, "is the mode of truth *(bden tshul)* of the ultimate. That is, ultimate truth does not deceive the world by posing one mode of appearance while existing in another mode."[138] Ultimate truth is described as "ultimate," not because it is absolute or higher than conventional truth, but simply because of its consistent character—its mode of appearance and its mode of being are the same—in contrast with the inconsistent character of conventional truth. Ultimate truth is nondeceptive for the same reason. Thus Candrakīrti writes, in his commentary on the *Yuktiṣaṣṭikā*: "[Interlocutor]: Why is nirvāṇa said to be the ultimate truth? [Reply]: Nirvāṇa is said to be ultimate truth based purely on worldly conventions—its nature does not deceive the world."[139]

To the cognizing consciousness, conventional truth presents itself as inherently existent. It appears to have substance, or essence, and therefore it deceives ordinary beings. "Insofar as conventional phenomena present themselves as more than conventional—as inherently existent—they deceive us. We take them to be what they are not—to be intrinsically identified, inherently existent entities. In that sense, they are false," writes Garfield. "But to the extent that we understand them as dependently arisen, empty, interdependent phenomena, they constitute a conventional truth."[140] Nāgārjuna also recognizes the deceptive nature of conventional truth in this sense: "The Victorious Conqueror has said that whatever is deceptive is false. Compounded phenomena are deceptive. Therefore they are all false."[141]

So far as Tsongkhapa is concerned, the rationale behind describing one of the two truths as ultimate, nondeceptive, or true, and the other as conventional, false, or deceptive, is to contrast the two truths on the basis of the consistency between their modes of appearance and existence. Since ultimate truth is, by definition, consistent with its mode of appearance, it is not deceptive, even to ordinary beings. However, since conventional truth is, by definition, inconsistent with its mode of appearance, it deceives ordinary beings. It is thus crucial to understand exactly what sense of falsehood is in play when the conventional is characterized as "deceptive," as Garfield rightly points out.[142]

Nevertheless this does not mean that ultimate truth can be considered epistemologically more significant than conventional truth. It is true that ordinary beings are deceived by the false and deceptive appearances of conventional truth, but the question is, are they deceived because of their knowledge of conventional truth or because they have no proper knowledge of conventional truth? The fact that conventional truth deceives ordinary beings, according to Tsongkhapa, demonstrates that they have not yet understood what conventional truth is.

Although ordinary beings experience false and deceptive conventional truth all the time, they remain oblivious to the inconsistent, and in this sense false and deceptive, nature of conventional truth. Thus instead of knowing such truths for what they are, ordinary beings perceive them to be essentially real—as if conventional truth were ultimate truth. Garfield explains:

> Yet one must bear in mind that, according to Nāgārjuna [and also for Tsongkhapa], perception untutored by Mādhyamika philosophy and rigorous practice delivers objects to consciousness as inherently existent. In this sense, the things that we see are wholly false. For most of us, the best that we can do is reason our way into knowing, but not seeing, their true nature. The goal of meditation on emptiness is to bring this knowledge into perceptual experience and, hence, to see things as they are.[143]

Tsongkhapa maintains an important distinction between knowledge of conventional truth and the ordinary experience of conventional truth. For him, they are not equivalent. Tsongkhapa contends that the ordinary being directly experiences conventional truth yet has no direct understanding of it. For ordinary beings, seeing physical forms, tasting flavors, smelling aromas, hearing sounds, touching tangible objects, and conceiving ideas are in themselves sufficient for leading a worldly life. Knowledge of conventional truth is not required. One may participate in mundane norms with mere perceptual or conceptual experiences of conventional truth—even reified ones.

Tsongkhapa likens the experience of conventional truths by ordinary beings to an audience held spellbound by a magic show. While the audience experiences the illusory animals conjured up by the magician, they may remain ignorant of the illusory nature of their experience. Knowledge of the reality is not necessary to experience the captivating effect. Similarly, so long as beings are ignorant of conventional truth, and thereby deceived by conventional truth, they are also ignorant of ultimate truth. Bodhidharma, the founder of Zen Buddhism, captures this point nicely: "Question: 'What are the two truths?' Answer: 'It is like the simmering of heated air. Deluded people see the air waving due to the heat and understand it as water, but it is really not water. It is simmering of heated air." And he continues: "The meaning of the two truths is also like this. Common men see the truth of the highest meaning as the worldly truth. Sages see the worldly truth as the truth of the highest meaning. Therefore, the *sūtra* says: 'When the Buddhas speak Dharma, they always rely upon the two truths.' The truth of the highest meaning is the worldly truth, and the worldly truth is the truth of the highest meaning."[144]

So, as long as we lack proper knowledge and understanding of either conventional or ultimate truth, Tsongkhapa insists, we have knowledge of neither. When we have proper knowledge of either of the two truths, we have proper knowledge of both.

Applying the Worldly Convention

Is it possible to reconcile Tsongkhapa's proposal that there are two actual truths with the Buddha's declaration that nirvāṇa is the only truth? In the *Cūlaviyūha Sutta,* the Buddha states: "The truth is one, there is no second about which a person who knows it would argue with one who knows. Contemplatives promote their various personal truths, that is why they do not say one thing and the same."[145] In the *Yuktiṣaṣṭikāvṛtti* [35], Candrakīrti raises the same question: "When the jīnas have stated that nirvāṇa alone is true, what learned person will then imagine that the rest is not false? How would you interpret that nirvāṇa alone is true and others are untrue?"[146] For the answer to this question Tsongkhapa relies on Candrakīrti's own explanation in the *Yuktiṣaṣṭikāvṛtti:*

> [Interlocutor]: Well, the Bhagavān states: "Oh monks! There is one noble truth. That is nirvāṇa, which is characteristically nondeceptive. What do you make of this statement?" [Reply]: Nirvāṇa is not like conditioned phenomena, which deceive the childish by presenting false appearances. For the existence of nirvāṇa is always consistent with its characteristic of the nonarising nature. Unlike conditioned phenomena, it never appears, even to the childish, as having a nature of arising *(skye ba'i ngo bo)*. Since nirvāṇa is always consistent with the mode of existence of nirvāṇa, it is explained as the noble truth, yet strictly in terms of worldly conventions.[147]

For Tsongkhapa the crucial point here is that Candrakīrti emphasizes that nirvāṇa is said to be the truth *strictly* in terms of worldly conventions. Let us briefly examine what Candrakīrti meant by this and why it is crucial for Tsongkhapa's position.

According to Candrakīrti and Tsongkhapa, in ordinary worldly discourse one may pose the question of whether phenomena such as a visual illusion, a mirage, a reflection of a face in a mirror, an echo of sound, and an image of the moon in a pool are *true?* To say that they are not true would not help to resolve the issue, since it would merely lead to the further question, why do they exist at all? The unicorn and the rabbit's horn are also false, yet they are nowhere to be found in the way that we find mirages, mirror images, and so forth. The real answer within the ordinary worldly convention (and therefore not from the Madhyamaka standpoint) must be something like this: "Entities such as illusions, mirages, reflections, and so forth are real, but they do not exist the way they appear to us. They all appear to be something other than they really are." It is the inconsistency between the appearance and the mode of existence that marks these entities as false, and since even the ordinary worldly consciousness understands this inconsistency, so visual illusions, mirages, mirror images, and so forth are described as false and deceptive phenomena. Thus, for Tsongkhapa, these are descriptions in *conventional* terms.

On the other hand, what constitutes the truth of an actual version of a face, moon, sound, and water, as opposed to an illusion or reflection?

Common sense suggests the answer would be that "because their appearances and modes of existence are consistent, they are true and nondeceptive." The nondeceptive nature of a face, moon, or sound is its ultimate truth from the perspective of worldly convention. Hence they are conventionally perceived as true or real instead of as false.

Both Candrakīrti and Tsongkhapa recognize this linguistic convention and mobilize exactly the same dialectical styles (as seen in Candrakīrti's quote above) in the Prāsaṅgika Madhyamaka system. Thus the Prāsaṅgika Mādhyamikas' insistence on conformity with the worldly conventions, at least according to Tsongkhapa's reading of it, has highly significant philosophical implications. Here are his arguments.

First, just as an illusion, a mirror image, etc., are real in an ordinary sense, despite the fact that they are deceptive and false, so, too, conventional phenomena in the Prāsaṅgika Madhyamaka sense are real, and can even be said to constitute truths, despite being recognized by the Mādhyamikas themselves as false and deceptive. Second, because the concept of ultimate truth is also taken from its ordinary application, nirvāṇa is spoken of as "ultimate" on the ground of its nondeceptive nature, in the sense that its mode of existence is consistent with its mode of appearance. The nondeceptive nature of the empty phenomenon itself constitutes its truth, and so it is conventionally described as ultimate in the Prāsaṅgika system.

Furthermore these worldly conventions, according to Tsongkhapa and Candrakīrti, further illustrate that there is no room for hierarchical ranking of the truths. Take the reflection of a face in the mirror, for instance, as opposed to the actual face. We might naïvely assume that because the reflection of a face is not an actual face and does not function as the actual face, it is of lesser importance or significance. But such logic would lead to the converse assumption that the actual face must also be of lesser importance or significance because it is not the reflection of the face, and therefore it does not function as the reflection of the face. The mere fact that the image is not something other than what it is (it is not what it reflects) should not diminish its significance. Understood as a reflection, the mirror image of the face has its own significance and even its own causal effectiveness, just as does the actual face. Moreover for Tsongkhapa the *causal effectiveness* of a thing is precisely what determines its being true. As a result of this determining factor, the thing is empirically functional, even if not necessarily consistent with its appearance, and therefore true in the ordinary sense, in its own right.

Now let us apply the same concept in the classic Prāsaṅgika context. If we claim that the conventional characteristics of a sprout, such as its color, shape, extension, size, and weight, are of lesser importance or significance because these characteristics are not identical with its emptiness, the reverse logic also applies. For the sprout's empty mode of being would not be able to function as the sprout's conventional truth, nor would it manifest itself as the sprout's conventional characteristics. Thus Tsongkhapa asserts that neither of the two truths is more or less significant than the other. Indeed, while the illusion only makes sense as illusion in relation to that which is not illusion, the reflection only makes sense as reflection in relation to that which is reflected. So, too, does the real only make sense as real in relation to the illusion, the thing reflected in relation to its reflection. This also holds in the case of discussions about the ultimate nature of things, such as the being of the sprout—it only makes sense inasmuch as it holds in discussions of ordinary phenomena. The only criterion that determines a thing's truth in the Prāsaṅgika Madhyamaka system, as represented by Tsongkhapa, is the causal effectiveness of the thing as opposed to mere *heuristic* significance. The sprout's empty mode of being and its being as appearance are both truths, insofar as both are causally effective, and thus both functional.

The two truths, understood as, respectively, the empty and the dependently arisen characters of phenomena, are on equal footing according to Prāsaṅgika Mādhyamikas of Tsongkhapa's persuasion. Nevertheless these truths have different designations—the sprout's empty mode is always described as "ultimate truth," while the conventional properties, such as color and shape, are described as "conventional truths." The former is accepted as *nondeceptive truth* while the sprout's conventional properties are accepted as *deceptive* or *false truth,* despite common sense dictating that they are true and real.

From the standpoint of an ārya's meditative equipoise, even what is accepted as empirically real in the ordinary sense is understood as false and deceptive truth. The sprout's conventional properties, for example, while having one mode of existence, present themselves to their cognizing consciousnesses with the conflicting modes of appearance. The sprout's empty mode, on the other hand, is accepted as nondeceptive truth from the standpoint of an ārya's meditative equipoise, for the way it exists and the way it appears to this consciousness are consistent.

Nevertheless, Tsongkhapa does not regard the worldly convention of ascribing different nomenclatures such as true or false, deceptive or nondeceptive, as bestowing truth on one and not the other. In Garfield's words: "It is important to note that they are introduced as two truths, and that they are introduced as distinct. This will be important to bear in mind...For it is tempting, since one of the truths is characterized as an ultimate truth, to think of the conventional as 'less true.'"[148] Just as ultimate truth is a form of truth, so, too is conventional truth—hence, for Tsongkhapa, there are indeed two truths.

Nevertheless, since the two truths are not conceptually or epistemologically identical in all respects, Tsongkhapa maintains they are rightly designated as "conventional truth" and "ultimate truth," rather than just as "truth."

The One and Only Truth

Let us now turn to Gorampa. In his view the two truths are binary opposites. Moreover, for Gorampa, whatever is false and deceptive cannot be truth—nondeception is thus the mark of truth. With this in mind, he argues: "Truth, in the end, cannot be divided into two. It therefore makes no sense to enumerate it. Therefore in the sūtra, it is said that 'there is only one noble truth, i.e., nirvāṇa, which is by nature nondeceptive.'"[149] Gorampa also cites Nāgārjuna's statement: "When the jīnas have stated that nirvāṇa alone is true, what learned person will then imagine that the rest is not false?"[150]

Gorampa rejects the authority of conventional truth by treating it as a projection of conventional mind—it is the ignorance of ordinary beings. As he writes:

> [Question]: If this were true, even the mere term *conventional truth* would be unacceptable, for whatever is conventional is incompatible with truth. [Reply]: Since [conventional] truth is posited only in relation to a conventional mind, there is no problem. Even so-called true conventionalities *(yang dag kun rdzob ces pa yang)* are posited as truth with respect to a conventional mind.[151]

This statement is based on the assumption that conventional truth is not actual truth. To justify the description of conventional phenomena as a form of truth, Gorampa argues that conventional truth is simply described to suit the "conventional mind," that is, the ignorant mind of an ordinary being experiencing the phenomenal world. In other words, conventional truth is described as "truth" only from the perspective of ignorance. It is a truth projected *(sgro brtag pa)* and taken for granted.

Gorampa equates the ontological significance of conventional truth with "the appearances of nonexistent entities like illusions."[152] As Sakya Paṇḍita puts it: "Conventional truths are like reflections of the moon in the water—despite their nonexistence, they appear due to thoughts."[153] And Sakya Paṇḍita further argues: "The defining characteristic of conventional truth constitutes the appearances of the nonexistent objects."[154] In this sense, conventional truths "are things apprehended by the cognition perceiving empirical entities [i.e., the ignorance of ordinary beings]. Those very things are found as nonexistent by the cognition analyzing their mode of existence that is itself posited as the ultimate."[155]

Most importantly, Gorampa argues that to describe conventional truth as "truth" has great pedagogical significance. Conventional truth is an expedient means to achieve ultimate truth, says Gorampa, and the Buddha described conventional truth as truth to suit the mentality of ordinary beings.[156] The two truths are thus categorized as a *means (thabs)* and a *result (thabs byung)*. Conventional truth, for Gorampa, is the means to attain the one and only truth that is nirvāṇa.[157] When conventional truth is provisionally designated as truth, it is contrasted with ultimate truth by treating the former as ignorant *(rmongs)*, or ignorance, and the latter as non-ignorant *(ma rmongs)*, or wisdom.[158]

According to Gorampa's view, any duality ascribed to truth is untenable. Since there is only one truth, it cannot be distinguished any further. Sakya Paṇḍita,[159] Longchen Rabjam,[160] Rendawa,[161] Rongtön Shakya Gyaltsen,[162] Taktsang Lotsawa,[163] Shakya Chogden,[164] and Gendün Chöpel[165] all agree with Gorampa that truth itself is not divisible. These scholars also agree that the distinction between the two truths is essentially between two conflicting perspectives, rather than any division within truth as such. As such Shakya Chogden, for example, writes:

> Precise enumeration *(grangs nges)* of the twofold truth explained by all earlier Tibetans rests on the precise enumeration of the mistaken cognition *(blo 'khrul)* and unmistaken cognition *(blo ma 'khrul)*. With this underpinning reason, they explained the precise enumeration through the elimination of the third alternative. There is not even a single figure to be found who claims the view comparable with the latter [Tibetan scholars, i.e., the Gelugpas], who assert a precise enumeration of the twofold truth based on the certification of valid cognitions.[166]

Among those who avowedly join Gorampa in claiming that the ultimate truth (i.e., nirvāṇa) is the sole truth and that the phenomenal world is utter illusion are Longchen Rabjam,[167] Shakya Chogden,[168] Taktsang Lotsawa,[169] Mipham Rinpoche,[170] Karmapa Mikyö Dorje,[171] and Gendün Chöpel.[172] Modern scholars such as Lindtner,[173] Singh,[174] Stcherbatsky,[175] and Murti[176] also follow the same line of argument. Although all of them are monists about truth, there is a differentiation to be made. Shakya Chogden[177] and Taktsang Lotsawa are nonabsolute monists. Although they maintain that ultimate truth is the sole truth, they do *not* claim it as a *truly established phenomenon (bden par grub pa),* one that withstands logical analysis. For example, Taktsang Lotsawa argues, "nirvāṇa, alone, is accepted as the truth and nondeceptive from the perspective of reasoning consciousness. Even then, when it is subjected to analysis, not only is nirvāṇa unestablished, but if anything at all superseded nirvāṇa, that should also remain [unestablished]."[178] Thus no phenomenon, according to Taktsang Lotsawa, withstands logical analysis. The rest are avowed absolute monists. For example, Mipham Rinpoche proposes with clarity and vigor that the ultimate truth is ultimately established and that it withstands logical analysis without being undermined:

> Reality is truly established. Conventional phenomena are established as false and deceptive. The ultimate, which is free from [falsity and deception], is established as truth of nondeception and nonfalsehood. If this remains unestablished, it would then be impossible to see the ārya's truth. Merely seeing false and deceptive objects like ordinary beings would never ever free anybody... Whatever is *dharmatā,* i.e., ultimate truth, is truly established, because it is established as the cognitive sphere of nondual wisdom. Besides, it withstands logical analysis, for no logical reasoning whatsoever can undermine it or destroy it. Therefore so long as it does not withstand logical analysis, it is not ultimate, because it would absurdly be conventional.[179]

Modern interpreters—such as Kalupahana,[180] Jay Garfield,[181] Jeffrey Hopkins,[182] Paul Williams,[183] Guy Newland,[184] Tom Tillemans,[185] and José Cabezón[186]—have in some of their works suggested a distinction between the two truths that is minimal and strictly epistemological in nature. Conventional truth and ultimate truth are, in their presentation of Madhyamaka philosophy, mutually entailing—the two truths are not ontologically hierarchical. Others modern interpretions treat conventional and ultimate as *levels* of truth or reality.[187] This view of the two truths, Newland argues, is no different from "an understanding of the two truths as alternative standpoints or perspectives."[188] In other contemporary works, scholars present a range of views.[189] It is apparent that there is neither consensus nor complete dissension on the issue of the relationship between the two truths.

This is not the case, however, with the views held by Tsongkhapa and Gorampa. Since Tsongkhapa views both truths as actual truths, he is fully committed to a nonparadoxical, mutually entailing, and nonhierarchical relationship between them. In contrast, since for Gorampa ultimate truth is the only truth, he is committed to a paradoxical, contradictory, and hierarchical relationship between the two truths.

Conclusion

The gulf between Tsongkhapa's and Gorampa's positions regarding the nature of the relationship between the two truths is evident from the outset and lays the groundwork for the debate between them. The key to Tsongkhapa's view is his insistence on the two-natures theory while for Gorampa it is the mere-mind theory. Tsongkhapa attempts to show that both truths have the two natures as their ontological reference, and so the distinction between them cannot be reduced to one of mere perspective or a purely epistemological or linguistic practice. In contrast, Gorampa's approach reinforces the conception of the two truths as founded in two contradictory perspectives. Consequently, for him, the distinction between the two truths is purely subjective and ultimately reducible to their cognizing consciousnesses—ignorance and wisdom.

When the analysis moves to the relationship between the two truths, the gap widens. By arguing that the two truths have a single ontological identity, even though they have different conceptual identities, Tsongkhapa shows that they have equal ontological status despite being verified along separate epistemic pathways. He also insists that they are equally significant in terms of their epistemological and soteriological values. Gorampa insists that the two truths are distinct and incompatible; he not only argues that they are ontologically distinct, but he also disparages conventional truth as less significant in terms of its epistemological and soteriological value. By casting the two truths hierarchically, Gorampa upholds a monistic and absolutist view. This is in contrast to Tsongkhapa's pluralist and nonabsolutist account that puts the two truths on equal footing. Yet Tsongkhapa and Gorampa both remain convinced of their consistency with Prāsaṅgika Madhyamaka thought.

2. Meanings and Definitions of the Two Truths

When asked "Great sage, what is the meaning of the truth?"
Mañjuśrī answered: "Son of heaven, the truth is no other than voidness. Thus voidness may be called the truth. Voidness is said to be the truth because it is without beginning and end, without decrease and increase. That [dharmas are] empty of nature is the truth. Suchness is the truth. The dharmadhātu is the truth. Reality is the truth. Thus such a truth is no truth [at all]."[190]

Introduction

THIS CHAPTER compares Tsongkhapa's and Gorampa's definitions of the two truths in two parts. The first part offers a detailed analysis of the meaning of the two truths.[191] This includes analyses of several important concepts related to the meaning of *conventional,* or *saṃvṛti (kun rdzob)*—namely, ignorance, mutual interdependence, and worldly conventions. These concepts and relations, as we will see, are critical in understanding the defining characteristics of the two truths. They are also key to clarifying the background to the discussion and addressing the significance of, and relationship between, the two truths.

Since the meanings and definitions of saṃvṛti proposed by Tsongkhapa and Gorampa are closely intertwined with their understanding of the scope and limits of the objects of negation, we will explore the nature of ignorance in relation to the concealers *(sgrib pa, āvaraṇas).* This will be followed by a brief, but nonetheless important, comparison of the various meanings of ultimate truth, or *paramārthasatya (don dam bden pa);* here the focus will be on whether the unconditioned and transcendent nature of paramārthasatya is epistemological or metaphysical.

The second part of this chapter is devoted to a comparative study of the definitions of the two truths offered by Tsongkhapa and Gorampa. Firstly, I will compare the criteria they each mobilize to determine the defining characteristics of the two truths. I will argue that for Gorampa, the two contradictory perspectives, namely, ignorance and wisdom, determine his definitions of the two truths, whereas for Tsongkhapa, this is determined by the empirically valid consciousness and ultimately valid consciousness. Secondly, through a comparison of the status of the two truths, Tsongkhapa's view that the two truths stand on an equal footing is reinforced. In his understanding all empirically given phenomena satisfy the defining characteristics of both truths, since they are equivalent to the dual natures verified by their corresponding consciousnesses. I will argue that for Gorampa, in contrast, the defining characteristics of the two truths are mutually excluding and hierarchical.

The Meanings of Saṃvṛti

We begin with Candrakīrti's explanation of the meaning of saṃvṛti. In the *Prasannapadā* he attributes three meanings to the term:

> *Saṃvṛti* means entirely obstructing. That is, ignorance is the concealer *(saṃvṛti, kun rdzob)* because it entirely covers up the suchness of all things. Or, *saṃvṛti* means interdependence; it has the sense of "due to being interdependent." Or, *saṃvṛti* means "term"; it is equivalent with "worldly convention." [In this sense,] it has the character of expression and expressed, consciousness and object of consciousness, etc.[192]

Tsongkhapa and Gorampa both comment on Candrakirti's three senses *(sgra bshad)* of *samvṛti:*[193]

- *ignorant consciousness,* which conceals the true nature of things either through the conception of essence or through the reification of essence;
- *that which is mutually interdependent (phan tshun brtan pa, paraparasaṃbhavana);*
- *worldly conventions ('jig rten tha snyad, lokavyavahāra).*

Tsongkhapa comments on these three meanings as follows:

> [1] *Kun rdzob (saṃvṛti)* is nescience or ignorance because it conceals *('gebs),* and thereby obstructs *(sgrib par byed pa)* reality. Since the [Sanskrit] equivalent of *kun rdzob (saṃvṛti)* also applies to the obstruction *(sgrib pa),* it is explained in these terms; this however is far from stating that all *kun rdzob* are obstructors. [2] Or, *kun rdzob* means mutually interdependent *(phan tshun brtan pa).* This means that, since [all phenomena] must be mutually interdependent, it is untrue that they possess self-instituting natures *(tshugs thub kyi rang bzhin pa).* The reason for this explanation of the term *[kun rdzob]* is also applicable to ultimate truth, yet the term *kun rdzob* does not apply [to ultimate truth, for it is not *kun rdzob*]. For example, the reason for the explanation of the term "lake-born" [lotus flowers] is applicable to frogs [since frogs are born in lakes], but the term "lake-born" does not apply to them [because they are not lotuses]. [3] Or, *kun rdzob* means terms *(brda, saṃket)*—i.e., worldly conventions *('jig rten gyi tha snyad, lokavyavahāra).* That too is explained as having characteristics of expresser and expressed, consciousness and object of consciousness, and so forth. Therefore *[kun rdzob]* must not held to be merely the object possessing conventions *(yul can gyi tha snyad),* consciousness, and expressions.[194]

Gorampa's explanation states:

> [1] *Kun rdzob* is that which obstructs all. The primal ignorance is described as *kun rdzob* because ignorance thoroughly conceals the reality of things. [2] Or, *kun rdzob* means mutually interdependent. It means [that things] are mutually interdependent. [3] Or, *kun rdzob* refers to terms, i.e., worldly conventions. That too is explained as having the characteristics of expresser and expressed, consciousness and objects of consciousness, and so forth.[195]

Both Tsongkhapa and Gorampa point out that these are connotations or implications saṃvṛti *(kun rdzob)* may bear in various contexts. In the following three sections, we will briefly consider the epistemological, ontological, and soteriological significance of each of these three meanings in turn.

Saṃvṛti as Ignorant Consciousness

In the first sense of saṃvṛti, the debate between Tsongkhapa and Gorampa centers primarily on the scope of ignorance and its implications for the system of conventional truths *(saṃvṛtisatya, kun rdzob bden pa).* Tsongkhapa argues that essences reified by ignorant consciousness are strictly epistemological, since they are purely conceptual reifications. Empirically, essences are nonexistent and, strictly speaking, do not have any ontological foundation. Despite the reifying agents themselves (ordinary beings) clinging to essences as realities or truths, those essences do not constitute empirical truths. The eradication of ignorance thus leads to the eradication of conceptually reified essences, but not to that of empirical truths themselves.

Gorampa argues that empirical truths are themselves essences reified by ignorance, and he therefore also denies that there are any so-called *conceptually reified* essences apart from what are empirically given. The eradication of ignorance, according to this view, leads to the eradication of empirical truth.

In the context in which saṃvṛti refers to ignorant consciousness, both Tsongkhapa and Gorampa maintain that saṃvṛti has the connotation of what Newland[196] calls a "concealer," for it specifically refers to a consciousness that conceals the true identities of phenomena. Phenomena, for both Tsongkhapa and Gorampa, are devoid of essences and are essentially empty of any substantial mode of being. Due to ignorance, however, as Tsongkhapa and Gorampa explain it, ordinary beings conceptually reify or superimpose *(sgro 'dogs pa)* onto phenomena the notion of an essential mode of existence. Tsongkhapa and Gorampa also agree that ignorance compels ordinary beings to unconsciously apply conceptually distorted identities to phenomena, and to confuse them with true identities. Since ignorance conceals the truth from being directly perceived, it is described as a "concealer."[197] Ignorance is also described as an "obscuring consciousness" *(rmongs par byed)* inasmuch as it literally obstructs sentient beings from seeing things as they really are. Gorampa, for example, argues:

> In the first [etymological explanation of] *saṃvṛtisatya, sam* is [an abbreviated form] of *samyag,* meaning "reality," and *vṛti* means "to conceal." Since it conceals the true meaning of reality, ignorance—the conception of true existence—is a model of *kun rdzob,* regardless of the difference between reified objects *(kun brtag pa)* and intuitive assumptions *(lhan skyes). Satya (bden pa)*

> means "truth." It is *truth* in the sense that it appears true from the perspective of the ignorant consciousness.[198]

However, Tsongkhapa and Gorampa soon diverge in their treatments of ignorance. Unlike Tsongkhapa, Gorampa goes on to argue that saṃvṛti in its connotation as ignorance is responsible for reifying *saṃvṛtisatya,* that is, for reifying the whole system of empirical truths *(tha snyad bden pa, vyāvahārikasatya).* Indeed, according to Gorampa's view, there is no cognitive process that does not reify *saṃvṛtisatya* at the same time as verifying it. Every cognitive event, either perceptual or conceptual, reifies or conceives essence, and therefore reifies or conceives all cognitions and cognized objects classified as objects of negation *(dgag bya).* Every cognition thus operates under the influence of ignorance.

Objects of negation, according to Gorampa, are of two types—soteriological objects of negation *(lam gyi dgag bya)* and epistemological objects of negation *(rig pa'i dgag bya).* We will leave the details of soteriological objects of negation for later consideration and first address the exact scope of epistemological objects of negation in Gorampa's account. In the following passage Gorampa clearly asserts that all subjects and objects, and thus all conventional truths, belong to epistemological objects of negation:

> The soteriological object of negation is constitutive of all deceptive appearances. The epistemological *(rigs pa)* and the scriptural *(lung)* objects of negation *(dgag bya)*...are comprised of apprehended objects and apprehending subjects. The former [apprehended objects] include two types [of objects of negation]: that which is grossly reified through philosophical misconception and that which is reified by virtue of innate misconception...The latter, the subjective object of negation, is comprised of all cognitions and distorted views—including concepts such as "this object," and "that object."[199]

Tsongkhapa also distinguishes between soteriological and epistemological objects of negation. However, for him epistemological objects of negation consist of "the conception of essence" and of "essence *per se.*"[200] Of the two, he sees the latter as fundamental, since the eradication of reified essence leads to the eradication of the consciousness that conceives or reifies essence. The erroneous conception of essence does not arise if its conceptual object, i.e., essence, is negated. The cognizing subject depends on its object to exist, since the existence of both subject and object is one of mutual interdependence.[201] In direct contrast with Gorampa's view, wherein empirical truths themselves are considered as epistemological objects of negation, Tsongkhapa argues that "whatever is [the epistemological] object of negation must have no empirical existence. For something that exists empirically cannot be repudiated by way of conceptual analysis."[202] This does not mean that repudiation of epistemological objects of negation is a futile exercise. Despite the nonexistence of essence *per se,* argues Tsongkhapa, "the misconceptions pertaining to the existence of essence still arise. This has to be repudiated."[203]

Given the more restricted scope of the first sense of saṃvṛti, Tsongkhapa equates it with ignorance and maintains that whatever is reified by ignorance must be included among epistemological objects of negation. It is thus crucial to note that, in this context, the term saṃvṛti should not be understood in its usual sense. The scope of saṃvṛti does not, therefore, include subjects and objects in any broad sense. Gorampa, again, argues that the first sense of saṃvṛti must include all conventional phenomena. He derives this argument from his Indian predecessor, Jayānanda (ca. 1200 C.E.). Jayānanda treats the entire system of *saṃvṛtisatya* as a reification of ignorance. In his commentary on the *Madhayamakāvatāra,* Jayānanda distinguishes between the two types of *concealers (sgrib pa, āvaraṇas)*—namely, deluded ignorance *(nyon mongs can gyi ma rig pa, kleśājñāna)* and nondeluded ignorance *(nyon mongs can ma yin pa'i ma rig pa, akleśājñāna).* The former is seen as responsible for causing the recurrence of saṃsāric life, while the latter is held responsible for the appearance of the conventional world.[204] Gorampa is in complete accord with Jayānanda on this issue.

Tsongkhapa considers the view held by Jayānanda, and therefore Gorampa, to be extremely problematic, at least as far as the Prāsaṅgika Madhyamaka is concerned. For Tsongkhapa, to identify ignorance as saṃvṛti "amounts to identifying saṃvṛti in terms of a perspective that refers to saṃvṛti, but this does not amount to identifying saṃvṛti in a general sense."[205] To describe saṃvṛti or ignorance as a concealer because it obstructs seeing true reality is "far from claiming that all saṃvṛti are concealers" according to Tsongkhapa.[206] It is acceptable for the Prāsaṅgika Madhyamaka to maintain that all phenomena are saṃvṛti, that is, conventionalities, and yet it is not acceptable to maintain that all phenomena are saṃvṛti, that is, concealers of reality. Hence "concealer of reality," in the case of Tsongkhapa, specifically refers to ignorant consciousness but not to phenomenal objects and sense perceptions.

Tsongkhapa does acknowledge, however, that saṃvṛti has another dimension. When saṃvṛti—ignorance as a concealer of reality—is understood in conjunction with the term *satya (bden pa),* then the two terms can be combined to form *saṃvṛtisatya (kun rdzob bden pa)*—literally, "truth for a concealer." In this context, *satya* should be taken as the object of consciousness, while *saṃvṛti* refers to the deluded consciousness itself. This very specific *saṃvṛtisatya,* according to Tsongkhapa, "is posited entirely by the power of a deluded ignorance."[207] In fact, this particular *satya,* as we are about to see, is said to be entirely fabricated by the deluded consciousness—it has no empirical objectivity whatsoever.

The question then arises: What is the ontological status of *satya,* i.e., truth reified by this saṃvṛti (deluded ignorance)? How is this particular truth as reified by ignorance different from other empirically given truths? Since Gorampa treats conceptually reified truth and empirically given truth as one and the same, these questions do not arise for him. But as Tsongkhapa insists on the radical distinction of conceptually reified truth from empirically given truth, his responses to the above questions are crucial:

> Under the influence of this *kun rdzob*—the conception of true existence—things such as blue colors appear to have essential existence, while in fact they have no essence whatsoever. False constructions fabricated [by the ignorance] appear so real to sentient beings that they are described by the Buddha as "truths for worldly beings," i.e., they are real [only] from the perspective of the erroneous consciousness of ordinary beings.[208]

In Tsongkhapa's view, *satya*—truth reified by ignorance—entails reified essence and the conception of essence. Essence fabricated by ignorance, which is truth or reality for deluded consciousness, is nevertheless utterly rejected by Madhyamaka thought. In fact, Tsongkhapa argues that it is one of the distinctive features of Prāsaṅgika (as opposed to Svātantrika) to proclaim that things do not have essences even conventionally. Although essence is recognized as truth by ordinary people—and thus described as a truth for ordinary beings, or "truth for a concealer"—it is nonetheless utterly nonexistent for the Prāsaṅgikas.

For Prāsaṅgikas "essence...is not a conventional truth."[209] Far from being empirical truth, Tsongkhapa insists that "anything that is posited by the reifying cognition is not even conventionally possible."[210] For while essence is reified by ignorance, it is empirically nonexistent. Essence superimposed or conceived through ignorance must not therefore have any empirical grounding *(tha snyad du 'ang mi srid).* For something to be qualified as *saṃvṛtisatya,* Tsongkhapa argues that "it must inevitably satisfy an empirical position."[211] Prāsaṅgika Mādhyamikas are unanimous in asserting the impossibility of things existing essentially, in and of themselves. This is because no nonreifying consciousness, such as perception, verifies the existence of essence. "This shows," Tsongkhapa concludes, "that essence is purely subjective."[212] Kalupahana also notes that, for the Mādhyamika, "the notion of a substance was rejected because it could not be identified with anything in experience."[213] For Tsongkhapa, then, reified essence and the conception of essence constitute the central epistemological objects of negation. This is why the distinction between the descriptions of phenomena as saṃvṛti on the one hand and ignorance (understood as a reifying perspective) as saṃvṛti on the other plays such a crucial role in Tsongkhapa's account.

This gives rise to the next question: what is the impact of eradicating ignorance and its reified essence, and so of eradicating epistemological objects of negation? Tsongkhapa and Gorampa agree that all phenomena conceived as essentially real by ordinary sentient beings are understood as conditioned and false by those who have eradicated ignorance. The essences fabricated by ignorance can only deceive immature beings, but these reified truths cannot deceive enlightened beings such as *ārya śrāvakas, ārya pratyekabuddhas,* and *ārya bodhisattvas.* Hence Tsongkhapa, for example, argues "since those beings no longer presuppose the existence of such essences, they see all phenomena as essentially unreal."[214] All conventional phenomena are "mere saṃvṛti, just like illusions, and they are perceived as dependently arisen."[215] Gorampa agrees.

In Tsongkhapa's view, although the three types of āryas are free from saṃvṛti—ignorance and its reified essence—their empirically valid cognitions consistently verify *saṃvṛtisatya,* conventional truths.[216] This means that although āryas understand all conditioned phenomena *(saṃskāra, 'du 'byed rnams)* as untrue, they do not reduce "conventional phenomena to nonconventional truths of some kind."[217] And those conventional truths are not concealers, whether they relate to subjective consciousness or to the object of that consciousness. But for Gorampa both subjective consciousness and objective phenomena, so long as they are saṃvṛti, are responsible for concealing the truth. Both subjective consciousnesses and the objects of consciousnesses are, according to this view, concealers of reality. "Objective appearances of the conditioned phenomena perceived by the three types of āryas in their postmeditative equipoise," Gorampa argues, "are also concealers of reality. For [those appearances] arise due to the power of the impressions or the apprehensions of duality."[218] Moreover Gorampa also claims that objective appearances obstruct the development of the meditative equipoise that transcends the apprehension of appearances.

While Tsongkhapa argues that empirical truths are not posited by ignorance but instead are certified by empirically valid consciousnesses, Gorampa takes empirical truths to be wholly posited by ignorance. Gorampa adopts this position from Jayānanda. When Jayānanda was asked, "But why are illusory objects like dependently arisen phenomena still apparent after the eradication of ignorance?" he replied, "The operation of mere ignorance conceals true knowledge *(jñeyāvaraṇa)*."[219] Gorampa shares this view.

Saṃvṛti as Mutually Interdependent

The second sense of saṃvṛti is *mutually interdependent (phan tshun brten pa, paraparasaṃbhavana)*. Tsongkhapa views this as a radical contrast with the first meaning of saṃvṛti, i.e., as ignorance. The mutual interdependence of the two truths here is both epistemological and ontological. For Tsongkhapa, even ultimate truth, let alone all empirically given truths, should be classified as categories of saṃvṛti in the sense of being mutually interdependent. Gorampa accepts that the second meaning of saṃvṛti applies to empirical truth in both ontologically and epistemologically, but he adamantly denies it applies to ultimate truth. For him ultimate truth is ontologically transcendent—it cannot be saṃvṛti at any level.

Let us turn to Tsongkhapa first. If the term *saṃvṛti* is taken to mean "mutually interdependent," he argues, saṃvṛti must apply exhaustively to *all* phenomena, including ultimate truth. At issue here is not merely the relation between phenomena and the apprehending consciousness; it is the ontological status of all phenomena. With respect to empirical or conventional truth, mutual interdependence entails an absence of essence. In other words, being mutually interdependent means that phenomena could not exist were they not relational and interdependent. "Since all phenomena arise through a network of causes and conditions, they are thereby empty of the self-defining characteristics."[220]

Mutual interdependence, in Tsongkhapa's view, is not restricted to empirical truths alone. Saṃvṛti in this sense refers also to the interdependence of ultimate truth and conventional truth. The mode of existence of ultimate truth is entirely dependent on its conventional counterpart. The two are like subject and predicate in that the latter cannot exist without the former and vice versa. In this sense *paramārthasatya,* ultimate truth, can be included in the categories of saṃvṛti—not because it fulfills the defining criterion of saṃvṛti, but because it is ontologically and epistemologically interdependent with conventional truth.

The notion of classifying ultimate truth as saṃvṛti is not sustainable, argues Tsongkhapa, if ultimate truth is given primacy—whether ontological or epistemological—over conventional truth. He himself accords *paramārthasatya* and *saṃvṛtisatya* equal status. *Paramārthasatya* is the ultimate nature, or ultimate mode, of empirically given truths.[221] Since ultimate truth is not possible without a characterized empirical object, *paramārthasatya* must be a dependently arisen phenomenon. Indeed, ultimate truth is none other than the ultimate mode of being of empirical truth. If *paramārthasatya* were not a dependently arisen phenomenon, it would then be ontologically absolute and therefore essentially real. In that case, *paramārthasatya* would be neither equivalent to an empty phenomenon nor categorizable as saṃvṛti—a mutually interdependent phenomenon.

Gorampa agrees with Tsongkhapa in recognizing empirical phenomena as mutually interdependent and as being dependently arisen and contingent. Gorampa explains *saṃ* as meaning "interdependent" *(brten pa)* or "relative" *(ltos pa)* and *vṛti* as "engaging" *('jug pa).*[222] The first two, *interdependent* and *relative,* reflect the idea of *ontological interdependence,* while the third, *engaging,* reflects the idea of *epistemological interdependence.* The point of contrast for Gorampa is that all interdependent phenomena, namely, all conventional and thus empirically given truths, are themselves the effects of ignorance—they arise as the result of ignorance. Although he takes saṃvṛti to mean mutually interdependent, Gorampa privileges dependence of object on subject and hence relativity to the subject. According to this view, the phenomenal world is ontologically dependent on the cognizing subject. Moreover, like Jayānanda, Gorampa argues that ignorance causally projects all empirical truths, either "through the impressions of primordial ignorance that conceives true existence," or "due to familiarity with flawed philosophical systems."[223]

So far as interdependence is concerned, Gorampa sees conventional and ultimate truth as radically distinct—ultimate truth is not in any respect ontologically dependent or interdependent. Firstly, ultimate truth is not projected by primal ignorance, for it is the only nondeceptive truth. Secondly, ultimate truth has ontological primacy over empirical truth. In other words, it is ontologically distinct and outranks empirical truth. Ultimate truth is ontologically free from the imperfections of empirical truths such as being conditioned, false, and deceptive, and thus also free of interdependence. It is ontologically transcendent and absolute. Hence, according to Gorampa, ultimate truth cannot in any circumstance constitute a category of saṃvṛti. In endorsing such a view, Murti states, "[Saṃvṛti] may also mean the mutual dependence of things—their relativity. In this sense it is equated with phenomena, and is in direct contrast with the absolute which is, by itself, unrelated."[224] Similarly, Jaideva Singh states: "The Absolute comprehended through the categories of thought is phenomena and phenomena stripped of these categories are the Absolute."[225]

There is yet another important distinction between Tsongkhapa and Gorampa. As far as the former is concerned, ontological interdependence *per se* is precisely what constitutes the *paramārthasatya,* the ultimate nature, of all phenomena. There is no *paramārthasatya* of phenomena apart from their being dependently arisen. To know phenomena as dependently arisen is tantamount to knowing ultimate truth. Gorampa argues the incompatibility of dependent arising and ultimate truth. The perception of phenomena as dependently arisen operates only under the spell of ignorance, whether deluded or nondeluded. Dependently arisen phenomena are ultimately reducible to the effects of ignorant consciousness, and hence cannot be the ultimate truth of any other phenomena.

Saṃvṛti as Worldly Conventions

> The Buddha said: "Good man, well said, well said! Just as you have said, the Buddhas, Tathāgatas, say that there are sentient beings, and so forth, in order to conform to conventions, even though they know that there is actually no no-self, saṃsāra, going, or coming. There is no dharma that can be nirvāṇa either. However, in order to [cause others to] realize the dharma leading to nirvāṇa, they discourse on nirvāṇa."[226]

The third meaning of saṃvṛti is *worldly convention ('jig rten gyi tha snyad, lokavyavahāra)*[227] or "terms" *(brda, saṅket).* This sense of saṃvṛti, according to Tsongkhapa, encompasses the labels we give to things along with the six consciousnesses and their objective referents. As Candrakīrti puts it, saṃvṛti as worldly convention "has the characteristics of expression and expressed object, consciousness and object of consciousness, and so forth."[228] Whereas the first meaning of saṃvṛti specifically equates it with reifying ignorant consciousness, Tsongkhapa argues that in the third sense saṃvṛti "must not be held to be merely subjective conventionalities—consciousness and expressions."[229] This third sense of saṃvṛti encompasses all cognitive resources, namely, the six senses—eye, ear, nose, tongue, body, and intellect—their six corresponding objects—form, sound, aroma, taste, tactile objects, and ideas—and the six consciousnesses—visual, auditory, etc.—that arise from the contact between the six senses and the six objects.

Gorampa agrees with Tsongkhapa on this meaning of saṃvṛti, explaining that *saṃ* refers to *saṅket (brda),* i.e., terms or expressions, while *vṛti* means "to posit." *Saṃvṛti* therefore refers here to "conventionalities posited by terms or expressions."[230] The second and third meanings of saṃvṛti—mutually interdependent and worldly conventions, respectively—in Gorampa's view, are closely tied to the first meaning of saṃvṛti. The whole system of worldly conventions—including cognizing consciousness, cognized objects, terms, and their referents, processes, events, etc.—are said to be the effects of ignorance, the first sense of saṃvṛti. Without ignorance neither the second nor the third meaning would be able to arise or make any sense. Gorampa also argues that *saṃvṛtisatya* is so described because it is true only from the vantage point of ignorant consciousness; the first sense of saṃvṛti is fundamental and overrides the significance of the other two. It is in this sense that objects are "conventional truths and are considered referents of linguistic conventions."[231]

This discussion concludes with a brief reflection on Tsongkhapa's and Gorampa's divergent readings of a crucial verse from Candrakīrti's *Madhyamakāvatāra:*

> Because ignorance conceals the true nature, it is (1) saṃvṛti.
> It conceives all conditioned phenomena as real.
> Thus, they are declared by [Śākya]mūnī as (2) *saṃvṛtisatya.*
> All conditioned things are (3) saṃvṛti.[232]

For each of these three uses of the term *saṃvṛti,* Tsongkhapa and Gorampa offer contrasting interpretations. Tsongkhapa maintains that the first use of the term differs significantly from the latter two uses, arguing that these uses "should not be taken as identical."[233] The first use of saṃvṛti, he claims, refers to subjective consciousness, *qua* ignorance, as a concealer. Ignorance, Tsongkhapa holds, "is a saṃvṛti because it is a reifying cognition that superimposes essential existence onto [contingent phenomena] by concealing the true mode of existence from being seen [by sentient beings]."[234] As was pointed out earlier, when saṃvṛti is understood with reference to *saṃvṛtisatya,* literally "a truth-for-a-concealer," the idea is, as Tsongkhapa puts it, "to identify [a specific] saṃvṛti, i.e., a perspective to which the saṃvṛti is being referred. However, strictly speaking this [identification] does not amount to identifying saṃvṛti in a general sense."[235] Tsongkhapa avers that saṃvṛti in this context refers specifically to an erroneous or a reifying cognition. Hence the first sense of saṃvṛti employed by Candrakīrti refers to a concealer, which is taken to mean "etymologically the same" *(skad dod)* as saṃvṛti.[236]

The second meaning of saṃvṛti has two senses. It refers to *essence* as it is conceptually reified by ignorant consciousness, which, Tsongkhapa argues, is empirically nonexistent. It can also refer to the empirical phenomena that act as the basis for the reification process, for example, to the table that is itself reified as an essential phenomenon. The third saṃvṛti, Tsongkhapa asserts, refers to all conventionalities in a much broader sense. All conditioned phenomena or dependently arisen phenomena, including ignorance itself and the conception of essence, come under the third category of saṃvṛti. However, not all conventionalities satisfy the criterion of being conventional truth. As Tsongkhapa argues, "if something is a conventional truth, it must necessarily meet the criterion of empirical existence."[237] Ignorance and all other dependently arising phenomena are conventional truths and are grounded in empirical evidence. While the essence projected by ignorance constitutes a conventional truth for ordinary beings, essence is not a conventional truth from the Madhyamaka standpoint. It does not meet the criterion of empirical truth. "It is thus unfounded even empirically."[238] Therefore, as Candrakīrti puts it, "[essence] and other things that are understood to be false even conventionally [e.g., the reflection of a face being an actual face, mirage being water, etc.,] are not considered as categories of conventional truths."[239] Nonetheless, they are considered as categories of conventionalities.

Gorampa's reading of same verse in the *Madhyamakāvatāra* is relatively straightforward in comparison with Tsongkhapa's. He takes the first sense of saṃvṛti to be synonymous with ignorance itself and the latter two as synonymous with the objects found or reified by such ignorance. In this respect, objects themselves are the essences, and there is no essence apart from what is empirically given. Dependently arisen phenomena, therefore, are the categories of objects that are projected by ignorance. In any case, as

Tom Tillemans rightly suggests: "Whatever be the translation, it is important that *saṃvṛtisatya* is not misunderstood as being just a purely conventional and arbitary agreement in the way in which the moon's being called 'that which has a rabbit' is just purely conventional agreement." For both Tsongkhapa and Gorampa the term *saṃvṛti,* while often translated into English as "conventionality," does not mean mere conventions.[240] Both hold the view that "What is true for the world, be it the impermanence of phenomena or the law of cause of effect, is so not just because of simple conventional agreements or arbitary words—whether we are Svātantrika or Prāsaṅgika, s*aṃvṛtisatya* is deeper than that."[241] The explanations of saṃvṛti by Tibetans like Longchen Rabjam,[242] Sakya Paṇḍita,[243] Shakya Chogden,[244] Rongtön Shakya Gyaltsen,[245] and their modern counterpart, Murti[246] largely accord with Gorampa's interpretation. All of them treat primal ignorance as the villain responsible for projecting the entire system of conventional truths. Consequently they also agree that the senses of saṃvṛti as conventional and as interdependent are entirely dependent upon the first meaning of saṃvṛti as ignorance.

Concealers: The Soteriological Objects of Negation

The scope and role of ignorance is a central issue in any exploration of the three meanings of saṃvṛti, and since the scope of the negative impact of ignorance is a crucial arena for Buddhists, we will briefly consider Tsongkhapa's and Gorampa's views on the *soteriological objects of negation (lam gyi dgag bya).*

Both Tsongkhapa and Gorampa maintain that it is the presence of the soteriological objects of negation—namely, the two types of obstructors, or concealers *(sgrib pa, āvaraṇas)*—that prevent sentient beings from attaining correct knowledge, and so from attaining enlightenment. The concealers comprise so-called deluded concealers *(mnyon sgrib, kleśṭāvaraṇas)* and nondeluded concealers *(nyon rmongs can ma yin pa'i sgrib pa, akleśṭāvaraṇa).* Nondeluded concealers are also called *concealers of true knowledge (shes bya'i sgrib pa, jñeyāvaraṇa).* These two types of concealers prevent cognizing beings from knowing phenomena as they actually are.

Deluded concealers are comprised of three main elements: craving, aversion, and ignorance, the so-called three poisons. The last, deluded ignorance, plays the chief role in concealing reality through either actively reifying essences or passively conceiving them, and sometimes both in conjunction. Either way, deluded concealers distort the ultimate truth of processes, events, and phenomena.[247]

The nondeluded concealers—concealers of true knowledge—are comprised of the predispositions or imprints left on our minds by the deluded concealers. For both Tsongkhapa and Gorampa the concealers of true knowledge make cognizing beings vulnerable to the reifying influence of deluded ignorance.[248] These subtle mental conditionings, unlike ignorance itself, do not themselves bring about active reification but are instead dispositions that may passively persist even when the *deluded* concealers have been eradicated. Just as the smell of the onion remains even after the onion itself has been removed, so the concealers of true knowledge remain after the removal of the deluded concealers; and just as it is much easier to dispose of the onion than its smell, so the deluded concealer is easier to get rid of than the nondeluded one.

Why are nondeluded concealers understood as ignorance? In Tsongkhapa's case, it is to the extent that they obscure subtle realities from direct perception—thus they prevent an ārya from grasping empty phenomena as empty or dependently arisen phenomena as dependently arisen. The nondeluded concealers thus constitute a form of ignorance even though they persist after the obliteration of deluded ignorance.

Gorampa distinguishes between deluded and nondeluded concealers very differently. He adopts Jayānanda's account according to which the types of ignorance are derived from different functions: "Ignorance is twofold, deluded and nondeluded. Deluded ignorance causes saṃsāra by generating clinging toward I and mine, whereas nondeluded ignorance merely causes the appearances of physical forms, and so forth. But it is not the cause of the conception of true existence [i.e., essence]."[249] The fact that the three types of āryas, according to Gorampa and Jayānanda, "cognize dependently arisen phenomena as mere conventionalities akin to illusions, and so forth, is precisely because they are still under the influence of nondeluded ignorance."[250] This nondeluded ignorance is called *nondeluded* because "it does not conceive of true existence, and therefore it does not give rise to other delusions, such as craving."[251] So far as Gorampa and Jayānanda are concerned, an enlightened being who has eradicated not only deluded concealers but also nondeluded concealers "does not have the perception of even mere conventionalities. Hence buddhas do not have any cognitive experience of phenomenal appearances such as that of blue color."[252]

Inasmuch as both deluded and nondeluded concealers are recognized as the soteriological objects of negation, there is no apparent disagreement between Tsongkhapa and Gorampa. Both vigorously argue for the negation of those concealers in order to attain the soteriological goal.

Recognizing all phenomena as essentially empty and selfless, and thus as dependently arisen, necessarily requires the eradication of the deluded concealers. Without the eradication of active reifying tendencies, Tsongkhapa maintains, it is not possible to know the selflessness of persons *(gang zag bdag med, pudgalanairātmya)* or the selflessness of phenomena *(chos kyi bdag med, dharmanairātmya).* By eradicating the deluded concealers, and thereby coming to direct knowledge of persons and phenomena as selfless and empty, the practitioner first attains total liberation from delusions and becomes an *arhat* (Tib: *dgra bcom pa*—one who has totally destroyed the enemies within). Eradication of the *nondeluded* concealers leads to the attainment of freedom from even the subtlest epistemic errors and cognitive and psychological conditioning *(bag chags, vāsanā).* In Tsongkhapa's view, thorough eradication of the soteriological objects of negation results in concurrent knowledge of the two truths. The chief consequence of eradicating the nondeluded concealers is the realization of full enlightenment—one becomes a buddha.

It is important to note that for Tsongkhapa the idea of essence, both of the self and of phenomena, is essentially an epistemic fabrication that also carries deep cognitive and psychological implications, and that it is a reification produced by deluded ignorance. As the Buddha says, "Monks, I do not envision even one other obstruction...like the obstruction of ignorance."[253] By eradicating ignorance at the cognitive level, along with its latent predispositions at the psychological level, the selflessness of both persons and phenomena are likewise eradicated.

Gorampa argues that the conception of the essential self of person is less subtle than that of phenomena. The deluded concealers are thus exclusively correlated with the conception of the essence of persons, whereas the concealers of true knowledge are correlated with the conception of the essence of phenomena.[254] While the eradication of the deluded concealers leads to the knowledge of selflessness of persons, Gorampa views the eradication of the concealers of true knowledge as leading to the knowledge of emptiness of phenomena.[255] Gorampa agrees with Tsongkhapa to the extent that the eradication of conception of the essential self of person does not require the eradication of empirical truths. But he denies that the eradication of the concealers of true knowledge, that is, the eradication of the idea of the essence of phenomena, is possible merely through cognitive or psychological transformation. What is actually required is the eradication of the ontological structures of empirical truths.

Thus, while Tsongkhapa maintains that eradicating the soteriological objects of negation does not eradicate empirical truths, Gorampa and his allies consistently argue that it does. Scholars such as Jayānanda,[256] Longchen Rabjam,[257] Rendawa,[258] Rongtön Shakya Gyaltsen,[259] Taktsang Lotsawa,[260] Shakya Chogden,[261] Mipham Rinpoche,[262] and Gendün Chöpel,[263] and their modern counterparts including Singh,[264] Poussin[265] Stcherbatsky,[266] Lindtner,[267] and Murti[268]—apart from some minor differences—all support Gorampa's argument that the eradication of the idea of the self of persons entails the eradication of afflictive emotions such as craving, aversion, and ignorance, while the eradication of the idea of the essence of phenomena brings the total eradication of dependently arising phenomena, thus conventional truths. Therefore, according to this view, all conventional phenomena are soteriological objects of negation. For instance, Gendün Chöpel writes:

> In short, the appearances that are apparent to us as ordinary beings, and that cannot be done away with even by way of dissecting into a thousand parts through the sevenfold reasonings, is itself the concealer for true knowledge. Or it is due to its power...The eradication of the deluded concealer culminates with the complete disappearance of the world of appearances from the perspective of conceptual mind while the eradication of the concealer of true knowledge culminates with complete disappearance [of the world of appearances] from the perspective of perceptual mind. Ācārya Candrakīrti therefore holds that a buddha, who has completely abandoned both concealers, experiences no such appearance...Inner clinging on to the table constitutes the deluded concealer, whereas the visual perception of the existence of the table constitutes the concealer of true knowledge.[269]

For Gorampa the eradication of the two types of ignorance—deluded and nondeluded—must lead to the eradication of the entire system of a dependently arisen world. Since all dependently arisen phenomena are objects of negation, what is then left is ultimate reality alone.

Tsongkhapa, on the other hand, argues that the eradication of the two types of ignorance cannot lead to the eradication of interdependent phenomena, since they are not the objects of negation. In Helmut Tauscher's words: "For Tsongkhapa's understanding of conventional existence *(tha snyad du yod pa),* which relates to both realities, it is crucial that only absolute existence *(don dam par yod pa)* is to be negated, but not conventional reality *(saṃvṛtisatya)* in the sense of conventionally real things or existence as such *(yod pa tsam),* for this would imply either substantialism or nihilism."[270] Other modern scholarly works of Thupten Jinpa[271] and Ruegg[272] on Tsongkhapa's position on the object of negation confirm that he does not treat conventionally existent phenomena as the object to be eradicated. Thus while Tsongkhapa argues that the eradication of the soteriological objects of negation entails the eradication of delusions rather than the ontological structures of empirical truths, Gorampa argues that the eradication of the soteriological objects of negation necessarily eradicates both delusions and the ontological structures of empirical truths.

The Meanings of Paramārthasatya

The most remarkable distinction between Tsongkhapa and Gorampa vis-à-vis the meaning of *paramārthasatya* lies in the criterion they apply to determine *parama (dam pa),* meaning "ultimate," and *artha (don),* meaning "object." For Tsongkhapa "ultimate" qualifies *artha,* that is, the object as such, whereas for Gorampa it is the apprehending consciousness that is *parama,* or ultimate. For Tsongkhapa *paramārtha* is the nature of both objects and the subjects that apprehend them, not something imposed upon the object by the subject. Gorampa argues that ultimate truth is none other than apprehending consciousness itself.

We first consider Candrakīrti's explanation of *paramārthasatya:* "Because it is an object, at the same time it is the ultimate, it is the ultimate object, and because it is truth, it is the ultimate truth."[273] Commenting on Candrakīrti's statement, Tsongkhapa argues that within the compound term *paramārthasatya, satya,* meaning truth, is that which is both *artha,* meaning object *(yul, viṣaya),* and *parama,* meaning ultimate. In this situation "both *artha* and *parama* are taken into account as the *paramārthasatya,* meaning ultimate truth *per se.*"[274] *Parama* is taken as the qualification of *artha,* the object, rather than the qualification of apprehending consciousness. In emphasizing this approach, Tsongkhapa is arguing that the meaning of *paramārthasatya* is not purely epistemological. Whether or not phenomena are considered in relation to their respective apprehending consciousnesses, the ultimate mode of the truth of phenomena doesn't change.[275] Tsongkhapa argues that ultimate truth is described as *truth* "because of its nondeceptive identity. Ultimate truth does not deceive sentient beings by presenting a mode of appearance that is different from its mode of being."[276] Conventional truth, on the other hand, *does* deceive ordinary sentient beings by presenting a mode of appearance that is contradictory to its mode of being.

If the term *ultimate* qualified the apprehending consciousness rather than the phenomena themselves, ultimate truth would have to be taken as simply imposed on phenomena by the apprehending consciousness. This would mean, however, that the Buddha would then be mistaken when he claimed in the *Dhammaniyāma Sutta* that "whether or not there is the arising of Tathāgatas, this property stands—this regularity of the Dhamma, this orderliness of the Dhamma: All processes are inconstant...All processes are *dukkha*...All phenomena are not-self."[277] Similarly, it would be erroneous for the Buddha to state in the *Paccaya Sutta:*

> Now, what is dependent co-arising? From birth as a requisite condition comes aging and death. Whether or not there is the arising of Tathāgatas, this property stands—this regularity of the Dhamma, this orderliness of the Dhamma, this this/that conditionality. The Tathāgata directly awakes to that, breaks through to that. Directly wakening and breaking through to that, he declares it, teaches it, describes it, sets it forth. He reveals it, explains it, makes it plain and says, "Look. From birth as a requisite condition comes aging and death."[278]

Both these passages suggest that for the Buddha the ultimate mode of phenomena is objective and invariable rather than subjective and imposed.

Unlike Tsongkhapa, Gorampa characterizes *parama* as a qualification of the apprehending consciousness, with *artha* as its corresponding object. The apprehending consciousness in this context refers to the very specific transcendent perspective *('jig rten las 'das pa'i ye shes, lokottarajñāna)* that belongs to āryas. The meaning of *paramārthasatya,* in Gorampa's view, grants primacy to the āryas' transcendent wisdom, which supersedes the ontological status of conventional phenomena. In Gorampa's words:

> *Artha* refers to reality *(chos nyid, dharmatā),* i.e., the object of engagement of an ārya's ultimate wisdom, for it is either cognizable

> or analyzable. Since there is no other object as supreme as this, it is the ultimate. It is [also] truth, for it is nondeceptive. Thus they are conjoined.[279]

Note the similarities between Gorampa's account of the meaning of *paramārthasatya* and Jayānanda's in his commentary on the *Madhyamakāvatāra:*

> *Parama* refers to transcendent wisdom, whereas *artha,* object, is its [apprehended] object, thus, [their conjunction forms] *paramārtha,* meaning *ultimate object.* This is also *satya (truth)* because it is nondeceptive. Or, *paramārtha* means "supreme object" *(mchog tu gyur ba'i don),* i.e., emptiness, for no other supreme object overshadows emptiness.[280]

Both Jayānanda and Gorampa consider *parama* as the ultimate qualification of an ārya's transcendent wisdom and *artha* as a corresponding object of that consciousness. In this sense, the subjective consciousness determines ultimate truth. Since no empirical object enters the equation of ultimate truth, the term *artha* is, in Gorampa's sense, more metaphorical than actual. "There is no realization and realized object, nor is there object and subject."[281] Taktsang Lotsawa is in agreement: "A wisdom without dual appearance is without any object."[282] Strictly speaking, transcendent wisdom itself becomes the ultimate truth. And since ultimate truth is the ārya's transcendent wisdom, *paramārthasatya* cannot have the ontological status advanced by Tsongkhapa.

The differences between Tsongkhapa's and Gorampa's analyses of the meaning of *paramārthasatya* are a significant factor in their profoundly divergent views on what is divided into the two truths. For Tsongkhapa, the division rests on the dual natures of each empirically given truth. Two truths are posited precisely because they are equivalent to the conventional and ultimate natures of each and every empirical phenomenon. For Gorampa, the division is between subjectivities,[283] and the two truths cannot be posited within the context of a particular empirical object. All empirical objects, according to him, have one and the same nature, and that nature is itself conventional truth. "Ultimate truth is to be experienced under a total cessation of dualistic appearance through an ārya's personal wisdom," and further, "Anything that has dualistic appearance, even omniscience, must not be treated as ultimate truth."[284] Longchen Rabjam,[285] Sakya Paṇḍita,[286] Shakya Chogden,[287] Rongtön Shakya Gyaltsen,[288] and Karmapa Mikyö

Dorje[289] all adopt Gorampa's line of argument in insisting on equating ultimate truth with an ārya's transcendent wisdom.

So far we have examined the meanings attributed to saṃvṛti and *paramārthasatya,* the nature and the scope of the objects of negation, and the significance of eradicating the objects of negation. In the second part of this chapter, an examination of Tsongkhapa's and Gorampa's respective positions on the definitions of the two truths will further clarify the differences between them.

Definitions of the Two Truths

The criteria for determining the definitions of the two truths are pivotal in contrasting the accounts of Tsongkhapa and Gorampa. Tsongkhapa claims the ontological status of each empirical phenomenon satisfies the definitions of both truths. Each phenomenon, as he sees it, possesses two natures that serve as the locus of the definitions of the two truths. Gorampa regards the ontological status of each empirical phenomenon as satisfying only the definition of conventional truth. He argues that each phenomenon has only an empirical nature rather than two natures, and that ultimate truth has a distinct ontological status.

Tsongkhapa also claims that each cognitive agent is potentially capable of knowing both truths exhaustively, being equipped with the requisite empirically and ultimately valid cognitions. Gorampa argues that each truth must be verified by a different individual, and that access to the two truths is mutually exclusive—a cognitive agent who knows conventional truth cannot know ultimate truth and vice versa.

Candrakīrti's Definition of the Two Truths

There are two slightly varying definitions of the two truths that we should take into account at this point, offered by Candrakīrti and Nāgārjuna respectively. We will deal with Candrakīrti's definitions in this section and Nāgārjuna's in the next. In the sixth chapter of the *Madhyamakāvatāra* Candrakīrti defines the two truths as follows:

> [The Buddha] said that all things have two natures—
> Those found by perceivers of reality and [those found by
> perceivers] of falsities *(brdzun pa).*

> Objects of perceivers of reality are things as they are;
> Objects of perceivers of falsities are conventional truths.[290]

Gorampa reads *brdzun pa* as modifying the perceiver as "false." However, as Guy Newland notes, Tsongkhapa reads *brdzun pa* as a reference to the perceived object and not the perceiver.[291] Consequently, Tsongkhapa defines conventional truth as an object "found by an empirically valid cognition that perceives false objects of knowledge,"[292] and defines ultimate truth as "an object found by reasoning consciousness perceiving, seeing reality."[293] In his commentary to Nāgārjuna's *Mūlamadhyamakakārikā,* Tsongkhapa applies these two definitions with respect to the two natures of the sprout:

> Each individual phenomenon—exterior or interior[294]—possesses dual natures—one of the ultimate and the other of the empirical. Consider the sprout, for example: it possesses a nature that is found by a reasoning consciousness perceiving reality, i.e., a nondeceptive knowable; and a nature that is found by an empirical consciousness perceiving a deceptive object, i.e., a false knowable. The former is the sprout's nature of ultimate truth, and the latter, the sprout's nature of empirical truth.[295]

A crucial point to be noted in Tsongkhapa's definition is his insistence on grounding the two truths in the two natures of each individual phenomenon. Candrakīrti remarks similarly: "The bhagavān buddhas, who flawlessly mastered the defining characteristics of each of the two truths, have shown that all phenomena, i.e., interior and exterior, such as conditioned phenomena and a sprout, have two natures."[296]

Two central ideas are embedded in Candrakīrti's and Tsongkhapa's grounding of the two truths on the two natures of each phenomenon. Firstly, the two truths are conceptual distinctions applied to a particular empirical phenomenon, since every phenomenon fulfills the criterion of both truths. Secondly, the two truths should not be construed as merely *one* specific nature of a phenomenon mirrored in two different perspectives. As each phenomenon, according to them, possesses two natures, so each verifying consciousness has a different nature as its referent, even though there is only one ontological structure involved. The two truths, argues Tsongkhapa, "indicate that if the characteristics of even one ontological structure—the sprout, for example—are divided, it has two natures, namely, conventional and ultimate. It does not however indicate that one nature *per se* is divided into the two truths with respect to [the contrasting perspectives] of ordinary beings and the āryas."[297]

Hence Tsongkhapa holds that a single ontological identity—a sprout, for instance—has two natures. Its conventional nature is its deceptive or false nature—it appears to have a self-sufficient existence while in reality it is a dependently arisen phenomenon. The ultimate nature of the sprout, however, is nondeceptive, appearing to its apprehending consciousness the way it actually exists.

Gorampa is equally convinced that Candrakīrti supports his view that the two truths are to be associated with two different perspectives. In arriving at this reading, Gorampa juxtaposes verses 6:23 and 6:28 of Candrakīrti's *Madhyamakāvatāra.* The first of these verses defines the two truths, whereas the second deals with the different senses of saṃvṛti. Gorampa regards the phrase *brdzun pa mthong ba,* meaning "perceiver of falsities," in verse 6:23 as synonymous with *gti mug,* meaning "ignorance," or "concealer," in verse 6:28. Similarly, he treats *kun rdzob bden pa,* "conventional truth as grasped by the perceiver of falsities," in verse 6:23, as synonymous with *kun rdzob,* "ignorance" or "concealer," in verse 6:28.

Like Huntington, who translates *yang dag mthong pa* as "correct perception" rather than "perceiver of reality," and *mthong ba brdzun pa* as "incorrect perception" instead of "perceiver of falsity," Gorampa reads *brdzun pa (falsity)* as an adjective referring to a perceiver as opposed to a perceived object.[298] The equating of *correct perception* with *perceiver of reality,* and *incorrect perception* with *perceiver of falsity,* plays a vital role in Gorampa's definition of the two truths. It allows him to argue that the underlying basis for the differentiation between the two truths is indeed a matter of conflicting perspectives:

> Since it is the cognition that grasps the two natures, ultimate truth is an object of a reality-perceiving cognition *(mthong ba yang dag)* whereas conventional truth is an object of a falsity-perceiving cognition *(mthong ba brdzun pa).*[299]
>
> When the Bhagavān Buddha disclosed reality as it is to his disciples from the empirical standpoint, he demonstrated that all phenomena are constitutive of the two natures—conventional and ultimate. And the doctrine of the two truths is based on the empty nature of all phenomena found by the wisdom of an ārya's meditative equipoise, and the existent nature found by

> the power of falsity—the false-perceiving cognition of ordinary beings.[300]

But then he states:

> Here in the Madhyamaka system, the object itself cannot be divided into two truths. Empirical truth and ultimate truth are divided in terms of the *mode of apprehension:* in terms of the *subject apprehending falsehood and subject apprehending truth,* or *mistaken and unmistaken apprehension,* or *deluded and undeluded apprehension,* or *erroneous and nonerroneous apprehension,* or *valid and invalid cognitions.*[301]
>
> All the Prāsaṅgikas and the Svātantrikas of India agree that [the two truths] are posited by the *object-possessing mind.* Because the two truths are posited in terms of the subjective mind, they depend on whether it is *deluded or nondeluded, a perception of falsity or a perception of truth,* or *a mistaken or an unmistaken cognition.*[302]

Although the first two paragraphs are somewhat ambiguous and do not expressly highlight distinctive features of Gorampa's view, the third and the fourth set forth the characteristic features with considerable clarity. As far as Gorampa is concerned, the definition of the two truths is entirely determined by the two contradictory cognitive perspectives associated with ignorance on the one hand, and wisdom on the other.

Gorampa also rejects Tsongkhapa's object-based definition explicitly:

> [If it were true that each phenomenon has two natures], it would absurdly follow that even one particular phenomenon, such as a sprout, must possess [two] empirically retrievable imputed objects [or natures] merely by designating the two truths. This must follow, for the sprout would have two natures, which would be the bases of the two truths. [If you accept this], it would then follow that the object found by the false-perceiving consciousness must also be absurdly found by an ārya's meditative equipoise. This must follow because [according to you] the object [verified by the false-perceiving consciousness] would be affirmatively grasped by the reality-perceiving consciousness since the two [apprehended] objects have a single ontological identity.[303]

Furthermore he states:

> The conventional nature of the sprout would absurdly become its ultimate nature, for the two [natures] have only one [phenomenal] characteristic. If you accept this, then it would follow that the nature verified by the false-perceiving consciousness would also be absurdly the nature verified by the reality-perceiving consciousness. If you accept this, it would then follow what is to be verified by the false-perceiving consciousness must absurdly be found by the reality-perceiving consciousness. If you accept this, then it must follow that these two [verifying cognitions] are not different insofar as their modes of verifying the natures of objects.[304]

While these two passages directly criticize Tsongkhapa's account of the two natures, they also shed light, albeit indirectly, on Gorampa's own definition. Gorampa argues that each empirical phenomenon has only one nature, namely, its conventional nature. The so-called ultimate nature, in his view, cannot be verified in any empirical phenomenon. If a sprout, for example, actually did possess two natures as proposed in Tsongkhapa's definition, then, according to Gorampa, each nature would have to be ontologically distinct. Since the ontological structure of the sprout cannot be separated into a so-called conventional and ultimate nature, the sprout must possess only one phenomenal nature, i.e., the conventional. As this nature is found only under the spell of ignorance, it can be verified only under the empirical cognitions of ordinary beings, and of unenlightened āryas not in meditative equipoise. This would be absurd because ultimate truth is totally beyond the reach of ordinary beings.

The two passages cited above also demonstrate, of course, that the defining characteristics of the two truths cannot, in Gorampa's view, be posited from within the framework of empirically given phenomena alone. Any such phenomenon can only satisfy the definition of conventional truth. The ontological status of the sprout, as sprout, is understood in terms of conventional truth, for it is false and deceptive. The ultimate truth of the sprout is beyond its conventional existence, beyond its existence merely *as sprout.* It is therefore not possible, in Gorampa's view, to confine the definition of ultimate truth to the framework of empirical phenomena.

Ultimate truth, for Gorampa, requires the metaphysical transcendence of empirical or conventional existence. Unlike conventional phenomena, it is neither presupposed nor projected by ignorance. Ultimate truth "is inexpressible through words and is beyond the scope of mind."[305] The mind, as Gorampa understands it, is always conceptual and thus deluded. "Yet ultimate truth," as he argues, "is experienced by āryas in their meditative equipoise, and is free from all conceptual categories. It cannot be expressed through definition, through any defined object, or through anything else."[306] Lindtner summarizes this view: "Reality *(tattva)* is beyond all ontological and epistemological dualities *(dvaya),* while the empirical world of origination, destruction, and so forth is illusory—due merely to ignorance *(avidya)*."[307]

Another important issue is the way Gorampa characterizes verifying cognitions. He agrees with Tsongkhapa on the need for two different cognitive resources—reality-perceiving cognition and falsity-perceiving cognition. Both thinkers agree that reality-perceiving cognition verifies ultimate reality, whereas falsity-perceiving cognition verifies conventional truth.[308] This agreement is, however, superficial. In contrast with Tsongkhapa, who argues that each cognitive agent may possess both cognitive modes, Gorampa argues that an enlightened being and an ordinary being have distinct cognitive modes. The only possible exception, for Gorampa, is the ārya that is not yet fully enlightened; such beings can access both types of consciousness. This general line of argument appears to originate directly from Jayānanda:

> Perceivers of reality consist of the bhagavān buddhas, who flawlessly understand the natures of things. [Ultimate] reality comprises their [apprehended] objects. However, their apprehended objects and subjects are comprised of unperceived objects and [unperceived] subjects...Perceivers of falsities are erroneous, for they do not realize reality. Besides, they grasp on to false things. Objects that they apprehend are conventional truths.[309]

Jayānanda argues that an enlightened being perceives only ultimate truth and possesses only transcendent wisdom. Ultimate truth is an object certified by transcendent wisdom. As Lindtner puts it, however, "the ultimate truth is the object of a cognition without an object *(advayajñāna),* and thus only an object metaphorically speaking *(upādāyaprajñapti)*."[310] Yet ultimate truth, "as it is beyond all categories of thoughts, is cognitively experienced without duality of subject and object."[311] And "in the ultimate context," says Jayānanda, "there is not even the slightest existence of object and subject."[312] These arguments are all in line with Gorampa's.

Thus for Tsongkhapa, the two natures of each empirical phenomenon define the two truths, while Gorampa considers wisdom and ignorance as the defining characteristics. Siding with Gorampa are Longchen Rabjam,[313] Sakya Paṇḍita,[314] Rendawa,[315] Mipham Rinpoche,[316] Shakya Chogden,[317] Taktsang Lotsawa,[318] Rongtön Shakya Gyaltsen,[319] Karmapa Mikyö Dorje,[320] and Gendün Chöpel,[321] all of whom formulate the definitions of the two truths in terms of the distinctions between the ignorant experiences of ordinary beings and the enlightened experiences of an ārya's wisdom. In like fashion, the definitions offered by modern interpreters such as Murti,[322] Singh,[323] Poussin,[324] Huntington,[325] and Williams[326] all ground the two truths in these two contradictory viewpoints.

Huntington and Williams, although emphasizing perception as the basis of the distinction, nevertheless attempt to preserve the compatibility between emptiness and dependent arising. "Emptiness," as Huntington puts it, "must resonate far down into the core of everyday experience."[327] Similarly, Williams argues that "emptiness and dependent origination mutually imply each other."[328] In arguing thus, Williams and Huntington seem to be straddling two contradictory positions, with one foot in Gorampa's camp and the other in Tsongkhapa's. Were empirical truth purely reified by delusory perceptions, then Huntington and Williams would have to deny that enlightened beings can perceive dependently arisen phenomena. Claiming that emptiness and dependently arisen phenomena are mutually entailing, on the other hand, means that an enlightened being, lacking any experience of dependently arisen phenomena, could have no cognitive experience of emptiness. Huntington and Williams must either relinquish their commitment to a mutual entailment, or else relinquish their definition of the two truths as based in incompatible cognitive capacities and experiences. They cannot plausibly retain both commitments. Neither Tsongkhapa nor Gorampa faces this dilemma.

To summarize: Tsongkhapa and Gorampa read Candrakīrti's definition of the two truths differently. Tsongkhapa considers the two natures of each phenomenon as the key factor. The conventional nature of an empirical phenomenon, as verified by an empirically valid consciousness, determines the definition of conventional truth; the ultimate nature of the same empirical phenomenon, as verified by an ultimately valid consciousness, determines the definition of ultimate truth. Since both truths are ontologically as well as epistemologically interdependent, knowledge of empirically given phenomena as dependently arisen suffices for knowledge of both truths. Gorampa, as we have seen, rejects Tsongkhapa's dual-nature account, treating each empirical phenomenon as satisfying only the definition of conventional truth and taking the definition of ultimate truth to be ontologically and epistemologically distinct from conventional truth. It is through the perception of either an ordinary being or an unenlightened ārya that the definition of conventional truth is verified—fully enlightened beings do not verify the defining characteristics of conventional truth in any respect. Similarly, no ordinary being can verify the definition of ultimate truth. Ultimate truth transcends conventional truth, and the knowledge of empirically given phenomena as dependently arisen could not satisfy the criterion of knowing ultimate truth.

Nāgārjuna's Definition of the Two Truths

Let us now consider Nāgārjuna's view:

> Not to be realized from the other, peaceful,
> Not elaborated by elaborations,
> Not conceptualized, and not a separate identity.
> That is the characteristic of [ultimate] reality.[329]

Tsongkhapa comments thus on this statement:

> [Ultimate truth] is not to be realized from another. Other persons can merely explain it, but cannot [make another person] directly realize it. Instead, it is to be personally realized through an undefiled wisdom. It is peaceful. Just as a person without cataracts does not see falling hairs, [ultimate truth] is free from inherent essence. It cannot thus be elaborated through the vocal elaborations, meaning, it cannot be expressed. "Conceptualization" refers to the operations of mind. At the point when the true nature of things as they are is consummated, the operations of mind temporarily cease. It is thus not conceptualized. However a phenomenon fulfills the criterion of ultimate truth, [the ultimate truth] of all other phenomena have the same identity. Thus, from the ultimate standpoint, there are no separate identities.[330]

Next Gorampa's comments:

> Ultimate truth cannot be realized as it actually is by naïve ordinary beings by means of the other's explanations or logical reasons. Instead, it is realized by an ārya's personal wisdom within

> meditative equipoise by way of not seeing anything at all. Since *nothing* is established primordially, it is peaceful. Since it is not an object to be expressed through vocal elaboration by way of clinging to it, [ultimate truth] is not elaborated. It is beyond the scope of mind and mental factors, thus no conception whatsoever can conceptualize it. Since no distinction whatsoever exists, there are no separate identities. These fivefold features are thus the defining characteristics of the reality of ultimate truth.[331]

Except for some minor linguistic differences, Tsongkhapa and Gorampa render Nāgārjuna's statement in terms that appear, on the face of it, to be virtually identical. A closer look at these two interpretations, however, reveals that they imply quite different and irreconcilable conclusions.

Gorampa interprets Nāgārjuna's account on the assumption that Nāgārjuna is making metaphysical claims about the nature of ultimate truth. Given Gorampa's commitment to a conception of ultimate truth as ontologically, epistemologically, and soteriologically transcendent of conventional truth, this is not surprising. In fact, Gorampa goes so far as to combine the definition of ultimate truth with that of *essence (rang bzhin, svabhāva).* In his commentary on the *Mūlamadhyamakakārikā,* in the chapter on the *Analysis of Essence* [15:2], Gorampa contentiously identifies ultimate truth with the defining characteristics of essence:

> [Question]: But what is the nature of the reality of phenomena? [Reply]: It is not possible to reveal its exact nature. However, to facilitate its understanding by the disciples, the real nature of phenomena is disclosed as the apprehended domain of the uncontaminated wisdom. Its nature has three defining characteristics: namely, it is not created by causes and conditions; it exists independently of conventions and of other phenomena; and it does not change. The reality of the transcendence of conceptual elaboration is its example.[332]

Gorampa's commitment to the absolute characterization of ultimate truth is nowhere expressed so overtly as here, where he uses Nāgārjuna's definition of essence as a means to define ultimate truth. Like Nāgārjuna's hypothetical essence, Gorampa argues that ultimate truth is *ontologically unconditioned,* and hence it is not a dependently arisen phenomenon; it is *distinct* from empirical phenomena in every sense of the word; it is *independent* of conceptual-linguistic conventions; it is an absolutely *timeless* and eternally *unchanging* phenomenon. Reading Gorampa's interpretation of Nāgārjuna's definition of ultimate truth against this background, it becomes apparent that for him Nāgārjuna's statement [18:9] is only concerned with metaphysically unitary and ineffable ultimate truth.

Gorampa applies the same metaphysical interpretation to the Buddha's following statement on ultimate truth:

> There is, monks, an unborn, unbecome, unmade, unfabricated. If there were not that unborn...there would not be the case that emancipation from the born, become, made, fabricated would be discerned. But precisely because there is an unborn...emancipation from the born...is thus discerned. The born, become, produced, made, fabricated, impermanent, composed of aging and death, a nest of illness, perishing, come from nourishment, and the guide [that is craving] is unfit for delight. The freedom from that is calm, permanent, beyond inference, unborn, unproduced, the sorrowless, stainless state, the cessation of stressful qualities, the stilling of fabrications, bliss.[333]

And as the Buddha also states:

> Freed, dissociated, and released from ten things, the Tathāgata dwells with unrestricted awareness, Vahuna. Which ten? Freed, dissociated and released from form...feeling...perception... processes...consciousness...birth...aging...death...dukkha... defilement, he dwells with unrestricted awareness. Just as a red, blue, or white lotus born in the water and growing in the water rises up above the water and stands with no water adhering to it, in the same way the Tathāgata—freed, dissociated, and released from these ten things—dwells with unrestricted awareness.[334]

For Tsongkhapa Nāgārjuna's definition and the Buddha's statements do not in any way present an account of the metaphysically transcendent nature of ultimate truth—although they have ontological implications, they directly attend to psychological, cognitive, and epistemic issues related to the *experiential* nature of ultimate truth. Since it is not possible for ultimate truth to be known merely by another's verbal explanations, so, Tsongkhapa argues, it is experienced personally within one's own psychophysical aggregates by one's own valid consciousness. In Kalupahana's words: "It is knowledge for which one does not depend upon another, primarily because it pertains to arising and ceasing of empirical phenomena. It involves personal verification, a verification that can be accomplished by someone before one begins to formulate any right view."[335] In this sense not only is ultimate truth beyond linguistic descriptions but it is also beyond the conceptual mind. Thus the Buddha explains how ultimate truth (here referring to nirvāṇa) is transcendently experienced:

> Monks, that sphere should be realized where the eye (vision) stops and the perception (mental noting) of form fades. That sphere is to be realized where the ear stops and the perception of sound fades...where the nose stops and the perception of aroma fades...where the tongue stops and the perception of flavor fades...where the body stops and the perception of tactile sensation fades...where the intellect stops and the perception of idea/phenomena fades: That sphere should be realized.[336]

To put the above considerations into clearer perspective, let us consider one final point: the relationship between the concept of dependent arising and the concept of ultimate truth. In highlighting the nature of dependent arising, Nāgārjuna states:

> Whatever arises in dependence upon whatever
> Is neither identical to it
> Nor different from it.
> It is, therefore, neither annihilated nor eternal.[337]

Tsongkhapa reads this statement as Nāgārjuna's definition of *worldly* or *mundane reality ('jig rten pa'i de kho na nyid kyi mtshan nyid),*[338] while Gorampa interprets it as the definition of *conventional reality (kun rdzob kyi de kho na nyid).*[339] Although there is a sharp difference in their usage of the terms at issue here—*mundane* versus *conventional* reality—this is not the key issue. In fact, both Tsongkhapa and Gorampa tend to use these two expressions interchangeably. In this context the focus is on what Tsongkhapa and Gorampa aim to achieve by means of their respective readings. By taking verse 18:10 as a definition of *worldly* or *mundane* reality, Tsongkhapa draws a contrast with verse 18:9, in which Nāgārjuna defines *transworldly* or *supramundane* reality *('jig rten las 'das pa'i de kho na nyid).* In making this contrast,

Tsongkhapa is also contrasting the truth verified by empirically valid consciousness (worldly or mundane consciousness) with truth verified by ultimately valid consciousness (supramundane or transcendent consciousness). In treating verse 18:10 as defining *conventional* reality, Gorampa, however, aims to contrast the truth verified by ignorance (incorrect perception) with the truth verified by wisdom (transcendent mind).

Although Tsongkhapa and Gorampa both apply the principle of dependent arising, and therefore of emptiness, to the most crucial issues—the compatibility between emptiness and dependent arising—the differences between their two positions are irreconcilable. Tsongkhapa mobilizes the principle of dependent arising, and so of emptiness, to establish the ultimate truth of all phenomena as dependently arisen, and therefore as empty. Gorampa on the other hand moblizes the principle of dependent arising and emptiness to argue that ultimate truth is not dependently arisen and therefore not empty.

For Tsongkhapa, just as there is an essential compatibility between dependently arisen and empty phenomena, so, too, is there an essential compatibility between the two truths. As dependently arisen, empty phenomena are not constructions of ignorant consciousness, so neither is conventional truth such a construction. Both truths are actual truths that stand on an equal footing. Moreover, according to this view, whosoever knows conventional truth, either directly or inferentially, also knows ultimate truth; whosoever knows ultimate truth, also knows phenomena as dependently arisen, and hence knows them as empty. Where there is no knowledge of conventional truth, the converse applies. For Gorampa, the incommensurability between dependently arisen and empty phenomena also applies to the two truths. Accordingly, whosoever knows conventional truth does not know ultimate truth, and one who knows ultimate truth does not know conventional truth; whosoever knows phenomena as dependently arisen does not know them as empty, whereas whosoever knows phenomena as empty does not know them as dependently arisen.

Let us briefly review. Granting ultimate truth a metaphysically independent status, Gorampa interprets both Nāgārjuna's definition and the Buddha's statements as demonstrations of its metaphysically unconditioned and transcendent nature. This allows him to formulate ultimate truth as ontologically absolute and to deny the credibility of dependently arisen phenomena. Since ultimate truth is transcendent of empirical truth in every sense, so, as Murti puts it, "the absolute is beyond the scope of discursive thought, language, and empirical activity...It is in fact the unutterable *(anabhilāpya),* the unthinkable, unteachable."[340] Since Tsongkhapa maintains the mutual interlocking of the two truths, he argues that both Nāgārjuna and the Buddha's positions on ultimate truth do not, in any way, affirm the metaphysical or transcendent ontological status of such truth. The Buddha and Nāgārjuna's statements, as Tsongkhapa sees the matter, point instead to the transcendent experience of the very same empirically given phenomenon (i.e. one's own psychophysical aggregates) as realized by means of valid consciousness. Thus Nāgārjuna writes: "Without relying upon empirical (truth), the meaning of the ultimate cannot be disclosed. Without realizing the meaning of the ultimate, nirvāṇa is not attained,"[341] and he adds: "Saṃsāra and nirvāṇa do not exist as two [individuals]. The exhaustive knowledge of saṃsāra is itself defined as nirvāṇa."[342]

Conclusion

Tsongkhapa's and Gorampa's definitions of the two truths are irreconcilable. This is most apparent in their respective accounts of the term *saṃvṛti.* Excluding essence superimposed by ignorance (i.e., a concealer), Tsongkhapa argues that all empirically given truths *(tha snyad bden pa, vyāvahārikasatya)* or conventional truths *(kun rdzob bden pa, saṃvṛtisatya)* are not posited by ignorance. Therefore empirical truths do not arise as a result of ignorance. Gorampa argues that all empirically given truths and their experiences, either perceptually or conceptually, are ultimately reducible to the effects of ignorance since they are wholly posited by ignorance. Whether the phenomenal world is described in terms of conventional truth or empirical truth, or even in terms of dependently arisen phenomena, so far as he is concerned, it is only under the spell of ignorance that we experience the empirical world.

Regarding their positions on the cognitive agents of the two truths, Tsongkhapa not only categorizes āryas and buddhas as the appropriate cognitive agents of ultimate truth, but he also allows that ordinary beings who are conceptually familiar with the Madhyamaka philosophy may be categorized in this way. Each cognitive agent, according to Tsongkhapa, is equipped with the necessary cognitive and epistemic resources—both ultimately valid and empirically valid consciousness—to verify both truths, and this is so despite the fact that the truths may be realized either directly or inferentially. In clear contrast, Gorampa refuses to accept ordinary beings as cognitive agents of ultimate truth or buddhas as cognitive agents of conventional truth. As he sees it, no ordinary being is able to realize ultimate truth and no buddha experiences conventional truth.

Since Tsongkhapa bases his definition of the two truths on the two natures of all empirically given phenomena, and treats empirically valid and ultimately valid consciousness as their determining criteria, the two truths are not reducible to contradictory perspectives. Although the defining characteristics of the two truths are verified through separate epistemic pathways, they are nonetheless everywhere inextricably conjoined. Thus the two truths, according to Tsongkhapa, stand on an equal epistemological and ontological footing. This allows him to argue that knowledge of conventional truth requires knowledge of ultimate truth and vice versa. The equal status of the two truths also facilitates Tsongkhapa's argument that knowledge of phenomena as dependently arisen amounts to knowing phenomena as essentially empty, and that the converse also holds. Gorampa grounds the definition of the two truths on the two contradictory perspectives associated with the cognitive experiences of ordinary beings on the one hand, and those of āryas on the other. Conventional truths are reducible to ignorance while ultimate truth is equated with transcendent wisdom. As ordinary beings are deluded beings, their experiences are, in their entirety, based on conventional truth, and thus they have strictly no access to ultimate truth. Fully enlightened beings, however, experience ultimate truth exclusively.

Closely tied to the meanings and definitions of the two truths is the nature and scope of the objects of negation—concealers—a major point of disagreement between Tsongkhapa and Gorampa. The implications of exactly how the objects of negation are understood have reverberated throughout this chapter. It is apparent that the meanings and definitions of the two truths proposed by Tsongkhapa and Gorampa are derived from their views regarding the objects of negation. As we have seen, Gorampa identifies empirical senses, their corresponding objects, and resultant consciousnesses, as the objects of negation, or, to be precise, as "concealers." Tsongkhapa categorically disagrees.

3. Language, Concepts, and Ultimate Truth

Introduction

IN THIS CHAPTER we compare the two Tibetan Prāsaṅgika accounts by asking: Is ultimate truth an object of knowledge of the conceptual mind (thought)? At issue here is whether ultimate truth is *linguistically expressible* and *conceptually knowable.* The first and second sections will analyze the limits of both language and conceptual mind in relation to ultimate truth, with particular reference to the often-cited "cataract" analogy. In the third section we will analyze the validity and significance of the conceptual "right view"—which is closely related to the issues concerning the limits of language and conceptual mind.

The analysis of the conceptual right view is important for two reasons. Firstly, its validity is closely connected to the capacity of conceptual mind to make the ultimate truth intelligible. Secondly, the idea of the right view is a central tenet in the Buddhist account of the path to perfection. The Buddha himself considers the right view as the forerunner of all spiritual practices. Such analysis will also enable us to clearly distinguish between Tsongkhapa's and Gorampa's views on the limits of the conceptual mind. It will also set the stage for the next chapter, which looks at the *nonconceptual* or *experiential right view.*

The Limits of Language and the Conceptual Mind: The Cataract Analogy and Its Applications

In much of the Madhyamaka philosophical literature the ineffability and inconceivability of ultimate truth is illustrated by employing, as an analogy, the contrast between impaired and healthy vision. For example, Candrakīrti states in the *Madhyamakāvatāra:* "Due to cataracts (or opthalmia), one sees illusions such as falling hairs, which are false with respect to the object. One with clear vision sees them as they are. [The perception of ultimate truth] must be understood in this way."[343] In commenting on this metaphor, Tsongkhapa[344] and Gorampa[345] agree that a person with cataracts might see hairs falling from the sky while the person with clear vision will see nothing of the sort. If someone with normal vision tells a visually impaired person "no hair is falling from the sky," that person's acceptance of the statement will nevertheless not prevent him from seeing the hairs. On this Tsongkhapa and Gorampa agree, but they disagree on its interpretation and, in particular, on whether the person with impaired vision would really understand the nonexistence of the hairs.

For both Tsongkhapa and Gorampa, the fact that mere assent to the illusoriness of a sensation does not typically prevent the illusion from being experienced indicates the limited power of language over our cognitive and perceptual processes, and thus also the limited power and role of conceptual mind.

A visually impaired person might understand the illusory character of the falling hairs, but he cannot perceive their nonexistence directly. The experience of falling hairs persists. The only solution—in the case of falling hairs—is to be cured of the cataracts. *Conceptual understanding* is not sufficient to the task. On the other side of the equation, the person whose vision is *not* impaired but who is unable to convey his conceptual understanding demonstrates the limits of *linguistic expression.*

So far as Tsongkhapa is concerned, a person with cataracts can form some conceptual understanding of the illusory character of the falling hairs by hearing an explanatory account of their illusoriness. Similarly, when ordinary beings listen to explanations concerning ultimate reality, they too can form some conceptual understanding of ultimate truth. Gorampa argues that a person with cataracts cannot form any understanding of the illusory nature of the falling hairs; such an understanding would actually require direct experience of the reality—that is, visual experience free of the illusory falling hairs. In the same way, he argues, ordinary beings cannot form any understanding concerning ultimate reality by merely listening to explanations—only an ārya, who directly experiences ultimate reality, can develop such an understanding.[346]

With the cataract analogy, both Gorampa and Tsongkhapa treat the cognitive abilities of ordinary beings on the model of impaired visual faculties, and the cognitive capacities of fully enlightened beings on the model of unimpaired visual faculties. The cognitive ability of ordinary beings is obscured by the presence of primal ignorance just as vision is impaired by the presence of cataracts. Moreover, just as a visually impaired person does not have direct access to the nonillusory visual experience, neither does an ordinary person have direct access to ultimate truth. Even a fully enlightened being will be unable to provide an ordinary being with the ability to perceive directly the nonexistence of essences.

The differences between ordinary and enlightened beings can be further elucidated through considering the limits of language. Tsongkhapa and Gorampa agree that the power of language is quite limited when it comes to expressing the nature of ultimate reality. Language depends upon linguistic convention, but ultimate reality goes beyond those conventions. Moreover linguistic discourse only makes complete sense when the listeners already have a certain degree of familiarity with what is being expressed, or the expressions used. Their ability to make sense of what is being said is thus dependent on prior knowledge.

Suppose the person with cataracts was born that way and has never seen the world without the illusion of hairs. This person cannot fully grasp the nonexistence of the hairs since he lacks any perceptual reference. The case is exactly the same for ordinary persons who have never had any experience of ultimate reality free from essences. The linguistic expressions used to explain ultimate reality only convey their full sense when the listener has had some direct experience of it. Inasmuch as ultimate reality is unknown to ordinary beings, linguistic discourse alone cannot fully bridge the gap between what is known and what is unknown to an ordinary being. In this sense, ultimate truth remains inexpressible. Explaining this limits to the Venerable Mahākoṭṭhita, the Venerable Śāriputra states: "As far, friend, as the six bases of sense contact *(phassāyatana)* reach, so far reaches the (explainable) world of diffuseness *(papañca);* and as far as the world of diffuseness reaches, so far reach the six bases of sense contact. Through the entire fading away and cessation of the six bases of sense contact, the world of diffuseness ceases and is stilled."[347]

If language is strictly inadequate to transmit the cognition of ultimate reality from one person to another, how does an ordinary person gain any understanding of ultimate reality whatsoever? Does the conceptual mind allow for some kind of grasp of ultimate truth? The answer depends on one's interpretation of the limits of conceptual thought and inference. Tsongkhapa argues that the conceptual mind, while it does not comprehend ultimate reality directly and fully, does comprehend ultimate reality conceptually and partially. In fact, he considers conceptual understanding as a stepping stone to direct realization. Gorampa argues that the conceptual mind has no capacity whatsoever to comprehend ultimate reality. "Ordinary beings," he asserts, "simply cannot understand ultimate reality, through listening to another's words, through reasoning, or through any other means."[348] Ultimate reality "cannot be elaborated through vocal expressions; hence it is beyond verbal elaborations. And it is also beyond the comprehension of mind and mental factors; no conceptual thought whatsoever can possibly encompass it."[349] As Gorampa sees it, ordinary beings are not cognitive agents of ultimate truth and are totally incapable of understanding ultimate reality. Hence listening to a discourse on ultimate reality cannot lead ordinary beings to comprehend ultimate reality. If, for some reason, they manage to form some ideas through inference, those ideas, and the knowledge that they comprise, must be thoroughly incoherent. "Go rams pa holds that...the actual ultimate is not accessible to thought and is thus utterly ineffable," writes Dreyfus.[350] Strictly speaking, the conceptual cognitions of ordinary beings are, according to Gorampa, completely inadequate to the task of comprehending ultimate reality.

The claim that conceptual cognition cannot access ultimate truth is based in large part on the fact that such cognition depends upon *universals.* Gorampa argues that "any cognition analyzing the nature of reality is simply the conceptual thought grasping at a conjunctive compound of the *term [universal] (sgra spyi)* and the *object universal (don spyi).*"[351] Conceptual thought is understood by Gorampa as comprising both conceptual/perceptual awareness and universals. The *term universal* is the concept of an object formed as a result of listening to descriptions of the object without actually seeing it. The *object universal,* on the other hand, is the concept of an object formed as result of seeing the object without having had any prior knowledge of it. Taken independently, neither universal makes much sense, since the former is description without reference, and the latter reference without description. Gorampa argues that these two universals work together to make language and thought function.

Conceptual thought, moreover, functions strictly within the conventional domain. It has no access whatsoever to ultimate truth since ultimate truth is utterly beyond any linguistic and conceptual conventions. All conceptual cognitions, as Gorampa understands them, "can focus on only one of the four extreme views at a time, and therefore it is impossible to repudiate the conceptual categories of the four extremes simultaneously."[352] Since the goal of enlightenment is to transcend the conceptual categories, the repudiation of the conceptual categories is absolutely essential. Moreover, conceptual cognitions are seen as multiplying the conceptual categories rather than assisting the process of transcendence.

Dreyfus writes that the Sakya tradition "insists that concepts apply only to conventional reality. Ultimate truth in Madhyamaka is completely beyond the reach of concepts. It is utterly ineffable, in the strong sense of the word."[353] Dreyfus also notes that "for the Sa-gya tradition in general and Go-ram-ba in particular, the key concept in Madhyamaka philosophy is not the absence of real existence, but freedom from elaborations *(prapañca, spros pa)*. Ultimate truth is utterly beyond the reach of elaboration."[354] On this matter, as on others, Gorampa exemplifies a more widely held view—one that is shared, notably by Shakya Chogden,[355] Taktsang Lotsawa,[356] Mipham Rinpoche,[357] Gendün Chöpel,[358] and Khenpo Künzang Palden.[359] Interestingly, however, some of his usual allies, such as Longchen Rabjam,[360] Sakya Paṇḍita,[361] and Rongtön Shakya Gyaltsen[362] are more sympathetic to Tsongkhapa's view on this account. Like Tsongkhapa, this latter group argues that logical inference paves the way to the direct realization of ultimate reality.

Given the close link between the limits of language and that of the conceptual mind, Gorampa argues that, just as an enlightened person cannot coherently explain ultimate reality, an ordinary being cannot realize ultimate reality: "It is not possible to explain ultimate truth through definition, through defined object, or through any other means in the manner it is experienced during the meditative equipoise, which is free from any conceptual elaborations. This is because ultimate truth is inexpressible through language and is not an apprehended object of the mind."[363]

Tsongkhapa only partly agrees with Gorampa on this point. He agrees that an ordinary being could not have a direct nonconceptual realization of ultimate reality; but, unlike Gorampa, he holds that an ordinary being can form a useful conceptual realization of ultimate reality.

An ordinary being does this, according to Tsongkhapa, by listening to discourses. While a conceptual understanding (an inferential knowledge) of ultimate reality is mistaken, since it assumes the universal of ultimate reality to be ultimate reality itself, it is nonetheless an essential prerequisite for the direct personal realization of ultimate truth. Here it is important to distinguish between Tsongkhapa's views on the *universal* of ultimate reality and ultimate reality *per se,* and so to distinguish between his views regarding the *universal* and the *particular.* The universal of ultimate reality is constructed through conceptual-linguistic conventions. Ultimate reality itself, however, is not a conceptual-linguistic construction. Thus, for example, the universal of ultimate truth pertaining to material form is constructed on the basis of linguistic descriptions and the conceptual grasping of emptiness of the material form, but the emptiness of the material form in itself is not constructed on the basis of conceptual-linguistic conventions. So even though the universal of ultimate truth of material form is constructed on the basis of conceptual-linguistic conventions, the ultimate truth of material form is not entirely dependent on conceptual-linguistic conventions. The ontological character of emptiness retains its true identity despite the fact that various universals, both coherent and incoherent, are imposed upon it.

Confusion between the *universal* of ultimate truth and ultimate truth itself—the *particular*—is somewhat analogous to the confusion that may arise between a face and its reflection. Just as we may mistake a reflection for an actual face, conceptual cognition mistakes the universal of ultimate truth for ultimate truth itself. The confusion here arises partly because the conceptual mind does not have direct access to ultimate truth, but only to the universal of ultimate truth, which mediates between the conceptual mind and emptiness. We may say that it thereby blocks direct access to ultimate truth, but at the same time, it also enables indirect access. The conceptual mind mistakes inferential knowledge via a universal for direct knowledge, but that does not make inferential knowledge fruitless. As we have already noted, for Tsongkhapa, if inferential knowledge of ultimate truth is based on valid empirical premises rather than mere fictions or imaginations, then inferential knowledge of ultimate truth provides the scaffolding that enables direct nonconceptual access to ultimate truth.

Tsongkhapa maintains a clear-cut distinction between direct nonconceptual realization of ultimate truth and conceptual realization of such truth. According to him, Candrakīrti's use of the cataract analogy indicates only "the listener's failure to realize exactly what is explained; it does not rule out [the listener's conceptual] realization of the nonexistence of hair."[364] By listening to descriptions, a person with cataracts could inferentially grasp the nonexistence of hairs despite not having the capacity to see this directly. Similarly, when ultimate truth is explained linguistically, ordinary beings afflicted by deluded ignorance cannot form an understanding of it to the level of those who are enlightened. So long as a person remains afflicted by deluded ignorance, he sees essences where none exist. A person afflicted in this way can never directly realize ultimate truth merely by listening to explanations. Yet since ultimate truth is not entirely ineffable,[365] and not entirely incomprehensible, explanations can lead to a conceptual view of ultimate reality. Tsongkhapa says:

> Although the explanation of ultimate truth through an analogy does not lead to its realization in the way [ultimate truth] is seen by those free from the affliction of the cloud of ignorance, this does not mean [Candrakīrti] accepts reality as nonrealizable in a general sense. Ultimate truth is not ineffable, for definitive scriptural texts and their verbal descriptions do embody its profound meanings. Furthermore it is not the case that [ultimate truth] is unrealizable by the mind associating with [verbal descriptions]. Therefore every single statement explaining the meaning of reality as beyond the scope of consciousness and verbal description must be understood in the same light.[366]

Tsongkhapa also argues for a significant role for language and conceptual mind in forming a bridge between conventional knowledge and ultimate knowledge. In this respect, an inferential understanding of ultimate truth is not only possible, but is, in fact, essential as a step on the path to the direct realization of ultimate truth. Conceptual realization, he argues, serves as the causal nexus between the naïve cognitive states of an ordinary being and the evolved wisdom of an ārya. Conceptual understanding of ultimate truth, no matter how trivial, acts as an epistemic bridge that transports us from the known—conventional truth—to the unknown—ultimate truth.

Inasmuch as it must be based on valid empirical premises, inferential knowledge of ultimate truth is linked to the experience of ordinary beings. Inasmuch as it involves an understanding of ultimate reality on the level of reason, it is linked to the transcendent experience of an ārya. In this way the conceptual realization of ultimate truth gradually paves the way for the most enlightened wisdom of buddhahood. Hence, for Tsongkhapa, the conceptual understanding of ultimate truth is absolutely required for the possibility of such enlightenment.

For Gorampa the realization of ultimate truth is perfectly *sui generis.* It spontaneously arises when a person attains the state of āryahood. And the realization must have no prior causal link with the conceptual experience of the ordinary being. Since conceptual knowledge contributes nothing to the eventual realization of the nonconceptual ultimate reality, nothing whatsoever is required to bridge the gap between the conventional knowledge of an ordinary being and the ultimate knowledge of an ārya. The transition is thus seen as a leap or as a spontaneous unfolding rather than as a gradual progression.

Another important point is that, for Gorampa, "the only nondeceptive subjective consciousness is the ārya's meditative equipoise. That which is nondeceptive from this perspective amounts to ultimate truth."[367] Therefore nothing whatsoever is capable of realizing ultimate reality except the wisdom of meditative equipoise. What is the cause of meditative wisdom? Is there a causal link between the ordinary cognitive state and the cognitive state of an ārya? For Gorampa, as pointed out earlier, the answer is simply *no*. An ārya's wisdom in meditative equipoise arises without any traceable prior causal event, such as a deluded cognitive state of an ordinary being. Direct nonconceptual realization of ultimate truth arises from nowhere.

Moreover Gorampa explicitly rejects the role of reasoning in realizing ultimate truth, arguing that valid reasoning consciousness belongs to the conventional realm and cannot bridge the two sides, even though a valid reasoning consciousness of ultimate truth is analogous to an ārya's realization during meditative equipoise.[368] Dreyfus also draws attention to this point: "When analyzing the way in which inference relates to emptiness, Go-ram-ba uses the concept of object universal.... Go-ram-ba's point is that inference does not apprehend emptiness itself.... Emptiness lies beyond the grasp of thought and language, which has access only to the object universal of emptiness."[369] Dreyfus argues that such a view, although familiar within the Dharmakīrtian tradition, "has no obvious place in Madhyamaka, especially when understood from Candrakīrti's perspective."[370] Dreyfus also notes that "the notion of object universal seems to be tied down to the foundationalist standpoint of the epistemologists. Nevertheless, Go-ram-ba is quite happy to use this notion to strengthen his analysis of emptiness as being beyond thought and language."[371]

So far as Gorampa is concerned, language and the conceptual mind have no soteriological value. Any knowledge founded on conventional truth, according to his view, is useful only within the conventional realm. Since, metaphysically speaking, ultimate truth stands beyond the conventional world, ultimate truth is completely inaccessible to the conventional constructions of language and conceptual mind. A correct understanding of ultimate truth unfolds only with the total eradication of the empirical world, and the only way to understand ultimate reality is through nonconceptual immediacy.

Tsongkhapa's argument for the soteriological value of language and the conceptual mind is examined in more detail below in the discussion of the Indian Mādhyamikas' views on the limits of language and conceptuality.

Ineffability and Inconceivability of Ultimate Truth

In the *Mūlamadhyamakakārikā,* while analyzing the ineffability and inconceivability of ultimate reality, Nāgārjuna writes:

> What is to be expressed has ceased
> For the domain of thought has ceased.
> Like nirvāṇa, the ultimate reality
> Is nonarisen and nonceased.[372]

In the *Prasannapadā* Candrakīrti glosses Nāgārjuna's statement:

> If there is something to be expressed here, indeed it should be explained. However, when what is to be expressed has ceased, and in the context where expressions do not have their referent objects, buddhas teach nothing whatsoever. Why is there no referent to be expressed? Because as it says, "the domain of thought has ceased." *Domain of thought* means "arena of conceptualization." Domain *(spyod yul)* is an object *(yul),* meaning an apprehended object *(dmigs pa).* If there were any domain of thought, one could argue that the superimposition of labels would make sense. As [ultimate reality] is not suitable to be a domain of thought, what could language possibly represent through logical projections?
>
> Why is there no domain of thought? Because, as it says, "like nirvāṇa, ultimate reality is nonarisen and nonceased." As the ultimate reality is nonarisen and nonceased, the nature of phenomena and the defining characteristics of phenomena are said to be equivalent to nirvāṇa. Thought therefore does not engage with [ultimate reality]. Without thought, there are no grounds whatsoever for linguistic superimposition. Furthermore, without having [a domain to be engaged], what would language refer to? For this reason, the statement "buddhas taught nothing whatsoever" still stands.[373]

Reflecting further on the same issue in the *Madhyamakāvatārabhāṣya,* Candrakīrti says that "because it is ineffable, and because it is not an object of consciousness, [ultimate truth] cannot truly be explained."[374]

Let us now consider the two Tibetan readings of these statements from

Nāgārjuna and Candrakīrti. Tsongkhapa emphasizes the distinction between the standpoints of the ultimate and of the empirical. As far as he is concerned, any realization, whether of conventional or ultimate truth, as well as any explanation of either of the truths, is possible only from the empirical standpoint. The ultimate standpoint is the perspective of transcendent wisdom. When transcendent wisdom engages with the transcendent mode of things, it does so by penetrating and transcending all conceptual categories. The fact that both Nāgārjuna and Candrakīrti take ultimate reality to be an inexpressible *(brjod par bya ba min pa)* and nonengaged domain of thought *(sems kyi spyod yul min pa)* means, according to Tsongkhapa, that they both can be interpreted as speaking exclusively from the ultimate perspective. "If there is anything expressible from the ultimate standpoint," Tsongkhapa says, "it should be expressed. From the ultimate standpoint, however, what is to be expressed has ceased, and thus it appears to be nonexistent."[375] Transcendent wisdom engages with the ultimate truth by dissolving all conceptual objects.[376] Consequently no phenomenon, he argues, retains its discreteness, shape, color, taste, etc., when penetrated by transcendent wisdom—by ultimate valid consciousness. All five aggregates are directly experienced by this wisdom as ultimately nonarisen and nonceased, not coming and not going, not permanent and not annihilated, peaceful and beyond thought constructions. This profound experience itself amounts to experiencing nịrvāṇa.[377] Tsongkhapa therefore sees no inconsistency in arguing that, from the perspective of the ultimate, "buddhas taught nothing whatsoever."[378]

Gorampa takes a very different view of the distinction between ultimate and empirical standpoints. For him the empirical standpoint refers strictly to the perspective of an ordinary being while the ultimate standpoint refers to an ārya's wisdom of the meditative equipoise. Ultimate truth is always inexpressible and inconceivable, and for Gorampa, ultimate truth is identical to the ultimate perspective—the transcendent consciousness of a buddha. They are one and the same. He argues that "eventually cognition itself becomes an undefiled cognitive sphere, and that itself is the ultimate buddha, who is adorned with the perfections of abandonment and realization,"[379] and further that "ultimate reality, empirical reality, and subjective wisdom—all three lose their distinctness," becoming one with transcendent consciousness.[380] *Tathāgata* is, he says, by definition a transcendent phenomenon, while conventionalities, are, by definition, mundane phenomena projected by ignorance.[381] "Proliferation *(spros pa, prapañca)* is a characteristic feature of causally effective things. The tathāgata [i.e., ultimate truth], however, is not a thing, hence it is not a category of proliferation but is transcendent of proliferation."[382]

In Gorampa's account, as in Jayānanda's, conventional truths include everything except what is ultimate. "Conventional truth," as the former puts it, "includes conceptual fabrications of phenomena, such as that of existence and nonexistence, by ordinary beings. Such [conceptually fabricated] natures are nonexistent, because existence, nonexistence, and so forth, are logically unacceptable."[383] As long as there is an existent, either a subject or an object, it cannot, according to Gorampa, be an ultimate truth. Subject and object, this and that, existence and nonexistence—all these dualities are categories of deluded thoughts, and ultimate truth transcends all dualities.

Since ultimate truth is beyond language and thought, it cannot be an object of knowledge. If it were knowable in this way, according to Gorampa, "then it should be expressible by language. However, because [ultimate truth] is not a domain of thought, no linguistic expression whatsoever can express it."[384] Ultimate reality is primordially nonarisen, nonceased, and nondual, not only epistemologically, but also in a metaphysical sense. Therefore "mind with dualistic appearances cannot by any means apprehend the aspect [of nondual ultimate reality]."[385] But why is an ultimate truth not a domain of mind? "Because nonarisen, nonceased, and nondual ultimate reality is itself the nature of phenomena. And since the nature of phenomena is posited as synonymous with nirvāṇa, mind cannot engage it."[386] Gorampa continues: "Since mind does not engage [ultimate reality], there is no reason [ultimate reality] should be linguistically expressed. As [mental engagement] is nonexistent, no words can capture it. In this sense 'buddhas taught nothing whatsoever.'"[387] Words convey meaning only if those words have a point of reference. Where no point of reference is verified by mind, there is simply no object to be expressed. The words are meaningless inasmuch as they have no affirmative message to convey. "If [ultimate truth] were at all expressible," says Gorampa, "there would be no reason why it should not be explained. However, because ultimate reality is free from any of the obsessions of linguistic determinations *(sgras bzhin pa),* [buddhas] refused to teach anything at all."[388]

Although Gorampa unequivocally maintains that ultimate truth is beyond the description of words and beyond the comprehension of thought, this claim does not prevent him from holding the view that buddhas do provisionally teach the doctrine of ultimate reality in conventional terms by employing what he describes as "linguistic superimposition" *(sgro brtag, samāropa).*[389] As Pettit describes it, Gorampa grants only "propaedeutic function" to the conceptual and linguistic formulation of ultimate truth. "This follows logically from his assumption that conventional reality is pervaded by conceptuality and that conceptuality is pervaded by ignorance."[390]

Gorampa and most of his Tibetan counterparts—such as Mipham Rinpoche[391] and Shakya Chogden[392]—are generally opposed to the distinction between ultimate and conventional standpoints as articulated by Tsongkhapa. In dealing with issues related to the ineffability and inconceivability of ultimate reality, they all treat this distinction as essentially metaphorical, and therefore maintain that ultimate truth is utterly ineffable and conceptually unknowable. Modern interpreters such as Murti, Singh,[393] and Narain also strongly endorse Gorampa's line of argument here.[394] Murti, for instance, argues that "the real is utterly devoid *(śūnya)* of these and other conceptual constructions; it is transcendent to thought and can be realized only in nondual knowledge—*prajñā* or Intuition, which is the Absolute itself."[395] Harsha Narain argues that Nāgārjuna's "whole endeavour is to demonstrate beyond the shadow of doubt that his *Śūnya* is totally transcendent to all possible categories of reason."[396]

If language is utterly incapable of disclosing ultimate truth, that raises another important question: What is the point of the Buddha's active teaching about ultimate truth, given the utter incapacity of words to express it, and the utter incapacity of the intellects of his disciples to grasp its meaning? Indeed, Gorampa himself fills several volumes with teachings about the ultimate truth. For Gorampa and his allies this is quite a formidable objection and one that he never fully resolves. As Narain puts it:

> The Mādhyamika finds it extremely difficult to give us even the remotest idea of the deliverance of the ultimate experience or of enlightenment called *Prajñāpāramitā* and can do little better than to mutter that it is of the nature of silence *(tūṣnīṃ-bhāva),* non-apprehension *(anupalambha)* and cessation of all expression *(prapañcopasama).* It has no knowing *whatsoever (yatra jñānasyāpa a-prcāraḥ).*[397]

However, by claiming that ultimate truth is *conceptually* unknowable, Gorampa does not mean to say that ultimate truth is *thoroughly* unknowable. For him ultimate truth is knowable by means of nonconceptual wisdom. In fact, no matter how much the two Tibetan Mādhyamikas are divided in their views regarding the intelligibility of language and the limits of conceptual mind, to the extent that they both accept ultimate reality as knowable by nonconceptual wisdom, they speak with a single voice. The details of nonconceptual knowledge will be discussed in the next chapter, but before we move on, we will briefly examine the validity of the conceptual right view.

The Validity of the Conceptual Right View

There are three issues crucial to the analysis of conceptual right view: (1) its defining characteristics; (2) its significance as the forerunner of the overall spiritual practices; and (3) its various types. Discussion of these will be followed by a more focused comparison of Tsongkhapa's and Gorampa's accounts.

First, let us turn to the scriptures and look briefly at what they have to say on right view. In the *Mahāsatipaṭṭhāna Sutta,* the Buddha offers the following definition: "What is right view? Knowledge of suffering, knowledge of the origin of suffering, knowledge of the cessation of suffering, and knowledge of the way of practice leading to the cessation of suffering. This is *right view.*"[398] Although this definition of right view undoubtedly reflects the Buddha's practical and soteriological concerns, the emphasis here is on the correct knowledge of the four noble truths. The reason for this is that liberation requires correct knowledge of the four noble truths, and this in turn depends on the correct view of the nature of self.

The nature of incorrect views is described in the Buddha's talk on "a thicket of wrong views" in the *Sabbāsava Sutta:*

> There is the case where an uninstructed, run-of-the-mill person...does not discern what ideas are fit for attention, or what ideas are unfit for attention. This being so, he does not attend to ideas fit for attention, and attends instead to ideas unfit for attention. This is how he attends inappropriately: "Was I in the past? Was I not in the past? How was I in the past? Having been what, what was I in the past? Shall I be in the future? Shall I not be in the future? What shall I be in the future? How shall I be in the future? Having been what, what shall I be in the future?" Or else he is inwardly perplexed about the immediate present: "Am I? Am I not? What am I? How am I? Where has this being come from? Where is it bound?"

> As he attends inappropriately in this way, one of six kinds of view arises in him: The view "I have a self" arises in him as true and established, or the view "I have no self"...or the view "It is precisely by means of self that I perceive self"...or the view "It is precisely by means of self I perceive not-self"...or the view "It is precisely by means of not-self that I perceive self" arises in him as true and established. Or else he has a view like this: "This very self of mine—the knower that is sensitive here and there to the ripening of good and bad actions—is the self of mind that is constant, everlasting, eternal, not subject to change, and will endure as long as eternity." This is called a thicket of views, a wilderness of views, a contortion of views, a writhing of views, a fetter of views. Bound by a fetter of views, the uninstructed run-of-the-mill person is not freed from birth, aging, and death, from sorrow, lamentation, pain, distress, and despair. He is not freed, I tell you, from suffering and stress.[399]

For the Buddha, right view is understood in thoroughly practical terms—it leads us to produce skillful virtues. Our perspective on reality has a bearing well beyond mere theoretical conviction. Our views govern our attitudes, our actions, and our whole orientation toward life. Our views might not be explicity expressed or clearly systematized—we might have only a hazy sense of our belief systems—but, as Bhikkhu Bodhi puts it, "these views have a far-reaching influence. They structure our perceptions, order our values, crystallize into the ideational framework through which we interpret to ourselves the meaning of our being in the world."[400] Our actions of body, speech, and mind may create the fabric of our lives, but all our actions, along with the consequences that follow from them, derive from the views we hold. Thus right view is the crucial difference between continued delusion on the one hand and progress on the path on the other. Views are not mere hypotheses, they imply an ontological commitment—they are our judgment of what is real and what is false. Those commitments drive our behavior and in consequence our entire experience.

The second issue to be discussed here concerns the role of right view as the forerunner of the entire Buddhist path, the guide for all the other factors. In recognition of its importance, the Buddha places right view at the very beginning of the noble eightfold path. "Bhikkhus, just as the dawn is the forerunner and first indication of the rising of the sun, so is right view the forerunner and first indication of the wholesome state."[401] Right view enables the practitioner to understand his or her starting point, destination, and the successive landmarks as practice advances. To engage in practice without a foundation in the right view is to risk getting lost in futile activities. It would be like driving somewhere you've never been without consulting a map or asking someone who has traveled there. You might get into the car and start to drive, but rather than approaching your destination, you are just as likely to move farther away from it. At the very least, you need some idea of the general direction and the roads that lead to it.

Success in the remaining elements of the eightfold Buddhist path depends on the orientation provided by right view: "For one of right view, bhikkhus, right intention springs up. For one of right intention, right speech springs up...For one of right knowledge, right deliverance springs up."[402] The Buddha also characterizes right view as the forerunner in that it leads to freedom from the wrong view: "How is right view the forerunner? One discerns wrong view as wrong view, and right view as right view...One tries to abandon wrong view and to enter into right view."[403]

The third issue concerns the different types or aspects of right view. In its fullest measure, right view involves a correct understanding of all phenomena—both mental and material—and thus its scope is equal to the full range of phenomena. Right view can also be understood in a more restricted sense. For example, in the *Sammādiṭṭhi Sutta,* Śāriputra considers sixteen different aspects of right view that pertain to the efficacy of moral and immoral actions, the four nutriments of life,[404] the four noble truths, the twelve factors of dependent arising,[405] and the taints *(āsava)* as the conditions for breeding ignorance. However, for practical purposes, all aspects of right view are broadly classified under a twofold division: *conceptual right view* and *experiential right view.*

Conceptual right view, in technical terms, is *lokika-saṃyagdṛṣṭi ('jig rten pa'i yang dag pa'i lta ba),* meaning "mundane right view." This view is primarily concerned with a correct conceptual understanding of those empirical truths that operate entirely within the confines of the world. In most circumstances, conceptual right view is equivalent to the understanding of the natural laws governing the material and spiritual worlds, particularly the understanding of how and why it is essential to act in accordance with the law of karmic cause and effect to achieve liberation.

Experiential right view is *lokottara-saṃyakdṛṣṭi ('jig rten las pa'i yang dag pa'i lta ba),* or "supramundane right view." This right view is primarily concerned with an immediate understanding of truths within the confines of one's own psychophysical aggregates. Although it, too, operates entirely within the confines of the mundane world, it penetrates, transcends, and directly reveals the supramundane nature within oneself.

For both Tsongkhapa and Gorampa, conceptual right view consists of the intellectual grasp of principles enunciated in the Buddha's teaching. It is called *right view* because it conforms with the truths, although it does not fully disclose those truths. Conceptual right view consists of the correct conceptual understanding of the truths arrived at by listening and studying the Buddha's teaching, followed by deeper personal analysis of their meanings on a conceptual level.

Experiential right view is the penetration of the truth enunciated in the Buddha's teachings within one's own immediate experience. For Tsongkhapa conceptual right view conforms to both ultimate and conventional truth, since the two truths are mutually interlocking. For Gorampa conceptual right view conforms only to conventional truth and is inconsistent with ultimate truth. Just as the two truths are mutually contradictory and hierarchical, so the two types of right view are also mutually contradictory and hierarchical.

As far as the scope and validity of conceptual right view are concerned, Tsongkhapa and Gorampa are clearly divided. For Tsongkhapa conceptual right view is critical to the development of experiential right view, whereas Gorampa regards conceptual right view to only refer to ordinary beings grasping conventional truths as truly existent—it is wholly invalid for developing experiential right view. Pettit in *Mipham's Beacon of Certainty* makes the same point, "Gorampa understands conceptuality *ipso facto* as involving apprehension of true existence, whereas Tsongkhapa," he argues, "does not."[406] These two opposing positions are not surprising; they are consistent with Tsongkhapa's and Gorampa's arguments above regarding the limits of language and of the conceptual mind.

As we have seen, ultimate truth is for Tsongkhapa an object of conceptual knowledge—to some degree it is both linguistically expressible and conceptually knowable. Consistent with that, he maintains that conceptual right view guides experiential right view, it acts as a forerunner to direct experience. In Bhikkhu Bodhi's words, "When...driven by keen aspiration to realize the truth embedded in the formulated principles of Dhamma, it [conceptual right view] serves as a critical phase in the development of wisdom *(pañña),* for it provides the germ out of which experiential right view gradually evolves."[407] Experiential right view, for Tsongkhapa, is essentially generated by the practice of insightful meditation guided by a correct conceptual understanding of the truths. One must thus begin with a correct conceptual grasp of the teachings in order to integrate the full scope of the Buddhadharma within one's immediate experience. By using a correct conceptual understanding and by cultivating the threefold training—morality, concentration, and wisdom—intellectual comprehension is eventually transformed into immediate perception.

Given Gorampa's commitment to ultimate truth as linguistically inexpressible and conceptually unknowable, conceptual right view must, according to him, be irrelevant in the journey to experiential right view. Conceptual right view is, in his sense, valid only within the conventions of ordinary beings and can provide no scaffolding for the development of experiential right view. Experiential right view comes only with penetration into a higher ultimate truth. Conceptual right view is properly so-called only in the sense that it is "right" or consistent with the conceptual-linguistic conventions of ordinary beings.

In Gorampa's view, just as there is only one truth, there is only one right view—and that is the experiential right view. Conceptual right view has no validity when it comes to realizing ultimate truth. The conceptual understanding of a table, for example, is a conceptual right view since it is acceptable within the conventions of ordinary beings. On the other hand, conceptually grasping the existence of a rabbit's horn or a mirage is a wrong view, for it is unacceptable even within the conventions of ordinary beings. Once a person becomes an ārya, his or her conceptual right view becomes obsolete. From an ārya's perspective, everything in the world is a projection of ignorance, and hence any conceptual view is only an obstruction to achieving experiential right view.

For Gorampa, experiential right view is "supramundane" in that it accesses that which is metaphysically higher. As a buddha accesses supramundane truth exclusively, only the supramundane right view applies. An ārya, on the other hand, accesses *both* mundane and supramundane truths, yet still possesses only the supramundane right view. Since an ārya realizes that the mundane truths are mere illusions and projections of ignorance, an ārya will always perceive such truths as flawed and mistaken. For right view implies an ontological commitment, and as Gorampa argues, āryas and buddhas are committed to the ontological status of ultimate truth alone. Ordinary beings, in contrast, are committed to the ontological status of mundane truths, so the mundane right view is valid for them.

Tsongkhapa maintains that conceptual right view, "though conceptual in nature, is closely connected with nonconceptual wisdom, since it serves as the causal condition for the arising of nonconceptual wisdom."[408] He argues that merely having a nonconceptual experience does not necessarily mean that it satisfies the criterion of nonconceptual wisdom—equivalent to experiential right view. For it to be valid nonconceptual experience, it must have the capacity to eradicate the reifying tendencies. Only then would it satisfy the criterion of nonconceptual wisdom. "Such nonconceptual wisdom," according to Tsongkhapa, "must be preceded by critical analysis through conceptual wisdom."[409]

The causal relationship between conceptual and experiential right view, or between mundane and supramundane right view, is crucial to Tsongkhapa's argument. In spite of the apparent discordance between the *views* at issue, Tsongkhapa claims there is nonetheless an inevitable causal relation between them. "Without this causal nexus," he argues, "it would be impossible for an uncontaminated path to arise from the contaminated ones. Thus no ordinary person could ever become an ārya."[410] There are infinite legitimate causal relationships that appear to be somewhat discordant but still are perfectly efficacious. Blue sprouts, for example, germinate from white seed, smoke arises from fire, man arises from woman, and so on.[411] A similar causal relationship is at work, argues Tsongkhapa, between conceptual and nonconceptual right view. "The ārya's nonconceptual wisdom directly realizes person and phenomenon to be selfless and empty. In order to arouse the ārya's nonconceptual wisdom realizing empty and selfless modes of person and phenomena, prior conceptual analysis of the identities of person and phenomena is essential. Only through developing a sound conceptual understanding can one actualize its meaning by engaging in nonconceptual meditation."[412]

Therefore, from Tsongkhapa's perspective, a person possessing right view can be any of the three kinds: ordinary person, ārya, or buddha. An ordinary person initially has no experiential right view. Beginning with a conceptual right view, his or her practices eventually culminate in the initial penetration of the supramundane experience on reaching the path of seeing (Tib. *mthong lam,* Skt. *darśanamārga*). The first phase of the direct culmination of the supramundane right view uproots all afflictive defilements, such as greed, aversion, and ignorance, transforming the person into an ārya, allowing him or her to enter irreversibly upon the path to liberation. An ārya has not only supramundane right view but also mundane right view. Following the path of seeing, an ārya enters the path of meditation (Tib. *bsgom lam,* Skt. *bhāvanāmārga*) and uproots even the latent predispositions of the earlier defilements. This leads to the attainment of *arhathood*—total personal liberation.

The path of meditation culminates with the attainment of perfect buddhahood—full enlightenment. This eradicates even the subtlest epistemic errors—the subtle misconception of dualistic appearances—conditioned by the earlier defilements. Unlike Gorampa, Tsongkhapa asserts that a buddha, like an ārya, possesses both supramundane and mundane right views. In fact, at the level of buddhahood, conceptual and nonconceptual right views are mutually entailing. Hence a buddha's conceptual knowledge of phenomena as dependently arisen and nonconceptual knowledge of phenomena as empty are synonymous.

Therefore the validity of conceptual right view and that of experiential right view, according to Tsongkhapa, are mutually reinforcing. The validity of conceptual right view applies for all cognitive agents—ordinary beings, āryas, and buddhas—while experiential right view (conforming to ultimate truth) applies only to āryas and buddhas. An ordinary person has yet to achieve direct penetration of the supramundane path. Therefore, Tsongkhapa avers, the right view, conceptually grasped by the wise ordinary being and transformed into direct perception with the attainment of the path of seeing, reaches its consummation with the arrival of the final goal of the Buddhadharma—the attainment of complete buddhahood. Conceptual right view is thus the forerunner of all subsequent achievements.

The Buddha himself explains that no single factor is as responsible for the arising of unwholesome states of mind as wrong view and no factor is as helpful for the arising of wholesome states of mind as right view; furthermore, no single factor is as responsible for the suffering of living beings as wrong view and no factor so potent in promoting the good of living beings as right view.[413] Therefore, in Bhikkhu Bodhi's words, "though our conceptual orientation toward the world might seem innocuous and inconsequential, when looked at closely it reveals itself to be the decisive determinant of our whole course of future development."[414]

In other passages, the Buddha seems to warn against the grasping of views altogether, and Nāgārjuna pays respect to the Buddha by endorsing this point: "I pay homage to Gautama who, out of compassionate mind, has taught the noble Dharma in order to relinquish all views."[415] On the surface this seems to support the position of Gorampa, who denies the capacity of any linguistic formulation to represent the ultimate view. A conceptual view, he would argue, can only obstruct us from the ultimate, and so we should discard it. Tsongkhapa, however, interprets Nāgārjuna's passage to mean that we should avoid the metaphysical commitments of both essentialism and nihilism.[416] For when the Buddha rejects views—as he does in the *Brahmajāla Sutta* (DN 1), for instance—he does so on the basis that they involve a metaphysical commitment to either the existence of essences or complete nonexistence. Tsongkhapa would argue that Gorampa's view is a commitment to nihilism, since it denies any validity whatsoever to conventional appearances. In Tsongkhapa's view, this goes too far. Let's examine this final point a little more closely.

Final Implications

Tsongkhapa and Gorampa arrive at radically different conclusions concerning the Buddha's and Nāgārjuna's positions on the limits of language and the validity of conceptual right view. Tsongkhapa infers that the Buddha and Nāgārjuna reject only metaphysical views—to be precise, wrong views—underpinned by an assumption of essence. Garfield adopts a similar stance: "[The Gelugpas] simply argue that when Nāgārjuna speaks of relinquishing 'all views,' he means 'all false views,' or 'all views according to which things are inherently existent.'"[417] Therefore Tsongkhapa argues that the Prāsaṅgika Mādhyamikas have positions based on right views, and so they do indeed have views to be considered. Garfield, for instance, suggests an example of one such view that Tsongkhapa would not relinquish: "Emptiness, for mādhyamika, is an ultimate truth. One *can* achieve a correct view—a view of things as they in fact are. Such as this view surely should not be relinquished, for this would be to relinquish the soteriological goal of all Buddhist practice."[418] Garfield points out that, therefore, "the dGe-lugs pas argue, one must read Nāgārjuna as suggesting straightforwardly, rationally, and without even a hint of paradox, that one should relinquish all false views, and that for the one who views emptiness as inherently existent there is no hope."[419]

Gorampa, again, concludes that the Buddha and Nāgārjuna categorically reject *all* views. Any view formulated on empirically given truths, Gorampa claims, is always underpinned by the assumption of essence. He argues that, from the Prāsaṅgika Madhyamaka perspective, any so-called correct understanding of empirically given truths amounts to a metaphysical view—it constitutes either the extreme view of existence or the extreme view of nonexistence.[420] Since the Prāsaṅgika Mādhyamikas do not, strictly speaking, have any views to be presented,[421] Gorampa maintains that "the Mādhyamikas do not have any position whatsoever."[422] Accordingly, apart from refuting the views presented by the non-Madhyamaka philosophers through *reductio ad absurdum,* the Mādhyamikas themselves take no affirmative position whatsoever.[423] Moreover, from Gorampa's standpoint, what is true for the Prāsaṅgika Mādhyamikas is something other than what is empirically given to sense experience, which is true and real only for ordinary beings. Therefore only ordinary beings adhere to views based on the understanding of empirical truths and thus they alone have views to be presented.

Tsongkhapa dismisses the assumption that the Buddha avoided propounding any view whatsoever. On Tsongkhapa's account, the Buddha's emphatic distinctions between right view and wrong view, coupled with his treatment of right view as the forerunner of all beneficial practices and of wrong view as the source of all problems, is sufficient to prove that the Buddha did not seek to relinquish all views indiscriminately. The criterion of right view is the correct conceptual understanding or immediate experience of empirically given truths. This holds true even for the Prāsaṅgika Mādhyamikas who, Tsongkhapa proposes, have views of their own and therefore certainly have views to be presented to their critics—such as Buddhist realists.

Another crucial distinction should be noted as well. For Tsongkhapa the transition from the ordinary state to buddhahood is smooth and gradual, an evolving chains of events—past practices generating present effects and present and past practices generating future effects. This is a gradual progression and enhancement of the conceptual right view of an ordinary being founded on the ordinary sense perception of the law of impermanence—the arising and cessation of the phenomenal world. This sense perception is not exclusive to āryas or buddhas. "The perception of arising and ceasing of phenomena conditioned by various factors," as Kalupahana puts it, "is available even to ordinary people who have not been able to completely free themselves from prejudices. Thus, there is a common denominator between the perceptions of an ordinary person and those of the enlightened one."[424]

Tsongkhapa therefore argues that all kinds of higher forms of knowledge, including the conceptual and experiential right view of the most enlightened person, have the conceptual right view of the ordinary state as their foundation. This is because wisdom, free from the conception of essence, depends on the conceptual understanding of the nonexistence of essence. Such understanding in turn develops from the correct conceptual analysis.[425] What makes the difference, however, is the fact that the perceptions, or the sense experiences of the ordinary person, are colored by defilements, whereas those of an enlightened being are totally free from such defilements and their latent dispositions.

Gorampa, unlike Tsongkhapa, views the transition from the ordinary state to buddhahood as thoroughly discontinuous and abrupt. The sensory experience of empirically given truths, including the arising and cessation of the phenomenal world, are mutually contradictory with the wisdom of an enlightened person. All empirical experiences, both perceptual and conceptual, are deluded. They simply cannot be causal conditions for enlightenment. There is thus no common denominator between the perceptions of an ordinary person and an enlightened one.

How then could an ordinary person elevate him- or herself to the enlightened state? It appears to involve, at least for Gorampa, a metaphysical leap from the conditioned world of empirical truths to an unconditioned world of nirvāṇa. Narain points out the inherent problem in such a view: "If all views are abolished, what remains? The truth, whatever it be like—truth, the apology for truth, the substitute for truth—is believed to transcend all speech and thought, to totally elude the grasp of reason, to be wholly incommunicable."[426] Narain also questions whether the truth could be as discontinuous with human reason as Gorampa would have it, and he adds: "If the answer is in the affirmative, Saṃsāra and Nirvāṇa turn out to be two different orders not only totally discontinuous and non-interactive but also impenetrably autonomous, thereby reducing the Mādhyamika to the status of an uncompromising dualist."[427]

Conclusion

In this chapter, we have seen that, insofar as the limits of language and conceptual mind are concerned, the two Tibetan Prāsaṅgikas have little common ground. By arguing that language can partly express ultimate truth, albeit not entirely, and that the conceptual mind has some degree of access to ultimate truth, although not fully, Tsongkhapa is able to postulate that ultimate truth can be an object of knowledge even with respect to the conceptual mind, thus allowing him to argue for the validity of conceptual right view. Gorampa, by arguing that language is wholly incapable of expressing ultimate truth and that the conceptual mind is equally incapable of knowing ultimate truth, advances the view that ultimate truth cannot possibly be an object of knowledge with respect to the conceptual mind, leading him to reject the validity of conceptual right view.

4. Realizing Ultimate Truth

Introduction

TSONGKHAPA and Gorampa are united in claiming that ultimate truth is an object of knowledge, at least inasmuch as it is accessible to nonconceptual wisdom. Not only they but all Tibetan Prāsaṅgika Mādhyamikas[428] are unanimous on this point. But Tsongkhapa and Gorampa diverge on *how* ultimate truth can be realized by nonconceptual wisdom. In this chapter, we will consider the issues in relation to three different epistemological approaches:

- seeing ultimate truth by way of *not seeing* it;
- seeing ultimate truth by *transcending conceptual elaborations;* and
- seeing ultimate truth *nondually.*

Although the emphasis is slightly different in each approach, they nevertheless all represent epistemic pathways geared toward the same nonconceptual realization of ultimate truth.

Since the aim of this chapter is to provide a comparative analysis of Tsongkhapa's and Gorampa's epistemological models, we will not, except in certain relevant respects, deal with their ontological positions. However, one question is worth asking in this regard: What motivates Tsongkhapa and Gorampa to adopt the radically opposing epistemological viewpoints we are about to explore? One possible answer can be found in their disagreement regarding the scope and nature of the objects of negation *(dgag bya ngos 'dzin).* As we saw in the second chapter, for Tsongkhapa, what obstructs our attaining transcendent knowledge is the defilements—craving, aversion, and delusion—and the essences we project onto things. Superimposed essences, which are driven by the defilements, are thus considered the objects of negation. Gorampa agrees with Tsongkhapa inasmuch as he recognizes the reifying tendencies of craving, aversion, and delusion as objects of negation, but he disagrees so far as the scope and nature of reified essence is concerned. While Tsongkhapa sees essence as a purely conceptual construction—as an empirically nonexistent and abstract entity that is projected and imposed *upon* conventional truth from within—Gorampa equates essence with conventional truth. Thus he views not merely essence but *both* essence *and* conventional truth as purely conceptual constructions projected from within due to the power of ignorance.

Tsongkhapa argues for eradicating both the underlying reifying tendencies—the defilements—and the conceptually reified essence. Gorampa argues for eradicating not only the underlying reifying tendencies, but also the entire matrix of the conventional world. This disagreement about the scope of the objects of negation, as we will see, informs their disagreements on epistemology and soteriology.

Unlike the more analytic language employed elsewhere, I favor a more descriptive style in some sections of this chapter. Given the nature of the topic—meditative experiences and their philosophical implications—a purely analytical approach is often inadequate to convey many of the crucial issues. Modern scholars working on Madhyamaka philosophy tend to set aside anything related to meditative experiences. In my view, such an approach does a serious injustice to the epistemological systems of the Mādhyamikas in general, and Tsongkhapa and Gorampa in particular. Since Tsongkhapa's and Gorampa's rather distinct epistemological models arise directly out of their different interpretations of the implications of certain meditative experiences, both descriptive and analytical styles are needed for any useful comparison.

Seeing Ultimate Truth by Way of Not Seeing It

> If you claim you see the Buddha,
> You see no Buddha at all.
> See the Buddha as you see the unseeable;
> See him like the trace of a bird flying in the sky.[429]

In the *Madhyamakāvatārabhāṣya* Candrakīrti explains the role of personal experience in realizing ultimate truth: "Only through exclusive personal experiences *(rang gi myong ba nyid du)* does the true nature [of ultimate reality] become clearer to those enthusiastic listeners," he writes.[430] And in the *Prasannapadā* he says:

> Because [ultimate reality] is not realized through another it is called *an unrealizable through another.* This means that it is not realized through another's explanation. Instead the meaning is that it is to be realized personally *(rang nyid).*[431]...One realizes ultimate reality personally by way of not realizing it. True nature pertaining to things is thus not realized through anyone else, and that itself is ultimate reality.[432]

The way in which ultimate truth is realized, or seen, by way of not seeing it is explained by Candrakīrti in the *Madhyamakāvatārabhāṣya:*

> [Question]: Is it not true that [ultimate reality] is not seen with characteristic of such [dualistic] appearance? So how do they [i.e., āryas] see it? [Reply]: Yes, it is true that [ultimate reality is not seen with dualistic appearances]. Yet [the Prāsaṅgika Mādhyamikas] assert that they see it by way of not seeing.[433]

Since "seeing it by way of not seeing" is a description of both the cognitive state of a meditator engaged in the meditation on ultimate truth and the meditative process itself, it is essential to understand both the process and the state arrived at. Tsongkhapa and Gorampa agree that, while noticing the bodily and mental processes as they arise and cease, a meditator also discerns the arising and passing away of the aggregates. When knowledge of the momentary and fleeting nature of aggregates becomes mature, keen, and strong, the initially discontinuous awareness of arising and cessation unfolds continuously. When keen knowledge thus proceeds and intensifies, then neither the arising of each bodily and mental process, nor its middle phase known as *presence,* nor the continuity of bodily and mental processes, nor the occurrence of unbroken flux is apparent to the meditator. Nor are the shape of the hand, the foot, the face, the body, and so on apparent to him. At this point, the meditator has entered single-pointed concentration on the ultimate truth. What is apparent to the meditator is only the ceasing of physical and mental processes, called *vanishing* or *dissolution.*[434] In the meditative state, all objects of meditation—bodily as well as mental—seem to the meditator to be entirely absent, to have become nonexistent. It appears to the meditator as if what is seen has vanished. Initially the meditator's consciousness takes familiar delight in conceptual elaborations, for instance, of shapes, concepts of individual identity derived from the continuity of serial phenomena, and collective concepts derived from the agglomeration of phenomena. Even up to the knowledge of arising and cessation, the meditator fastens on to structures or features—such as any mark, sign, idea, or image—of objects conceived or perceived. All graspable conceptual objects remain apparent to the meditator's senses. But once the knowledge of ultimate truth, or emptiness, is achieved as described above, no such conceptual formations or structures appear to consciousness.[435] Since, at this point, cognition does not involve any graspable object but is nonetheless engaged, albeit with an empty cognitive sphere, so the process is fittingly described as "seeing by way of not seeing."

Tsongkhapa and Gorampa agree with the account thus far. Before embarking on an examination of Tsongkhapa's view, we need to address a key issue that forms the backdrop to his interpretation of Candrakīrti. Tsongkhapa makes a crucial distinction between conceptual wisdom—otherwise known as *empirically valid cognition* or *empirical wisdom*—and nonconceptual wisdom—otherwise known as *ultimately valid cognition* or *ultimate wisdom*. The former, as Tsongkhapa characterizes it, cognizes things that are presented to it without analyzing their ultimate mode of being, while the latter cognizes the ultimate nature of things by way of such a critical analysis. Despite distinguishing between these two valid cognitions, he maintains that they are mutually entailing. Whether the subjective consciousness is that of a buddha, another ārya, or even an ordinary being, these distinctions and the mutually supportive relation between them remain epistemically important.

Against this background, Tsongkhapa explains the position taken by Candrakīrti as follows:

> Yes, it is true that [the nonconceptual wisdom] does not see [ultimate reality] by way of [seeing] dualistic appearances, because dualistic appearances do not withstand the critical perspective of the [wisdom] realizing things as they truly are. However, [the Prāsaṅgika Mādhyamikas] assert that āryas see [ultimate truth] by way of not seeing.[436]

The key issues raised in Candrakīrti's passages concern how, and in what ways, ultimate truth is realized. As a result, the distinction between the two cognitive faculties, and the way ultimate and conventional truth relate to them, is of central importance. Tsongkhapa insists that ultimate truth is the object of nonconceptual wisdom. He argues that from the vantage point of nonconceptual wisdom, all dualistic appearances of conventional truths disappear. Such wisdom sees phenomena as having no discrete identities, no positive or affirmative qualifications whatsoever. All phenomena present themselves to such wisdom initially as in flux, as insubstantial, and, eventually, as selfless and empty. The empty mode of phenomena is seen by nonconceptual wisdom through the penetration of all dualistic appearances.

Tsongkhapa argues, in fact, that a direct realization of the empty mode of phenomena is possible only by piercing through all conventional truths by ultimate wisdom. Hence "the mode of realizing realities as they truly are is by way of not seeing the appearances of conventionalities, such as the psychophysical aggregates."[437] In other words, ultimate wisdom realizes ultimate truth by directly perceiving the ultimate characteristics of phenomena (i.e., their empty mode) without actually perceiving the characterized phenomena as such.[438] This means that the ultimate truth of phenomena, such as the psychophysical aggregates, is indeed seen by way of not seeing those phenomena.

Let us now turn to Gorampa, for whom the distinction between conceptual and nonconceptual wisdom has significance only in the case of an unenlightened ārya's mode of cognition. He considers such an ārya, one who is still in training, as the sole cognitive agent who conceives both conventional and ultimate truth. For buddhas and ordinary beings, the distinction between conceptual and nonconceptual wisdom has no relevance or application. A buddha cognizes ultimate truth exclusively, and thus requires only nonconceptual or ultimate wisdom. An ordinary being, however, has no access to ultimate truth, and thus does not require nonconceptual or ultimate wisdom. Conceptual or empirical wisdom serves as the sole epistemic resource for ordinary beings.

What is at issue here is not just a matter of distinguishing between the consciousnesses of an ārya and a buddha, but also the role of ultimate wisdom as shared by the two. Gorampa maintains that, from the vantage point of nonconceptual wisdom, all conventionalities disappear. Ultimate wisdom, he argues, "does not apprehend even the slightest dualistic appearance [both in the conventional and the ultimate sense], for it is thoroughly free from all epistemic misconceptions, including predisposition without any trace."[439]

When it comes to the question of how ultimate reality is realized, at least insofar as it can be described in words, Tsongkhapa and Gorampa thus seem quite close. Like Tsongkhapa, Gorampa argues that ultimate truth is realized by way of not seeing it—namely, by way of dissolving all dualistic appearances of conventionalities or by abjuring any positive account of ultimate truth. Both hold that conventional truth is always realized by way of engaging with dualistic appearances, while ultimate truth is realized by way of dissolving all dualistic appearances. Yet whereas Tsongkhapa posits the mutually supportive relation between conceptual and nonconceptual wisdom, even in the realization of ultimate truth, Gorampa maintains that nonconceptual wisdom alone is capable of such realization. In fact, he claims the exact opposite of Tsongkhapa: Gorampa argues that nonconceptual wisdom—ultimate wisdom—can have no empirical grounding, and in gaining access to ultimate truth, it must operate entirely without reliance on empirical input.

Tsongkhapa's and Gorampa's divergence on the status of empirical wisdom stems from their disagreement about the efficacy of conventional truth, which in turn is informed by their dissension on the nature and extent of the objects of negation, and thence by their fundamental discord on the relationship between the two truths. Tsongkhapa argues for unity between the two truths and thus does not consider conventional truths as objects of negation. Gorampa insists on disunity between the two truths and does consider conventional truths as objects of negation. Similarly Tsongkhapa argues for unity between the two cognitive faculties, so that even a buddha is said to be equipped with both empirical and ultimate wisdom. Gorampa argues for disunity between the two cognitive faculties, so that a buddha is said to have only ultimate or nonconceptual wisdom.

How exactly does a similar understanding of the nature of nonconceptual wisdom—seeing by not seeing—lead to such different conclusions? The answer lies in how they parse this expression. Tsongkhapa reads the phrase "seeing by way of not seeing" as the same idea expressed in the claim: "without seeing constitutes the noble seeing."[440] The phrase "seeing by way of not seeing" is not contradictory, for in Tsongkhapa's view, the Prāsaṅgikas "do not accept seeing nothing as seeing [the ultimate reality]."[441] For Tsongkhapa the terms *seeing* and *not seeing,* used within the same phrase, imply two different objects of reference, and for this reason, he argues, "not seeing conceptual elaborations is itself posited as seeing the transcendence of conceptual categories."[442] The term *seeing* has "transcendence of the conceptual elaborations" *(spros dral, aprapañca)* as its referent, while the term *not seeing* has "conceptual categories" *(spros pa, prapañca)* as its referent. In other words, that which is seen is the empty mode of being of phenomena, while that which is not seen is the conventional mode of existence of those phenomena. Since the phrases "seen" and "not seen" take different objects, the phrase need not be contradictory (or mystically paradoxical). It appropriately describes how ultimate truth appears to its cognizing consciousness.

In some sense, Gorampa agrees with this latter point.[443] Although he does not elaborate much on the phrase, he also understands the terms *seeing* and *not seeing* to take different referents. *Seeing* refers to ultimate reality, or the transcendence of conceptual categories, while *not seeing* refers to empirical reality, or conceptual categories.

How then does Gorampa differ from Tsongkhapa in understanding the phrase "seeing it by way of not seeing"? Does seeing the ultimate by way of not seeing it constitute an engagement with a particular cognitive *content,* or is it simply the engagement with a total *absence?*

Transcendence

Since seeing ultimate truth by way of not seeing also means transcending conceptual elaboration, the distinctions between Tsongkhapa's and Gorampa's positions on realization of ultimate truth can be further articulated by considering the criterion that determines the transcendence of conceptual elaboration. A key issue here is whether the transcendence of conceptual elaboration calls for a total obliteration of conceptual categories. Is there a way of transcending conceptual elaborations without actually eliminating them?

Proliferation of Conceptual Elaboration

First let us look more closely at what is meant by *conceptual elaboration,* itself only a rough translation of the Sanskrit term *prapañca* (Pāli *papañca,* Tib. *spros pa*).[444] A precise English equivalent for the term presents difficulties. This is partly because the concept expressed by the term *prapañca* is totally foreign to the English-speaking world and partly because none of the texts in the Buddhist canon offers a clear and precise definition. However, the Buddhist canon does give a clear analysis of how *prapañca* arises in us, how it leads to conflict within and without, and how it can be ended.[445]

Despite variation in some details, the texts all depict the essential basis that gives rise to prapañcas. Although part of a larger causal nexus, the unskillful mental habit called *prapañca* lies at the heart of all conflicts—both within and without. Prapañca is essentially the blind tendency of thoughts to proliferate due to a mistaken sense of self. Prapañca distorts the normal processes of cognition because of a fundamental error. Consequently phenomena present themselves to consciousness in a way they don't actually exist—they appear as substantial, self-subsistent, isolated units with an immutable essence.

Prapañca is felt most immediately on the experiential level—that is, the domain of the psychophysical aggregates. This domain is putatively divided into two—a cognitive or subjective element comprised of consciousness and its adjuncts, and a cognized or objective element comprised of cognitive data. Although the subjective and objective elements are interlocking and mutually dependent, the operation of prapañca leads to the conceptual bifurcation of those elements into subject and object. Just as the subject is split off from experience, and is erroneously conceived as distinct from the cognitive act itself, so also the objective element, conceived as the external world of objects, is equally divorced from cognitive experience. This error leads consciousness to view itself as an immutable ego standing against the world of changing phenomena—it solidifies the idea of the self as substantial and independently existing. Thanissaro Bhikkhu thus suggests "that the root of the categories of *papañca* is the perception, *I am a thinker.*"[446]

Once the ego is solidified through the processes of prapañca, it constantly seeks self-affirmation and self-aggrandizement. Yet because the ego is an utter illusion, utterly empty, utterly void, so the appearance of selfhood itself generates a nagging sense of insufficiency—the ego cannot be adequate to that which it projects itself as being. Consequently, on both emotional and intellectual fronts, the ego experiences an aching sense of incompleteness, an inner lack requiring perpetual fulfillment, and the lurking suspicion of an ultimate lack of identity. The result is an inner disquietude and a chronic anxiety that is expressed in a compulsion to build and to fortify the sense of self. This process leads to greed, to desire, to relentless craving—for pleasure, wealth, power, and fame—all as a means to satisfy the need for self-security. In turn, this results in hatred, selfishness, and violence. Thus, through the process of prapañca, the agent becomes a victim of his own ignorance and misconception.[447]

When the sense of self arises in relation to experiences, then based on the feelings arising from sensory contact, some feelings will naturally seem appealing and others will seem unappealing. "From this there grows desire, which comes into conflict with desires of others who are also engaging in papañca. This is how inner complications breed external contention."[448]

This analysis of prapañca and the way it victimizes the agent is fundamental to the Buddhist phenomenology of suffering and therefore largely accepted by both Tsongkhapa and Gorampa. Where they part company is regarding the scope of prapañca and how it is brought to an end. Tsongkhapa holds that prapañca is a reifying cognitive process that originates in habitual clinging to the substantiality and essences of things:

> [Question]: Ending what leads to the end of defilements?
> [Response]: Reproductive karma, which causes birth in saṃsāra, arises from defilements. Although defilements in themselves are not self-evidently existent, they arise from the erroneous conceptions engaging with the false notions such as "appealing" and "not appealing." Erroneous conceptions engaging with the false notions, in turn, arise from the beginningless habituation with grasping at true existence in relation to the diverse categories of prapañca. These include cognitions and cognized objects, expressions and expressed, jars and mattresses, male and female, gain and loss, and so forth. Prapañca, which grasps at the true existence of these things, can be eradicated through practice directed toward seeing the emptiness of those things.[449]

Ultimate wisdom is the only means by which the cognitive distortions perpetuated by prapañca can be eradicated, and so Tsongkhapa and Gorampa both approach the categories of prapañca from the vantage point of this wisdom rather than from a more generalized perspective. Consequently, in the context of ultimate wisdom, Tsongkhapa takes prapañca to mean not only the categories that are conceptually reified through the assumption of the existence of essences (those that are generally classified as the objects of negation), but also "the categories of appearances."[450] Gorampa follows suit, asserting that "far from being only truly existent entities or negative entities, *prapañca* includes all signs of phenomena, both positive and negative, that provoke mental engagements and distractions."[451] As Dreyfus puts it: "By *elaboration [prapañca],* Gorampa means more than holding to things as really existing or understanding emptiness to imply a commitment to a positive entity. He means all signs, positive or negative, through which objects can be conceptualized."[452]

As we have seen now on several occasions, an initial agreement between Tsongkhapa and Gorampa is often underlaid by a deeper discord. The same is true for their characterizations of prapañca. Tsongkhapa offers two context-dependent characterizations. One emphasizes an epistemic process—the mental tendency to *essentialize* that leads to the proliferation of the categories of prapañca; the other emphasizes something more ontological—the contents of categories of prapañca as viewed by transcendent wisdom. Gorampa offers only a single characterization of prapañca, which places the emphasis solely on its contents. The characterization of prapañca as an epistemic process allows Tsongkhapa to argue that conventional phenomena are not the objects of negation, while Gorampa's ontological approach, looking only at the ultimate nature of categories and contents, allows him to argue that the objects of negation comprise all conventional phenomena.

Transcending Conceptual Elaboration

> [Mañjuśrī said]: Subhūti, the five aggregates belong to causes and conditions. If they belong to causes and conditions, they do not belong to oneself or others. If they do not belong to self and others, they have no owner. If they have no owner, there is no one who grasps them. If there is no grasping, there is no contention, and noncontention is the practice of religious devotees. Just as a hand moving in empty space touches no object and meets no obstacles, so the bodhisattvas who practice the equality of emptiness transcend the mundane world.[453]

The contention between Tsongkhapa and Gorampa on the understanding of prapañca becomes clearer as we enter the second phase of the analysis, namely, that of the *transcendence of prapañca*. As we noted above, when Tsongkhapa approaches prapañca from the perspective of ultimate wisdom, he classifies all conventional appearances within the categories of prapañca. In his view, however, the transcendence of the categories of prapañca cannot be equated with "the absence of the prapañca of appearances."[454] Instead he holds that "transcendence of the categories of prapañca should be understood as a dissolution of all dualistic appearances from the standpoint of the direct perception of things as they really are."[455]

Although it is not entirely without ontological implications, Tsongkhapa does not view the transcendence of the categories of prapañca as a metaphysical transcendence. What is transcended is the conventional understanding associated with the dualistic appearance of things—but without entailing the nonexistence of those things. This follows from his prior commitment to a transcendent epistemological perspective as the basis on which the essenceless, relational, and contingent nature of phenomena is established. So while the cognitive agent experiences a total transcendence of the categories of prapañca in the realization of ultimate truth during meditative equipoise, Tsongkhapa takes this experience of transcendence to operate strictly within the epistemic domain—within the psychophysical aggregates, which are not themselves transcended or dissolved. Transcending the categories of prapañca is not metaphysical transcendence.

The characterization of *prapañca* offered by Gorampa, however, has strong metaphysical implications. "*Prapañca,*" he says, "is the characteristic feature of causally effective things. The tathāgata, however, is not a thing, hence the categories of prapañca do not apply to it. Therefore the tathāgata is transcendent of prapañca."[456] Gorampa makes it very clear that just as he does not regard prapañca as merely a cognitive process, neither is the transcendence of prapañca merely epistemic—it is not simply a change in one's perspective. Prapañca is constitutive of *all* causally effective phenomena, and so the transcendence of the categories of prapañca means the transcendence of *all* empirical phenomena, including the empirical consciousness—as they are all causally effective. Thus the transcendence of prapañca is a transcendence of the very structures that constitute cognition, and so, one might say, even of cognition itself (or at least as it is part of the system of conventional appearances).

Like Gorampa, many of his traditional allies—Rendawa,[457] Rongtön Shakya Gyaltsen,[458] Shakya Chogden,[459] Karmapa Mikyö Dorje,[460] Mipham Rinpoche,[461] and Gendün Chöpel[462]—also treat prapañca as simply synonymous with the system of conventional truth. This camp equates prapañcas with the entire system of conventionalities and the latter with ignorance and the effects of ignorance. Thus they all maintain, like Gorampa, that prapañcas, such as the impressions of existence and nonexistence, appear as long as metaphysical transcendence is not achieved.[463]

There is no doubt that Tsongkhapa and Gorampa differ markedly in their understanding of what the transcendence of the categories of prapañca entails. For Gorampa it is contradictory to hold that one can retain any connections with the conventional world while transcending the categories of prapañca—any relation with the conventional world is seen as detrimental to the pursuit of liberation. The transcendence of the categories of prapañca means, therefore, the total ontological and epistemological *separation* from the conventional world.[464] Given Gorampa's insistence on the primacy of ultimate truth and ultimate wisdom over conventional truth and empirical wisdom, his insistence on the need for metaphysical transcendence is hardly surprising—it is consistent with his overall agenda.

In contrast, Tsongkhapa's philosophy is not committed to maintaining the primacy of ultimate truth and ultimate wisdom over conventional truth and empirical wisdom—the two truths and their cognitive counterparts are seen as interdependent and mutually entailing, and this holds true even in the case of transcendent epistemology. In Tsongkhapa's view, the mutual interconnection of the two truths and the coordination between the two cognitions is not severed even in transcending of the categories of prapañca. "Because the characteristic of reality and the prapañca of the characterized appearances are mutually inseparable, the existence of ultimate truth would be impossible [without the characterized objects as its basis]," he contends.[465] His insistence on the epistemic rather than metaphysical character of the transcendence at issue is thus clearly consistent with his emphasis on the unity between the two truths.

While the consistency of their respective positions may be evident, it nevertheless remains for us to account more fully for the radically different accounts of transcendence adopted by Tsongkhapa and Gorampa. The issues come into sharpest relief when we consider the prapañcas of personal identity—the five psychophysical aggregates. In Gorampa's epistemology, the transcendence of the categories of prapañca requires a total elimination of all five psychophysical aggregates, since these are identified with the categories of prapañca. The transcendent wisdom that is arrived at through such transcendence is ontologically independent of the conventionalities of the five psychophysical aggregates, and occurs only after every connection with conventional knowledge has been severed. The dissolution of those aggregates is therefore a necessary condition for the achievement of transcendent wisdom and does not undermine it. In Tsongkhapa's epistemology, the transcendence of the prapañcas of personal identity must be achieved *within* the five psychophysical aggregates. The transcendence of the prapañcas of personal identity is soteriologically significant only if personally experienced within the bound of one's psychophysical aggregates. Such transcendence must, therefore, be epistemic and psychological; it cannot entail complete metaphysical transcendence of conventionalities, or their total dissolution.

As espoused by Tsongkhapa, ultimate valid cognition is *transcendent wisdom* in the sense that it is directed to the transcendent sphere—toward ultimate truth, supramundane or unconditioned nirvāṇa—but it is nevertheless mundane in terms of its scope and nature. Transcendent wisdom still operates entirely within the range of the conditioned world—it is itself dependently arisen and does not imply a shift to a metaphysically unconditioned sphere. Only reality as it is given within their own five aggregates is accessible to yogis and knowable directly through their personal experience. The transcendence of the categories of prapañcas is directed toward just such direct, personal wisdom. It is this wisdom, according to Tsongkhapa, that liberates beings from the obsession with conceptual elaborations such as those associated with the notions of an independent and substantial self—*me* and *mine*.

The true and essential characteristic of transcendent knowledge thus consists in a precise understanding of the conditioned world itself. In Bhikkhu Bodhi's words: "Though the realization of the unconditioned requires a turning away from the conditioned, it must be emphasized that this realization is achieved precisely through the understanding of the conditioned."[466] Whereas Gorampa argues that a practitioner must break off all ties with the conditioned world in order to attain unconditioned nirvāṇa, Tsongkhapa claims that the practitioner must view things as they are by means of direct awareness. This idea is again nicely captured by Bhikkhu Bodhi: "Nibbāna cannot be reached by backing off from a direct confrontation with saṃsāra to lose oneself in a blissful oblivion of the world."[467] Emphasizing the same point, Nāgārjuna also claims that "saṃsāra and nirvāṇa are not distinct. The understanding of saṃsāra is itself posited as nirvāṇa."[468]

It is crucial for Tsongkhapa to emphasize the connection between transcendent and empirical wisdom, and therefore also the connection between saṃsāra and nirvāṇa, since it is on this basis that he argues that transcendent knowledge is equivalent to the knowledge of phenomena as dependently arisen. Hence he argues that "dependently arisen, i.e., reality in its true nature, as seen by an ārya, is free from all categories of prapañca, such as expression and expressed objects, definitions and defined objects, and the like."[469] In other words, as Bhikkhu Bodhi puts it, "the path to liberation is a path of understanding, of comprehension and transcendence, not of escapism or emotional self-indulgence. Nibbāna can only be attained by turning one's gaze towards saṃsāra and scrutinizing it in all its starkness."[470]

For Tsongkhapa the transcendence of the categories of prapañca need not and does not threaten the symbiotic relationship between the two truths. The transcendent experience remains firmly grounded in empirical reality while also allowing for epistemic transcendence: transcendent wisdom, underpinned by right view and firm ethical foundations, directs the mind upon the unconditioned so as to penetrate and cut through all the categories of prapañca. Transcendent wisdom therefore destroys the mental tendencies for the proliferation of prapañca, but it leaves the categories of prapañca intact. To borrow a simile from Buddhaghosa, just as a lamp simultaneously burns the wick, dispels the darkness, creates light, and consumes the oil, so transcendent wisdom simultaneously understands things as they are, abandons ignorance and the obsessions to proliferate prapañcas, realizes nirvāṇa, and develops the path to liberation. The key to transcendent knowledge, therefore, lies in the wisdom capable of penetrating the conceptual world—penetrating the five psychophysical aggregates of the knower. Such wisdom, Tsongkhapa argues, involves a direct experience that operates within the confines of one's own five psychophysical aggregates and yet sees through those aggregates.

Gorampa's transcendent epistemology, as we have seen, is geared toward metaphysical transcendence. This leads him to argue in favor of the absolute existence of the transcendent tathāgata, the latter taken as identical with transcendent wisdom,[471] while also insisting on the elimination of all the categories of prapañca—of the entire conventional system. While Tsongkhapa does argue in favor of epistemic transcendence, he also insists that transcendent knowledge does not actually eliminate all conceptual categories: "The transcendence of conceptual categories means dissolving all the categories of prapañca—dualistic appearances—from the perspective of the transcendent wisdom capable of directly realizing ultimate reality."[472] Once transcendent knowledge is achieved, the meditator still makes use of dualities in practical contexts—to distinguish between, for instance, skillful and unskillful action, afflictions and nonafflictions—and yet the habitual tendency toward prapañca ceases, for the meditator now sees such dualities as part of ongoing processes rather than as inherently persisting discrete entities.

Gorampa's alternative transcendent position derives from his emphasis on the two truths and their cognitive counterparts as completely distinct from one another and hierarchically related. Since ultimate truth and transcendent wisdom are viewed as ontologically and epistemologically independent of their conventional counterparts, they must also be completely transcendent of those counterparts—both epistemologically *and* ontologically. Likewise, Tsongkhapa's contrasting emphasis on the unity of the two truths is the basis for his insistence on the merely epistemic character of transcendence. The unity of the two truths, and the modes of understanding associated with them, are not violated even at the climax of the transcendent experience.

It may be said that while Gorampa mobilizes his transcendent epistemology to enable a nonduality that is metaphysical, Tsongkhapa does so to enable the formulation of a nonduality that is merely epistemic. This brings the idea of nonduality itself to the fore.

Nondual Epistemology

> [Mañjuśrī said:] Subhūti, the basic nature of the five aggregates is emptiness. If that nature is emptiness, there is neither "I" nor "mine." If there is neither "I" nor "mine," there is no duality. If there is no duality, there is neither grasping nor abandoning. If there is neither grasping nor abandoning, there is no attachment. Thus free of attachment, one transcends the mundane world.[473]

The two Tibetan Prāsaṅgikas agree that the direct personal realization of ultimate truth requires the transcendence of all prapañca, and this in turn depends on the attainment of what is known as *nondual knowledge.* Thus a detailed analysis of nonduality is crucial to our discussion. This analysis will involve *how* and *when* the nondual state is attained; whether the nonduality at issue is epistemic or metaphysical; and what is implied by the attainment of the nondual state—particularly in relation to the dichotomy of subject and object.

Tsongkhapa regards the nondual realization of ultimate truth as an epistemic event. In his understanding nondual realization is possible, yet the apprehending consciousness—transcendent wisdom—retains its ontological distinctness as subject, and the cognitive sphere—ultimate reality—likewise retains its ontological distinctness as object. Gorampa contends that nondual realization forms a single metaphysical reality—a total integration of subject and object. Only such a complete integration, according to him, resolves the problem of duality. Thus Tsongkhapa and Gorampa agree that, from the standpoint of nondual wisdom, the meditator experiences a total dissolution of even the subtle duality between subject and object, but they disagree on the implications of this nondual experience. Tsongkhapa does not hold the achievement of nondual wisdom as equivalent to the cessation of cognitive activity, whereas for Gorampa it means exactly that.

Tsongkhapa's description of the way the meditator arrives at nondual understanding is as follows. The cognitive agent experiences a fusion of subjectivity and its object, which refer here not to self and outside world but rather to elements within the meditator's own psychophysical aggregates.

The meditator remains introspective, not engaging the outside world, but the outside world as such does not disappear. What occurs is instead a total cessation of the dualities between subject *I* and object *mine,* between *thinker* and *thought,* between *feeler* and *feelings,* between *mind* and *body,* between *seeing* and *seen,* and so forth.[474] Initially a meditator perceives, for instance, that in each act of seeing, two factors are always present: the object seen and the act of seeing it. While each single act of seeing involves dissolution, the object seen and the act of seeing actually consist of numerous physical and mental processes that are seen to dissolve serially and successively.[475] Eventually, the meditator also notices the dissolution of the dissolution itself. In other words, the meditator first realizes the fluctuating and transitory character of the five aggregates, which is then followed by the further realization of the aggregates as empty and selfless, and finally by the realization of the emptiness of even the empty and selfless phenomena. Nondual knowledge is thus arrived at, in Tsongkhapa's view, through the direct experience of seeing the truths within one's own aggregates, rather than through being convinced of the truth of certain abstractions through rational argument or persuasion. Since the process here is a cognitive experience that operates entirely within the domain of one's own psychophysical aggregates, it is therefore an epistemic but not a metaphysical nonduality.

This is how, according to Tsongkhapa, an ārya has direct nonconceptual and nondual access to the transcendent nature of his own five psychophysical aggregates during meditative equipoise. In the wake of meditative equipoise, an ārya engages with dualistic worldly activities, such as taking part in philosophical discourse, practicing different social conventions, and so on. The ārya will thus make use of socio-linguistic conventions, but since the ārya has eradicated all reifying tendencies, even these worldly dualistic engagements will be seen as consistent with nondual wisdom. Both nondual and dual wisdoms, especially in the case of a buddha, Tsongkhapa argues, are fully commensurate.

As far as Gorampa is concerned, however, no dichotomy can be reconciled with nonduality and so with nondual knowledge. The key to attaining nondual knowledge is to eschew the dichotomy between ultimate reality as object and transcendent wisdom as subject. Gorampa maintains that it is impossible to achieve nonduality as long as the dichotomy between subject and object persists. His nonduality is thus a metaphysical unity requiring the fusion of transcendent wisdom with ultimate reality. They become a single entity, which he alternately describes as "transcendent wisdom," "buddha," "tathāgata," "ultimate truth," or "ultimate reality."

"Because one has realized emptiness and attained a perfect integration with it," says Gorampa, "the adventitious stains wear out. Eventually the cognition itself becomes an undefiled cognitive sphere. This itself is the ultimate buddha, who is adorned with the perfections of abandonment and realization."[476] From this point onward, "ultimate reality, empirical reality, and subjective wisdom—all three lose their contradistinctions"—they all literally become one unified phenomenon.[477]

Gorampa argues that existence, nonexistence, both, and neither constitute the four extreme conceptual elaborations. "Once they are simultaneously eliminated, the individuality of cognizing mind and cognized reality ceases to appear."[478] He claims that "the cognizing mind inseparably embraces the transcendence of conceptual elaboration as its object, and that itself is designated as ultimate truth."[479] In other words, as Shakya Chogden puts it: "The actual cognitive sphere of the [nondual] wisdom of meditative equipoise directly realizing emptiness is the wisdom itself."[480] For both Gorampa and Shakya Chogden, then, "this wisdom is the ultimate truth, for it is the actual cognitive domain of the wisdom of the meditative equipoise...This holds true because this wisdom is the direct personal wisdom."[481]

The advocacy of such an absolute nondual wisdom is not unique to Gorampa and Shakya Chogden. Despite minor differences, several Tibetan Prāsaṅgikas hold a similar view. Like Gorampa, Karmapa Mikyö Dorje emphasizes the synthesis between transcendent wisdom and ultimate truth, arguing that "there is neither separate ultimate truth apart from the transcendent wisdom, nor transcendent wisdom apart from the ultimate truth."[482] Mipham Rinpoche, on the other hand, employs a more idealistic route to absolute nonduality: "In the end, there are no external objects. It is evident that they appear due to the force of mental predisposition...All texts that supposedly demonstrate the existence of external objects are provisional [descriptions of] their appearances."[483] Consequently whatever is posited as existent, according to Mipham Rinpoche, "is like a horse or an elephant appearing in a dream. When it is subjected to logical analysis, it finally boils down to the interdependent inner predispositions. And this is at the heart of Buddhist philosophy."[484] The climax of this absolute nonduality, for these thinkers, is the absolute realization of transcendent wisdom and the complete collapse or dissolution of the entire conventional system. Identical with ultimate truth, transcendent wisdom survives as the one and only truth. Transcendent wisdom becomes timeless, absolute, and unaffected by change. Even the concept of time is no longer applicable, since transcendent wisdom endures eternally—"it neither arises nor ceases," as Gorampa puts it.[485]

Central to Gorampa's doctrine of nonduality are several key idealistic conceptions. He does not hesitate to reconcile conceptions derived from the Yogācāra or Vijñānavāda School—such as that of *vijñaptimātra (rnam rig tsam)* (representation) or of *cittamātra (sems tsam)* (mind only)—with Prāsaṅgika Madhyamaka.[486] He contends that the external world is a system of purely mental constructs and that the five sensory consciousnesses perceiving the phenomenal world arise from the foundational consciousness, or *ālayavijñāna (kun gzhi rnam shes)*.[487] This latter idea is one of the fundamental elements of Yogācāra idealism. *Ālayavijñāna* is characterized as devoid of intentional activity, self-luminous and self-knowing, and is seen as the primary cause of all sensory experience. For the ālayavijñāna is the storehouse of all past karmic seeds—both defilements and virtues, which ripen as unpleasant or pleasant experiences upon meeting with the appropriate conditions. Ālayavijñāna is thus regarded as the foundation of both saṃsāra and nirvāṇa. According to both Gorampa and the proponents of Yogācāra idealism, it is transcendent of the dualism of subject and object, existence and nonexistence, death and birth, purity and defilements, arising and cessation, and is described as *dharmadhātu,* nirvāṇa, or *tathāgatagarbha* (buddha nature).

In defending the conception of the foundation consciousness, Sogyal Rinpoche, for example, writes: "There is the very nature of mind, its innermost essence, which is absolutely and always untouched by change or death. At present it is hidden within our own mind, our *sems,* enveloped and obscured by the mental scurry of our thoughts and emotions," but, he goes on, "just as clouds can be shifted by a strong gust of wind to reveal the shining sun and wide-open sky, so, under certain special circumstances, some inspiration may uncover for us glimpses of this nature of mind."[488] Sogyal Rinpoche also explains that, despite having varying depths and degrees, these glimpses each bring some light of understanding, meaning, and freedom. "This is because the nature of mind is the very root itself of understanding. In Tibetan we call it *Rigpa,* a primordial, pure, pristine awareness that is at once intelligent, cognizant, radiant, and always awake. It could be said to be the knowledge of knowledge itself."[489] This is in complete accord with Gorampa's views.

So in brief, in the nondualism postulated by Gorampa, the ultimate task of wisdom is to break through the diversity of appearances in order to discover the unifying nondual reality. This way of understanding the task of wisdom abolishes the validity of all conventional dualities, including the duality between subject and object. In Lindtner's terms: "Reality *(tattva)* is beyond all ontological and epistemological dualities *(dvaya),* while the empirical world of origination, destruction, and so forth is illusory—due merely to ignorance *(avidyā).*"[490] By using the epistemology of nonduality, Gorampa argues for a metaphysics of nonduality. As we will see in the next section, the formulation of his metaphysical nonduality reaches its culmination with the proposition of *nothingness* in place of *emptiness.*

Unlike Gorampa, Tsongkhapa holds that even the highest level of wisdom preserves duality and diversity. He asserts that Prāsaṅgika Madhyamaka draws our attention to empirical dualities—among them the duality of morality and immorality—and takes them as the indispensable basis for any genuine search for liberating wisdom. For Tsongkhapa, then, nonduality must be taken as a strictly epistemic process. In the section after next this view will be reinforced by showing that for Tsongkhapa even nondual knowledge is consistent with knowing phenomena as empty. It follows, therefore, that nondual knowledge is equivalent to knowing phenomena as dependently arisen, and is thus consistent with dual knowledge.

Seeing Phenomena as Nothing

Gorampa sees transcendent wisdom as an absolute, and he also holds that the attainment of this wisdom amounts to the realization of nondual reality. But what does that realization consist of? Does transcendent wisdom involve any cognitive activity? If the answer is positive, so that transcendent wisdom, understood as "seeing by not seeing," is indeed taken to involve cognitive activity, then why should the "seeing" in this case be characterized as "not seeing"? If the answer is negative, meaning an absence of any cognitive activity, then why is the "not seeing" of transcendent wisdom characterized as "seeing"? To phrase it slightly differently: transcendent wisdom involves either a form of cognition, in which case it requires a distinction between cognizer and cognized, or else there is no distinction between cognizer and the object of cognition, in which case transcendent wisdom is not a form of cognition.

Even among his closest allies, Gorampa's treatment of the transcendent nature of conceptual elaboration in a nondual state is highly contentious. It revolves around two important moves: firstly, he argues that the transcendence of conceptual elaborations in a nondual state is equivalent to engaging with an *utter absence* or *nothingness;* and secondly, he argues that ultimate cognition does not depend upon a dichotomy between subject and object. Gorampa writes that "the transcendence of conceptual elaboration is equivalent to an utter absence of any established entity," but he also insists that "in order to ensure the realization of that *utter absence* per se by the devotees, the transcendence of conceptual elaboration is presented as an arbitary model of ultimate truth."[491] According to this view "a model that actually represents the characteristic [of ultimate truth] cannot exist."[492] However, for the benefit of devotees, "ultimate truth is said to have been provisionally presented by means of the threefold conventional fabrications—definition *(mtshan nyid, lakṣaṇa),* definiendum *(mtshon bya, lakṣman),* and the defined model *(mtshan gzhi, lakṣya).* In this sense alone ultimate truth can be treated as the counterpart of conventional truth."[493] It transpires, therefore, that ultimate truth is not an object of knowledge in the sense that it can become known to its cognizing consciousness. It is simply an utter absence of anything empirical.

In order to establish the nondual character of ultimate cognition, Gorampa attempts to resolve the apparent dichotomy between transcendent wisdom (the putative subject) and emptiness (the putative object):

> [Question]: When you earlier defined *transcendence of conceptual elaboration,* you mentioned that it is free from all symbols of expression and objects of expression, from object and subject, and from negation and affirmation; here you praised it thus. Is this not like describing the qualities of the "sky flower" [i.e., a nonexistent entity], which cannot be known?
>
> [Gorampa]: Yes, [you are right. Talking about the transcendence of conceptual elaboration is exactly like describing the qualities of something nonexistent]. However, its description, even in this context, is not meant to suggest the existence of [duality] between the consciousness realizing [the transcendence of conceptual elaboration] and its experienced object or an object to be experienced [in the nondual state]...The elimination of conceptual elaboration in its entirety by an ārya's nonconceptual wisdom is itself considered the realization of emptiness, or is merely expressed as seeing the truth. If any object, either to be conceptualized or to be experienced, were involved [in the nondual state], it would, at best, be a universal or a thing [but not ultimate truth].[494]

Given his commitment to a metaphysical nonduality, any subject-object duality presents a problem for Gorampa. He is therefore determined to eliminate all possible dichotomies, which he achieves by equating the status of apprehended objects with universals. Here *universal* does not have the usual sense of abstractness but rather refers to the objects themselves. Gorampa therefore argues that if, in the nondual state, there is an object to be either conceptualized or experienced, then "at best it would be a universal or a thing." Since thing, and therefore universal, cannot be an ultimate truth, emptiness, in Gorampa's sense, must mean the utter absence of empirical truth. In this way transcendent wisdom is undifferentiated from nothingness. This undifferentiated transcendent wisdom does indeed satisfy the definition of being nondual in the most complete sense—it is beyond all cognitive activities, both perceptual and conceptual. It would seem that as long as the cognitive activities between cognizing subject and cognized object persist, the mind must always remain caught up in perceptual or conceptual operations. Moreover both thought and perception operate always within the domain of duality between subject and object. Since the persistence of such dualities constitute, in Gorampa's view, obstacles to the achievement of the nondual state, then those obstacles must be removed if that state is to be achieved.

In the nondual system advocated by Gorampa, there can be no transcendent cognitive *content* apart from transcendent cognition, since this would constitute a version of what is, for Gorampa, the highly problematic dichotomy between subject and object. Since the presence of any cognitive activity between subject and object threatens the achievement of nonduality, Gorampa insists that emptiness must be an utter absence—it cannot be an object of knowledge or a cognitive content, and nondual wisdom must embrace it without any duality or dichotomy. "Grasping and nongrasping are two," says the *Vimalakīrtinirdeśa Sūtra,* and that is dualistic. "Thus, the inaction and noninvolvement of all things is the entrance into nonduality."[495] By treating emptiness as an utter absence rather than a cognitive content, and nondual wisdom as a *contentless* cognition, Gorampa effectively resolves the problem of the apparent dichotomy between the objectivity of ultimate reality and the subjectivity of transcendent wisdom. Thus what remains is an absolute, nondual, and transcendent subject itself.

The view that equates emptiness with an utter absence is, once again, not unique to Gorampa. In fact, Taktsang Lotsawa,[496] along with Gendün Chöpel, explicitly endorses this view. Gendün Chöpel, for instance, argues that in the meditative equipoise there is no apprehended object whatsoever: "When it is fused with the appearance in the postmeditative equipoise, the union is formed in between the *nothingness* during the meditative equipoise and the *appearances* of something during the subsequent attainment."[497] This is how "the meaning of the *establishment of ultimately nothing* and the *establishment of empirically something* should be understood."[498]

This view that equates emptiness with nothingness is vigorously challenged, not only by numerous Gelug philosophers—such as Tsongkhapa,[499] Khedrub Jé,[500] and Jamyang Shepai Dorje[501]—but also by several non-Gelug thinkers, such as Sakya Paṇḍita,[502] Rongtön Shakya Gyaltsen, and Mipham Rinpoche. In criticizing the doctrine, Rongtön Shakya Gyaltsen, for example, points out that the equation of *seeing nothingness* with the *nondual state* in meditative equipoise would entirely incapacitate the purgative potency of *vipaśyanā*—penetrating wisdom. As the most important task of the wisdom of vipaśyanā is the eradication of latent defilements, this is a serious objection. If meditative equipoise were equivalent to seeing nothingness, "like a nondiscerning meditative trance," then meditative equipoise "would utterly lack the active penetrating insight of vipaśyanā seeing emptiness."[503] Moreover if the equivalence of meditative equipoise with seeing nothingness were accepted, "even sleep, falling into coma, and so on, would equally purge [the latent defilements], since they also possess mere nondiscernment."[504] In similar fashion, Mipham Rinpoche joins Rongtön Shakya Gyaltsen in challenging the equation of seeing nothingness with the nondual wisdom of meditative equipoise. While reinforcing Rongtön Shakya Gyaltsen's criticisms, Mipham Rinpoche brands Gorampa's view as nothing short of quietism—a view, also attributed to the Chinese Hva Shang, that takes cognitive disengagement to be a matter of ceasing all cognitive activities.[505] To take the validity of meditative equipoise as consisting in seeing nothingness is equivalent, in Mipham Rinpoche's view, to endorsing Hva Shang's insistence on stilling thoughts and becoming almost zombie-like: "It is the stilling of mind to attain the quietism without analysis, but that would lack the illuminating power of vipaśyanā. Thus, like a stone on the ocean bed, one eternally remains in the ordinary state."[506] The attainment of total freedom from latent impurities would then become impossible. Mipham Rinpoche reveals another absurdity inherent in the doctrine that equates emptiness with nothingness:

> If one maintains *not seeing* as *seeing emptiness,* since the mode of reality is so profound, there is an acute danger of erring. As mind is not an object bearing a physical form, nobody is able to see its color and so forth. To think that merely not seeing constitutes realizing emptiness is certainly committing a grave error. It is not

> possible to see a cow's horn on a man's head even after analyzing it a hundred times. It would be easy indeed for anyone, were not seeing itself sufficient to realize emptiness.
>
> ...For the erroneous view that apprehends nothing whatsoever, no thing whatsoever is established. There is no way to develop the ascertainment. It will have thus no capacity whatsoever to eliminate obstructions [of nirvāṇa and buddhahood]. Therefore, just as fire is inferred from smoke, the difference between the two [vipaśyanā and seeing nothingness] should be understood on account of its conduciveness to the realization [of reality] and the abandonment [of defilements].[507]

In short, by proposing, as we saw in the previous section, a doctrine of absolute transcendent wisdom, and by proposing, as we have seen here, a doctrine of nothingness, Gorampa argues that a nondual state, strictly speaking, must refer to a transcendent wisdom that is totally free of all cognitive activity. His insistence on metaphysical nonduality leads him to discount all cognitive content and activity as utterly inconsistent with such nonduality. Because he takes nonduality to be absolute, Gorampa must insist on the complete elimination of the phenomenal world as the object of negation, he must equate emptiness with nothingness,[508] and he must also take the full realization of nonduality as arrived at only when the subject-object dichotomy completely collapses. Harvey describes it as "the experience of transcendent knowledge, which is an undifferentiated unity, beyond the subject-object duality and a concept of any kind, even 'thought.' It is thought which is no longer what is usually meant by 'thought,' as it is without object, contentless."[509] Small wonder then that the water analogy strikes Gorampa so powerfully. Just as two jars of clear water form an inseparable mixture, Gorampa's nondualism requires a total fusion of subject and object. Tsongkhapa, on the other hand, does not equate emptiness with nothingness—yet he insists that it is possible, nevertheless, to achieve nondual awareness.

Seeing Phenomena as Empty

> [The Buddha said]: "Mahākāśyapa, to one who has the true insight, things are empty, not because one contemplates them as empty; they are empty by nature. Things are signless, not because one contemplates them as signless; they are signless in themselves.

> Things are unsought, not because one contemplates them as unsought; they are unsought in themselves. Things are devoid of origination, arising, entity, and self-nature; they are impossible to grasp, not because one contemplates them as such; they are so in themselves. This understanding is called true insight."[510]

As we have seen, Tsongkhapa is entirely opposed to the formulation of a metaphysical nonduality and instead directs his efforts toward the defense of an epistemic nonduality. Thus he posits that it is possible to attain nondual awareness even though the metaphysical distinction between subjectivity and objectivity remains. But how credible is Tsongkhapa's nonduality if it retains the metaphysical duality of subject and object?

To see ultimate truth nondually is, in his view, to see phenomena as empty, and given the conceptual unity between emptiness and dependent arising, so, in experiential terms, to see phenomena as empty is also to see phenomena as dependently arisen. It is critical therefore to understand the nature of the conceptual unity between emptiness and dependent arising, for the same principle of conceptual unity must be applied on the experiential level to resolve the tension between knowing phenomena as empty, therefore nondually, and knowing them as dependently arisen, therefore dually. Here the issue of the unity of the two truths becomes central.

Candrakīrti and Tsongkhapa both defend the validity of nondual epistemic access to ultimate truth by applying the conceptual unity between emptiness and dependent arising on the empirical, experiential level. In commenting on Āryadeva's *Catuḥśataka* (15:10), Candrakīrti argues that seeing phenomena as empty should *not* be equated with seeing "the son of an infertile woman"—which is to say that seeing phenomena as empty should not be construed as seeing nothingness or the mere absence of empirical realities.[511] Given the compatible relationship between dependent arising and emptiness, "a correct seeing of phenomena as dependently arisen should lead to seeing them as illusory, and strictly not as the son of an infertile woman."[512] Candrakīrti argues that "Prāsaṅgika Mādhyamikas…posit things as illusory and the like because they fear that it might otherwise absurdly lead to undermining the existence of dependently arisen phenomena. They do not agree with such [nihilistic] advocates."[513] Candrakīrti further explains: "When things are subjected to logical analysis… because the essence of things remains unestablished, the illusory-like nature of each individual object should remain as the remainder."[514] Tsongkhapa also reiterates that "there is no inconsistency whatsoever should the repudiation of the essence be followed by a cognition of objects as having mere illusory meaning. It is in fact vital."[515]

However, the cognition of anything positive by the ultimately valid consciousness as opposed to empirically valid consciousness—even the cognition of an illusory object—is problematic from that ultimate perspective. All the Prāsaṅgika Mādhyamikas agree that the ultimately valid consciousness does not itself positively affirm any object. For it to do so would be tantamount to an affirmation of the existence of essence in the face of analysis, but this would be radically inconsistent with the central metaphysics of the Prāsaṅgika Madhyamaka, namely, the thesis that nothing in the world has an essence that can defy or withstand critical analysis. "It would therefore be inconsistent for the reasoning consciousness—analyzing whether essence exists—itself to cognize the existence of even a merely illusory object."[516] This process of engaging with ultimate truth by not affirming anything in particular, rather actively eliminating everything, is precisely what is *med dgag* (Skt. *prasajyapratiṣedha*). In Dreyfus's words: "For Tsong kha pa, emptiness is a negation *(dgag pa, pratiṣedha)* and must be understood in terms of the negation of the putative object of negation *(dgag bya)*."[517]

For Tsongkhapa's critics, however, "this approach to emptiness is questionable," as Dreyfus observes. They interpret Tsongkhapa's use of the term *med dgag* as "absolute negation" (to use Pettit's phrase) in the metaphysical sense, and assume that he is clinging to ultimate truth as an absolute negation (because he recognizes the identity of emptiness and ultimate truth). From his critics' point of view, Tsongkhapa stands accused of advocating the doctrine of Madhyamaka nihilism. Gorampa, in the *Lta ba ngan sel (Eliminating the Erroneous View),* accuses Tsongkhapa of being "seized by demons" *(bdud kyis zin pa)* and in the *Lta ba'i shan 'byed (Distinguishing Views)* decries him as a "nihilistic Mādhyamika" *(dbu ma chad lta ba)* who is spreading "demonic words" *(bdud kyi tshig)*.[518] Tsongkhapa, on the contrary, argues that his notion of *med dgag* is an epistemic one, although not denying its ontological implication. To be precise, *med dgag* is an epistemic elimination of all prapañcas in order to have a direct vision of emptiness.

Just as not seeing ultimate reality by the dual empirically valid consciousness does not imply the nonexistence of ultimate truth, so, too, argues Tsongkhapa, "not seeing conventionalities in the nondual state does not lead to the breakdown of the unity between characterized objects and their characteristics since their relationship is not posited from the vantage point of the reasoning consciousness realizing ultimate reality."[519] From the perspective of the empirically valid cognition that verifies things such as color and shape, ultimate truth is nonexistent. But it does not follow from this that ultimate truth is itself nonexistent. Similarly, as Pettit encapsulates Tsongkhapa's points: "If an ultimate analysis finds no sprouts, that does not mean that sprout does not exist at all, but only that it is empty of inherent existence." He further adds: "If a conventional analysis finds a sprout, that is not the same as finding an inherent existence *(svabhāva, rang bzhin)* of a sprout, which could only be found by an analysis of the ultimate status of a sprout—and of course never is."[520] These epistemic paradigms demonstrate, according to Tsongkhapa, that while ultimate truth and its verifying transcendent wisdom are directly related, dual empirical wisdom and nondual ultimate truth are related indirectly[521]—they are, in fact, mutually supportive. Indeed, without mutual support between empirical wisdom and transcendent wisdom, the attainment of a nondual state is, in Tsongkhapa's view, impossible. Since the two truths and the two modes of understanding are mutually interlocking, so, despite the nonduality of experience during the meditative equipoise, this nondual experience still operates within the epistemic domain and therefore has to have an empirical ground.

Thus, although nondual transcendent wisdom gives access to ultimate truth, Tsongkhapa argues that this wisdom does not do so in isolation from dual empirical wisdom. Nondual transcendent wisdom is itself an empirical phenomenon, and it is not therefore an empirically transcendent truth, as Gorampa would have it. Just as nondual wisdom requires dual empirical wisdom as its grounding, so dual empirical wisdom requires nondual wisdom to validate its epistemic authority. In this way both cognitive resources mutually support each other, thereby enabling the agent concerned to realize the truth pertaining to the five aggregates from both dual and nondual standpoints. Just as seeing phenomena as empty and seeing them as dependently arisen interlock in all circumstances, so, Tsongkhapa contends, the nondual knowledge of ultimate truth and the dual knowledge of conventional truth universally interlock epistemologically and ontologically.

Were Tsongkhapa to argue that the ultimate reasoning consciousness, in isolation from empirical consciousness, sees things as dependently arisen, then he would incongruously be obliged to suppose that an ārya or a buddha sees conceptual elaborations while in the nondual state, and so to deny the possibility of the transcendence of conceptual elaborations even in that state; this would then force him to accept conceptual elaborations as withstanding or defying ultimate analysis, which would imply the existence of their essences. According to the standard Madhyamaka position accepted by Tsongkhapa, a failure to transcend conceptual elaborations by nondual or transcendent wisdom would mean a failure to grasp the true meaning of ultimate reality. "If ultimate truth were seen in terms of discrete objects, such as the psychophysical aggregates, seeing them, for instance, as the domain of touch, of expression, and of mind from the perspective of consciousnesses realizing the ultimate rather than seeing them by way of not seeing," then, Tsongkhapa argues, "ultimate truth would not be beyond conceptual elaborations."[522] Seeing ultimate truth as free from any duality is coherent and noncontradictory from the perspective of nondual wisdom, but not from the perspective of dual empirical wisdom.

It is important to note, however, that to see ultimate truth as nondual wisdom sees it, without seeing phenomena in discrete terms, does not mean that nondual wisdom is seeing *nothing* or is devoid of cognitive content or activity. For Tsongkhapa nondual wisdom *sees* the empty or ultimate mode of one's identity, and of one's five psychophysical aggregates, while dual wisdom sees the conventional, dependently arisen mode of one's identity, and of one's five aggregates. The only contrast between these two modes of seeing is that the former sees its object negatively while the latter sees its object positively. The dual and nondual knowledge of an ārya buddha, in particular, are equally valid—the wisdom that understands phenomena as empty also understands them as dependently arisen, and vice versa. A nondual experience of ultimate truth does not undermine the status of conventional truth, since the realization of ultimate truth is equivalent to that of conventional truth. It follows therefore that if nondual knowledge is a correct knowledge of ultimate truth, it should necessarily be equivalent to the dual knowledge of phenomena as dependently arisen.

Tsongkhapa therefore sees no contradiction in claiming that, from the empirical standpoint, nondual wisdom constitutes the subjective pole of consciousnesses with ultimate truth as its objective counterpart.[523] From the ultimate vantage point, on the other hand, nondual wisdom and ultimate truth "are free from the duality of act *(bya ba)* and object acted upon *(byed pa)*."[524] In the nondual state even the cognitive interplay between subject and object appears, from the meditator's point of view, to cease completely. This is because, as Tsongkhapa points out, "duality of act and object acted upon is posited strictly from the perspective of empirical cognition."[525] The dual appearances of subject and object completely dissolve from the perspective of nondual wisdom, and thus the meditator does not experience the mutual interaction between distinct and separate elements—between the seer and the seen—but the meditator nonetheless engages in an act of *mere seeing*. As the Buddha explains to Bahiya:

> In reference to the seen, there will be only the seen. In reference to the heard, only the heard. In reference to the sensed, only the sensed. In reference to the cognized, only the cognized. That is how you should train yourself...then Bahiya, there is no you in terms of that. When there is no you in terms of that, there is no you there. When there is no you there, you are neither here nor yonder nor between the two. This, just this, is the end of stress.[526]

The experience of mere seeing in a nondual form is valid only when it is empirically grounded and when there is cognitive activity occurring between nondual wisdom and nondual ultimate truth. Tsongkhapa maintains, in fact, that the activity between subject and object is inevitable in any acquisition of valid knowledge. It is thus consistent to argue that nondual wisdom involves a knowing subject and ultimate truth involves a known object.[527]

Tsongkhapa's main purpose in attaining nondual knowledge is not to eschew the subject-object dichotomy. The purpose, as he sees it, is rather to purify deluded cognitive states and destroy ego-tainted emotions in the service of *bodhicitta*—the goal of attaining full enlightenment in order to free all beings from suffering and its causes. Both the dual and nondual perspectives are required for success on the path, and that is why Tsongkhapa creates no hierarchy between them. One cannot eliminate negativity without a proper appreciation for empirical cause and effect, and one cannot eliminate the root delusion about an essential self without penetrating the ultimate truth.

We can thus summarize our discussion of nonduality as follows. Tsongkhapa's account of nondual knowledge rests largely on the unity of the two truths and therefore of emptiness and dependent arising. The attainment of nondual knowledge, according to his view, requires an eradication of ignorance and other reifying tendencies, and does not require any metaphysical shift. More specifically, such attainment does not require the establishment of a metaphysical unity between subject and object, nor the eschewal of conventionalities.

Gorampa, however, differs in claiming that nondual wisdom necessarily undermines the validity of conventionalities. Indeed, as long as dependently arisen phenomena are recognized, he holds that nondual knowledge will be impossible. This would be so even for an ārya or a buddha, who instead of experiencing ultimate truth during meditative equipoise would experience only conceptual elaborations, that is, conventionalities. The fact that conventionalities are not seen during meditative equipoise, argues Gorampa, suggests that their ontological status is wholly undermined by the attainment of nondual wisdom. Dependently arisen phenomena are effectively eradicated by nondual transcendent wisdom, and excluded from the nondual wisdom of an ārya or a buddha. From Gorampa's perspective, the nondual knowledge of ultimate reality is valid only when that knowledge is totally divorced from the realization of phenomena as dependently arisen; from Tsongkhapa's perspective, such knowledge is valid only when linked with the realization of phenomena as dependently arisen.

In the *Mahāratnakūṭa Sūtra* the Buddha reminds us of the poignant dangers associated with the doctrine of emptiness: "If one thinks that he has realized emptiness and becomes attached to emptiness, then he regresses in the pursuit of the Buddhadharma."[528] From a soteriological and ethical perspective, entertaining a view of self is better than an attachment to a nonview, namely, a view of selflessness: "Thus, Kāśyapa, it is better for one to take a view of the self as massive as Mount Sumeru than to take a view of emptiness and becoming arrogant. Why? Because all views can be eliminated by emptiness, but if one gives rise to the view of emptiness, there is no way to do away with it."[529] Emptiness is prescribed to eliminate all views, as the patient is prescribed medicine to eliminate illness. However, just as there is no cure for the illness if the medicine itself turns to poison, there will be no elimination of views if emptiness itself becomes another view—"Kāśyapa, all views can be eliminated by emptiness, but the view of emptiness cannot be eradicated," says the Buddha.[530]

Conclusion

In the *Condensed Perfection of Wisdom Sūtra* the Buddha says:

> Forms are not seen, and sensations are also not seen; unseen is recognition, and unseen is mind. Wherever consciousnesses *(shes pa, jñātā),* mind *(sems, citta),* and mental cognition *(yid, manas)* are unseen, that itself is explained as seeing Dharma by tathāgatas. Using words, sentient beings say that [they have] seen space.

> Examine how they see space. The Tathāgatā explains that seeing Dharma [ultimate reality] is similar. No other metaphor could illustrate the seeing of [ultimate reality].[531]

Tsongkhapa and Gorampa basically agree in recognizing ultimate truth as an object of knowledge and recognizing nonconceptual wisdom as the corresponding subject; they both accept the negative approach—seeing by way of not seeing—as necessary to arrive at knowledge of ultimate reality; and they both view the achievement of ultimate truth by its cognizing consciousness as possible only through the transcendence of conceptual categories. A huge gulf nevertheless exists between these two thinkers on these issues. Tsongkhapa argues for an epistemic nonduality while avoiding a metaphysical nonduality. Despite taking ultimate reality to be realized by way of not seeing any duality, Tsongkhapa draws no metaphysical conclusion and does not abolish the dichotomy of subjectivity and objectivity. Gorampa, on the other hand, employs an epistemic model of nonduality to arrive at a metaphysical nonduality. Since ultimate reality is seen without seeing any dualistic appearance, Gorampa argues, the contradistinctions between subjectivity and objectivity are henceforth lost; the transcendent subject and the transcendent object form a single metaphysical unity that can be interchangeably described as transcendent wisdom, buddha, or tathāgata.

Tsongkhapa consistently never abandons the idea of cognitive interaction between ultimate truth and ultimate wisdom throughout his transcendent epistemology. Ultimate truth is consistently recognized as an object of knowledge, while transcendent wisdom is recognized as its subjective counterpart. In Gorampa's case, since he upholds a metaphysical nonduality, absolute transcendent wisdom can have no separate cognitive sphere associated with it. For him, the claim that ultimate reality is an object of knowledge is merely a metaphor; the only true and reliable knowledge is completely nondual. Hence Gorampa consistently eschews the cognitive resources of conventional knowledge and its counterpart, conventional truth. To ensure that there is no duality whatsoever, he even rejects the dichotomy between the transcendent sphere and transcendent wisdom—the transcendent sphere, namely, emptiness, is equated with nothingness, while transcendent wisdom is itself a becoming one with that nothingness. Thus Gorampa is able to formulate an account of nondual wisdom as being without both content and activity—involving no object of knowledge distinct from the cognizing consciousness. Transcendent wisdom itself becomes both subject and object such that, strictly speaking, there is nothing to be known and only the nondual knower remains.

Both Tsongkhapa and Gorampa describe nondual knowledge as being like a process of "mixing water." They contend that the fusion between subjectivity and objectivity, from the meditator's point of view, is like mixing clean water from two different jars by pouring it all into one jar. Thus Tsongkhapa argues: "From the vantage point of the wisdom that directly realizes ultimate reality, there is not even the slightest duality between object and the object-possessing consciousness. Like mixing water with water, [the yogi] dwells in the meditative equipoise."[532] He insists, however, that this metaphor should not be taken too far or too literally. It refers only to the cognitive process and does not indicate a metaphysical unity. Gorampa, on the other hand, insists on taking this analogy in its most literal sense: just as the clean water from the two separate jars, when poured together, merge without any trace of their prior separation, so, with the achievement of transcendent wisdom and the realization of ultimate reality, the elements that previously appeared separate are merged in a single, complete, metaphysical unity. As he sees it, only if it is grounded in such a metaphysical basis can the dissolution of the duality between subject and object be meaningful.

5. Enlightenment

[Mañjuśrī said to the Buddha]: "So be it, World-Honored One. If good men and good women wish to know the state of buddhahood, they should know that it is not a state of the eye, the nose, the tongue, the body, or the mind; nor is it a state of forms, sounds, scents, tastes, textures, or mental objects. World-Honored One, the nonstate is the state of buddhahood. This being the case, what is the state of supreme enlightenment as attained by the Buddha?" The Buddha said: "It is the state of emptiness, because all views are equal. It is the state of signlessness, because all signs are equal. It is the state of wishlessness, because three realms are equal. It is the state of nonaction, because all actions are equal. It is the state of the unconditioned, because all conditioned things are equal."[533]

Introduction

TSONGKHAPA and Gorampa are both committed to the standard Madhyamaka position on the unique cognitive abilities of a fully enlightened being. They agree that a buddha is an all-knowing cognitive agent and that enlightenment represents an unparalleled cognitive achievement. Yet, although both agree also that an enlightened being is able to know all objects of knowledge in the span of a single temporal instant, they disagree on a number of crucial issues concerning the nature of enlightenment, including the question of exactly how, and in what ways, an enlightened wisdom knows all objects of knowledge.

In this final chapter we compare Tsongkhapa and Gorampa's positions regarding the nature of enlightenment, the characteristics of enlightened knowledge, and how such knowledge is different from and superior to the knowledge of the other āryas. In the course of this comparison we will see that for Tsongkhapa the unparalleled cognitive potential of enlightenment lies in its ability to access the two truths simultaneously within a single event of wisdom, whereas for Gorampa it lies in its capacity to access just one truth—metaphysically transcendent ultimate truth—within a single cognitive event.

We begin by analyzing what is called the universality of ultimate truth. This universality is directly related to the way an enlightened wisdom knows reality as it pertains to all objects of knowledge. Both Tsongkhapa and Gorampa hold that it is precisely because the universality of ultimate truth is exhaustively embraced by an enlightened wisdom that such wisdom can be said to know the ultimate truth of all objects of knowledge.

The Universality of Ultimate Truth

> [The Buddha speaks to Mañjuśrī] "All the Dharmas I teach are of one taste—the taste of detachment, liberation, and ultimate quiescence. What is taught by a good man or a good woman who has acquired the Single Deed Samādhi is also of one taste—the taste of detachment, liberation, and ultimate quiescence—and is unerringly consistent with the true Dharma. Mañjuśrī, a great Bodhisattva who has acquired the Single Deed Samādhi has fulfilled all the conditions conducive to his swift attainment of supreme enlightenment."[534]

Before turning to the two Tibetans, we will first consider Candrakīrti's comments on the universality of ultimate truth. In explaining the unique way an enlightened being realizes reality, Candrakīrti writes in the *Madhyamakāvatāra*, "Despite the divisions created by vessels, space is itself without any divisions. Similarly, any division created by things is not present in ultimate reality. Hence," he adds, "by fully accomplishing the realization of the uniformity [of all phenomena], you noble knower comprehend all objects of knowledge in a single instant."[535]

Tsongkhapa and Gorampa use similar terminology in commenting on this passage. Despite the fact that space is variously divided by containers and other objects, the space inside those containers is characterized as a "mere absence of all obstructing entity." The space inside the vessels thus remains uniformly "undivided." Similarly, although there are manifold divisions of phenomena produced by their respective causes and conditions, the ultimate truth pertaining to them shares the same uniform nature. The ultimate truth of each conditioned phenomenon possesses the characteristic of *nonarising,* a characteristic uniformly shared by all phenomena. In this sense, ultimate reality is shared by all phenomena without any division, just as the space inside various vessels is one and the same space.

Thus far Tsongkhapa and Gorampa agree,[536] but a closer examination reveals striking differences. Ontologically, Tsongkhapa maintains a pluralistic standpoint in contrast to the monism of Gorampa. Despite his commitment to the universality of ultimate truth, according to which ultimate truths share similar natures, Tsongkhapa asserts that each empirical truth has its own ultimate truth. Gorampa, however, precisely because of his commitment to the universality of ultimate truth, insists there is only one ultimate truth for all empirical phenomena. Epistemologically, Tsongkhapa argues that enlightened wisdom accesses the universality of ultimate truth by virtue of having knowledge of *both* the empirical and ultimate truths; Gorampa argues that the enlightened person has knowledge of ultimate truth alone. Let's look at these claims more closely.

We first consider matters from the ontological standpoint. Although all empirically given truths—such as the aggregates of form, feelings, and so on—are contingently produced and have diverse conventional characters, all of them, according to Tsongkhapa, are ultimately empty of inherent existence. They share this universal characteristic, literally, "one taste" *(ro gcig, ekarasa).* The Buddha, for example, makes this statement: "Just as the great ocean has but one taste, the taste of salt, even so does this Dharma and discipline have but one taste, the taste of release."[537] The *Samādhirājasūtra* also tells us: "By knowing one, all are known. And by seeing one, all are seen. Despite many things being said about [ultimate truth] in conventional terms, no arrogance should arise from it."[538] Furthermore, "Just as you have recognized *('du shes)* [the true nature of your own] personality, so you should apply the same insight to all [phenomena]. All phenomena are of the [same] nature like clear space."[539] In the *Gaganagaṃjasamādhi Sūtra* it is stated: "Whoever by meditating on one phenomenon knows all phenomena as apprehensible like illusions and mirages, and knows them as hollow, false, and ephemeral, will before long reach the *summum bonum (snying po)* of enlightenment."[540] And Āryadeva also says: "Whosoever sees one is said to see all. That which is emptiness of one is the emptiness of all."[541] Referring to this last passage from Āryadeva, Candrakīrti comments:

> The emptiness of the essence of form is itself the emptinesses of the essences of the aggregates such as feeling. Similarly, the

> emptiness of the essence of the eye-source is itself the emptinesses of the essences of all twelve sources. Likewise, the emptiness of the essence of the eye-constituent is itself the emptinesses of the essences of all eighteen constituents. Equally so are [the emptinesses of the essences of] the infinite categories of things due to the distinct divisions in things, locations, times, and contexts. For whatever is the emptiness of the essence of one thing is itself the emptinesses of the essences of all things. In spite of the fact that jars and bowls for example are distinct, space is not distinct. While things such as form are distinct, insofar as they all lack the essential arising of form, and so on, they are not distinct. By understanding the lack of the essential arising of merely one phenomenon, one understands the lack of the essential arising of every phenomenon.[542]

As we have seen, Tsongkhapa argues that since all phenomena are empty of any substance or essence, they are necessarily dependently arisen and relational entities.[543] Endorsing the claim that the ultimate nature of all phenomena is fundamentally the same does not, in his view, make one a monist. Tsongkhapa remains committed to a pluralistic view. "A pluralistic view of the world," as Kalupahana puts it, "is not incompatible with dependent arising *(pratītyasamputpāda)*. Pluralism in the context of dependent arising does not imply the existence of self-contradictory truths. It need not necessarily lead to a notion of an Absolute that transcends such self-contradictory truths."[544] Tsongkhapa maintains that the ultimate reality of, for instance, the table in front of one's eyes cannot be treated as simply identical with the ultimate reality pertaining to the chair that one is sitting on. The empty table cannot be equated with the empty chair, since the emptiness of the table is constitutive, not only of the empty table, but of the empty conceptual-linguistic conventions imposed upon it as well. Those conventions belong exclusively to the ultimate truth of the table and are not present in the chair. Tsongkhapa, however, does not regard this concession as an impediment to arguing for the universality of ultimate truth. Just as different objects occupy different spaces, and yet the space those objects occupy has the same nonobstructive characteristic, so the ultimate realities of both table and chair are different, notwithstanding that the two ultimate realities have identical natures—they share "the same taste." Both of these emptinesses imply insubstantiality and lack of essence in the negative sense, as well as dependently arisen and relational nature in the affirmative sense.

It can therefore be said that, according to Tsongkhapa, an identical nature is universally shared by the ultimate realities of every empirical phenomenon. When the Buddha says that "the truth is one, there is no second,"[545] Tsongkhapa infers a reference to the dependently arisen as the criterion of truth rather than to an absolute truth that transcends all forms of duality and plurality. He remarks that "whatever you (the Buddha) have spoken has reference to dependent arising. For this leads to nirvāṇa. None of your actions fails to lead to peace."[546] He further argues that the Buddha has surpassed everyone in terms of his knowledge and teachings of dependent arising: "Among teachers the one who teaches dependent arising reigns supreme, and among knowledge the wisdom of dependent arising reigns supreme. These two are like the powerful monarchs ruling the world systems."[547] Given that each dependently arisen phenomenon occupies a different space and time, the universality of ultimate reality does not threaten Tsongkhapa's pluralism.

Gorampa takes the contrary approach by mobilizing the universality of ultimate reality to reinforce his monism. "Since its nature is one and the same like space," he asserts, "it has no divisions."[548] Gorampa sees a clear incompatibility between a pluralistic account of ultimate reality and the commitment to its having a single uniform nature. Then again, his commitments to both a monistic ontology *and* the universality of ultimate truth are seen to be compatible, and, indeed, as mutually reinforcing.

Gorampa regards the ultimate reality of the table as wholly equivalent to that of all other phenomena. There is no difference at all between the ultimate reality of the table and that of the chair—or of anything else for that matter. Just as space is the same for all the different objects that occupy it (it is, one might say, the objects that differ, and not the space), so it is one and the same ultimate reality that universally underlies all empirical phenomena. The universality of ultimate truth could not, from Gorampa's perspective, be maintained if the same ultimate reality were not shared by all empirical phenomena. If there were an ultimate truth that pertained to each phenomenon individually, then so would the ultimate truths of those phenomena, like the phenomena themselves, be confined within the bounds of those phenomena. There would then be no universal ultimate truth, no universally applicable characteristics. Any pluralistic account of ultimate reality is thus seen by Gorampa as contradictory to the notion of the universality of ultimate reality.

We will now address the epistemological aspect of the universality of ultimate truth. Since ontology and epistemology are typically interdependent, the two ontological positions discussed above provide the basis for the two epistemological positions. For Tsongkhapa, the inseparable ontological unity between the two truths means that knowledge of one necessarily entails knowledge of the other. A fully enlightened being "perfectly knows the universality of [ultimate truths] within a single moment of wisdom."[549]

In Gorampa's view, an enlightened wisdom accessing the universality of ultimate truth operates entirely independently of any empirical truths. Thus he holds that an enlightened wisdom must necessarily sever all epistemic connections with empirical knowledge. "When the universality of ultimate truth of all phenomena is understood as dharmadhātu," he says, "a single event of wisdom knows this within a single moment. This is followed by the disappearance of distinctions between ultimate reality, empirical reality, and apprehending wisdom."[550] Consequently these latter three form a nondual, absolute, and independent transcendent wisdom wherein all dualities fuse. As such the knowing wisdom and the object known literally become one.

For an ārya who is yet to be fully enlightened, the wisdom of the universality of ultimate truth arises only during the meditative equipoise and not during the postmeditative equipoise. For a fully enlightened being, there is no postmeditative equipoise—such a being, as Gorampa holds it, remains eternally absorbed with the universality of ultimate truth. As he sees it, this is the highest cognitive virtue of an enlightened being.[551] It is crucial to note that for Gorampa knowing the universality of ultimate truth is not a matter of engaging with it. On attainment of full enlightenment, the duality between subject and object totally disappears. The interaction between what is to be known and the knower comes to an end. The knower—transcendent wisdom—alone survives. In Gorampa's view, this is the way an enlightened being directly and personally knows the universality of ultimate reality without any duality. In more explicit terms, knowing the universality of ultimate truth means to become one with the unconditioned and transcendent ultimate truth. The knower becomes timeless, neither arising nor ceasing.[552]

If it is true that an enlightened being knows all objects of knowledge within a single instant, as both Tsongkhapa and Gorampa claim, the question then arises: How is this possible? To arrive at an answer, we will first explore why other sentient beings (particularly the three types of āryas, namely, *ārya śrāvakas, ārya pratyekabuddhas,* and *ārya bodhisattvas*) do not know all objects of knowledge within a single instant, and then revisit the analysis of an enlightened being's superior ways of knowing. Like Tsongkhapa, Gorampa[553] acknowledges the value of exploring the ways an nonenlightened ārya knows the two truths. A precise evaluation of the cognitive framework within which nonenlightened beings operate is seen as pedagogically useful for the analysis of the enlightened cognition.

How an Ārya Knows the Two Truths

Consistent with the standard Madhyamaka position, both Tsongkhapa and Gorampa maintain that, with the sole exception of buddhas, all beings, including ārya śrāvakas, ārya pratyekabuddhas, and ārya bodhisattvas of the tenth level *(bhūmi)* and below, are subject to varying degrees of misconception regarding the two truths. Ordinary beings are predominantly influenced by reifying ignorance and afflictive defilements. These cognitive agents superimpose absolute characteristics, such as essences, substantiality, or permanence, on to impermanent and insubstantial things, processes, or events. However, ārya bodhisattvas (on the eighth bhūmi and below) are free from active reifying tendencies and afflictive defilements. They have directly experienced ultimate truth, and so they have eradicated all negative emotions, including deluded ignorance, but they are still under the influence of latent defilements. Due to the continued and sustained orientation toward ultimate truth that is directly and personally realized in meditative equipoise, ārya śrāvakas, ārya pratyekabuddhas, and the ārya bodhisattvas of the eighth to tenth bhūmis are, however, totally free of even the subtlest latent reifying tendencies.[554] Yet these three types of āryas are still subject to what is called *nondeluded ignorance*—the conditioned state of mind predisposed by the previously existent latent conception of essence *(bden 'dzin gyi bags chags)*. Thus, although these three types of āryas—śrāvakas, pratyekabuddhas, and bodhisattvas of the eighth to tenth bhūmis—no longer have even the latent reifying psychological tendencies, they are yet to be fully enlightened, and they still have very subtle cognitive limitations. They remain predisposed to the assumption of dualities (rather than the reification of dualities) that was deeply habituated by the previously existent latent reifying tendencies. Often the subtle misconceptions possessed by them are described as "predisposed misconceptions of dualistic appearance" *(gnyis snang 'phrul ba'i bag chags)*.[555]

To this point both Tsongkhapa and Gorampa are in agreement. But what constitutes the "misconception of dualistic appearance"? And how should it be defined? To begin with, both Tibetan Mādhyamikas pinpoint the misconception of dualistic appearance as a very subtle tension between the mode of phenomenal existence and how that existence is understood—it involves a minimal conflict between ontological status and the corresponding epistemic state. However, on closer observation, it becomes evident that Tsongkhapa and Gorampa offer strikingly different accounts of what is at issue here: Tsongkhapa's ontology of ultimate truth has to accommodate the status of conventional truth, and consequently his nondual epistemology must encompass the understanding of conventional truth as well; Gorampa's ontology of ultimate truth necessarily excludes the status of conventional truth, and consequently his nondual epistemology must exclude the understanding of conventional truth.

This *dualistic appearance,* as Tsongkhapa understands it, is a subtle misconception that pertains to the nature of both truths. It is described as "dualistic appearance" because of the persisting subtle conflict between the ontological status of ultimate truth and its concurrent epistemic status due to the presence of the subtle epistemic error. The solution lies, therefore, in eliminating the epistemic error. A mere dichotomy between the subject and the object, in Tsongkhapa's view, is not part of the problem. In fact, the mere dichotomy between subject and object is, as he understands it, inevitable for even the most evolved wisdom. No knowledge whatsoever is possible without the interaction between cognition and cognitive field. In the *Dvaytānupassanā Sutta,* the Buddha also points out that dualities in themselves are not problems, provided they are understood properly:

> Monks, if there are any who ask, "Your listening to teachings that are skillful, noble, leading onward, going to self-awakening is a prerequisite for what?" they should be told, "For the sake of knowing qualities of dualities as they actually are." "What duality are you talking about?" "This is dukkha. This is the origination of dukkha": this is one contemplation. "This is the cessation of dukkha. This is the path of practice leading to the cessation of dukkha": this is the second contemplation. For a monk rightly contemplating this duality in this way—heedful, ardent, and resolute—one of the two fruits can be expected: either gnosis right here and now, or—if there be any remnant of clinging-sustenance—non-return...
>
> Now, if there are any who ask, "Would there be the right contemplation of dualities in yet another way?" they should be told, "There would." "How would that be?" "Whatever dukkha

> comes into play is all from ignorance as a requisite condition": this is one contemplation. "From the remainderless fading and cessation of that very ignorance, there is no coming into play of dukkha": this is a second contemplation. For a monk rightly contemplating this duality in this way—heedful, ardent, and resolute—one of the two fruits can be expected: either gnosis right here and now, or—if there be any remnant of clinging-sustenance—non-return.[556]

Like Tsongkhapa, Gorampa's account of dualistic appearance also refers to a conflict between the ontological status of ultimate truth and the concurrent epistemic state. Gorampa differs, however, in viewing the conflict as between the ultimate subject and the ultimate object. From his perspective, the subject-object dichotomy is at the heart of the problem, and the only solution is to eschew the objective element in order to embrace a metaphysical nonduality—so long as the interaction between the apprehending consciousness and apprehended object is maintained, so also is the misconception of the subtle dualistic appearance perpetuated.

Having explained dualistic appearance, the next question is: What harm does this duality actually cause? What is wrong with maintaining this subtle dualistic appearance? Both Tsongkhapa and Gorampa argue that it is the presence of the misconception of dualistic appearance that prevents the three types of āryas from accomplishing the simultaneous realization of the universality of ultimate reality; in the presence of such misconception, conventional truths and ultimate truth can only be known sequentially.

Gorampa maintains the three types of āryas perceive empirical truths in their postmeditation entirely because of the misconception of dualistic appearance. "Because they have not yet eradicated the predisposition of dualistic appearance," Gorampa asserts, "their subsequently attained wisdom *(rjes thob ye shes, pṛṣṭha labdha jñāna)* perceives the plurality of characterized objects *(chos can, dharmin)* associated with arising and cessation."[557] As long as the perception of characterized objects with the characteristics of arising and cessation persists, it is not possible for the three types of āryas to engage with the universality of ultimate reality. The plurality that these āryas experience during postmeditation thus prevents them, according to Gorampa, from accessing ultimate reality; the wisdom of the meditative equipoise, on the other hand, immediately presents them with that reality: "During meditative equipoise, they realize ultimate reality; hence neither arising nor cessation is perceived."[558] The alternation between the knowledge of conventionalities and ultimate reality, as Gorampa sees it, "is an indication that these āryas have yet to accomplish the perfection of knowing the universality of all phenomena in terms of their dharmadhātu."[559]

Tsongkhapa's take is very different. It is worth recalling here Tsongkhapa's emphatic distinction between ultimately valid cognition—transcendent wisdom, nonconceptual wisdom—and empirically valid cognition. Certainly it is true, according to him, that when the three types of āryas directly and personally know ultimate truth by means of ultimately valid cognition, they do not concurrently know conventional truth; and the converse also applies. Hence Tsongkhapa argues that "so long as buddhahood is not attained, it is not possible for a single cognition simultaneously to perceive characterized phenomena each individually while at the same directly cognizing ultimate reality within a single temporal instant." Instead, "these two kinds of knowledge come about sequentially."[560] This does not mean, however, that, in the direct knowledge of ultimate truth, the ultimately valid cognition of the three āryas operates independently of its empirical counterpart; neither is it suggested that for such āryas empirically valid cognition operates independently of ultimate valid cognition. Realizing the two truths, either alternately or simultaneously, always requires mutual support between the two valid cognitions. Tsongkhapa regards this mutual collaboration as an essential condition for any coherent knowledge. Without such coordination, realization of neither ultimate truth nor conventional truth is possible. This mutual support in itself does not require that the cognitive agent concerned has simultaneous knowledge of both truths. Even sequential knowledge of the two truths by these āryas demands mutual support between the two cognitive resources. Indeed, any knowledge of the two truths, whether sequential or simultaneous, depends on the same epistemic conditions.

Tsongkhapa posits two approaches to the question of how, and in what ways, the subtle misconception of duality limits the knowledge of the three āryas. It can be approached from either meditative equipoise (the ultimate standpoint) or postmeditation (the empirical standpoint). From the former standpoint, the issue is how the subtle misconception of duality restricts the scope of these āryas' knowledge of all phenomena as empty. From the latter standpoint, the issue is how such misconception impedes these āryas' knowledge of all phenomena as dependently arisen.

Approaching it from the standpoint of meditative equipoise, Tsongkhapa maintains that while the āryas dwell in the meditative state, they have direct knowledge of ultimate truth, and consequently they know that all phenomena are empty. Because of the limits imposed by the subtle misconception of duality, however, they still do not have direct knowledge of the emptiness of emptiness itself. To know emptiness itself as empty, these āryas have to know directly all empty phenomena as equivalent to dependently arisen phenomena from the ultimate standpoint. This insight requires the most profound understanding of how nonconceptual knowledge of phenomena as empty is equivalent to conceptual knowledge of phenomena as dependently arisen. This depends on simultaneous knowledge of the two truths. However, as long as āryas' knowledge is circumscribed by the subtle misconception of duality due to previously existent mental predispositions, simultaneous knowledge of the two truths is not possible. Since these āryas still have tendencies toward the dichotomization of the two truths, they also retain those tendencies toward empty and dependently arisen phenomena.

Approaching from the postmeditation standpoint, Tsongkhapa maintains that when the three types of āryas are engaging in practical activities in postmeditation, they directly know conventional truth, hence āryas know that all phenomena are dependently arisen. However, because of the limits imposed by the subtle misconception of duality, they still do not see the dependently arisen nature of dependent arising itself. The latter knowledge requires direct understanding of how dependently arisen phenomena are empty from the conventional standpoint, without relying on inference. This in turn requires the most profound understanding of how the conceptual knowledge of phenomena as dependently arisen is equivalent to the nonconceptual knowledge of all phenomena as empty. In other words, āryas have to know the compatibility between the ultimate and the conventional views of Madhyamaka. Again, as in the first approach, this understanding depends on the simultaneous knowledge of the two truths. But because āryas of the three kinds are not yet free from the tendency to dichotomize the two truths, and therefore to dichotomize empty and dependently arisen phenomena, simultaneous knowledge is not yet possible for them.

Based on these arguments, Tsongkhapa maintains that āryas of the three kinds have only alternating knowledge of the two truths. Either they directly know conventional truth in the postmeditation, or they directly know ultimate truth in the meditative equipoise. These three types of āryas could not have concurrent knowledge of both the truths, and therefore could not have concurrent knowledge of empty and dependently arisen phenomena, and thus the scope of knowledge of the three types of āryas is limited. Only perfectly enlightened beings are held capable of having direct knowledge of both truths simultaneously, and hence capable of knowing empty and dependently arisen phenomena concurrently.

In short, both Tsongkhapa and Gorampa agree that all āryas, except ārya buddhas, are incapable of knowing the universality of ultimate truth within a single cognitive event. They also agree that it is due to the influence of the subtle misconception of duality that āryas of the three kinds do not have an exhaustive knowledge of all knowable objects. The two Tibetans nevertheless disagree inasmuch as Gorampa insists that the subtle misconception of duality causes āryas to mistakenly perceive empirical truths in postmeditation, while Tsongkhapa insists the subtle misconception prevents the āryas from knowing the two truths simultaneously.

A Buddha's Exceptional Mode of Knowing the Two Truths

Our focus in the next two sections will be on the exceptional cognitive scope of the fully enlightened being who, according to both Tsongkhapa and Gorampa, is free from even the subtle misconception of duality. Given that their treatments of this topic are distinct, we will discuss them separately. We will start with Gorampa's treatment.

Knowing the Two Truths from the Two Conflicting Perspectives

For Gorampa the subtle misconception of dual appearance is, as argued earlier, none other than the conception of the duality of subject and object. This duality is the subtlest object of negation, also called the "subtlest obstruction of knowledge" *(shes bya'i sgrib pa phra mo)*.[561] The fact that an ārya experiences empirical truths as objects of knowledge during postmeditation, and cannot embrace the universality of ultimate truth in all circumstances, is, argues Gorampa, due entirely to this misconceived dichotomy. Enlightenment therefore culminates with eradication of the subject-object dichotomy. Enlightenment means absolute nondual wisdom. This wisdom, as Gorampa would have it, is metaphysically transcendent, free from any empirical basis.

In Gorampa's epistemology, enlightened wisdom involves two distinct ways of knowing—knowing things from an *enlightened perspective* and knowing things from the nonenlightened, *other's perspective.* The chief feature of enlightened knowledge is its capacity to cognize the universality of ultimate truth. Eradicating the subject-object dichotomy, in Gorampa's view, is the only possible way to eschew empirical truth and the empirically valid consciousness that verifies it. Hence Gorampa asserts that "conventional truths enunciated in those contexts [e.g., in the texts of Nāgārjuna and Candrakīrti] are nonexistent [from an enlightened consciousness]. Since there is no erroneous apprehending subject, its corresponding object — [conventional truth]—does not exist."[562] The "erroneous apprehending subject" in this context refers to all empirically valid consciousnesses. The empirically valid consciousness verifying empirical truths is, he maintains, representative of the ignorant cognitive activities that involve the subject-object dichotomy. Since an enlightened person is free from ignorance, so the empirically valid consciousness is also absent. Thus empirical truths projected by ignorance and verified by the empirically valid consciousness are not verified by an enlightened wisdom:

> Despite the fact that [a buddha] does not perceive appearance of the conventional categories—arising, cessation, and so on—explained to the disciples, [a buddha] does perceive the appearance of the nondifferentiated being *(dbyings)* of the ultimate reality...Even then, there is no appearance that leads to duality in perception, for even the slightest fallacious inclinations [of committing to duality] have already been eliminated....
>
> In short, the eight entities, including arising, cessation, and so on, discussed in the preamble of the *Mūlamadhyamakakārikā* are all conceptual elaborations; so are the twenty-seven analyzable factors—from the conditions up to views—examined throughout the twenty-seven chapters, and the entire conventional system, including all empirical entities. In the buddharealm, they are realized by an enlightened being within a single instant of enlightened wisdom. Although those conceptual elaborations remain unseen, there is no contradiction in saying that they are perceived as dharmadhātu, inalienably fused with the universality of ultimate truth.[563]

Jayānanda,[564] Rendawa,[565] Shakya Chogden,[566] Taktsang Lotsawa,[567] Kunkhyen Pema Karpo, Karmapa Mikyö Dorje,[568] Mipham Rinpoche,[569] Gendün Chöpel[570]—all are proponents of Gorampa's view that enlightenment is transcendent of empirical experiences. For example, Pema Karpo writes:

> To the extent the remaining obstructions exist, to that extent multifaceted appearances are perceived as illusory, etc., during the postmeditative state. However, from the moment all latencies [of

> previously existent defilements] are exhaustively [eliminated], conventional phenomena are eternally not perceived. Instead one eternally dwells on the essence of the meditative equipoise.[571]

Gorampa's account of enlightened wisdom—metaphysically absolute, nondual, and transcendent—arises from his efforts to graft the *ālayavijñāna,* the foundation consciousness[572] of Yogacāra idealism, onto the Prāsaṅgika Madhyamaka system. "The Prāsaṅgika Madhyamaka," he claims, "must accept the empirical existence of the ālayavijñāna, since it is revealed in the Bhagavān's discourses. Ācārya [Candrakīrti] also says that it is an empirical truth[573] and a vehicle to understand ultimate truth."[574] Ālayavijñāna is a "sheer luminous consciousness. Though it is not totally distinct from the six aggregates," according to Gorampa, "it endures uninterruptedly through to the level of buddhahood right from the [ordinary state of] sentient beings."[575] The enlightened wisdom is recovered, then, from the foundational consciousness that is already existent in each and every being. It is this wisdom that alone exists after the total elimination of the empirical system, and it exists unconditionally and nonrelationally: "The process of arising and cessation is not perceived, hence it is neither a conditioned nor an impermanent phenomenon."[576]

Elsewhere Gorampa argues that "because every conditioned phenomenon is momentary, it arises and ceases. Hence both [arising and cessation] are untenable [as features of enlightened wisdom]."[577] He continues: "Whatever is conditioned would inevitably bear false and deceptive characteristics. And, so long as the perception of arising and cessation exists, the meaning of dependently arisen would not be one of nonarising."[578] And as Gendün Chöpel puts it: "To the extent the appearance of conventionalities are not ceased, and to the extent the referent of consciousness is not done away with, to that extent, despite having had a direct knowledge of emptiness, one is forced to accept one's earlier [essentialist] views."[579]

Furthermore, Gorampa contends, while "impermanent, conditioned, false, and deceptive phenomena are experienced by āryas in lower levels of the noble path, they must be nonexistent for an enlightened wisdom."[580] Phenomena are nonexistent not only in the ultimate sense but also in the empirical sense at this point. "The ultimate nonexistence of [conditioned] phenomena is also experienced even by āryas in the lower scale of the noble path," therefore it does not demonstrate any exceptional cognitive qualities on the part of an enlightened person.[581] But the nonexistence of impermanent, conditioned, false, and deceptive phenomena from the empirical standpoint does indeed demonstrate the exceptional qualities of enlightened wisdom.

To reinforce the nondual character of enlightened wisdom, Gorampa argues for nondifferentiated integration between wisdom and ultimate truth. Here he uses two slightly different approaches: first, he argues that, with the attainment of buddhahood, consciousness itself is transformed into the ultimate truth. "Having realized emptiness, and having it thoroughly familiarized, all adventitious stains are eradicated," he states, adding that "mind itself is transformed into the uncontaminated sphere *(zag med kyi dbyings)*. This is the ultimate buddha, an embodiment of the virtues of the abandonment [of wrong views] and the realization [of ultimate truth]."[582] Secondly, he explicitly delineates the fusion between enlightened wisdom and ultimate truth:

> Having burnt all the fuels of the conceptual elaborations—the objects of knowledge such as arising and cessation, permanence and annihilation—through the vajra-like meditative stabilization, dharmadhātu, free from all conceptual elaborations, sustains. So, too, the continuum of the previously existent consciousness becomes free from conceptual elaborations, such as arising and cessation. The [enlightened] wisdom is thus formed by the inseparable nature.[583]

In the *Mahāratnakūṭa Sūtra* Mañjuśrī takes a very similar, if not identical, position to Gorampa regarding the identity of *dharmadhātu* and *bodhi*. Śāriputra asks Mañjuśrī: "Does the Buddha not realize supreme enlightenment through the dharmadhātu?" The latter replies: "No, Śāriputra. Why? Because the World-Honored One is the dharmadhātu itself. It is absurd to say that the dharmadhātu realizes the dharmadhātu. Śāriputra," he continues, "the nature of the dharmadhātu is bodhi. Why? Because in the dharmadhātu, there is no trace of sentient beings and all dharmas are empty. The emptiness of all dharmas is bodhi, because they are not two and are not different."[584] Consider also the implications of this dialogue, where the Buddha asks Mañjuśrī: "You call me the Tathāgata. Do you really think that I am the Tathāgata?" Mañjuśrī answers: "No World-Honored One, I do not think you are the Tathāgata. There is nothing about suchness that distinguishes it as suchness, nor is there a Tathāgata's wisdom capable of knowing suchness." Mañjuśrī goes on to explain: "Because the Tathāgata and wisdom are not two. Emptiness is the Tathāgata; therefore the Tathāgata is only an arbitrary name. How, then, can I regard anyone as the Tathāgata?"[585] While the first quote emphasizes the identity of bodhi and dharmadhātu and the latter Tathāgata and wisdom, the point is clear. For Gorampa, this means that an ultimate truth, as a knowable, and an enlightened consciousness, as a knowing subject, are identical.

Gorampa, however, takes this identity even further. In defending his idea of the nondifferentiated character of enlightened wisdom and ultimate reality, he even dismisses the existence of the mind and mental factors that might otherwise be thought to persist in an enlightened person. So long as "mind and the mental factors exist, the subject-object duality is inevitable... Thus would exist differentiation on the basis of the perception of objects ...."[586] However, "once a nondifferentiated consciousness—which is free from all conceptual elaborations, the objects of knowledge, such as arising and cessation—is attained there is not the slightest dualistic appearance. Not even different modes of perception exist."[587] Since nonduality is seen as the chief qualification of enlightened knowledge, so "the slightest involvement of duality, even in the case of enlightenment, denies ultimate truth."[588]

This absolute nondualistic account gives rise to several pertinent questions. If it is true that an enlightened wisdom does not see anything from its own perspective, how could an enlightened being interact with others, with his followers, for example? How could a buddha determine what discourse is beneficial and appropriate for others if he does not see others? In response to these questions, Gorampa introduces what he calls *knowing from the other's perspective (gzhan ngor shes pa)*. Although Gorampa claims that an enlightened being does not experience anything empirical from an enlightened perspective, such a being nonetheless recognizes and identifies empirical phenomena and interacts with other people from the other's perspective. For example, when the Buddha sees one of his disciples, say Śāriputra, he sees and interacts with Śāriputra from the disciple's own perspective. Likewise, when the Buddha sees phenomenal objects and engages with them, he does this from his disciples' points of view. Therefore knowledge from the other's perspective, although it is the secondary form of knowledge of an enlightened being, is not part of the cognitive operation of enlightened wisdom.

Thus Gorampa maintains that knowledge from the enlightened perspective and knowledge from the other's perspective are contradictory and mutually exclusive. From an enlightened perspective, as he argued earlier, a buddha experiences nothing whatsoever, neither ultimately nor empirically. Gorampa, in fact, dismisses the distinction between the empirical and ultimate standpoints at the level of buddhahood: "The empirical standpoint is accepted merely from the other's perspective. The distinction between the empirical and ultimate standpoints does not apply to the enlightened perspective."[589]

Gendün Chöpel illustrates the concept of other's perspective by using a metaphor:

> When a magician conjures up an illusory elephant, the audience sees it as a real elephant. The magician plays his tricks in order to see something non-elephant as if it is a real elephant. Now, when the audience asks the magician: "is this a real elephant?" [The magician] replies "yes." In this case, the magician accepts the elephant from the other's perspective.[590]

Thus the world of empirical truths, reified by ignorance, is spontaneously experienced by an enlightened person from the other's perspective. Gorampa thus claims that "both ultimate arising and empirical arising exist [for an enlightened person] from the other's perspective. That which is said to be nonarising is with reference to a buddha's own perspective. From this perspective neither ultimate arising nor empirical arising exists."[591] It is worth reflecting on the key phrase he uses here—when a buddha engages with the world from the other's perspective, then he, like naïve ordinary beings, is said to reify not only empirical arising but also ultimate arising. So in this context even an enlightened being is an essentialist or a reificationist, like ordinary beings. Gorampa certainly posits that "from a buddha's own perspective, since arising and cessation are not perceived, there are neither conditioned nor impermanent phenomena." However, he also argues that "from the other's perspective, the perspective of his disciples, [an enlightened being experiences] arising and cessation, since arising and cessation of virtues exist."[592] Although Gorampa insists that enlightened beings experience arising and cessation from the other's perspective, "it does not follow that an enlightened wisdom is itself characterized by arising and cessation. It simply shows how they appear to the minds of disciples."[593] An enlightened person, as mentioned earlier, "perceives arising and cessation from the other's perspective *(gzhan snang)*, but certainly not from his own perspective *(rang snang)*."[594]

Supporters of Gorampa's doctrine of other's perspective include Mipham Rinpoche,[595] Taktsang Lotsawa,[596] and Karmapa Mikyö Dorje.[597] They also advocate that the exceptional quality of enlightened knowledge consists in not experiencing anything empirical from the enlightened perspective, but experiencing everything from the other's—nonenlightened—perspective.

What stands out as the essential feature of knowledge from the other's perspective is that it is, in every sense, equivalent to the knowledge of ordinary beings. Just as an ordinary person reifies essence, claims Gorampa, so too does an enlightened being. Rongtön Shakya Gyaltsen, who is otherwise one of Gorampa's traditional allies, ridicules the doctrine of the other's perspective. To claim that the attaining of enlightenment requires knowledge from the perspective of ordinary beings is, according to Rongtön Shakya Gyaltsen, tantamount to claiming that ordinary beings are accomplished enlightened beings, and that enlightened beings are ordinary beings. Without expending any effort, ordinary beings are born with the ordinary perspectives, and they should therefore be inherently possessed with enlightened knowledge.[598]

Knowing the Two Truths Simultaneously

Tsongkhapa is in accord with Gorampa that the attainment of buddhahood culminates with total eradication of the subtle object of negation—the misconception of duality. Among the numerous exceptional qualities of an enlightened person, Tsongkhapa singles out the cognitive ability to have direct and simultaneous realization of the two truths within a single instant. In his view, the coordination between a buddha's ultimately and empirically valid cognition is absolutely essential to achieve this simultaneity. Without this coordination, he argues, it is not possible for an enlightened person to realize either of the two truths. The ultimately valid consciousness of an enlightened person is not capable of realizing ultimate truth in the absence of empirically valid cognition; similarly, empirically valid consciousness is not capable of realizing conventional truth in the absence of ultimately valid consciousness.[599]

Thus the two valid cognitive resources of an enlightened person are always mutually entailing. Not only they do not function independently of each other, but they no longer know the two truths alternately, as do other āryas. "When every misconception is eradicated without a trace," Tsongkhapa explains, "each individual moment of every single enlightened consciousness *(ye shes)* embodies an interplay of dual consciousness that arises uninterruptedly with the identical characteristics."[600] By knowing empirical truth, then, an enlightened being knows ultimate truth, and by knowing ultimate truth, a buddha also knows empirical truth. In this way an enlightened being knows the two objects of knowledge simultaneously within a single moment of wisdom. This is possible here because the ultimately valid consciousness and the empirically valid consciousness of a buddha perform their functions in a way that makes them inseparable. The uncritical cognitive engagement of every single empirically valid consciousness of an enlightened person is accompanied by the critical cognitive engagement of every single ultimately valid consciousness of a buddha and vice versa. Recognizing these mutually inclusive cognitive resources of a buddha, Tsongkhapa argues that every single moment of enlightened consciousness knows both truths directly.

From a slightly different perspective, it can also be said that the previously alternating engagements between meditative equipoise and subsequent attainment[601] now, with true enlightenment, achieve a perfect equilibrium. Previously, the wisdom of meditative equipoise was directed more toward ultimate truth, while the wisdom of the subsequent attainment, or postmeditation, was directed more toward empirical truth. The knowledge of the two truths was thereby somehow isolated, not integrated. However, with the attainment of buddhahood, the cognitive capacity to engage with ultimate truth and that of engaging with conventional truth become simultaneous. Tsongkhapa argues: "Once the predisposition of the conception of true existence is thoroughly eradicated, one attains buddhahood. Thereafter," he explains, "[a buddha] continuously abides in the meditative equipoise, directly realizing ultimate truth. Thereafter the alternate [realization]—i.e., not abiding in meditative equipoise in subsequent attainment—no longer applies."[602] In other words, whether a buddha appears to be in meditative equipoise or engaged in other activities, the mind of an enlightened being does not deviate from direct knowledge of the two truths. Tsongkhapa therefore claims that there is no qualitative distinction whatsoever between a buddha's wisdom of meditative equipoise and his wisdom of subsequent attainment, or postmeditation:

> Because there is no wisdom of subsequent attainment realizing phenomenal objects that is qualitatively distinct from the wisdom of meditative equipoise, it should be accepted that a single moment of wisdom knows all objects of knowledge comprising the two truths.[603]

With the end of the alternating realization of two truths,[604] the usual qualitative distinction between the cognitive status of meditative equipoise and that of postmeditation no longer applies. Every enlightened cognitive activity is a correct knowledge of ultimate truth.

Tsongkhapa's claim gives rise to a couple of questions: If every moment of enlightened consciousness knows both truths directly, is a buddha's empirically valid cognition able to cognize ultimate truth independently of his ultimately valid cognition? Similarly, is a buddha's ultimately valid cognition able to cognize conventional truth independently from his empirically valid cognition?

In response to the first question, Tsongkhapa argues that the empirically valid consciousness of a buddha does not know ultimate truth independently from ultimately valid consciousness, and that this is so for two reasons. First, an affirmative answer would render the cognitive role of a buddha's ultimately valid consciousness redundant, and thus contradict Tsongkhapa's view that designates the verification of ultimate truth as the function of ultimately valid consciousness. Second, if this were so, it would threaten the internal consistency of Tsongkhapa's definitions of ultimate truth, since he has previously defined ultimate truth in relation to the cognitive function of ultimately valid consciousness. In response to the second question, Tsongkhapa says that it is not possible for the ultimately valid consciousness of a buddha to know conventional truth independently of empirically valid consciousness, and that again this is so for two reasons analogous to those just cited. First, if this were possible, it would render the cognitive role of a buddha's empirically valid consciousness redundant, again contradicting Tsongkhapa that the function of verifying empirical truths belongs to empirically valid consciousness. Second, if this were so, it would threaten the internal consistency of Tsongkhapa's own definitions of conventional truth, since he defines conventional truth in relation to the function of empirically valid consciousness. Tsongkhapa claims, therefore, that the two valid consciousnesses of an enlightened being do not involve knowledge of ultimate truth independently of one another.

Tsongkhapa denies that this poses any contraction—insofar as both wisdoms are invariably valid representations of ultimate truth, the wisdom of the meditative equipoise and of postmeditation are both accepted as qualitatively identical *(ngo bo gcig)*. According to him, this identity does not make either wisdom redundant or threaten the internal consistency of the definitions of the two truths. While qualitatively identical, the two wisdoms are also distinct in terms of their mode of cognitive activity:

> Because [an object] is found by the wisdom knowing truths as they truly are *(je lta ba mkhyen pa'i ye shes)*, it is a wisdom knowing

> truths as they truly are *(je lta ba)* with respect to that object. And because [an object] is found by wisdom knowing phenomenal objects *(je snyad pa mkhyen pa'i ye shes),* it is a wisdom knowing phenomenal objects *(je snyed pa)* with respect to that object. Therefore an enlightened mode of knowing ultimate and conventional truths should be understood with reference to the individual objects *(yul so so la ltos nas).*[605]

Although the ultimately valid consciousness of an enlightened being is a coherent representation of conventional truth, still, according to Tsongkhapa's view, conventional truth *per se* is not found or verified by such consciousness. Rather, the function of such consciousness is to critically verify the ultimate truth of the empirically given phenomena that is found by empirically valid consciousness. Because of its critical cognitive function, the ultimately valid consciousness of a buddha cannot provide a holistic view of the world. But a holistic view is essential to establish the validity of conventional truth. In the light of its critical function, the ultimately valid consciousness of an enlightened being is consistently described as the "wisdom that knows phenomena as they truly are" *(ji lta ba bzhin du mkhyen pa'i ye shes, yathābhūtajñāna).* Likewise, although the empirically valid consciousness of an enlightened being is a coherent representation of ultimate truth, ultimate truth *per se* is not found or verified by such consciousness. Instead, the function of such consciousness is to verify conventional truth. Because of its uncritical cognitive function, the empirically valid consciousness of a buddha consistently represents its corresponding objects holistically. It is therefore always described as the wisdom that realizes "the plurality of phenomenal objects" *(ji snyed pa mkhyen pa'i ye shes, yavātajñāna).* Understanding that the two different types of cognition, in Tsongkhapa's view, "have different spheres of authority," Pettit notes that "consciousness that investigates conventional phenomena *(tha snyad dpyod pa'i tshad ma)* is not authoritative for determining the ultimate status of phenomena, nor is an analysis of the ultimate status of phenomena *(don dam dpyod pa'i tshad ma)* authoritative for their conventional status."[606] This is like saying that an ear consciousness is not authoritative for visual objects. The sphere of authority for each consciousness derives from its function, and therefore its authority should not be viewed as absolutely inherent and independent of the others.

It is quite apparent that even the "exceptional way of knowing the two truths by a buddha" does not, according to Tsongkhapa, contradict the definitions of the two truths. Neither does it make the cognitive functions of the two valid consciousnesses of an enlightened person redundant. The empirically valid consciousness of an enlightened person uncritically verifies empirical truths, while ultimately valid consciousness critically verifies the ultimate mode of empirical truths. But because the two cognitive resources are inextricably interwoven, every enlightened consciousness is a culmination of the two wisdoms. Every event of enlightened consciousness coherently represents things as they truly are. This is how, in Tsongkhapa's view, even the most enlightened wisdom operates within the framework of the definitions of the two truths, while nevertheless achieving the realization of both truths simultaneously. In so doing, it avoids all contradictions. "Such is the exceptional qualities of a bhagavān, a buddha,"[607] says Tsongkhapa:

> With the reference to dharmatā, it is a wisdom knowing things as they are. Here, every dual appearance dissolves from the vantage point of that cognition. Thus this wisdom, just like pouring water into water, embraces universality *(ro gcig)*. However, with respect to the phenomenal objects, it is a wisdom knowing empirical truths. At this point, though the dualistic appearances perceiving distinct subject and object are involved, they are unmistaken dualistic appearances. Since the predisposition of the misconception pertaining to dualistic appearance is uprooted without trace, dualistic appearances no longer misconceive the perceived object.[608]

In Tsongkhapa's view, then, an enlightened being has two ways of knowing ultimate truth. One is to realize it during the meditative equipoise by transcending all dualities, described as knowing *space-like emptiness (nam mkha' lta bu'i stong nyid)*.[609] As the Buddha explains:

> Monks, that sphere should be realized where the eye (vision) stops and the perception (mental noting) of form fades. That sphere is to be realized where the ear stops and the perception of sound fades...where the nose stops and the perception of aroma fades...where the tongue stops and the perception of flavor fades...where the body stops and the perception of tactile sensations fades...where the intellect stops and the perception of ideas fades: That sphere should be realized.[610]

For Tsongkhapa this sphere of nondifferentiated, space-like experience does not in any way represent a metaphysical transcendence. The experience of such nature is entirely possible within the meditator's own body. This transcendent state can be directly and personally experienced, but it cannot be intellectually known or linguistically described from the outside, and neither can an enlightened person, even when actually experiencing it, offer any criterion to describe it. The Buddha articulates this point:

> There is, monks, that sphere where there is neither earth nor water, nor fire, nor wind, nor sphere of the infinitude of space, nor sphere of the infinitude of consciousness, nor sphere of nothingness, nor sphere of neither perception nor nonperception, nor this world, nor the next world, nor sun, nor moon. And there, I say, there is neither coming, nor going, nor stasis, nor passing away, nor arising: without stance, without foundation, without support (mental object). This, just this, is the end of *dukkha* [Ud 8.1].[611]

The other way of knowing ultimate truth is during the subsequent attainment in the wake of meditative equipoise. Tsongkhapa describes this way of realizing ultimate truth as knowing *illusion-like emptiness (sgyu ma lta bu'i stong nyid).*[612] In this mode of knowing, argues Tsongkhapa, phenomena are perceived as relational, interdependent, and illusory. Although the duality between subject and object is involved, it is thoroughly compatible with the nondual enlightened knowledge.[613] The Buddha explains, in the *Paccaya Sutta,* why knowing phenomena as dependently arisen does not constitute a misconceived duality:

> When a disciple of the noble one has seen well with right discernment this dependent co-arising and these dependently co-arisen phenomena as they are actually present, it is not possible that he would run after the past, thinking, "Was I in the past? Was I not in the past? What was I in the past? How was I in the past? Having been what, what was I in the past?" or that he would run after the future, thinking, "Shall I be in the future? Shall I not be in the future? What shall I be in the future? How shall I be in the future? Having been what, what shall I be in the future?" or that he would be inwardly perplexed about the immediate present,

> thinking, "Am I? Am I not? What am I? How am I? Where has this being come from? Where is it bound?" Such a thing is not possible. Why is that? Because the disciple of the noble ones has seen well with discernment this dependent co-arising and these dependently co-arisen phenomena as they are actually present.[614]

Since the duality between subject and object in this context is totally free from any misconception, the mere presence of duality is not a problem. It is, in fact, an inevitable ground for coherent knowledge. "Once this point is understood," says Tsongkhapa, "one can correctly understand how the meditation on the space-like emptiness during the meditative equipoise reinforces the understanding of illusion-like emptiness in the subsequent attainment."[615] The validity of knowing the illusion-like emptiness—conventional truth—and the validity of knowing the space-like emptiness—ultimate truth—are therefore compatible in every respect.[616] By knowing phenomena as conventionally illusory, a buddha knows that phenomena are ultimately empty; by knowing phenomena as ultimately empty a buddha knows that phenomena are conventionally illusory. Hence, in Tsongkhapa's view, "there is no contradiction in saying that every single enlightened wisdom captures all objects of knowledge."[617]

Conclusion

For both Tsongkhapa and Gorampa, enlightenment is the *summum bonum* of Buddhism—the most sublime wisdom and the perfection of all virtues and spiritual trainings. This chapter showed how Tsongkhapa's and Gorampa's differences in explaining the nature of the two truths culminate in divergent understandings of enlightenment itself. Giving the two truths equal status, Tsongkhapa argues that enlightenment is the culmination of the simultaneous realizations of the two truths by every single moment of enlightened wisdom. Gorampa, on the other hand, argues for the primacy of ultimate truth and ultimate wisdom over empirical truth and empirical consciousness. Consequently, for him, the achievement of enlightenment is the achievement of nondifferentiated and nondual ultimate truth by ultimate wisdom through transcending empirical truths and empirical consciousness.

Enlightenment, according to Tsongkhapa, means seeing empirical truths as they actually are. Knowledge without an empirical grounding is, he argues, flawed and erroneous, and such knowledge cannot be the basis of enlightenment. Knowledge of empirical truths as they are is equivalent to knowing ultimate truth; the two are not contradictory. For Gorampa, enlightenment is precisely freedom from empirical truth and empirical knowledge, which are conditioned by ignorance. Knowing empirical truths and knowing ultimate truth are thus contradictory and independent of one another—indeed, the former has no soteriological significance at all.

Ordinary beings, according to Tsongkhapa, have no direct knowledge of empirical truth, for they always reify truth and presuppose the existence of essence. Only noble beings—āryas and buddhas—have direct knowledge of empirical truth, and only buddhas are said to possess simultaneous knowledge of both truths. Indeed this is the distinctive cognitive capacity of an enlightened person. According to Gorampa, however, ordinary beings have direct knowledge of empirical truths, but such knowledge serves no soteriological purpose. In fact, he treats direct knowledge of empirical truths as objects to be negated. Gorampa argues that direct knowledge of empirical truths inhibits ārya bodhisattvas (from the eighth to tenth bhūmis), ārya śrāvakas, and ārya pratyekabuddhas from embracing the nondual and transcendent ultimate truth. Only when all the objects of negation are abolished—the entire system of empirical truth and the empirical senses—does the sublime wisdom of enlightenment dawn. The distinctive cognitive capacity of an enlightened being is, according to Gorampa, the complete transcendence of the empirical world.

An enlightened wisdom, in Tsongkhapa's view, manifests itself in two modes of knowing that are mutually compatible and mutually reinforcing. Enlightened wisdom knows ultimate truth by way of knowing phenomena as dependently arisen. In such wisdom, and the knowledge associated with it, there remains a duality between subject and object. But because this duality does not comprise even the subtlest misconception, it is not in any way a hindrance. The second mode of knowing by an enlightened wisdom is by way of transcending dualities. This transcendence is, however, strictly epistemological in nature. It operates entirely within the framework of the psychophysical aggregates of the enlightened person, and is in no way a metaphysical transcendence. Gorampa also postulates two modes of knowing by the enlightened being: knowing from one's own perspective and knowing from the other's perspective. But in contrast to Tsongkhapa's account, these modes of knowing are fundamentally contradictory. Knowing from others' (nonenlightened) perspective is irrelevant to actual enlightenment and is equated with the knowledge of ordinary beings. Just as ordinary beings reify essence, so does this mode of knowing. However, when an enlightened being knows from his own perspective, then the knowledge is strictly nondifferentiated, nondual, and transcendent. Such knowledge does not allow for any duality between subject and object. Instead a fusion is achieved between metaphysically transcendent ultimate truth and ultimate wisdom. This nondual state is itself considered to be ultimate knowledge.

6. Conclusion

There are undeniable similarities that run throughout the philosophical systems of Tsongkhapa and Gorampa—they share identical soteriological objectives, employ similar methodologies, employ the same Indian Prāsaṅgika Madhyamaka sources, and work within the same linguistic and dialectical conventions. Their disagreement about the nature of the two truths, however, leads them to an equally pervasive set of differences between their two systems. These have been cataloged and summarized in the preceding chapters, and we won't revisit all the separate points of disagreement here. Nonetheless, let's briefly review the major differences between Tsongkhapa's and Gorampa's accounts in regard to each of the main areas: soteriology and psychology, ontology, and epistemology, and look at the implications for these on their approach to moral conduct.

Soteriology and Psychology

Neither Tsongkhapa nor Gorampa recognizes nirvāṇa as the highest goal. Since both are Mahāyāna Buddhists, their highest ideal is the bodhisattva ideal of buddhahood for the sake of all beings, rather than the arhathood of śrāvakas and pratyekabuddhas. They also agree that buddhahood, or full enlightenment, culminates with the attainment of the two buddha bodies, the *rūpakāya*—the consequence of the accumulation of moral virtues—and *dharmakāya*—the consequence of the accumulation of wisdom. However, they each conceive of buddhahood in radically different ways. Even at the level of buddhahood, Tsongkhapa argues for a harmonious relationship between the two truths, while Gorampa insists on the absolute character of ultimate truth and the rejection of conventional truth. Tsongkhapa contends that buddhahood provides the most coherent epistemic access to the unity of the two truths, and simultaneous knowledge of the two truths is possible only for fully enlightened beings. In contrast, Gorampa maintains that buddhahood severs all connections between the two truths, and those who reach the highest goal access only ultimate truth. For Tsongkhapa, a tathagāta—one who achieves the highest goal—is a conventional and dependently arisen phenomenon. For Gorampa, however, whosoever achieves the highest goal is nonempirical and entirely unconditioned. Hence a tathagāta for him is a transcendent and nondual being.

Tsongkhapa and Gorampa both take the prior attainment of nirvāṇa as one of the essential conditions for the attainment of buddhahood. Tsongkhapa and Gorampa even appear to agree on the psychological transformations that arise as a result of achieving nirvāṇa. The unhealthy psychological dispositions of the ordinary state—saṃsāric predispositions—are replaced by the healthy psychological dispositions of the liberated state—the attainment of nirvāṇa. Saṃsāra, the cycle of birth, death, and rebirth driven by suffering, comes to mean psychological bondage, moral corruption, and a state of constant restlessness induced by craving, aversion, and delusion. Nirvāṇa, the end of such suffering, means psychological freedom, and it represents moral perfection as well.

For Tsongkhapa nirvāṇa is antithetical to saṃsāra, particularly when the emphasis is placed on their psychological and moral underpinnings. Moreover, nirvāṇa is not equated with ultimate truth, nor is saṃsāra equated with conventional truth. Since saṃsāra and nirvāṇa are, in this context, contrasted on the basis of their psychological and moral contents, they cannot be equated with the ontology of the two truths. Saṃsāra represents moral bankruptcy, while nirvāṇa represents moral perfection; the former represents psychological ills, while the latter represents freedom from such ills. Gorampa, on the other hand, given his commitment to the idea of ālayavijñāna, which he calls the fundamental root of both saṃsāra and nirvāṇa, appears on a psychological level to blur the distinction between saṃsāra and nirvāṇa. Saṃsāra and nirvāṇa are both states of consciousness, as Tsongkhapa would agree, and for Gorampa all states of consciousness have their root in the ālaya. Gorampa's point is that the saṃsāra-nirvāṇa dichotomy is a duality, and from that perspective both are transcended in ultimate truth—clinging to the difference is an obstacle to the nondual realization.

Ontology

Tsongkhapa's ontology treats the two truths as mutually entailing. He argues that they share the same ontological status, and that they are empty and dependently arisen. The same principle applies to his ontology of saṃsāra and nirvāṇa. Since both saṃsāra and nirvāṇa are dependently arisen and empty, they have equal ontological status. Gorampa's ontology treats the two truths as hierarchical and contradictory. He argues that conventional truth and ultimate truth each have their own distinct and independent ontological status. The same distinction is applied in the way he treats saṃsāra and nirvāṇa ontologically. While conventional truth and saṃsāra are treated as dependently arisen, and thus as ontologically conditioned *('dus byas, saṃskṛta),* Gorampa argues that ultimate truth and nirvāṇa are ontologically unconditioned *('dus ma byas, asaṃskṛta)* and transcendent. The spirit of Gorampa's transcendent ontology is well expressed in Spiro's words: "From an ontological point of view, Buddhism [in this case, Gorampa] postulates the existence of two planes which, like parallel lines, never meet. On the one hand there is saṃsāra, the worldly ([Pāli:] *lokiya*) plane; on the other hand there is nirvāṇa, the otherworldly *(lokuttara)* or transcendent plane."[618]

Epistemology

The two kinds of knowledge, that of conventional truth and that of ultimate truth—of saṃsāra and nirvāṇa—are, according to Tsongkhapa's epistemology, complementary. They are yoked together and cannot be isolated from one another. Just as the knowledge of conventional truth depends on that of ultimate truth, so the true knowledge of saṃsāra depends on the realization of nirvāṇa. One who directly knows conventional truth and saṃsāra as dependently arisen and empty thus also knows ultimate truth and nirvāṇa as dependently arisen and empty. Likewise, without knowing ultimate truth and nirvāṇa as dependently arisen and empty, it is not possible to know conventional truth and saṃsāra as dependently arisen and empty. In contrast, according to Gorampa's epistemology, knowledge of either of the two truths—of saṃsāra or nirvāṇa—is incompatible with knowledge of the other. The knowledge of conventional truth and saṃsāra as dependently arisen is distinct from knowledge of ultimate truth and nirvāṇa. The knowledge of conventional truth and saṃsāra as dependently arisen is a mundane one based on knowing conventional truth and saṃsāra as ontologically conditioned, whereas the knowledge of ultimate truth and nirvāṇa constitutes transcendent knowledge, since it is based on knowing ultimate truth and nirvāṇa as ontologically transcendent.

In terms of the epistemological resources by which the two truths are verified, the distinctions are again sharply drawn. Tsongkhapa considers empirically valid cognition and ultimately valid cognition as the two verifying consciousnesses. Although empirically valid cognition verifies conventional truth and ultimately valid cognition ultimate truth, Tsongkhapa holds that empirically valid cognition does not know conventional truth by itself. Likewise, ultimately valid cognition itself is not a sufficient condition for knowledge of ultimate truth. Coherent knowledge of either truth, Tsongkhapa argues, requires the two verifying consciousnesses to support each other. While Tsongkhapa sees such mutual support between the two cognitive resources as indispensable for developing correct knowledge of both truths, Gorampa adopts a very different approach. He considers ignorance and wisdom as the two verifying consciousnesses—and he sees those two consciousnesses as contradictory and as operating autonomously.

Ethical Implications

Although this book does not directly explore Tsongkhapa's and Gorampa's treatment of morality, the comparative analysis of the doctrine of the two truths would be incomplete without some reflection on the ethical implications of the competing perspectives on the two truths. Tsongkhapa's commitment to the mutually compatible relationship between the two truths and the two corresponding cognitive processes means he is also committed to the mutually compatible relationship between nonconceptual wisdom (meditative equipoise) and conceptual wisdom (postmeditation). He argues that the dualistic cognitive engagements of an enlightened being—practical activities in the world—are consistent with nonconceptual wisdom. In this way, Tsongkhapa holds that the elements of the threefold training—in morality, concentration, and wisdom—are mutually supportive. Wisdom arises from a concentrated mind, and a concentrated mind arises from a firm moral foundation. Each element makes its own vital contribution to the path.

Tsongkhapa maintains that the factors of moral discipline—right speech, right action, and right livelihood—keep the tendencies toward moral transgression in check, and thus thwart even the thought of immoral conduct. On this basis, he argues, the three factors of concentration—right effort, right mindfulness, and right concentration—firmly anchor the mind and enable the cognitive agent to realize the impermanent, selfless, and empty characteristics of persons and phenomena, leading to the growth of the two types of penetrating wisdom. First is the unfolding of experiential wisdom—the experiential right view—which enables the meditator to visualize the five aggregates nonconceptually, and thus nondually. Second is the unfolding of conceptual wisdom—the conceptual right view—which enables the cognitive agent to make correct conceptual judgments—ontological, moral, and epistemological. The resulting benefits of the development of the two types of penetrating wisdom show themselves in the purity of psychological, moral, and cognitive states.

For Tsongkhapa, the stages of the path are only linear in a metaphorical sense. Morality is not merely a platform to enable some form of soteriological leap into the ultimate, whereupon one discards it. It is at the heart of the goal itself. The stages of the path and the perfections are cumulative, according to Tsongkhapa, and the beginning and end of spiritual development must take place within a single being's mental continuum.

For all these reasons, Tsongkhapa consistently retains a sharp and clear distinction between moral and immoral conduct, and their consequences, all the way through to the highest spiritual development. In fact, according to Tsongkhapa, a buddha embodies the highest moral integrity and wisdom, in both spirit and action. This unity between wisdom and morality arises naturally out of the harmonious relationship between the two truths.

The lesser role accorded to morality in Gorampa's soteriology is not immediately evident. Like Tsongkhapa, Gorampa affirms the importance of moral conduct as the starting point of the path. The essential disagreement between them emerges only later—in the way they evaluate the role of morality in the path's advanced stages. Morality and enlightenment, as far as Gorampa is concerned, are discrete. Morality may lead one in the direction of enlightenment, but it must ultimately be discarded before enlightenment can be attained. Since Gorampa argues that conventional truths are projections of ignorance, conventional practices, including adherence to moral values, must inevitably be seen as objects to be discarded in pursuit of the final realization. Morality, ultimately, is not relevant for the attainment of buddhahood, which transcends mundane moral conduct.

Gorampa's transcendent thesis seems to echo the Buddha's parable of the raft, where the Buddha states that "the Dhamma is similar to a raft, being for the purpose of crossing over, not for the purpose of grasping. Bhikkhus, when you know the Dhamma to be similar to a raft, you should abandon even the teachings, how much more so things contrary to the teachings."[619] Moreover, since transcendent wisdom as such is seen as identical with ultimate truth—which Gorampa characterizes as an absolute that is timeless and unaffected by change—no amount of moral or immoral activity can influence its basic nature. On this account, morality is gratuitous and without soteriological power. In enlightenment, distinctions between good and bad, moral and immoral, and skillful and unskillful lose their validity. Such distinctions are valid only at the conventional level, the level of an ordinary discourse, not the level of a buddha's final realization. This leads to the conclusion that unethical behaviors are binding on the trainee, but cannot defile the realized being, who is beyond such distinctions.

According to this view, the conduct of an enlightened being cannot be circumscribed by moral principles. Having transcended all conventional distinctions of moral and immoral, good and bad, an enlightened being acts spontaneously from his or her intuition of the ultimate nonduality. Commitment to a conventional moral code and all that it represents can only inhibit and obstruct the final realization. As Winston King proposes, "[the enlightened being] must kick away from under him the laboriously built ladder of kammic merit from which he has risen toward sainthood, and take to the transcendental flight on the wings of super-normal (super kammic) wisdom." The moral virtue itself, "which raises one to such a realm, and the love even of the highest kind of goodness...no matter how much preferable to the love of evil," explains King, "bind him more subtly and dangerously than before to the realm of time and space, that is, birth, death, and suffering."[620] Morality is seen as a necessary condition for the attainment of enlightenment, but it is also seen, paradoxically, as a hindrance to such attainment. Paradoxical though such a conclusion may appear, it is a natural outgrowth of Gorampa's attitudes toward and treatment of conventional truth.

The positions on the two truths taken by these two Tibetan Prāsaṅgika Mādhyamikas are distinct and, finally, irreconcilable. Tsongkhapa's commitment to the unity between the two truths, and the unity between the two corresponding epistemic pathways, lays the foundation for his entire philosophical system. In contrast, Gorampa's commitment to the contradictory relationship between the two truths and the respective verifying cognitions leads to significantly different implications. While they both claim to be the heirs of the Indian Prāsaṅgika Madhyamaka tradition, their interpretations of the two truths lead to fundamentally different approaches to ontology, epistemology, soteriology, and, not least, morality.

Abbreviations

Abbreviations for non-Tibetan works appear at the end of this table.

Bdag med sgrub rigs	Shakya Chogden, *Theg pa chen po dbu ma rnam par nges pa'i bang mdzod lung rigs rgya mtsho las bdag med sgrub rigs le'u brgyad pa*
Bden gnyis gnas 'jug	Shakya Chogden, *Bden pa gyis kyi gnas la 'jug pa nges don bdud rtsi'i thigs pa*
Bden gnyis rnam gzhag	Shakya Chogden, *Theg pa chen po dbu ma rnam par nges pa'i bang mdzod lung rigs rgya mtsho las bden pa gnyis kyi rnam bzhag le'u bzhi pa*
Bden gnyis rnam gzhag	Gyaltsab Jé, *Bden gnyis kyi rnam gzhag dang lta ba'i 'khrid yig rin po che'i phrin pa*
Dbu 'jug rnam bshad	Rendawa, *Dbu ma 'jug pa'i rnam bshad de kno na nyid gsal ba'i sgron ma*
Bka' gdams bces btus	Potowa, *Legs par bshad pa bka' gdams rin po che'i gsungs gi gces btus nor bu'i bang mdzod.*
Brgal lan nyin byed	Mipham Rinpoche, *Brgal lan nyin byed snang ba*
Bshes spring 'grel ba	Rendawa, *Bshes pa'i spring yig gi 'grel pa don gsal*
Bzhi rgya'i 'grel ba	Rendawa, *Dbu ma bzhi brya ba'i 'grel pa*
Dag brgyud grub pa'i shing rta	Mikyö Dorje, *Dbu ma la 'jug pa'i rnam bshad dpal ldan lus gsum mkhyen pa'i zhal lung d'ag rgyud grub pa'i shing rta*

Dam chos dogs sel	Mipham Rinpoche, *Rdo grub pa dam chos zhes pas gzhan gyi zer sgros bsdus nas mkhas su re ba'i 'khyar ngag de dag mi mkhas mtshang phud du kho rang nas skul ba bzhin nyams mtshar du bkod pa*
Dbu 'jug rnam bshad	Shakya Chogden, *Dbu ma 'jug pa'i rnam bshad nges don gnad kyi ṭīkā*
Dbu ma'i 'byung tshul	Shakya Chogden, *Dbu ma'i byung tshul rnam par bshad pa'i gtam yid bzhin lhun po*
Dbu ma'i phan yon	Shakya Chogden, *Theg pa chen po dbu ma rnam par nges pa'i bang mdzod lung rigs rgya mtsho las 'bras bu sku gnyis zung 'jug le'u bcu gcig pa dang dbu ma'i phan yon bstan pa'i le'u bcu gnyis pa*
Dbu rtsa'i 'grel ba	Maja Jangchub Tsöndü, *Dbu ma rtsa ba shes rab kyi 'grel ba 'thad pa'i rgyan*
Dbu rtsa'i mchan 'grel	Mipham Rinpoche, *Dbu ma rtsa ba'i mchan 'grel gnas lugs rab gsal*
Dbu rtsa'i rnam bshad	Shakya Chogden, *Dbu ma rtsa ba'i rnam bshad skal bzang 'jug ngogs*
Dbu tsa'i rnam bshad	Rongtön Shakya Gyaltsen, *Dbu ma tsa ba'i rnam bshad zab mo'i di kho na nyid snang ba*
Dbu ma'i lta khrid	Rongtön Shakya Gyaltsen, *Dbu ma'i lta khrid kyi bsdus don snying po'e gsal byed*
Dgongs pa rab gsal	Tsongkhapa Lobsang Dragpa, *Dbu ma dgongs pa rab gsal*
Dka' gnas brgyad bshad	Tsongkhapa Lobsang Dragpa, *Rtsa ba shes rab kyi dka' gnas chen po brgyad kyi bshad pa*
Don dam rnam bshad	Shakya Chogden, *Theg pa chen po dbu ma rnam par nges pa'i bang mdzod lung rigs rgya mtsho las don dam rnam bshad le'u drug pa*

Dpyod 'jug tshig 'grel	Künzang Palden, *Byang chub sems pa'i dpyod pa la 'jug pa'i tshig 'grel 'jam dbyangs bla ma'i zhal lung bdud tsi'i thig pa*
Drang nges	Geshe Yeshe Tabkhé, *Shar tsong kha pa'i drang ba dang nges pa'i don rnam par 'byed pa'i bstan bcos legs bshad snying po*
Gang zag bdag med	Shakya Chogden, *Theg pa chen po dbu ma rnam par nges pa'i bang mdzod lung rigs rgya mtsho las gang zag bdag med le'u bdun pa*
Grub mtha' kun shes	Taktsang Lotsawa, *Grub mtha' kun shes nas mtha' bral sgrub pa zhes bya ba'i bstan cos*
Grub mtha' mdzes rgyan	Changkya Rölpai Dorje, *Grub mtha' thub stan lhun po'i mdzes rgyan*
Grub mtha' mdzod	Longchen Rabjam, *Grub mtha' rin chen mdzod*
Grub mtha'i rnam bshad	Taktsang Lotsawa, *Grub mtha' kun shes nas mtha' bral sgrub pa zhes bya ba'i stan cos rnam par bshad pa legs bshad rgya mtsho*
Grub mtha'i rnam bshad	Jamyang Shepai Dorje, *Grub mtha'i rnam bshad kun bzang zhing gi nyima*
Gzung gsum gsal byed	Kunkhyen Pema Karpo, *Dbu ma'i gzung gsum gsal bar byed pa nges don grub pa'i shing rta*
Gzhung lugs legs bshad	Sakya Paṇḍita, *Gzhung lugs legs par bshad pa'i bstan bcos*
Jug pa'i dka' gnad	Shakya Chogden, *Dbu ma 'jug pa'i dka' ba'i gnad rnam par bshad pa ku mud phren mrdzes*
Klu sgrub dgongs rgyan	Gendün Chöpel, *Dbu ma'i zab gnad snying por dril ba'i legs bshad klu sgrub dgongs rgyan*
Kun rdzob rnam bshad	Shakya Chogden, *Theg pa chen po dbu ma rnam par nges pa'i bang mdzod lung rigs*

	rgya mtsho las kun rdzob bden pa'i rnam bshad le'u lnga pa
Lam rim chen mo	Tsongkhapa Lobsang Dragpa, *Byang chub lam gyi rim pa chen mo*
Las thabs shes bzung 'jub	Shakya Chogden, *Theg pa chen po dbu ma rnam par nges pa'i bang mdzod lung rigs rgya mtsho las thabs shes bzung 'jub le'u bcu pa*
Legs bshad snying po	Tsongkhapa Lobsang Dragpa, *Drang ba dang nges pa'i don rnam par 'byed pa'i bstan bcos legs bshad snying po*
Lta ba'i 'od zer	Gorampa Sönam Sengé, *Dbu ma rtsa ba'i shes rab kyi rnam pa bshad pa yang dag lta ba'i 'od zer*
Lta ba'i gnas	Shakya Chogden, *Theg pa chen po dbu ma rnam par nges pa'i bang mdzod lung rigs rgya mtsho las lta ba'i gnas le'u dgu pa*
Lta ba'i shan 'byed	Gorampa Sönam Sengé, *Lta ba'i shan 'byed theg mchog gnad gyi zla zer*
Nges don rab gsal	Gorampa Sönam Sengé, *Dbu ma spyi don nges don rab gsal*
Nges shes sgron me	Mipham Rinpoche, *Nges shes rin po che' sgron me*
Prasannapadā	Candrakīrti, *Mūlamadhyamakavṛttiprasannapadā*
Rigs lam rab gsal	Mipham Rinpoche, *Gzhan gyis brtsad pa'i lan mdor bsdus pa rigs lam rab gsal de nyid snang byed*
Rigs tsogs dka' gnad	Rongtön Shakya Gyaltsen, *Dbu ma rigs pa'i tsogs kyi dka' ba'i gnad stan pa rigs lam kun gsal*
Rten 'brel stod pa	Tsongkhapa Lobsang Dragpa, *Rten 'brel stod pa legs bshad snying po*

Rtsa shes ṭīk chen	Tsongkhapa Lobsang Dragpa, *Rtsa shes ṭīk chen rigs pa'i mgrya mtso*
Sgom gsum rab dbye	Sakya Paṇḍita, *Sgom gsum rab tu dbye ba'i stan bcos*
Sgom rim 'khrul spong	Shakya Chogden, *Dbu ma chen po'i sgom rim 'khrul spong dbyangs kyi rnga sgra*
Shes 'grel ke ta ka	Mipham Rinpoche, *Shes rab le'ui 'grel pa ke ta ka*
Shes rab ral gri	Mipham Rinpoche, *Don rnam par nges pa shes rab ral gri*
Shes nying rnam bshad	Rongtön Shakya Gyaltsen, *Shes rab sying po'i rnam bshad yum don rab gsal*
Spros bral bshad pa	Shakya Chogden, *Zab mo spros bral gyi bshad pa stong nyid bdud rtsi'i lam po che*
Spyod 'jug 'grel bshad	Thubten Chödrag, *Spyod 'jug gi 'grel bshad rgyal sras yon tan bum bzang*
Stong thun chen mo	Khedrub Jé, *Dbu ma'i stong thun skal bzang mig 'byed*
Stong thun chung ba	Shakya Chogden, *Stong thun chung ba dbang po'i rdu rje blo gsal mgu byed*
Thub pa dgongs gsal	Sakya Paṇḍita, *Thub pa'i dgongs pa rab tu gsal ba*
Zab don mig 'byed	Khensur Pema Gyaltsen, *Zab don gdams pa'i mig 'byed gser gyi thu ma*
Zla ba'i zhal lung	Mipham Rinpoche, *Dbu ma 'jug pa'i 'grel pa zla ba'i zhal lung dri med shel phreng*
Toh.	*A Complete Catalogue of Tohoku University Collection of Tibetan Works on Buddhism.* 1934 and 1953 (ed.). Sendai, Japan: Prof. Yensho Kanakura.

Tokyo-Kyoto Edition	*Tibetan Tripiṭaka.* 1959 (ed.). Tokyo-Kyoto: Tibetan Tripiṭaka Research Foundation.

AN *Aṅguttara Nikāya*

Dhp *Dhammapada*

DN *Dīgha Nikāya*

Iti *Itivuttaka*

Khp *Khuddhaka Nikāya*

MN *Majjhima Nikāya*

Ps *Paṭisambhidāmagga*

SN *Saṃyutta Nikāya*

Sn *Sutta Nipata*

Ud	*Udāna*
CIHTS	Central Institute of Higher Tibetan Studies

Notes

1 The famous Chinese monk Chih-i (538–97), the architect of the T'ien-t'ai School (Tendai in Japan), proposed the oneness of *three* truths, where the third truth dialectically reconciles the extremes of the two truths. Understanding *things are* as the conventional truth and *things are not* as the ultimate truth, he treats them as binary opposites, and proposes both *things are* and *things are not* as well as *things neither are nor are not* as the third truth. The third truth is also called the *middle truth.* Matthew Kapstein, "The Trouble with Truth: Heidegger on *Alétheia,* Buddhist Thinkers on *Satya,*" in his *Reason's Traces: Identity and Interpretation in Indian and Tibetan Buddhist Thought* (Boston: Wisdom Publications, 2001), p. 221; Donald Mitchell, *Buddhism: Introducing the Buddhist Experience* (New York: Oxford University Press, 2002), pp. 190–94.

2 See Georges B.J. Dreyfus and Sara L. McClintock, eds., *The Svātantrika-Prāsaṅgika Distinction: What Difference Does a Difference Make?* (Boston: Wisdom Publications, 2003). In this recent book commentators have argued that the doxographical distinction between the Svātantrika and Prāsaṅgika Madhyamaka emerged in Tibet in the eleventh to twelfth centuries. See, for example, José Ignacio Cabezón's article, "Two Views on the Svātantrika-Prāsaṅgika Distinction in Fourteenth-Century Tibet," on Tsongkhapa and Gorampa's analyses on this matter, pp. 289–315. For more on Tsongkhapa's view, see Chizuko Yoshimizu, "Tsongkhapa's Reevaluation of Candrakīrti's Criticism of Autonomous Inference," pp. 257–88, as well as D.S. Ruegg's "Indian and the Indic in Tibetan Cultural History, and Tsoṅ khapa's Achievement as a Scholar and Thinker: An Essay on the Concepts of Buddhism in Tibet and Tibetan Buddhism," *Journal of Indian Philosophy* 32 (2004): 321–43.

3 The distinction between the use of *Mādhyamika* versus *Madhyamaka* is not rigid. However, throughout the book, when the word is used in association with the person who holds the view, I use Mādhyamika, and when the term is used in association with the view itself, or the literature, system, or tradition reflecting the view, I tend to use Madhyamaka.

4 Most sources agree that the Buddha lived for eighty years some time in the fifth and sixth century B.C.E., but they disagree on his precise date of birth. Theravādins put his birth at around 624 B.C.E., while most Western scholars put it sometime between 566 and 558 B.C.E. For a detailed analysis, see Hirakawa Akira, *A History of Indian Buddhism: From Śākyamuni to Early Mahāyāna* (Delhi: Motalal Banarsidass, 1998), pp. 21–37.

5 Nāgārjuna is often regarded as the founder of the Mahāyāna tradition, and of the Madhyamaka school in particular. For the traditional life stories of these Indian adepts, see *Tāranātha's History of Buddhism in India,* trans. and ed. by Chimpa and Chattopadhyaya (Delhi: Motilal Banarsidass, 1990). Western scholars argue that the Tibetan account of Nāgārjuna's life conflates the philosopher with a tantric yogi of the same name who lived several centuries later. In the *Encyclopedia of Indian Philosophies,* vol. 8, ed. by Karl H. Potter (Delhi: Motilal Banarsidass, 2002), pp. 97–182, Christian Lindtner provides useful summaries of each of Nāgārjuna's major writings.

6 Āryadeva was a contemporary to Nāgārjuna and is recognized as the latter's foremost pupil. Tom Tillemans has offered the most recent analysis of his life and works in *Materials for the Study of Āryadeva, Dharmapāla, and Candrakīrti* (Vienna: Arbeitskreis für Tibetische und Buddhistische Studien, 1990). See also Karen Lang's excellent summaries of Āryadeva's principal works in Potter's *Encyclopedia of Indian Philosophies,* vol. 8.

7 Very little is known of Candrakīrti's life. The conclusion drawn in Ruegg's *The Literature of the Madhyamaka School of Philosophy in India* (Wiesbaden: Otto Harrassowitz, 1981), p. 228, from the rather scarce evidence available is ca. 600–50.

8 I use the term *empirically given phenomena*—meaning empirically verifiable—as interchangeable with the Tibetan *tha snyad du grub pa'i chos* or *tha snyad pa'i chos.* The intention is to contrast *tha snyad du grub pa'i chos* with *kun rdzob kyi chos,* which is rendered into English as "conventional phenomena." Tsongkhapa and Gorampa use both these terms. However, while the latter treats *tha snyad du grub pa'i chos* (or *tha snyad pa'i chos*) and *kun rdzob kyi chos* as basically the same, the former distinguishes them. For Tsongkhapa, *kun rdzob kyi chos* is inclusive: it refers not only to empirically given phenomena but also to conceptually constructed phenomena—such as the horn of a rabbit—that are not verifiable through the senses. For Tsongkhapa, *tha snyad du grub pa'i cho* is less inclusive because it excludes all purely conceptually constructed enties. This distinction is crucial for Tsongkhapa. Using this criterion, he differentiates between what is *kun rdzob tsam* and *kun rdzob bden pa.* Not all *kun rdzob kyi chos,* he argues, satisfy the criterion of *kun rdzob bden pa.* A rabbit horn, for example, is conceptually constructed with no empirical base and therefore does not necessarily need to be certified by valid cognitions. All *tha snyad du grub pa'i chos,* on the other hand, since they are not merely conceptual projections, do satisfy the criterion of *kun rdzob bden pa,* and they are all certified by valid cognitions.

9 For a brief biographical account of Tsongkhapa, see Don rdor and Bstan 'zin chos grags, *Gang ljongs lo rgyus thog gi grags can mi sna* (Bod ljongs mi dmangs Press, 1993), pp. 434–41; a detailed Tibetan biographical account is in Rgyal dbang Chos rje, *'Jam mgon chos kyi rgyal po Tsongkhapa chen po'i rnam thar* (Sarnath: Gelugpa Students' Welfare Fund Committee, 2000). An English-language biography is in Robert Thurman's *Life and Teachings of Tsong Khapa* (Dharamsala: Library of Tibetan Works and Archives, 1982). On Tsongkhapa's achievements, see Ruegg's "Indian and the Indic in Tibetan Cultural History, and Tsoṅ kha pa's Achievement as a Scholar and Thinker," and Thupten Jinpa's "Delineating Reason's Scope for Negation: Tsongkhapa's Contribution to Madhyamaka's Dialectical Method," *Journal of Indian Philosophy* 26 (1998): 275–308.

10 This work is now available in English translation as *The Great Treatise on the Stages of the Path to Enlightenment* (Ithaca, NY: Snow Lion Publications) in three volumes: vol. 1 (2000), vol. 3 (2002), and vol. 2 (2004).

11 For an English translation, see R.A.F. Thurman, *Tsongkhapa's Speech of Gold in the Essence of True Eloquence* (Princeton: Princeton University Press, 1984).

12 This latter work has been translated by Jay L. Garfield and Geshe Ngawang Samten in *Ocean of Reasoning: A Great Commentary on Nāgārjuna's Mūlamadhyamakakārikā* (New York: Oxford University Press, 2006).

13 For an account of his life, see Don rdor and Bstan 'zin chos grags, *Gang ljongs lo rgyus thog gi grags can mi sna,* pp. 535–37.

14 A critical edition and translation of this work appears in José Cabezón and Geshe Lobsang Dhargyay's *Freedom from Extremes: Gorampa's "Distinguishing the Views" and the Polemics of Emptiness* (Boston: Wisdom Publications, 2007).

15 José Cabezón, in *A Dose of Emptiness: An Annotated Translation of the sTong thun chen mo of mKhas grub dGe legs dpal bzang* (Albany: State University of New York Press, 1992), provides a useful list of some of the major polemical works and polemical authors, p. 398n26; p. 403n40. See also his introduction to *Freedom from Extremes,* pp. 18–33.

16 See Guy Newland, *The Two Truths* (Ithaca, NY: Snow Lion Publications, 1992), pp. 59–75; and Jeffrey Hopkins, *Meditation on Emptiness* (Boston: Wisdom Publications, 1996), pp. 413–17.

17 "'Thing,' in its most general sense, is interchangeable with 'entity' or 'being' and is applicable to any item whose existence is acknowledged by a system of ontology, whether that item be particular, universal, abstract, or concrete." See Ted Honderich, *The Oxford Companion to Philosophy* (New York: Oxford University Press: 1995), p. 871.

18 Sun, Tang-yi, *Bod rgya tshig mdzod chen mo* (Peking: Mi Rigs Press, 1993), p. 633: *ngo bo/ rang bzhin dang gnas lugs/.*

19 *Rang bzhin tha mi thad pa.* Sun, *Bod rgya tshig mdzod chen mo,* p. 633: *ngo bo gcig pa/ rang bzhin tha mi dad pa/ dper na bum pa dang mi rtag pa lta bu'o/.*

20 Sun, *Bod rgya tshig mdzod chen mo,* p. 633: *ming gi rnam grangs la rang bzhin gcig pa dang/ bdag nyid gcig pa'o//.*

21 Cabezón also translates *ngo bo cig* as a "single-nature" in *A Dose of Emptiness,* p. 364.

22 See Hopkins, *Meditation on Emptiness,* p. 413, and Newland, *The Two Truths,* p. 59.

23 Cabezón, *A Dose of Emptiness,* p. 364: "The two truths are of the same nature but have different opposites."

24 Dreyfus, Georges B.J., *Recognizing Reality: Dharmakīrti's Philosophy and Its Tibetan Interpretations* (Albany: State University of New York Press, 1997), pp. 165–70.

25 Sun, *Bod rgya tshig mdzod chen mo,* p. 1458: *rtog pa rigs mi mthun pa'am tha dad pa las log par snang ba'i chos/ dper na/ bum pa ma yin pa las log tsam gyi cha ni bum pa'i ldog pa yin pa ste rtog pa la snang ba'i gzugs lta bu'o//.*

26 Dreyfus, *Recognizing Reality,* p. 166.

27 Dreyfus, *Recognizing Reality,* p. 165.

28 Sun, *Bod rgya tshig mdzod chen mo,* p. 663: *ngo bo gcig la ldog pa tha dad pa/ rang bzhin so so ba ma yin zhing rang gi ldog pa tha dad du gnas pa ste/ bum pa dang shes bya gnyis dang/ mi rtag pa dang dngos po/ mi dang mi'i nyer len gyi bum po'o//.*

29 'Jam dbyangs bzhad pa'i rdo rje, *Grub mtha'i rnam bshad kun bsang zhing gi nyi ma* (hereafter, *Grub mtha'i rnam bshad*) (Tsho ngon: Kan su'i Mi Rigs Press, 1992), pp. 849–52. The translations here are drawn from Jeffrey Hopkins' *Meditation on Emptiness,* pp. 406–12. Hopkins also considers Jamyang Shepai's objections to those six different positions regarding the basis of the divisions of the two truths.

30 Newland, *The Two Truths,* pp. 40–50.

31 *Dbu ma dgongs pa rab gsal* (hereafter, *Dgongs pa rab gsal*) (Sarnath: Gelugpa Students' Welfare Committee, 1984), p. 176: *bden pa gnyis kyi dbye gzhi la 'dud tshul me 'dra ba mang mod kyang/ 'dir shes bya la bya ste//.* His followers unanimously accept the *objects of knowledge* as the basis of the division of the two truths. For example, Khedrub Jé (Mkhas grub Rje) (see Cabezón, *A Dose of Emptiness,* pp. 357–60) not only proposes *objects of knowledge* as the basis of the division of the two truths but also refutes the position of Ngog Loden Sherab (Rngog Blo ldan shes rab, 1059–1109) who denies objects of knowledge as the basis for determining ultimate truth. See also Changkya Rölpai Dorje (Lcang skya Rol pa'i rdo rje), *Gub mtha' thub stan lhun po'i mdzes rgyan* (hereafter, *Grub mtha' mdzes rgya*) (Tsho sngon: Kan su'i Mi Rigs Press, 1989), pp. 317–18, and Jamyang Shepai Dorje, *Grub mtha' rnam bshad,* pp. 849–52.

32 *Ngo bo gcig la ldog pa tha dad.* Helmut Tauscher, "Phya pa chos kyi seng ge as a Svātantrika," in Dreyfus and McClintock, eds., *The Svātantrika-Prāsaṅgika Distinction,* p. 235.

33 Tauscher, "Phya pa chos kyi seng ge as a Svātantrika," p. 235.

34 As Mathew Kapstein notes in his article "Abhayākaragupta on the Two Truths" in *Reason's Traces: Identity and Interpretation in Indian and Tibetan Buddhist Thought* (Boston: Wisdom Publications, 2001), p. 395, the term *saṃvṛti (kun rdzob)* is variously translated as "relative, conventional, transactional, superficial, occluded, ostensible, concealer." I have opted to render *saṃvṛti* as "empirical" in most contexts to preserve its nonarbitary character, and therefore to stress the phenomena that are accessible to the senses. The term *empirical* here is more restricted than its general sense of what is experimentally verifiable. I am thankful to Dr. Gareth Sparham for pointing out the need to defend my usage. See also note 8 above on "empirically given."

35 A Complete Catalogue of Tohoku University Collection of Tibetan Works on Buddhism (hereafter, Toh.), Prof. Yensho Kanakura, ed. (Sendai, Japan: 1934 and 1953) no. 60, Dkon brtsegs nga, f. 62b: *'de ltar de bzhin gshigs pas kun rdzob dang don dam pa gnyis thugs su chud de/ shes bar bya ba yang kun rdzob dang don dam pa'i bden pa 'der zad de/ de yang bcom ldan ldas kyis stong pa nyid du rab tu gzigs rab tu mkhyen/ legs par mngon du byas pas de'i phyir thams cad mkhyen pa zhes bya'o//.* Cited in Tsongkhapa, *Dgongs pa rab gsal,* p. 176; and by Khedrub Jé in Cabezón, *A Dose of Emptiness,* p. 357.

36 Toh no. 60, *Dkon brtsegs nga,* f. 61b. Cited in Tsongkhapa, *Dgongs pa rab gsal,* p. 178: *'jig rten mkhen pa'i gzhan la ma gsan par/ bden pa de gnyis nyid kyis stong par mrzad/ gang gi kun rdzob de bzhin don dam tse/ bden pa gsum pa gang yang ma mchis so//.*

37 Sun, *Bod rgya tshig mdzod chen mo,* p. 2862*: shes bya/ blo'i yul du bya rung ba ste/ ka ba dang bum pa la sogs pa'i chos gang dang gang yin rung kyang/ sems can nas sangs rgyas kyi bar gyi blo spi'i yul du bya rung ba'o//.*

38 Hopkins, *Meditation on Emptiness,* p. 418.

39 *Dgongs pa rab gsal,* p. 173: *'des ni myu gu lta bu gcig gi ngo bo la yang phye na kun rdzob yin pa dang/ don dam yin pa'i ngo bo gnyis yod par ston gyi…//.* As Tsongkhapa further explains, "The ultimate reality of the sprout is its [ultimate] characteristic, thus it is called sprout's nature. The sprout's color, shape, etc., are also its features, therefore they too are its nature." *Rtsa shes ṭīk chen,* p. 406: *myu gu'i chos nyid ni de'i rang bzhin yin pas de'i ngo bo zhes bya la myu gu'i kha dog dang dbyibs la sogs pa yang myu gu'i bdag nyid yin pas de'i ngo bo'o//.*

40 *Dgongs pa rab gsal,* p. 173: *myu gu'i ngo bo gcig nyid so skye dang 'phags pa la ltos nas bden pa gnyis su bstan pa gtan min no//. Āryas ('phags pa)* are no longer ordinary beings because they have had a direct realization of the nature of ultimate truth. This ensures their eventual release from the cycle of suffering rebirth and frees them from believing in their perception of intrinsic essences. Their perception is purified of all traces of delusion when they reach buddhahood, or full enlightenment.

41 Hopkins also states that "the division of the two truths is not an ontological division…The division of the two truths emphasizes two types of objects of consciousness, truths and falsities. Both, however, are falsely existent or falsely established because neither is independent; each depends on its imputing consciousness and on the other." See *Meditation on Emptiness,* p. 418.

42 Newland, *The Two Truths,* p. 49.

43 Newland, *The Two Truths,* p. 49.

44 Gorampa Sönam Sengé, *Dbu ma spyi don nges don rab gsal* (hereafter, *Nges don rab gsal*), *The Complete Works of the Sakya Scholars,* vol. 12. (Tokyo: Toyo Bunko, 1969), p. 374a–b.

45 *Nges don rab gsal,* p. 374a–b.

46 *Nges don rab gsal,* p. 374a–b: *yul gyi gnas tshul gyi ngos nas bden pa gyis su med kyang blos gnas tshul mthong ba dang ma mthong ba'i sgo nas bden pa gnyis su dbye zhes pa'i don du snang bas shin tu legs so// des na gnas tshul rang ngos nas mtshan mtshon dang/ dbye gzhi dang dbye ba sogs byar med kyang tha snyad bden par sgro brtag nas gdul bya la bstan pa'i dbye ba'i ya gyal yod pa ltar bdye gzhi'ang yod par bya dgos//.*

47 *Nges don rab gsal,* p. 374b: *gsung rub kyi brjod bya tsam dbyer gzhir byas na shin tu'ang 'thad te…dbu ma'i zhung lugs 'dir sgras bstan du med kyang tha snyad du sgras bstan pa dang/ bden pa gnyis po dbyir med kyang gdul bya la dbye ste bstan pa sogs gzhung 'grel gye dgongs pa gong 'og sgrigs na 'de nyid 'thad par sems so//.*

48 *Nges don rab gsal,* p. 374a–b: *gnas tshul rang ngos nas mtshan mtshon dang/ dbye gzhi dang dbye ba sogs byar med kyang tha snyad bden par sgro btags nas gdul bya la bstan pa'i tshe bye ba'i ya gyal yod pa ltar dbye bzhi yod par bya dgos…//.*

49 Christian Lindtner, *Nagarjuniana: Studies in the Writings and Philosophy of Nāgārjuna* (hereafter *Nagarjuniana*) (New Delhi: Motilal Banarsidass, 1987), p. 19.

50 *Nagarjuniana,* p. 19n49.

51 *Nges don rab gsal,* p. 374b: *bden pa gnyis ste/ yul can gyi blo sgo nas kun rdzob gyi bden pa dang don dam bden pa gnyis yin la//.*

52 *Nges don rab gsal,* p. 375b: *dbu ma'i gzhun lugs 'dir ni yul rang ngos nas bden pa gnyis su dbyer med…//*

53 *Lta ba ngan sel, The Complete Works of the Sakya Scholars,* vol. 13 (Tokyo: Toyo Bunko, 1969), f. 611: *de yang gzhi gcig nyid snang tshul gyi sgo nas so sor phye ba yin*

gyi yul gyi ngos nas so sor yod pa zhig ma yin no//. Also see f. 603: *de ltar blo'i sgo nas ngo bo gnyis 'dzin pa'i mthong ba yang dag pa'i yul ni don dam bden pa yin la/ thong ba rdzun pa'i yul ni kun rdzob bden pa'i//.*

54 *Nges don rab gsal,* p. 375b: *brdzun pa mthong ba dang/ yang dag mthong ba gnyis sam/ 'khrul ma khrul gnyis/ rmongs ma rmongs gnyis/ phyin ci log ma log gnyis sam/ tshad ma yin min gnyis kyis mthong tshul gyi sgo nas kun rdzob den pa dang/ don dam bden pa gyis su phye ba ste//.* Also see p. 375b–d for his detailed authentication of each of these assertions through various citations.

55 *Nges don rab gsal,* p. 384c: *bden pa gnyis yul can gyi blo rmongs ma rmongs sam brdzun pa mthong ba dang/ yang dag mthong ba'am/ 'khrul ma 'khrul gyi sgo nas 'jog dgos pas yul can gyi blo'i sgo nas 'jog pa ni rgya gar gyi thal rang thams cad mthun par snang la//.*

56 He argues that the division of the two truths is made depending on "mistaken cognition" *(blo 'khrul ba)* and "unmistaken cognition" *(blo ma 'khrul ba).* See Longchen Rabjam (Klong chen Rab 'byams), *Grub mtha' rin chen mdzod* (hereafter, *Grub mtha' mdzod*), vol. 6. (Gangtok, Sikkim: Khentse Labrang, 1983), ff. 201–2.

57 Sakya Paṇḍita (Sa skya Paṇḍita), *Gzhung lugs legs par bshad pa* (hereafter, *Gzhung lugs legs bshad*), the *Sakya bka' 'bum,* vol. 5 (Tokyo: Toyo Bunko, 1968), p. 72d: *yul can gyi blo 'khrul pa dang/ ma khrul pa gnyis la ltos nas bden pa gnyis su nges pa yin no//.*

58 Mipham Rinpoche's (Mi pham Rin po che) treatment of the two truths is quite inconsistent. Sometimes his view appears strikingly similar to Tsongkhapa's, particularly in the *Nges shes rin po che' sgron me* (hereafter, *Nges shes sgron me*), *The Collected Writings,* vol. 8. (Gangtok: Sonam Topgyal Kazi, 1976), ff. 95–97, and his commentary to Candrakīrti's *Madhyamakāvatāra, Dbud ma 'jug pa'i 'grel pa zla ba'i zhal lung dri med shel phreng* (hereafter, *Zla ba'i zhal lung*) (Sarnath: Nyingma Students' Welfare Committee, 1977), ff. 81, 169. In the *Sher 'grel ke ta ka* (Sarnath: Nyingmapa Students' Welfare Committee, 1993), pp. 3–4, 90–92, however, Mipham explicitly endorses the perspective-based division of the two truths. In his article "Would the True Prāsaṅgika Please Stand," in *The Svātantrika-Prāsaṅgika Distinction,* p. 321, Dreyfus notes the same problem: "despite this openness, Mi pham is in limited agreement with Tsongkhapa, and on many issues he sides with the latter's critics." Furthermore, Mipham is an explicit critic of Tsongkhapa. As John Pettit points out in *Mipham's Beacon of Certainty: Illuminating the View of Dzogchen, the Great Perfection* (Boston: Wisdom Publications, 1999), p. 136, "Although the substance of Mipham's and Go ram pa's critiques of Tsongkhapa and their formulations of Mādhyamika systems are for the most part the same, there is a notable difference in tenor."

59 Rongtön Shakya Gyaltsen (Rong ston Śākya rgyal tshan), *Dbu ma rigs pa'i tsogs kyi dka' ba'i gnad stan pa rigs lam kun gsal* (hereafter, *Rigs tsogs dka' gnad*) (blockprint, n.d.), f. 7: *bden pa gnyis po yang yul la chos gnyis yod pa'i dbang gyis bzhag pa min gyi/ shes ngo gynis la ltos nas gzhag pa ste//.* See also f. 11.

60 Although Taktsang Lotsawa (Stag tsang Lo tsā ba) claims "mere objects of knowledge" *(shes bya tsam)* as the basis of the division of the two truths, it is obvious that he is more committed to a division based on two different perspectives. See *Grub mtha' kun shes nas mtha' bral sgrub pa zhes bya ba'i bstan cos* (hereafter, *Grub mtha'*

kun shes) (blockprint, n.d.), f. 27; and its commentary *Grub mtha' kun shes nas mtha' bral sgrub pa zhes bya ba'i stan cos rnam par bshad pa legs bshad rgya mtsho* (hereafter, *Grub mtha'i rnam bshad*) (blockprint, n.d.), f. 206, where Taktsang argues that the Prāsaṅgikas accept all conventionalities based on the perspectives of ordinary beings.

61 Despite the fact that Shakya Chogden (Śākya Mchog ldan) claims "mere truth" *(bden pa tsam)* as the basis of the division, his explanation is rooted in the notion that the two truths are distinguished on the basis of correct perception and incorrect perception. See *Theg pa chen po dbu ma rnam par nges pa'i bang mdzod lung rigs rgya mtsho las bden pa gnyis kyi rnam bzhag le'u bzhi pa* (hereafter, *Bden gnyis rnam gzhag*), *The Complete Works*, vol. 15 (Thimphu, Bhutan: Kunzang Tobgey, 1975), f. 15; also see ff. 3–4 for his objections to Tsongkhapa's position that objects of knowledge *(shes bya)* is the basis of the division.

62 Karmapa Mikyö Dorje (Karma pa Mi skyod rdo rje) argues that there are not two truths in the Madhyamaka system; truths are posited purely from the perspective of ordinary beings. See *Dbu ma la 'jug pa'i rnam bshad dpal ldan lus gsum mkhyen pa'i zhal lung dag rgyud grub pa'i shing rta* (hereafter, *Dag brgyud grub pa'i shing rta*) (blockprint, n.d.), ff. 5, 306: *'jig rten pa gang dag de kno na nyid rtogs ched du 'jig rten gyi bden brdzun gyi tha snyad sogs dang sgo bstun nas de ngor gcom ldan 'das kyis bden gnyis kyi rnam gzhag mdzad kyi/ bdu ma pa rang lugs kyis grub pa ni ma yin no//.*

63 In his preface to *Mādhyamika Dialectic and the Philosophy of Nāgārjuna*, ed. by S. Rinpoche (Sarnath: CIHTS, 1985), pp. xxiv–xxvi, Murti writes: "*Paramārthasatya*, or Absolute Truth is the knowledge of the real as it is without any distortion...*Saṃvṛtisatya* is Truth so-called; Truth as conventionally believed in common parlance...There are not two different spheres or sets of objects...the difference is in our manner of looking at things."

64 In his article "Madhyamaka" in *Mādhyamika Dialectic and the Philosophy of Nāgārjuna*, pp. 152–53, Poussin describes, "*Dharmas* are like the hairs that a monk with diseased eyes thinks he sees in his alms bowl...This is proved by the fact that a man with undiseased eyes has no thought about these hairs at all."

65 "The Absolute and the Empirical...are not two sets of separate realities set over against each other...The Absolute or Nirvāṇa viewed through the thought-constructions *(vikalpa)* is saṃsāra, the world or saṃsāra viewed *sub specie aeternitatis* is the Absolute or Nirvāṇa itself." Introduction to Theodore Stcherbatsky's *The Conception of Buddhist Nirvāṇa* (Delhi: Motilal Banarsidass, 1989), p. 30.

66 He interprets Candrakīrti as saying that all phenomena possess only one nature and that the second nature is obtained on the strength of false perceptions of common people. See *The Emptiness of Emptiness: An Introduction to Early Indian Mādhyamika* (Honolulu: University of Hawaii Press, 1994), pp. 39, 40, 231.

67 Newland, *The Two Truths*, p. 47.

68 Hopkins, *Meditation on Emptiness*, p. 419.

69 In the *Rtsa ba phyogs bsdus* (Varanasi: Sakya Students' Welfare Committee, 1996), p. 155: *dngos kun yang dag brdzun pa mthong ba yis/ dngos rnyed ngo bo gyis ni 'dzin par 'gyur/* 6:23/. This passage is also cited in Candrakīrti, *Madhyamakāvatārabhāṣya* (Varanasi: Sakya Students' Welfare Committee, 1994), p. 98.

70 *Madhyamakātarabhāṣya,* p. 98: *'du byed dang myu gu la sogs pa nang dang phyi ro gyi dngos po thams cad kyi rang gyi ngo bo rnam pa gnyis nye bar bstan te//.* Cited in Tsongkhapa, *Rtsa shes ṭīk chen,* p. 406.

71 Mkhas grub Rje, *Dbu ma'i stong thun skal bzang mig 'byed* (hereafter, *Stong thun chen mo*) (Dharamasala: Sherig Press, n.d.), f. 429: *'jug pa las/ dngos rnyed ngo bo gnyis ni 'dzin par 'gyur/ zhes sogs rtsa 'grel gis gsung pa ltar kun rdzob dang don dam gyi chos thams cad la ngo bo yod la/ ngo bo yod na ngo bo gcid dang tha dad gang rung yin dgos ste yod na gcig dang tha dad gang rung yin dgos pa'i phyir ro//.* I borrowed the translation of this passage from Cabezón, *A Dose of Emptiness,* p. 363.

72 Tsongkhapa argues that there are only two possibilities: either the two natures are identical *(ngo bo gcig)* or distinct *(ngo bo tha dad);* there cannot be a third. See *Dgongs par rab gsal,* p. 176: *'der ni gnyis ka la ngo bo yod la/ de la ngo bo gcig dang tha dad gang yang min pa mi srid pa'i phir/.*

73 *Dgongs pa rab gsal,* p. 176: *byas pa dang mi rtag pa lta bu ste//.*

74 See Gyaltsen Namdol (Rgyal mtshan rnam grol), ed. and trans., *Ācārya Nāgārjuna's Bodhicittavivaraṇa and Ācārya Kamalaśīla's Bodhicittabhāvanā,* Bibliotheca Indo-Tibetan Series 23 (Sarnath: CIHTS, 1991), pp. 45–45: *kun rdzob las ni tha dad par// de nyid dmigs pa ma yin te/ 67/ kun rdzob stong pa nyid du bshad// stong pa kho na kun rdzob yin// med na mi 'byung nges pa'i phir// byas dang mi rtag je bzhin no/ 68//.* Cited in Tsongkhapa, *Dgongs pa rab gsal,* p. 176; Khedrub Jé, *Stong thun chen mo* (see Cabezón, *A Dose of Emptiness,* p. 364), and Newland, *The Two Truths,* p. 61.

75 *Dgongs pa rab gsal,* pp. 176–77: *rkang pa dang po bzhi'i don ni kun rdzob las ngo bo that dad par de kho na nyid yod pa min te/ kun rdzob pa rnams bden pas stong pa yin pa'i phir dang/ bden stong nyid kyang gzhi kun rdzob la 'jog pa'i phir zhes pa 'o// de nas gnyis kyis ni de ltar yin dang med na mi 'byung ba'i 'brel ba nges la/ de yang bdag gcig pa'i 'brel pa yin pas byas mi rtag bzhin du ngo bo gcig par bstan no//.*

76 See Robert Thurman, trans. and ed., *Life and Teachings of Tsongkhapa* (Dharamsala: Library of Tibetan Works and Archives, 1982), p. 74.

77 *Stong thun chen mo,* f. 429: *de'i phyir bden gnyis ni ngo bo gcig la ldog pa tha dad cing med na mi 'byung ba bdag gcig 'brel grub pa byas mi rtag lta bu yin te...//.* See Cabezón, *A Dose of Emptiness,* p. 364, for a slightly different translation of this passage.

78 Newland, *The Two Truths,* p. 60.

79 Cabezón, *A Dose of Emptiness,* p. 516n1128.

80 Garfield, J.L. *The Fundamental Wisdom of the Middle Way: Nāgārjuna's Mūlamadhyamkakārikā.* (New York: Oxford University Press, 1995), p. 276.

81 *Nges don rab gsal,* p. 375d: *spyir gnyis su dbye ba thams cad la bum snam ltar rdzas tha dad dam/ byas mi rtag ltar ngo bo gcig la ldog pa tha dad dam/ zla ba dang bsil zer byed pa ltar rnam grangs pa'i tha dad dam/ dngos po dang ngos med ltar gcig pa bkag pa'i tha dad yin zhes bya ba 'de dpyad dgos pas bden pa gnyis la'ang de dpyad par bya'o//.* See also Sakya Paṇḍita, *Thub pa'i dgongs pa rab tu gsal ba* (hereafter, *Thub pa dgongs gsal*), the *Sakya 'bka'' bum,* vol. 5 (Tokyo: Toyo Bunko, 1968), p. 31d.

82 *Nges don rab gsal,* p. 376d: *mdo las gcig dang tha dad la skyon brjod pa ni don dam gyi dbang du byas pa yin pas don dam par gcig dang gnyis las grol la//;* also p. 376a: *'o na ci ltar gnas zhe na gcig dang tha dad las grol bar gnas te/.*

83 *Nges don rab gsal,* p. 377a: *don dam par gcig dang tha dad las grol ba dang/ 'phags pa'i mnyam gzhag gi ngor gcig dang tha dad las grol ba don gcig pa'i phir...//.*

84 *Nges don rab gsal,* p. 377a: *tha snyad du dngos po dang dngos med ltar gcig pa bkag pa'i tha dad yin ces gsungs pa 'de nyid rigs pas 'thad par mngon te//.*

85 See *Nges don rab gsal,* p. 376d, and *Lta ba ngan sel,* ff. 604–5, for more on such criticisms.

86 *Nges don rab gsal,* p. 376d: *bden pa gnyis ngo bo gcig yin na dpe'i sgo nas rab rib can gyis mthong ba'i skra shad dang/ mthong ba dag pas skra shad med par mthong ba gnyis ngo bo gcig tu thal te/ bden pa gnyis ngo bo gcig yin pa'i phir//.*

87 *Nges don rab gsal,* p. 375d: *mdo sde dgongs 'grel las/ bden gnyis gcig pa dang tha dad pa'i phyogs la skyon bzhi bzhi gsungs te//.*

88 *Nges don rab gsal,* pp. 375d–376a: *dang po ni bden pa gnyis gcig yin na/1/ byis pas kun rdzob gzugs dang sgra la sogs pa mngon sum du mthong ba de bzhin du don dam pa'i bden ba'ang mngon sum mthong bar thal ba dang/2/ kun rdzob las gzugs sgra la sogs pa spros ba'i dbye ba du ma yod pa de bzhin don dam pa la yang dbye ba du ma yod par thal ba dang/3/ kun rdzob kun nas nyon mongs pa'i rang bzhin nam mtshan nyid yin ba ltar don dam yang de ltar 'gyur ba dang/4/ kun rdzob byis pas mthong ba la sogs pa'i don logs su btsan du med pa de bzhin du don dam pa'i bden pa'ang de ltar thal ba'o//.*

89 *Nges don rab gsal,* p. 376a: *gnyis pa ni bden pa gnyis tha dad yin na.../1/ 'phags pa rnams kyis don dam mngon sum du rtogs kyang kun rdzob kyi 'ching ba las mi grol bar thal ba dang/2/ chos nyid don dam de kun rdzob kyi spyi'i mtshan nyid ma yin par thal ba dang/3/ 'du byed kun rdzob rab tu ma grub pa'am/ bdag med de don dam a ma yin par thal ba dang/4/ gang zag gcig gi rgyud la kun nas nyon mongs kyi mtshan yid dang/ rnam byang gi mtshan nyid gnyis dus gcig tu so sor grub par thal ba'o//.*

90 *Zab don gdams pa'i mig 'byed gser gyi thur ma* (hereafter, *Zab don mig 'byed*), vol. 3 (Mundgod: Drepung Loselling Printing Press, 1984), p. 323: *ldog pa gcig yin na yang /1/ bum pa'i chos nyid mngon sum du rtogs pa'i so skye yod pa dang/2/chos nyid de la dmigs nas chags sogs nyon mongs skye ba dang/3/de la kha dog dang dbyibs sogs grub par 'gyur zhing/4/rnal 'byor pas chos nyid sgom pa'i 'bad pa don med du thal/ bum pa dang bum pa'i chos nyid ldog pa gcig yin pa'i phir//.*

91 The radical division of the two truths is due to Dölpopa's controversial doctrine of the "extrinsic emptiness" *(gzhan stong),* the subject of an ongoing intensive debate between its allies (both explicit and implicit) and its critics. According to Cabezón, *A Dose of Emptiness,* pp. 423–24n108, the exponents of the doctrine of extrinsic emptiness include Dölpopa, Tāranātha, Shakya Chogden, the eighth Karmapa Mikyö Dorjé, and the figures from the *ris med* ecumenical movement in eastern Tibet. The broadest study of Dölpopa and his legacy is Cyrus Stearns' *The Buddha from Dolpo: A Study of the Life and Thought of the Tibetan Master Dolpopa Sherab Gyaltsen* (Albany, NY: SUNY Press, 1999), and Jeffrey Hopkins recently translated Dölpopa's masterwork in *Mountain Doctrine: Tibet's Fundamental Treatise on Other-Emptiness and the Buddha-Matrix* (Ithaca, NY: Snow Lion Publications, 2006). Several short works are also available on *gzhan stong:* Cabezón, "The Canonization of Philosophy and the Rhetoric of Siddhānta in Indo-Tibetan Buddhism," in *Texts in Context: Traditional Hermeneutics in South Asia,* ed. J. Timm (Albany: SUNY Press, 1991); Kapstein, "The Trouble with Truth," pp. 223–25; Kapstein, "From Kun-mkhyen Dol-po-pa to 'Ba'-mda' Dge-legs: Three Jo-nang-pa Masters on the Interpretation of the *Prajñāpāramitā*" in his *Reason's Traces,* pp. 301–4; D.S. Ruegg, "The Jo nang pas: A School of Buddhist Ontology According

to the *Grub mtha' shel gyi me long,*" *Journal of American Oriental Society* 83 (1963): 73–91; and M. Broido, "The Jo-nang-pas on Madhyamaka: A Sketch," *Tibet Journal* 14, no. 1. (1989): 125–45.

92 Cited in Kapstein, "The Trouble with Truth," p. 223, from *Dolpopa,* vol. 5 (series vol. VII), pp. 812–15.

93 Kapstein, "The Trouble with Truth," p. 223.

94 Kapstein, "The Trouble with Truth," p. 224.

95 *Stong thun chen mo,* f. 429: *ngo bo tha dad yin na 'brel med don gzhan du 'gyur dgos te/ ngo bo tha dad la bdag gcig 'brel mi srid pa'i phyir dang/ chos nyid 'dus ma byas yin pas de dang de 'byung du 'brel ba mi srid pa'i phyir ro//.* I borrowed the translation of this passage from Cabezón, *A Dose of Emptiness,* p. 363.

96 Thupten Chödak (Thub stan chos grags), *Spyod 'jug gi 'grel bshad rgyal sras yon tan bum bzang (Spyod 'jug 'grel bshad)* (Tsho sngon: Mi rig Parkhang, 1990), pp. 701–2. Also see Newland, *The Two Truths,* pp. 63–66, for his comments on the works of Jamyang Shepai Dorje and Ngawang Palden (Nga dbang dpal ldan) on the same issue.

97 *Zab don gdams pa'i mig 'byed,* pp. 322–23: */1/bum pa bden ston bum pa'i gnas lug min pa dang/2/bum pa bden stong rtogs pas bum ba bden 'dzin gyi sgro 'dogs mi gcod ba dang/3/bum pa bum pa bden grub kyi dgag gzhi yin pa sogs mi 'thad cing/4/sangs 'phags kyi rgyud la bum pa bden stong rtogs pa'i ye shes dang bum pa bden 'dzin gnyis lhan cig tu med pa sogs mi thad par thal/ bum pa dang bum pa bden stong ngo bo tha dad yin pa'i phir//.*

98 Kapstein, "The Trouble with Truth," p. 224.

99 *Grub mtha' mdzod,* ff. 192–93: *des na don dam pa'i bden pa spros pa thams cad dang dral ba de kun rdzob kyi bden pa las dngos po gzhan dang de nyid du'ang brjod du med pa/ gcig pa bkag tsam gyi tha dad yin no//.* See ff. 191–92 for his criticisms of other views.

100 *Rigs tsogs dka' gnad,* ff. 21–22: *tha snyad du gcig pa bkag pa'i tha dad de/ skra shad dang skra shad kyis dben pa' tha dad bzhin no//.* As he states: "It is like the difference between the [perception of] arrows of hair and [the perception of] no hairs."

101 Mipham Rinpoche, *Dbud ma 'jug pa'i 'grel pa zla ba'i zhal lung dri med shel phreng* (hereafter, *Zla ba'i zhal lung*) (Sarnath: Nyingma Students' Welfare Committee, 1977), f. 84: *rnam grangs min pa kho na don dam dang/ tha snyad shes brjod 'jug gsum gyi yul gyur thams cad kun rdzob byas na bden gnyis gcig pa bkag ba'i tha dad yin nam snyam//.* In this passage Mipham agrees with Longchen Rabjam, his predecessor, for the latter argues that "From the standpoint of the provisional ultimate *(rnam grangs kyi don dam)* or from the conventional standpoint, the two truths are distinct and incompatible *(gcig pa dkag pa'i tha dad).*" However, Mipham does not maintain this position consistently. Elsewhere he argues that the two truths have a single ontological identity but different conceptual identities *(ngo bo gcig la ldog pa tha dad)* from the standpoint of the nonprovisional ultimate *(rnam grangs min pa'i don dam).* See Mipham, *Zla ba'i zhal lung,* f. 81: *bden pa gnyis ngo bo gcig la ldog pa tha dad pa'i ngo bo gcig pa de/ snang stong dbyer med ngo bo gcig yin la/ de ni bden gnyis dpyod pa'i tshad mas grub ste gang snang 'de stong/ stong pa de snang ba las tha dad du yod na/ chos de'i ngo bo mi stong bar 'gyur bas de gnyis tha dad du med do// ngo bo dbyer med par grub pa'i ngo bo ni rnam grangs min pa'i don dam ste/ de la gang du'ang brjod mi shes te so sor rang rig gi yul lo//.* Also see Mipham, *Shes 'grel ke ta ka,* p. 4,

for his criticism of the notion that the two truths are distinct or identical. Note the sentence structure, however. He argues that "if the two truths are ultimately distinct *(don dam par tha dad)* and conventionally identical *(kun rdzob tu gcig),*" then there would be four fallacies for each position. Although Mipham's dialectic seems to be compatible with Tsongkhapa's, the underlying assumptions are totally different. From Mipham's definitions of the two truths, it is clear that the two truths must not have equal status. If this is unconvincing, see *Zla ba'i zhal lung,* f. 159: *mthar ni 'phi don med de bag chags kyi snang ba tsam yin par dngos stobs kyis grub ste/.*

102 The criticisms Gendün Chöpel advances against Tsongkhapa's view are considered here primarily as a means to indicate Gendün Chöpel's rejection of the view that holds the mutual compatibility between the two truths. These criticisms are legitimate from the point of view held by Gorampa, Gendün Chöpel, and Tsongkhapa's other critics. According to them, the two truths are reducible to ignorance and wisdom. While for Tsongkhapa, the two truths must not be reducible to ignorance and wisdom since both have their ontological references. Therefore the legitimacy of these criticisms should be understood by having proper perspectives of both systems before applying them directly against Tsongkhapa's view.

103 Gendün Chöpel, *Dbu ma'i zab gnad snying por dril ba'i legs bshad klu sgrub dgongs rgyan* (hereafter, *Klu sgrub dgongs rgyan*) (Lhasa: Bod ljongs bod yid dpe rnying khang, 1990), p. 215: *bden gnyis zung 'jug bya ba 'de 'phags pa'i ye shes dang 'jig rten phal pa'i rnam rtog gnyis 'gal med zung du 'jug pa'i dus gcig srid na de dus 'ong bar nges kyi gzhan du nam yang srid pa'i skabs med do//.* Also, p. 217: *kun rdzob dang don dam mi 'gal bya ba 'de bden gnyis gang gi dpyod lungs byed na yang thar pa'i go skabs ga la yod//.* A translation of Gendün Chöpel's work appears in Donald Lopez's *The Madman's Middle Way: Reflections on Reality of the Tibetan Monk Gendun Chopel* (Chicago: University of Chicago Press, 2006).

104 *Klu sgrub dgongs rgyan,* pp. 220–22: *don la blun po'i mthar thug pa'i 'jig rten phal ba'i bsam mno dang/ mkhas pa'i mthar thug pa'i sangs rgyas kyi mkhyen lugs gnyis 'gal med zung 'jug te khas blang pa yin la/ de 'dra byed tshe ma rigs pa dang rigs shes gnyis kyi yul yang 'gal med zung 'jug tu mkhas blang na ci la mi chog/ ...mdor na bden gnyis 'gal med du 'dod pa 'de sangs rgyas nas sems can gyi bar bsam mno thams cad 'gal med du 'dod pa'i lugs yin no//.*

105 *Thub pa dgongs gsal,* p. 32a: *don dam dang tha snyad pa'i rnam bzhag gnyis las/ dang po ni gcig dang tha dad kyi spros pa dang bral ba yin te...gnyis pa tha snyad pa'i rnam gzhag ni/ gzhan sel gyi ngor ngo bo byed med ldog pa tha dad ces bya ba'am de nyid dang gzhan du brjod du med pa zhes bya ba gsungs pa de kho na khas blang ngo//.* Sakya Paṇḍita expressly rejects the notion of "distinct that is incompatible with their unity" *(gcig pa bkag pa'i tha dad).* See his *Gzhung lugs legs par bshad pa* (hereafter, *Gzhung lugs legs bshad*), the *Sakya bka' 'bum,* vol. 5 (Tokyo: Toyo Bunko, 1968), p. 73a: *gcig pa bkag pa'i tha dad kyang ma yin te/ gang rung dgnos por thal ba'i phir/ des na de nyid dang gzhan du brjord ba med de//.* Gorampa, on the other hand, ascribes this view to Sakya Paṇḍita. See Gorampa, *Nges don rab gsal,* p. 376d: *gsum pa ni dpal ldan Sa skya Paṇḍita'i bshad pa....*

106 *Dbu ma 'jug pa'i rnam bshad de kno na nyid gsal ba'i sgron ma* (hereafter, *Dbu 'jug rnam bshad*) (Sarnath: Sakyapa Students' Union, 1995), pp. 121–21: *bden pa gnyis po 'de dag gcig gam tha dad ce na/ gcig pa'am ma yin/ tha dad pa'am ma yin te/ 'de dag phan tshun ltos nas rnam par 'jog pa'i phir ro/ gang zhig gang la ltos pa de ni de dang*

gcig ma yin te/ rang nyid rang la ltos pa la dgos pa med pa'i phir ro/ /gzhan nyid kyang ma yin te/ ltos pa po ma grub na ltos sa las gzhan nyid kyang ma yin la/ /grub na gzhan las ltos me dgos pa'i phir ro//. The two truths can be expressed neither as identical nor as different; they are relative as opposed to being ontologically interdependent. Were the relationship between the two truths not understood in terms of subjective relativity, Rendawa says, he would contradict the definitions of the two truths he provided earlier based on two conflicting perspectives.

107 Shakya Chogden maintains that the two truths are inexpressible *(brjod par bya ba ma yin pa)* in terms of how they relate to each other. They can be expressed neither as identical nor as distinct in terms of their nature. This inexpressibility, he says, applies both in terms of the conventional stance and in terms of the ultimate stance. See his *Theg pa chen po dbu ma rnam par nges pa'i bang mdzod lung rigs rgya mtsho las bden pa gnyis kyi rnam bzhag le'u bzhi pa* (hereafter, *Bden gnyis rnam gzhag*), *The Complete Works,* vol. 15 (Thimphu, Bhutan: Kunzang Tobgey, 1975), f. 33: *myu gu dang de'i chos nyid stong pa nyid ni ngo bo gcig dang tha dad gang du yang brjod par bya ba ma yin te/ kun rdzob tu yang der brjod par bya ba ma yin don dam du yang der brjod par bya ba ma yin pa'i phir//.* See his objections to the notion of identity or difference based on his interpretation of the *Saṃdhinirmocana Sūtra,* ff. 33–35; and his objections to Tsongkhapa's position that the two truths have a single ontological identity with different conceptual identities, ff. 30–32. His criticisms of Tsongkhapa, though, rest on many factors, notably his absolute denial of the very coherence of the so-called "ontological identity" or "single-nature" relationship in the Madhyamaka system. For example, in the *Bden gnyis rnam gzhag,* ff. 31–32, he writes: *chos thams cad ngo bo nyid med pa zhes bya ba 'de dbu ma'i lugs yin pa'i phir/ de yang dbu ma par rang lugs 'chad pa na kun rdzob kyi rang gi ngo bo ni rnam pa thams cad du 'gog pa kho nar nges la/ don dam pa'i ngo bo ni gnas skabs gcig tu khas blangs kyang/ de ngo bo mtshan nyid pa ma yin la/ de yang mthar 'gog pa'i phir/ byang chub sems 'grel las/ med na mi 'byung nges pa'i phir/ /zhes 'byung ba de yang/ kun rdzob kyi ngo bo med pa'i shes byed yin te/ gzhung der kun rdzob kyi ngo bo med pa nyid don dam par bshad pa'i phir//.*

108 *Dag brgyud grub pa'i shing rta,* ff. 287–88: *kho bo cag dbu ma pa la ni rnam par dpyad pa na bden gnyis gzhi grub pa dang ma grub pa gang du'ang smra bsam brjod pa dang dral pa'i phir/ bden gnyis ngo bo gcig dang tha dad gang du'ang rtog par ga la byed ces shes par bya'o//.* Also see his objections to Dölpopa's notion of the distinct nature of the two truths, ff. 281–85; and the objections to Tsongkhapa's notion of identical ontological characters of the two truths, ff. 285–87.

109 Taktsang Lotsawa holds that the two truths are like *characteristic* and *characterized,* and that they are characteristically inseparable. See *Grub mtha'i rnam bshad,* f. 268: *kun rdzob rang stong dang don dam bzhan stong du 'dod pa ltar ngo bo tha dad ma yin gyi/ cho can dang de'i chos nyid dam gnas lugs yin pas bden gnyis ngo bo dbyer med du gnas shing//.* However, given his commitment to the subjective distinctions, it is unclear how he could consistently sustain the argument that the two truths resemble characteristic and characterized.

110 *Rtsa shes ṭik chen,* p. 406: *myu gu'i chos nyid ni de'i rang gzhin yin pas de'i ngo bo zhes bya la myu gu'i kha dog dang dbyibs la sogs pa yang myu gu' bdag nyid yin pas de'i ngo bo'o//.*

111 *Mūlamadhyamakakārika* 24:10, in the *Rtsa ba phyogs bsdus* (Varanasi: Sakya Students' Welfare Committee, 1996), p. 64: *tha snyad la ni ma brtan par/ /dam pa'i don ni bstan mi nus/ /dam pa'i don ni ma rtogs par/ /mya ngan 'das pa thob m 'gyur //.* Lindtner's *Master of Wisdom: Writings of the Buddhist Master Nāgārjuna* (Oakland, CA: Dharma Publishing, 1986) provides useful critical studies of the texts included in the edition.

112 *Mūlamadhyamakakārika* 24:14, p. 64: *gang la stong pa nyid rung ba/ /de la thams cad rung bar 'gyur/ /gang la stong nyid mi rung ba/ /de la thams cad rung mi 'gyur//.*

113 In the *Rtsa ba phyogs bsdus,* v. 70 (Varanasi: Sakya Students' Welfare Committee, 1996), p. 135: *gang la stong pa nyid srid pa/ /de la don rnams thams cad srid/ /gang la stong nyid mi srid pa/ /de la ci yang mi srid do//.*

114 *Mūlamadhyamakakārikā* 24:18, p. 65: *rten cing 'brel bar 'byung ba gang/ /de ni stong pa nyid du bshad/ /de ni brten nas gdags pa ste/ /de nyid dbu ma'i lam yin no//.*

115 *Vigrahavyāvartanī* 71, p. 135: *gang zhig stong dang rten 'byung dag/ / dbu ma'i lam du don gcig par/ /gsungs mchog mtshungs pa med pa yi/ / sangs rgyas de la phyag 'tshal lo//.*

116 *Mūlamadhyamakakārikā* 24:19, p. 65: *gang phyir rten 'byung ma yin pa'i/ /chos 'ga' yod pa ma yin pa/ /de phyir stong pa ma yin pa'i/ /chos 'ga' yod pa ma yin no//.* Similarly other verses in the *Mūlamadhyamakakārikā,* notably 24:10–11, 24:20, 24:36–37, 24:39–40, reinforce Nāgārjuna's commitment to the mutually compatible relationship between the two truths.

117 Candrakīrti, *Madhyamakāvatāra* 6:37, p. 158: *dngos po stong pa gzugs brnyan la sogs pa/ /tshogs la ltos nas ma grags pa yang min/ /ji ltar der ni gzugs brnyan sogs stong las/ /shes pa de yi rnam pa skye 'gyur ltar//.*

118 *Madhyamakāvatāra,* p. 158: *de bzhin dngos po thams cad stong na yang/ stong nyid dag las rab tu skye bar 'gyur//.*

119 *Madhyamakāvatāra* 6:38, p. 158: *bden pa gnyis su'ang rang bzhin med pa'i phyir/ /de dag rtag pa ma yin chad pa'ang min//.*

120 Tsongkhapa, *Rten 'brel stod pa legs bshad snying po (Rten 'brel stod pa).* In Ācārya Gyaltsen Namdol and Ācārya Ngawang Samten, trans. and ed., *Pratītyasamutpādastutisubhāṣitahṛdayam of Ācārya Tsongkhapa,* Dalai Lama's Tibeto-Indological Series, vol. 3 (Sarnath: CIHTS, 1994), vv. 11–12: *kyod ni nam gzhig stong pa nyid/ /rten 'byung don do mthong pa na/ /rang bzhin gyis ni stong pa dang/ /bya byed 'thad pa'ang mi 'gal zhing// de las bldog par mthong ba na/ stong la bya ba mi rung zhing/ /bya dang bcas la stong med pas/ mya ngan gyang du ltung bar bzhed//.*

121 *Rten 'brel stod pa,* v. 15: *de phyir rten nas 'byung ba las/ /ma gtogs chos 'ga' yod min pas/ /rang bzhin gyis ni stong pa las/ /ma gtogs chos 'ga' med par gsungs//.*

122 *Rten 'brel stod pa,* v. 18: *rang bzhin 'ga' yang med pa dang/ /'de la rten nas 'de 'byung pa/ /rnam gzhad thams cad 'thad pa gnyis/ /mi 'gal 'du ba smos ci dgos//.*

123 *Rten 'brel stod pa,* v. 27: *de phyir rten nas 'byung ba gang/ /rang bzhin gyis ni gdod ma nas/ /rnam par dben yang der snang bas/ /'de kun sgyu ma bzhin du gsungs//.*

124 Tsongkhapa, *Lam gtso rnam gsum gyi rtsa ba,* v. 13 (hereafter, *Lam gtso rnam gsum*), in the *Dbu ma'i lta khrid phyogs bsdebs* (Sarnath: Gelugpa Students' Welfare Committee, 1985), p. 252: *gzhan yang snang bas yod mtha' sel ba dang/ /stong pas med mtha' sel zhing stong pa nyid/ /rgyu dang 'bras bur 'char ba'i tshul shes na/ /mthar 'dzin lta bas 'phrog par me 'gyur ro//.*

125 *Lam gtso rnam gsum,* v. 11, p. 252: *snang ba rten 'drel blu ba med pa dang/ /stong pa khas len dral ba'i go ba gnyis/ /ji srid so sor snang ba de srid du/ da dung thob pa'i dgongs pa rtogs pa med//.*

126 *Lam gtso rnam gsum,* v. 12, p. 252: *nam zhig ris 'jog med par cig car du/ /rten 'brel mi bslur mthong ba tsam nyid nas/ /nges shes yul gyi 'dzin stangs kun zhig na/ de tshe lta ba'i dpyad pa rtogs pa lags//.*

127 The two bodies of a buddha—namely, the *rūpakāya (gzugs sku),* literally "form body," accomplished as a result of the exhaustive accumulation of meritorious deeds *(bsod nams, pūnya),* and the *dharmakāya (chos sku),* literally "nature body," or "truth body," accomplished as a result of the exhaustive accumulation of penetrative wisdom *(ye shes, jñāna).*

128 *Grub mtha'i rnam bshad,* p. 898–99: *bden pa gnyis la nye ring mi rig te/ bden pa gnyis gang las nyams na phung par yang 'dra/ mthar ltong par 'dra/ ma nyams na tshogs gnyis rdzogs pa dang sku gnyis thob pa'i bar 'dra ba'i phyir te/ kun rdzob khas ma blangs par nyams na skur 'debs kyi mthar ltong dge rtsa gcod 'bras bu ngan 'gror ltong/ gsugs sku sgrub byed dang de'i 'bras bu las nyams par 'gyur.../ des na bden gnyis zung 'brel gces te/ de la mthar mi ltong ba dang mi phung ba dang tshogs gnyis dang de'i sku gnyis thob pa'i bar yin phyir te...//.*

129 *Yuktiṣaṣṭikā* 60, in the *Rtsa ba phyogs bsdus* (Varanasi: Sakya Students' Welfare Committee, 1996), p. 96: *dge ba 'de yis skye bu kun/ /bsod nams ye shes tshogs bsags te/ /bsod nams ye shes las byung ba'i/ /dam pa gnyis ni thob par shog//.* Cited in Candrakīrti, *Yuktiṣaṣṭikāvṛtti, Dbu ma* vol. *ya pa,* 26 of of Sde dge Paljor Edition of the Bstan 'gyur, The Tasmanian University Collection (Dharamsala: Paljor Press Edition, 1997–98), f. 59.

130 SN 5:437. Cited in *The Path of Purification: A Translation of Visuddhimagga by Bhadanācariya Buddhaghosa,* Bhikkhu Ñāṇamoli, trans. (Taipei, Taiwan: The Corporate Body of the Buddha Educational Foundation, 2001), p. 809.

131 See "The Trouble with Truth," p. 217.

132 The noble truth of suffering, the noble truth of the origin of suffering, and the noble truth of the path leading to the cessation of suffering come under the conventional truth, while the noble truth of the cessation of suffering is categorized under ultimate truth.

133 *Bden gnyis rnam gzhag,* p. 140: *ye shes chos sku dang longs spyod rjogs pa'i sku gnyis dngos rgyu tshogs pa'i tshar gcig la rags las kyi 'brel pa grub pa yin la/ dus cig car du mngon du byed pa yin no/ /...des na gzhi'i bden pa gnyis zung du 'jug pa dang/ /lam tshogs gnyis zung du 'jug pa dang/ 'bras bu cho gzugs gnyis zung du 'jug pa rigs pa'i lam nas drangs....*

134 *Nāgārjuna: The Philosophy of the Middle Way,* p. 69.

135 In contrast Garfield, *The Fundamental Wisdom of the Middle Way,* p. 297n108, argues, "Despite their ontic unity, the ultimate truth is epistemologically and soteriologically more significant than the conventional."

136 Candrakīrti, *Mūlamadhyamakavṛttiprasannapadā* (hereafter, *Prasannapadā*) (Rajpur: Sakya College, 1993), p. 416: *sangs rgyas bcom ldan las rnams kyis chos bstan pa ni/ bden pa gnyis po 'de la brten nas 'jug pa yin no//.*

137 *Madhyamakāvatārabhāṣya,* p. 69: *bden pa bzhan gang cung zad cig yod pa de yang ci rigs par bden pa gnyis kyi khongs su gtogs pa kho nar nges par bya'o//.*

138 *Rtsa shes ṭīk chen,* p. 411: *don dam bden pa'i bden tshul ni/ mi slu ba yin la de yang gnas tshul gzhan du gnas shing snang tshul gzhan du snang nas 'jig rten la mi slu ba'i phir//.*

139 *Yuktiṣaṣṭīkāvṛtti,* f. 14: *gal te de lta na'ang je ltar myang ngan las 'das pa don dam pa'i bden par gsungs she na/ de'i bdag nyid du 'jig rten la mi slu ba'i phir 'jig rten gyi tha snyad kho nas de don dam pa'i bden par gsungs so//.* Cited in the *Rtsa shes ṭīk chen,* p. 411.

140 Garfield, *The Fundamental Wisdom of the Middle Way,* p. 208.

141 *Mūlamadhyamakakārikā* 13:1, p. 31: *bcom ldan 'das kyi chos gang zhig/ slu ba de ni brdzun zhes gsungs/ /'du byed thams cad slu ba'i chos/ /de na de dag 'rdzun pa yin//.* I borrowed the translation from Garfield, *The Fundamental Wisdom of the Middle Way,* p. 206.

142 Garfield, *The Fundamental Wisdom of the Middle Way,* p. 208.

143 Garfield, *The Fundamental Wisdom of the Middle Way,* p. 208.

144 Jeffrey Broughton, trans., *The Bodhidharma Anthology: The Earliest Records of Zen* (Berkeley: University of California Press, 1999), p. 19.

145 Sn 4.12, trans. by Thanissaro Bhikkhu.

146 *Rtsa shes ṭīk chen,* p. 412: *'o na rigs pa dgrug cu pa las/ myang ngan 'das pa bden gcig bu/ rgyal ba rnams kyis nam gsungs pa/ de tshe lhag ma log min zhes/ mkhas pa su zhig rtog par byed/ ces myang 'das gcig bu bden gyi gzhan rnams mi bden zhes gsungs pa je ltar drangs snyam na//.*

147 *Yuktiṣaṣṭikāvṛtti,* ff. 14–15: *'o na bcom ldan ldas kyis/ dge slong dag bden pa dam pa 'de ni gcig ste/ 'de lta ste mi slu ba'i chos can mya ngan las 'das pa'o/ /zhes gang gsungs pa de ji ltar zhe na/ /je ltar 'dus byas log par snang bas byis pa rnams la slu bar byed pa yin pa de bzhin du/ /mya ngan las 'das pa ni ma yin te/ rtag tu skye ba med par'i rang bzhin gyis ngo bo kho nar gnas pa nyid kyi phir ro/ /de ni byis pa rnams la yang 'dus byas ltar skye ba'i ngo gor nam yang mi snang ngo/ /de'i phir mya ngan las 'das pa ni rtag tu kho nar mya ngan las 'das pa nyid du gnas pa'i phir jig rten gyi tha snyad kho nas bden pa dam par gsungs kyi…//.* Cited in the *Rtsa shes ṭīk chen,* p. 312, and in Khedrub Jé's *Stong thun chen mo* (see Cabezón, *A Dose of Emptiness,* p. 360).

148 Garfield, *The Fundamental Wisdom of the Middle Way,* pp. 296–97.

149 *Nges don rab gsal,* p. 377a: *mthar thog bden pa gnyis su dbyer med pas grangs nges byar med de/ mdo las bden pa dam pa ni gcig kho na ste/ 'de lta ste/ mi slu ba'i chos can gyi myang ngan las 'das pa'o//.*

150 *Yuktiṣaṣṭikā* 35, pp. 91–92: *mya ngan 'das pa bden gcig bu/ rgyal ba rnams kyis nam gsungs pa/ de tshe lhag ma log min zhes/ mkhas pa su zhig rtog par byed//.* I borrowed the translation of this verse straight from Lindtner, *Master of Wisdom,* p. 35.

151 *Lta ba ngan sel,* f. 606: *'on na kun rdzob bden pa zhes pa'i tha snyad kyang mi 'thad par 'gyur te/ kun rdzob yin na bden pa yin pa 'gal ba'i phir/ de ni blo kun rdzob pa'i ngo bor bden ba la 'jog pas skyon med do/ yang dag kun rdzob ces pa yang/ blo kun rdzob pa la ltos nas yang dag tu 'jog pas skyon med do//.*

152 Gorampa, *Yang dag lta ba'i 'od zer* (hereafter, *Lta ba'i od zer*), *The Complete Works of the Sakya Scholars,* vol. 12 (Tokyo: Toyo Bunko, 1969), p. 287c: *med bzhin du snang ba sgyu ma dang tshungs//.*

153 Sakya Paṇḍita, *Gzhung lugs legs par bshad pa* (hereafter, *Gzhug lugs legs bshad*), the *Sakya bka' 'bum*, vol. 5 (Tokyo: Toyo Bunko, 1968), p. 72a: *kun rdzob tu chos thams cad chu'i zla ba ltar med bzhin du snang par rtog pa yin la//.*

154 *Gzhug lugs legs bshad*, p. 72b: *kun rdzob kyi bden pa'i mtshan nyid ni yod pa ma yin pa'i don snang ba'o//.*

155 *Nges don rab gsal*, p. 377a: *thabs dang thabs byung gi dbang du byas na tha snyad mthong pa'i blos dngos por gzung ba de nyid la gnas lugs dpyod pa'i blos ngos po ma rnyed pa nyid la don dam du 'jog dgos pa'i phir//.*

156 *Nges don rab gsal*, p. 370b: *'o na gdul byas don dam pa rtogs pa'i thabs med par 'ghur ro snam na gdul byas de rtogs pa'i don du tshig gyi brtod bya dang/ sems kyi spyod yul du tha snyad kyi bden par sgro btags nas bstan pa ste//.*

157 *Nges don rab gsal*, pp. 370a–371a: Gorampa offers an explicit and lengthy discussion on the superimposition of conventional truth and how it serves the purpose of reaching the ultimate truth.

158 When the truth is explained from the standpoint of ordinary disciples *('dul bya'i ngor)*, Gorampa maintains the four precise enumerations of the truth. They are apprehending subjects *(yul can)*, apprehended objects *(yul)*, actions *(byed pa)*, and potentials *(nus pa)*. See *Nges don rab gsal*, p. 377a–b: *gdul bya ngor bstan pa'i tshe/ yul can dang/ yul dang/ byed pa dang/ nus pa'i sgo nas grangs nges pa dang bzhi las dang po ni...yul can gyi blo la rmongs mar mongs sogs gnyis su grangs nges pa'o/ gnyis pa ni gzhugs sogs kyi snang ba gcig nyid la'ang ma dpyad pa'i blo ngor de dang der bden pa dang/ dpyad na mi rnyed pa gnyis su nges pa'o/ gsum pa ni 'ching bar byed pa dang/ grol bar byed pa gnyis su nges pa'o/ bzhi pa ni bsod nams kyi tshogs bsag pa dang/ ye shes kyi tshogs bsag pa'i gzhir gyur pas skyu gnyis thob pa gnyis su zhugs pa'o//.*

159 Sakya Paṇḍita stresses the notion that the enumeration of truth represents two conflicting perspectives, and thus they are contradictory. A mistaken cognition and an unmistaken cognition are contradictory. For him there is neither a thing that belongs to both categories that can be positively affirmed, nor a thing that does not belong to either of the two categories that can be repudiated. Hence the existence of the third alternative is not possible. Therefore twofold truth is, according to him, a precise enumeration. See *Thub pa dgongs gsal*, p. 32a–b: *bden pa bzhi dang bcu drug la sogs pa gsungs bzhin du gnyis su grangs nges pa'i rgyu mtshan ci yin zhe na/ ...'dir ngos 'gal gyi mtha' rnam par dpyod pa las gnyis su nges te/ 'de ltar blo 'khrul ma 'khrul gnyis dngos 'gal yin la/ de'i sar na gnyis ka yin bsgrub phyogs dang/ gnyis ka ma yin pa dgag phyogs kyi phung po gsum pa mi srid pas bden ba gnyis su grangs nges so//; Gzhung lugs legs bshad*, p. 72d: *yul can gyi blo 'khrul pa dang/ ma khrul pa gnyis la ltso nas bden pa gnyis su nges pa yin no//.*

160 Longchenpa proposes an enumeration based on a direct contradiction between the transcendence and the nontranscendence of elaborations *(spros pa las grol ma grol)*. See *Grub mtha' mdzod*, ff. 205–6: *spros ba las grol ma grol dngos 'gal du nges pas bsgrub phyogs dang dgag phyogs kyi phung po gsum ba khegs pas gnyis su grangs nges so// rnam pa gcig tu na yul rnam ni yul can las ltos nas 'jog pa na yul can ni mthar mthog pa 'khrul pa'i blo dang/ mthar thog pa ma 'khrul pa'i blo gnyis las mi 'da'/ de la 'khor ba'i chos rnams ni 'khrul pa dang chos nyid ni ma 'khrul pa'i yul yin pas blo'i dbang gis gnyis su bzhag ste//.*

161 *Dbu 'jug rnam bshad*, p. 122: *bden pa la ltos nas brdzun par rnam par 'jog la/ brdzun pa la ltos nas bden par rnam par 'jog pa'i phir ro//.*

162 *Dbu ma tsa ba'i rnam bshad zab mo'i di kho na nyid snang ba (Dbu tsa'i rnam bshad)* (Sarnath: Sakya Students' Union, 1995), p. 287: *yul can mthong ba brdzun pa dang/ mthong ba yang dag pa gnyis su nges pas/ gnyis su grangs nges par bzhad ste//.* Also see Rongtön, *Rigs tsogs dka' gnad,* f. 22: *yul can gyi blo la gnas tshul la zhugs ma zhugs gnyis su nges pa'i dbang gis yul gnyis su nges par bzhag ste/ phung po gsum pa gzhan med pa'i phir blo la ltos nas bden pa gnyis su nges so//.*

163 *Grub mtha'i rnam bshad,* f. 263: *'di'i dbye bar bya ba'i ngo bo'am ris ni gnyis kho na ste/ slu chos kun rdzob kyi bden pa dang/ bslu med don dam gyi bden pa'o...rig pa yang/ thabs phyogs gtso bor byas pa'i blang dor la kun rdzob ming du mi rung zhing/ blang dor gtso bo rnam dag gi dmigs pa la don dam med du mi rung bas nyung na mi 'du zhing de tsam gyis skyes bu'i don thams cad tshogs par 'gyur bas mang mi dgos pa'i phir ro//.*

164 Shakya Chogden is a monist regarding the truth. He rejects the enumeration of truth while arguing the logical plausibility of a single truth. See *Theg pa chen po dbu ma rnam par nges pa'i bang mdzod lung rigs rgya mtsho las bden pa gnyis kyi rnam bzhag le'u bzhi pa* (hereafter, *Bden gnyis rnam gzhag*), *The Complete Works,* vol. 15 (Thimphu, Bhutan: Kunzang Tobgey, 1975), ff. 7–8: Here Shakya Chogden attacks Khedrub Jé's account of the precise enumeration of the two truths. Yet he does enumerate the truth based on contradictions between the deceptive and the nondeceptive standpoints. For this see Shakya Chogden, *Dbu ma rtsa ba'i rnam bshad skal bzang 'jug ngogs* (hereafter, *Dbu rtsa'i rnam bshad*), *The Complete Works,* vol. 5 (Thimpu, Bhutan: Kunzang Tobgey, 1975), f. 222: *grangs nges pa yin te/ bslu mi slu phan tshun spangs te gnas pa'i 'gal ba yin pas so//.*

165 *Klu sgrub dgongs rgyan,* pp. 214–15, 222, 277.

166 Shakya Chogden, *Bden gnyis rnam gzhag,* ff. 9–10: *bod snga ma rnams kyi bden pa gnyis kyi rnam gzhag 'chad pa de ni yul can gi blo 'khrul ma 'khrul gnyis su grangs nges pa'i rgyu mtshan gyis de gnyis la phung sum sel ba'i rnam gzhag mdzad pa yin gyi/ phi rabs pa rnams 'chad pa ltar yul bden pa gnyis kyis grangs nges tshad mas grub par 'chad pa ni gcig kyang mi snang no//.*

167 *Grub mtha' mdzod,* f. 145: *kun rdzob bden pa'i mtshan nyid ni chos can gang zhig rig pas dpyad mi bsod pa/ don dam bden pa'i mtshan nyid gang zhig rig pas dpyad bzod pa//.* Also f. 200: *de ltar rigs shes rjes dpag gyi rang bzhin skye med spros pa la dpyad bzod don dam bden pa'i mtshan nyid yin no shes dbu ma rang rgyud par rnams 'dod pa yin no//.*

168 *Bden gnyis rnam gzhag,* f. 6: *mdor na dbu ma'i rang lugs la kun rdzob bden pa yod par khas len pa 'de ni zla ba'i zhabs kyi phyogs snga sma ba kho na yin te/ sems tsam pas gzhan dbang kun rdzob tu bden grub yin par rang lugs su bshad pa dang khyad par mi snang pa'i phir dang/ rang lugs la bden pa gcig kho nar nges gsung pa dang 'gal ba'i phir//;* f. 7: *shes bya thams cad bden pa gnyis su grangs nges pa zhes bya ba 'de dbum ma'i rang lugs ma yin te/ dbu ma'i rang lugs la gnas skabs su bden pa ni gcig khno na yin par...//;* f. 8: *mdor na/ dbu ma'i rang lugs la gnas skabs kyi bden ba don dam pa'i bden pa gcig pu yin la//.*

169 *Grub mtha'i rnam bshad,* f. 305: *legs par dpyad na myang'das dang de las lhag pa'i chos kyang grub pa med mod rig shes kyis cung zad dpyad ngor bslu med ni/ mya ngan 'das pa bden gcig pur// gang tshe sangs rgyas rnams gsung ba// zhes pa ltar/ myang 'das kno na yin par bzhed pa'i phir//.*

170 Mipham Rinpoche, *Dam chos dogs sel* (Sarnath: Nyingmapa Students' Welfare Committee, 1993), p. 602: *de lta bu'i de bzhin nyid dam de ni bden par grub pa yin*

te/ kun rdzob rnams mi bden pa rdzun pa blu ba'i chos su grub la/ de dang dral ba don dam ni bden pa rdzun med pa mi slu ba'i chos su grub ste/ de ma grub na 'phags pa'i bden pa mthong ba'ang mi srid de rdzun pa bslu ba'i don mthong bas tha mal pa ltar su yang grol bar mi 'gyur ro/ mgon po klus/ bcom ldan 'das kyis chos gang zhig/ rdzun pa de ni bgrub par gsungs shes dang/ /mya ngan 'das pa bden gcig pur/ /rgyal ba rnams kyis gang gsungs pa/ /de tshe lhag ma log pa zhes/ /mkhas pa su zhig rtog mi byed/ /ces gsung pa bzhin no//. In this passage Mipham not only attempts to show that ultimate truth is the only truth but also takes one step further to show that ultimate truth is an absolute, therefore truly existent *(bden par grub pa).*

171 *Dag brgyud grub pa'i shing rta,* f. 302: *des na grub mtha gong 'od thams cad kyi lugs gang la rigs pas gnod pa med cing dpyad bzod ni don dam dang des las ldog pa kun rdzob.../I.*

172 *Klu sgrub dgongs rgyan,* pp. 214–15, 222, 277.

173 "Ontologically, nirvāṇa is a world beyond saṃsāra," he writes in *The Master of Wisdom,* p. 321.

174 In his introduction to *The Conception of Buddhist Nirvāṇa,* see pp. 51–59. Also see p. 70: "In Mahāyāna we have, on the other hand, a denial of real elements *(dharma-nairātmya),* and an assertion of the absolute Whole *(dharma-kāya).* In Hīnayāna, we have a radical pluralism; in Mahāyāna, we have a radical monism"; and p. 72: "Just as Mahāyāna moved towards radical Monism, even so Brāhmanism moved towards radical Monism. It is most probable that Mahāyāna is indebted to some Upaniṣadic influence."

175 See *The Conception of Buddhist Nirvāṇa,* p. 19: "...the system of pluralism which is taught in Hīnayāna and to the monist view which is the central conception of Mahāyāna."

176 His introductory notes to *The Mādhyamika Dialectic and the Philosophy of Nāgārjuna,* p. xxvi, state: "In fact, there is only one truth—the Absolute. The other—saṃvṛtisatya, is truth so-called in common parlance, it is totally false from the Absolute standpoint." And on p. 20: "In early Buddhism they correspond to a pluralistic universe, in Mahāyāna to a monistic"; p. 47: "The Mādhyamika system started with an entirely different conception of reality. Real was that possessed as reality of its own *(sva-bhāva),* what was not produced by causes *(akṛtaka=asaṃskṛta),* what was not dependent upon anything else *(paratra nirpekṣa).*"

177 *Bden gnyis rnam gzhag,* ff. 15–16*: 'phags pa'i mnyam gzhag la ltos nas ni bden pa gcig kyang ma gzhag ste/ des ni bden pa phar zhog gang du yang ma gzhigs pa'i phir ro/ /mthar spros pa thams cad dang dral ba'i rjes kyi shes pa la ltos nas ni bden ba gcig kyang ma gzhag ste/ de'i tshe ni shes bya'i mtshan ma ji snyed pa thams cad brdzun par bzhag dgos pa'i phir ro// ...de ltar na mthar thug la ltos nas bden pa mi srid la/ gnas skabs su bden pa mtshan nyid pa don dam pa'i bden pa dang btags pa kun rdzob kyi bden pa'o/ /de'i shes byed kyang bden 'dzin gyi ngor bden na bden par 'gal pa la thug pa yin no//.* Here Shakya Chogden reinforces the idea that ultimate truth is the only real truth from the Madhyamaka standpoint. However ultimate truth is not treated as the absolute truth. "Ultimately," he says, "it is to be proven false, because every object of knowledge is posited as false." Although he talks about the conventional truth in great detail, he does not take truth from the Madhyamaka standpoint. Hence his monistic position still stands. Another crucial point to be noted here is his

categorical rejection of the dual objective basis of the two truths. He writes, f. 17: *chos can gcig gi steng du kun rdzob kyi rang bzhin dang don dam pa'i kyi rang bzhin gnyis ka bden pa mi srid pa'i phir//.* For further clarification, see ff. 17–18, 21–22.

178 *Grub mtha'i rnam bshad,* f. 305: *legs par dpyad na myang'das dang de las lhag pa'i chos kyang grub pa med mod rig shes kyis cung zad dpyad ngor bslu med ni/ mya ngan 'das pa bden gcig pur// gang tshe sangs rgyas rnams gsung ba// zhes pa ltar/ myang 'das kno na yin par bzhed pa'i phir//.*

179 Mipham Rinpoche, *Dam chos dogs gsel,* ff. 602–3: *de lta bu'i de bzhin nyid dam de ni bden par grub pa yin te/ kun rdzob rnams mi bden pa rdzun pa bslu ba'i cho su grub la/ de dang dral ba don dam ni bden pa rdzun med pa mi bslu ba'i chos su grub ste/ de ma grub na phags pa'i bden pa mthong ba'am mi srid de rdzun pa bslu ba'i don mthong bas tha mal ba ltar su yang grol bar mi 'gyur ro/ ... yang dag kun rdzob lta bu tha snyad du bden pa yin kyang gnyis snang dang bcas pa'i blo yi yul kun rdzob ba de dag rigs pas dpyad mi bzod pa yin pa'i phir bden grub min la/ chos nyid don dam par gang yin pa ni bden grub yin te/ gnyis snang med pa'i blo ye shes kyis yul du grub pa gang zhig/ /de la rigs pa gang gis kyang gzhig cing gzhom pa'i rgyu ba mi 'jug pa'i dpyad bzod pa yin pa'i phir/ /de na rigs pa'i dpyad mi bzod pa ji srid du ni don dam ma yin de/ kun rdzob tu thal ba'i phir//.*

180 *Nāgārjuna: The Philosophy of the Middle Way,* p. 69: "*Artha* as well as *paramārtha* are truths *(satya).* The former [conventional truth] is not presented as an un-truth *(a-satya)* in relation to the latter [ultimate truth], as it would be in an absolutistic tradition. Neither is the former sublated by the latter; there is no indication whatsoever that these are two truths with different standing as higher and lower."

181 *Empty Words: Buddhist Philosophy and Cross-Cultural Interpretation,* pp. 24–25: "This dual thesis of the conventional reality of phenomena together with their lack of inherent existence depends upon the complex doctrine of the Two Truths or Two Realities—a conventional or nominal truth and an ultimate truth—and upon a subtle and surprising doctrine regarding their relation. It is, in fact, this sophisticated development of the doctrine of the Two Truths as a vehicle for understanding Buddhist metaphysics and epistemology that is Nāgārjuna's greatest philosophical contribution."

182 *Meditation on Emptiness,* pp. 418–19: "...the division of the two truths is not an ontological division. Both exist only conventionally *(saṃvṛtisat, kun rdzob tu yod pa)* with *saṃvṛti* here referring to a valid dualistic cognizer; both truths exist for valid dualistic cognizers and not in ultimate analysis. The division of the two truths emphasizes two types of objects of consciousness, truths and falsities. Both, however, are falsely existent or falsely established because neither is independent; each depends on its imputing consciousness and on the other...The division into two truths on epistemological grounds is a call to eradicate ignorance and to attain the highest wisdom."

183 *Mahāyāna Buddhism: The Doctrinal Foundations* (London: Routledge, 1996), p. 71: "Conventional and ultimate are not two distinct realities, two realms opposed to each other. It should be clear that the ultimate, emptiness, is what is ultimately the case concerning the object under investigation. It is what makes the object a conventional entity and not an ultimate one, as we think it is. Emptiness makes the conventional conventional. Conventional and ultimate are thus not separate."

184 Newland, *The Two Truths,* p. 60: "That the two truths are 'different isolates' means, for example, that a table and its emptiness can be distinguished in terms of how they are understood by a conceptual consciousness. To say that two things are different isolates is to make only the most minimal distinction between them."

185 "Metaphysics for Mādhyamikas," in Dreyfus and McClintock, eds., *The Svātantrika-Prāsaṅgika Distinction,* pp. 114–15: "It is important that *saṃvṛtisatya* is not misunderstood as being just a purely conventional and arbitary agreement in the way in which the moon's being called 'that which has a rabbit' *(śaśin)* is just a purely conventional agreement. What is true for the world, be it the impermanence of phenomena or the law of cause and effect, is so not just because of simple conventional agreements on arbitrary words—whether we are Svātantrika or Prāsaṅgika, *saṃvṛtisatya* is deeper than that." This statement clearly suggests that Tillemans does not consider *saṃvṛtisatya* is entirely a projection of one's mind in that it has an ontological basis.

186 Cabezón, *A Dose of Emptiness,* p. 516n1128: "Although having the same referent, they [the two truths] have different names, different designations, being the opposites of different entities *qua* names."

187 D.S. Ruegg, *The Literature of the Madhayamaka School of Philosophy in India* (Wiesbaden: Otto Harrassowitz, 1981), pp. 3, 16; J.W. de Jong, "The Problem of the Absolute," *Journal of Indian Philosophy* 2: 3; Paul Williams, "Tsong-khapa on kun-rdzob-bden-pa," in Aris and Aung, eds., *Tibetan Studies in Honour of Hugh Richardson* (New Delhi: Vikas, 1980), p. 325; Nathan Katz's diagram, demonstrating conventional truth as a subdivision of truth, in Hajime Nakamura, *Indian Buddhism* (Hirakata City: Kansai University of Foreign Studies Press, 1980), p. 285.

188 Newland, *The Two Truths,* p. 262.

189 See Cabezón, *Dose of Emptiness,* pp. 355–79 on Khedrub Jé and 514–19 on his research findings on this issue of the two truths; Helmut Tauscher, "Phya pa chos kyi senge ge as a Svātantrika," in Dreyfus and McClintock, eds., *The Svātantrika-Prāsaṅgika Distinction,* pp. 207–38; Kapstein, "The Trouble with Truth," pp. 205–20; Kapstein, "Abhayākaragupta on the Two Truths," pp. 393–417; M. Sprung, ed., *The Problem of the Two Truths in Buddhism and Vedanta* (Dordrecht: Reidel, 1973), for a collection of useful articles; C.W. Huntington, "The System of Two Truths in the *Prasannapadā* and the *Madhyamakāvatāra:* A Study in Madhyamaka Soteriology," *Journal of Indian Philosophy* 11 (1983): 77–106; F. Streng, "The Buddhist Doctrine of Two Truths," *Journal of Indian Philosophy* 1 (1971): 262–71; Christian Lindtner, "Atiśa's Introduction to the Two Truths, and Its Sources," *Journal of Indian Philosophy* 9 (1981): 161–214; and G.M. Nagao, "An Interpretation of the Term *Saṃvṛti* (Convention) in Buddhism," *Silver Jubilee Volume of the Zinbun Kagaku Kenkyo,* pp. 550–61; Guy Newland, *The Two Truths,* provides a detailed analysis of Gelugpas' presentation of the two truths; Geshe Sopa and Jeffrey Hopkins, *The Practice and Theory of Tibetan Buddhism,* offers a summary of Gelugpas' view on this subject.

190 *Mahāratnakūṭa Sūtra* 4:7, Garma C.C. Chang, trans., *A Treasury of Mahāyāna Sūtras: Sections from the Mahāratnakūṭa Sūtra* (Delhi: Motilal Banarsidass, 2002), p. 64.

191 "Meaning" and "sense" are here being used to translate the Tibetan term *sdra bshad,* which normally refers not merely to meaning but also has connotations of

"etymology." Since most of the discussion focuses on the various senses or meanings associated with the two truths, rather than on any strict etymological analysis, I have chosen to discuss just meaning or sense rather than etymology.

192 Candrakīrti, *Prasannapadā*, p. 415: *kun nas sgrib pas na kun rdzob ste/ mi shes pa ni dngos po'i de kho na nyid la kun nas 'gebs par byed pa'i phir kun rdzob ces bya'o/ yang na phan tshun brten pas na kun rdzob ste/ phan tshun brten pa nyid kyis na zhes bya ba'i don to/ yang na kun rdzob ni brda ste/ 'jig rten gyi tha snyad ces bya ba'i tha tshig go/ de yang brjod pa dang brjod bya dang/ shes pa dang shes bya la sogs pa'i mtshan nyid can no//.* The translation of this passage is borrowed from Newland, *The Two Truths,* p. 76.

193 See Garfield, *The Fundamental Wisdom of the Middle Way,* p. 297, for his brief reflection on the three distinct meanings; Newland, *The Two Truths,* pp. 77–89, also offers his reading of Gelugpas' presentation of the three meanings of *saṃvṛti.*

194 Tsongkhapa, *Rtsa shes ṭīk chen,* pp. 402–3: *[1] kun rdzob ni mi shes pa'm ma rig pa ste dgnos po'i de kho na nyid 'gebs shing sgrib par byed pa'i phir ro/ 'di ni kun rdzob kyi skad dod sgrib pa la'ang 'jug pas de'i cha nas bshad pa yin gyi kun rdzob thams cad sgrib byed du bshad pa min no/ [2] yang na kun rdzob ni phan tshun brten pa yin pa'i don no/ 'di ni phan tshun brten dgos pas na rang la tshugs thub kyi rang bzhin yod pa mi bden pa'i don no/ tshul de'i sgra bshad pa'i rgyu mtshan don dam bden pa la yang yod mod kyang kun rdzob pa'i sgra 'jug pa ni min te/ dper na mtsho skyes kyi sgra bshad pa'i rgyu mtshan sbal pa la yod kyang mi 'jug pa bzhin no/ [3] yang na kun rdzob ni brda ste 'jig rten gyi tha snyad do/ 'de yang brjod bya dang rjod byed dang shes pa dang shes phya la sogs pa'i mtshan nyid can du bshad pas yul can gyi tha snyad shes brjod tsam la bzung ngo//.* My translations of the three meanings of *saṃvṛti* are largely taken from Newland, *The Two Truths,* pp. 77–86.

195 Gorampa, *Nges don rab gsal,* p. 377b*: [1] kun nas grib pas na kun rdzob ste/ mi shes pa ni dngos po'i de kho na nyid la kun nas 'gebs par byed pa'i phir kun rdzob ces bya'o/ [2] yang na phan tshun brtan pas na kun rdzob ste/ phan tshun brtan ba nyid kyis na zhes bya ba'i don te/ [3] yang na kun rdzob ni brda ste/ 'jig rten gyi tha snyad ces bya ba'i tha tshig go/ de yang brjod pa dang brjod bya dang/ shes pa dang shes bya la sogs pa'i mtshan nyid can no//.*

196 Newland, *The Two Truths,* p. 77, consistently translates *saṃvṛtisatya (kun brdzob bden pa)* as "concealer-truth" and seems to treat *saṃvṛtisatya* and *concealer-truth* as equal, assuming it as the Gelugpas' standard reading. I use his term *concealer-truth* in the context where *saṃvṛti* is specifically referred to as primal ignorance; however, I do not consider them equivalent. Especially for Tsongkhapa, *saṃvṛti* carries a much wider application. All phenomenal objects can be described as *saṃvṛtisatya* but certainly not as concealer-truth, because phenomenal objects themselves do not conceal truth. Rather they are the truths. However Newland's rendition is consistent with Gorampa's reading, for in the case of Gorampa, every *saṃvṛtisatya* amounts to concealing the underlying truth. Phenomena are seen as total illusions.

197 Tsongkhapa, *Dgongs pa rab gsal,* p. 185. Also see *Rtsa shes ṭīk chen,* p. 403–4. Khedrub Jé (see Cabezón, *A Dose of Emptiness,* p. 361) offers a similar explanation.

198 Gorampa, *Nges don rab gsal,* p. 377b: *dang po ni/ saṃvṛtisatya zhes pa'i saṃ ni samyag ste yang dag pa/ vṛti ni sgrib par byed pa ste yang dag pa'i don la sgrib par byed pas na kun brtags dang lhan skyes so sor ma phye ba'i bden 'dzin gyi gti mug ni kun rdzob kyi*

mtshan gzhi ste yang dag pa'i don la sgrib par byed pa'i phir ro/ satya ni bden pa ste blo de'i ngor bden par snang bas na bden pa'o//.

199 *Lta ba ngan sel,* ff. 595–96: *lam gyi dgag bya ni 'khrul ba'i snang ba mtha' dag yin la/ 'der lung rigs kyi dgag bya gnyis las/ dang po yang kun btags kyi ma rig pas btags pa dang/ lhan skyes kyi ma rig pas btags pa gnyis...gnyis pa yul can ni/ yul de dang der rtog pa'i blo dang lta ba ngan pa thams cad yin te//.*

200 *Lam rim chen mo,* p. 651–52: *phyin ci log gi 'dzin pa la dgag byar gsungs pa dang des bzung pa'i rang bzhin yod pa la dgag byar mdzad pa gnyis yod do//.*

201 *Lam rim chen mo,* p. 652: *'on kyang dgag bya'i gtso bo ni phyi ma yin te/ yul can phyin ci log ldog pa des bzung pa'i yul thog mar dgag dgos pa's so//.*

202 *Lam rim chen mo,* p. 652: *dgag bya 'di ni shes bya la med pa zhig dgos ste/ yod na dgag par mi nus pa'i phyir ro//.*

203 *Lam rim chen mo,* p. 652: *de lta yin na yang yod par 'dzin pas sgro 'dogs skye bas dgag dgos la//.* For more elaborations on Gelugpas' position on the epistemological and soteriological objects of negation, see Geshe Yeshe Tabkhé (Dge shes Ye shes thabs mkhas), *Shar tsong kha pa'i drang ba dang nges pa'i don rnam par 'byed pa'i bstan bcos legs bshad snying po* (hereafter, *Drang nges*) (Sarnath: CIHTS, 1997), pp. 161–62; Jamyang Shepai Dorje ('Jam dbyangs Bzhad ba'i rdo rje), *Grub mtha'i rnam bshad kun bzang zhing gi nyi ma* (hereafter, *Grub mtha' rnam bshad*) (Tsho sngon: Kan su'i Mi rigs Press, 1992), pp. 811–16; Changkya Rölpai Dorje (Lcang skya Rol pa'i rdo rje), *Gub mtha' thub stan lhun po'i mdzes rgyan* (hereafter, *Grub mtha' mdzes rgyan*) (Tsho sngon: Mtsho sngon Mi rigs Par khang, 1989), pp. 284–88; Thub stan chos grags, *Spyod 'jug gi 'grel bshad rgyal sras yon tan bum bzang* (hereafter, *Spyod 'jug 'grel bshad*) (Tsho sngon: Mi rigs Press, 1990), pp. 720-24; and Khedrub Jé (see Cabezón, *A Dose of Emptiness*), pp. 92–96, 161–62.

204 Jayānanda, *Madhyamakāvatārasyaṭīkā* (Tokyo: University of Tokyo, 1978), p. 73d: *sgrib pa ni nram pa gnyis te/ nyon mongs pa'i sgrib pa can gyi dang/ nyon mongs pa can ma yin par ma rig pa'o/ de la nyon mongs pa can gyi ma rig pa ni 'khor ba'i rgyun 'jug ba'i rgyu yin la/ nyon mongs pa can ma yin pa'i ma rig pa ni gzugs la sogs pa snang pa'i rgu yin no//.*

205 *Dgongs pa rab gsal,* p. 185: *kun rdzob pa gang gi ngor 'jog pa'i kun rdzob ngos 'dzin pa yin gyi/ kun rdzob pa spyi ngo 'dzin pa min no//.*

206 See Tsongkhapa, *Rtsa shes ṭīk chen,* p. 402, for his first sense of *kun rdzob.*

207 *Rtsa shes ṭīk chen,* p. 404: *nyon mongs pa can gyi ma rig pa'i dbang gis kun rdzob kyi bden pa rnam par bzhag go//.*

208 *Dgongs pa rab gsal,* p. 186: *kun rdzob bden 'dzin de'i mthus sngon po la sogs pa gang zhig/ rang bzhin gyis grub ma med bzhin du der snang bar bcos pa'i bcos ma sems can rnams la bden par snang ba de ni/ sngar bshad pa'i 'jig rten gyi phyin ci log gi kun rdzob pa de'i ngor bden pas 'jig rten gyi kun rdzob gyi bden pa zhes thub pa des gsungs te//.*

209 *Dgongs pa rab gsal,* p. 186: *rang zhin de...ni kun rdzob kye bden pa ma yin no//.*

210 *Dgongs pa rab gsal,* p. 188: *bden 'dzin des bzhag pa ni rang gi tha snyad du yang mi srid par bzhad pa'i phir ro//.*

211 *Rtsa shes ṭīk chen,* pp. 404–5: *nyon mongs pa can gyi ma rig pa ni bden 'dzin yin pas dis bzung pa'i don tha snyad du yang mi srid pa'i phir dang/ kun rdzob kyi bden pa yin na tha snyad du yod pas khab pa'i phir ro//.*

212 *Dgongs pa rab gsal,* p. 404: *dnos po la bden par grub pa me srid pas bden par 'jog pa ni blo'i ngor yin la/ bden 'dzin min pa'i blo ngor bden par gzhag tu med pa'i phir ro//.*

213 Kalupahana, *Nāgārjuna,* p. 85.

214 Tsongkhapa, *Rtsa shes ṭīk chen,* p. 404: *bden pa ni ma yin te bden par mngon par rlom pa med pa'i phir ro//.*

215 *Rtsa shes ṭīk chen,* p. 404: *byis pa rnams ni slu bar byid pa yin la des las gzhan pa rnams la ni sgyu ma la sogs pa ltar rten cing 'brel par 'byung ba nyid kyis kun rdzob tsam du 'gyur ro//.*

216 *Rtsa shes ṭīk chen,* p. 405: *nyon mongs can gyi ma rig pa'i kun rdzob spangs pa rnams la/ gang gi ngor bden par 'jog pa'i bden zhen gyi kun rdzob med pa'i rgyu mtshan gis/ 'du 'byed rnams de dag gi ngor mi bbden par bsgrubs kyi kun rdzob bden pa ma yin par ma bsgrubs pa'i phir ro//.*

217 *Rtsa shes ṭīk chen,* p. 405: *nyon mongs can gyi ma rig pa'i kun rdzob spangs pa rnams la/ gang gi ngor bden par 'jog pa'i bden zhen gyi kun rdzob med pa'i rgyu mtshan gis/ 'du 'byed rnams de dag gi ngor mi bden par bsgrubs kyi kun rdzob bden par ma yin par ma bsgrubs pa'i phir ro//.*

218 *Lta ba ngan sel,* f. 611: *'phags pa gsum gyi rjes thob la snang ba'i 'du 'byed kyi cha de yang yang dag sbrib gyed de gnyis snang gyi bag chags kyi dbang gyis byung bas snang med kyi mnyam gzhag la sgrib par byed pa'i phir ro//.* Jaideva Singh, *The Conception of Buddhist Nirvāṇa,* p. 53, echoes Gorampa's view when he says: "Phenomena are characterized as *saṃvṛti,* because they throw a veil over Reality."

219 *Madhyamakāvatārasyaṭīkā,* p. 73b–c: *gal te nyon mongs pa can gyi ma rig pa log pa yin na de'i tshe sgyu ma la sogs pa ltar rten cing 'brel par 'byung pa rnams ci ltar snang zhe na/ . . . shes bya'i sgrib pa'i mtshan nyid can ma rig pa tsam kun du spyod pa'i phir//.*

220 Tsongkhapa, *Drang nges legs bshad snying po* (hereafter, *Legs bshad snying po*). In Geshe Yeshé Tabkhé's *Shar tsong kha pa'i drang ba dang nges pa'i don rnam par byed pa'i bstan bcos legs bshad snying po* (Sarnath: CIHTS, 1997), p. 138: *de ltar rgu dang rkyen la brten nas 'byung ba'i gtan tshigs nyid kyis chos rnams las rang gi mtshan nyid kyis grub pa'i rang bzhin med do//.*

221 *Legs bshad snying po,* p. 141: *chos can rten 'brel dang chos nyid don dam pa'i bden pa gnyis rten dang rten par yod pa ni tha snyad pa'i shes ngor yin la. . ./ chos can med na chos nyid yan gar ba gnas pa'i mthu med. . ./.*

222 *Nges don rab gsal,* p. 377c: *saṃ zhes pa ni rten pa'am ltos pa la 'jug la vṛti ni 'jug pa ste brten nas 'jug pa'am ltos nas 'jug pa 'o//.*

223 *Nges don rab gsal,* p. 382b: *thog ma med pa'i bden 'dzhin gyi bag chags sam tshe 'der grub mtha' ngan pa thos pa'i rkyen gyis yod med sogs kyi mtha' gang rung gcig bzung nas dngos po de'i ngor sgro btags pas na rnyed ces pa'i tha snyad 'jog ste//.*

224 Murti, T.R.V., *The Central Philosophy of Buddhism* (London: Allen & Unwin, 1955), pp. 244–45.

225 See his introduction to *The Conception of Buddhist Nirvāṇa,* p. 53.

226 *Mahāratnakūṭa Sūtra,* 1. See Chang, *Mahāyāna Sūtras,* p. 20.

227 Tom Tillemans, following Mark Siderits, adopts "customary" for *saṃvṛti* in place of conventional. See Tillemans, "Metaphysics for Mādhyamikas," p. 114, n. 4.

228 *Prasannapadā,* p. 415: *yang na kun rdzob ni brda ste/ 'jig rten gyi tha snyad ces bya ba'i tha tshig go/ de yang brjod pa dang brjod bya dang/ shes pa dang shes bya la sogs pa'i mtshan nyid can no//.*

229 *Rtsa shes ṭīk chen,* p. 403: *Yul can gyi tha snyad shes brjod tsam la mi bzung ngo//.*

230 *Nges don rab gsal,* p. 377c: *saṃ ni saṅket zhes pa brda yin la vṛti ni snga ma ltar te brda 'jug pas na kun rdzob ste//.*

231 *Nges don rab gsal,* p. 377c: *de gnyis la'ang satya zhes pa sbyar ba'i tshe ltos nas 'jug pa'ang yin blo 'khrul ba'i ngor bden pa'ang yin pas na kun rdzob bden pa dang/ brda 'jug pa yin//.*

232 Candrakīrti, *Madhyamakāvatāra* 6:28, p. 156. Also cited in the *Madhyamakāvatārabhāṣya,* p. 102: *gti mug rang bzhin sgrib phir kun rdzob ste// des gang bcos ma bden par snang de ni// kun rdzob bden zhes thub pa des gsungs te// bcos mar gyur pa'i dngos ni kun rdzob tu'o//.* I disagree with Huntington's translation of this stanza. He clearly equates the first *kun rdzob* and the latter *kun rdzob,* treating both as having the same meaning, and thus unambiguously renders both with what he describes as the "screen," a Tibetan equivalent of *sgrib byed.* See *The Emptiness of Emptiness,* p. 160.

233 *Dgongs pa rab gsal,* p. 186: *rkang pa dang pos stan pa'i kun rdzob dang/ rkang pa phyi ma gnyis kyis bstan pa'i kun rdzob gnyis gcig tu me bya ste//.*

234 *Dgongs pa rab gsal,* p. 185: *rang bzhin gyis yod par sgro 'dogs par byed pa yin lugs kyi rang bzhin mthong ba la sgrib pa'i bdag nyid can ni kur rdzob bo//.*

235 *Dgongs pa rab gsal,* p. 185: *kun rdzob pa gang gi ngor 'jog pa'i kun rdzob ngos 'dzin pa yin gyi/ kun rdzob pa spyir ngos 'dzin pa min no//.*

236 *Dgongs pa rab gsal,* p. 185: *kun de ni kun rdzob kyi skad dod sgrib byed la yang 'jug pas sgrib byed do//.*

237 *Rtsa shes ṭīk chen,* pp. 404–5: *kun rdzob kyi bden pa yin na tha snyad du yod pas khyab pa'i phir ro//.*

238 *Rtsa shes ṭīk chen,* p. 404: *nyon mongs can gyi ma rig pa ni bden 'dzhin yin pas dis bzung ba'i don tha snyad du yang mi srid pa'i phir//.*

239 *Madhyamakāvatārabhāṣya,* p. 103: *de'i phir de dang gang zhig kun rdzob tu yang rdzun pa ni kun rdzob kyi bden pa ma yin no//.*

240 Tillemans, "Metaphysics for Mādhyamikas," p. 114n4.

241 Tillemans, "Metaphysics for Mādhyamikas," p. 115.

242 *Grub mtha' mdzod,* f. 193: *saṃvṛti zhes bya ba sgrib par byed pas na kun rdzob ste/ yang dag pa'i don la sgrib par byed pa 'khrul pa'i shes pa'o/ de'i yul du bden pas na bden pa ste gzugs la sogs pa sna tsogs pa'i chos snang pa'i ngo bo rmi lam dang 'dra ba 'de nyid do//.*

243 *Gzung lugs legs bshad,* f. 72b: *kun rdzob bden pa'i ngo bo ni/ snang ba yul dang yul can te/ gzung 'dzin gyis bsdus pa'i chos thams cad do/ de dag la ci'i phyir kun rdzob kyi bden pa zhes bya zhe na/ kun ni shes bya'i gnas yin la/ rdzob ni sgrib ba ste//.* Sakya Paṇḍita's dialectical structure seems to differ slightly in the sense that for him, *kun* refers to the mode of being of all objects and *rdzob* refers to all objects of knowledge because they are the ones that conceal their own mode of being. Also see his *Thub pa dgongs gsal,* f. 32b.

244 *Bden gnyis rnam gzhag,* f. 30: *dbang po'i ni... ma rig pa la kun rdzob ces bya zhing/ de la'ang nyon mongs pa can yin min gnyis las/ dang po'i ngor bden pa na bden pa zhes bya'o// gnyis pa ni/ phan tshun brten pas na kun rdzob ces bya ste mi bden pa zhes bya ba'i don to// gsum pa ni/ 'jig rten gyi tha snyad kyis bzhag pas ni kun rdzob ces bya ste/ don dam par ma grub pa zhes bya ba'i don to// gsum po de yang/ go rim bzhin du

saṃvṛti zhes dang/ saṃketu zhes dang/ saṃbhar zhes bya ba'i sgra las drangs pa'o//. Also see ff. 30–31 for more on this issue.

245 *Dbu tsa'i rnam bshad zab mo,* p. 288.

246 In his introduction to *Mādhyamika Dialectic and the Philosophy of Nāgārjuna,* p. xxv, he argues that "as etymology shows, *saṃvṛti* is that which covers up entirely the real nature of things and makes them appear otherwise. In this sense it is identical with *avidyā,* the categorizing function of the mind-reasoning...It may also mean the mutual dependence of things—their relativity. In this sense it is equated with phenomena, and is in direct contrast with the absolute, which is, by itself, unrelated. The third definition of *saṃvṛti* is that which is of conventional nature *(saṃketa),* depending as it does on what is usually accepted by the common folk *(lokavyavahāra).*"

247 *Dgongs pa rab gsal,* p. 190: *nyon mongs can gyi ma rig pa ni... 'gal zla mi thun phyogs gangs zag dang chos rang bzhin gis grub par sgro 'dogs pa'o//.* Tsongkhapa maintains that the Prāsaṅgikas' identification of a deluded concealer *(nyon sgrib, kleśāvaraṇas)* is unique and has to be contrasted with the positions of the Abhidharmikas and even of the Svātantrikas. The Abhidharmikas and Svātantrikas contrast the conception of the essence of self, and the conception of essence of phenomena. They categorize only the latter under the umbrella of deluded ignorance and the former under the umbrella of the view of the substantial "I" and "mine" *('jig tshogs la lta ba, satkāyadṛṣṭi).* See pp. 190, 191–95.

248 *Dgongs pa rab gsal,* p. 196: *nyon mongs pa'i bag chags rnams shes sgrib yin te/ de'i 'bras bu gnyis snang 'khrul pa'i cha thams cad kyang der bsdu'o/ /nyon mongs kyi sa bon la bag chags su bzhag pa gcig dang/ nyon mongs gyi sa bon min pa'i bag chags gnyis las shes sgrib tu 'jog pa ni phyi ma te/ nyon mongs kyi sa bon thams cad zad pas bden 'dzin mi skye yang/ bag chags kyis bslad pas snang yul la 'khrul pa'i blo skyed pa'o//.* See pp. 195–98 for details.

249 Jayānanda, *Madhyamakāvatārasyaṭīkā,* p. 73c: *ma rig pa rnam pa gnyis te/ nyon mongs pa can dang/ nyon mongs pa can ma yin pa'o/ de la nyon mongs pa can ni mi shes pa gang bdag dang bdag ge'o snyam pa'i mngon par zhen pa skyed pa'i sgo nas 'khor ba'i rgyu gyur pa'o/ nyon mongs pa can ma yin pa ni gang gzugs la sogs pa rnams snang ba tsam gyi rgu yin gyi bden par mnong par zhen pa'i rgu ni ma yin no//.*

250 Jayānanda, *Madhyamakāvatārasyaṭīkā,* p. 73c: *de la nyon mongs pa can ma yin pa'i ma rig pa tsam kun du spyod pa'i phyir nyan thos la sogs pa rnams la sgyu ma la sogs pa bzhin du rten cing 'grel par 'gyung ba rnams kun rdzob tsam du snang ba yin no//.* The three types of āryas are the śrāvaka āryas, the pratyekabuddha āryas, and the bodhisattva āryas.

251 Jayānanda, *Madhyamakāvatārasyaṭīkā,* p. 73c*: bden par zhin par med pa nyid kyis 'dod chags la sogs pa'i nyon mongs pa rnams skyed par mi byed pas nyon mongs pa can ma yin pa'o zhes bya'o//.*

252 Jayānanda, *Madhyamakāvatārasyaṭīkā,* p. 73c: *sngon po la sogs pa'i rnam pa dang bcas pa'i shes pa nyams su myong ba mi mnga' ba'i sangs rgyas bcom ldan 'das rnams la ni kun rdzob tsam snang ba med pa'o//.*

253 *Itivuttaka* 1:14. See Thanissaro Bhikkhu, p. 3.

254 *Nges don rab gsal,* p. 389a–d explains his own position; he also offers his objections to Tsongkhapa's view. See p. 38b–d and pp. 390a–393b.

255 *Lta ba ngan sel,* ff. 540–58, 727–29, 738.

256 *Madhyamakāvatārasyaṣṭikā,* p. 73a–d.

257 *Grub mtha' mdzod,* f. 269: *sems rab tu ma zhi bar byed pa gang mi dge ba'am/ sgrib pa lung du ma stan pa'i ngo bo ser sna la sogs pa ni nyon sgrib yin la/ khor gsum la bden zhin dang ma dral ba gang bde ba zag bcas sam ma sgribs lung ma stan gyi ngo bo gzung 'dzin gyi rtogs pa yul yul can ni shes sgrib yi no//.*

258 *Dbu 'jug rnam bshad,* pp. 127–29: *de la ma rig pa ni gnyis te/ nyon mongs pa can dang/ nyon mongs pa can ma yin pa'o/ /dang po ni bdag dang bdag gi bar mngon par zhen pa'i sgo nas 'khor ba'i rgyur gyur pa'o/ /gnyis pa ni gzugs sogs chos su mngon par zhen pa'i sgo nas yul dang yul can du snang ba skyed pa'o/ /dang po ni gang zhag gi bdag med pa sgoms pas spongs ngo/ /phyi ma ni chos su bdag med pa goms pas spong ngo//.*

259 *Rigs tsogs dka' gnad,* ff. 109–23.

260 *Grub mtha'i rnam bshad,* ff. 236–37, 274–78.

261 See Shakya Chogden, *Dbu ma 'jug pa'i dka' ba'i gnad rnam par bshad pa ku mud phren mrdzes* (hereafter, *'Jug pa'i dka' gnad*), *The Complete Works,* vol. 5 (Thimphu, Bhutan: Kunzang Tobgey, 1975), ff. 477–86, for a detailed analysis of the definitions of the two concealers *(sgrib gnyis); Dbu 'jug rnam bshad,* ff. 328–33 for his account; *Theg pa chen po dbu ma rnam par nges pa'i bang mdzod lung rigs rgya mtsho las don dam rnam bshad le'u drug pa* (hereafter, *Don dam rnam bshad*), *The Complete Works,* vol. 15 (Thimphu, Bhutan: Kunzang Tobgey, 1975), ff. 169–71, for his critique of the Gelug view; *Theg pa chen po dbu ma rnam par nges pa'i bang mdzod lung rigs rgya mtsho las kun rdzob bden pa'i rnam bshad le'u lnga pa* (hereafter, *Kun rdzob bden pa'i rnam bshad*), *The Complete Works,* vol. 15 (Thimphu, Bhutan: Kunzang Tobgey, 1975), ff. 126–43, for further critique of the Gelug view; and ff. 143–50, for more on his own position.

262 Mi pham Rin po che, *Brgal lan nyin byed snang ba (Brgal lan nyin byed)* (Sarnath: Nyingmapa Students' Welfare Committee, 1993), p. 518: *gang zag gi bdag med rtogs pas nyon sgrib dang chos kyi bdag med rtogs pas shes sgrib spong ba' lang sems tsam nas thal 'gyur ba'i bar de bzhed pa la khyad med cing brjod tshul phra mo re mi 'dra ba yang don khyad med pa yin pas thams cad lam gyi gnad la dgongs pa gcig ces brjod do//.* He argues that there is no difference between the positions of Cittamatrins, Svātantrikas, and Prāsaṅgikas insofar as they all accept that knowledge of the selflessness of person eradicates deluded concealers and that knowledge of the selflessness of phenomena eradicates concealers of true knowledge. In his *Brgal lan nyin byed snang ba,* pp. 487–518, Mipham provides detailed objections on the view held by Lobsang Rabsel (Blo bzang Rab gsal).

263 *Klu sgrub dgongs rgyan,* p. 182.

264 In *The Conception of Buddhist Nirvāṇa,* p. 34, he argues: "The Mahāyānist says that Reality is veiled not only by *kleśāvaraṇa* but also by *jñeyāvaraṇa* or the veil that hides true knowledge. The removal, therefore, of *jñeyāvaraṇa* is also necessary. This is possible by the realization of *dharmanairātmya* or *dharmaśūnyatā,* the egolessness and emptiness of all elements of existence."

265 In his article "Madhyamaka," he argues: "The Madhyamaka school claims to find the true 'middle way' by declaring, not only the unreality of the individuals *(pudgala nairātmya),* but also the unreality of the dharmas themselves; it denies the existence of not only the beings who suffer, but also of pain. Everything is void." See the *Mādhyamika Dialectic and the Philosophy of Nāgārjuna,* p. 150; also see pp. 149, 151.

266 "In the Absolute...all elements of existence have vanished, because all of them, whether they be called defilers, or the creative power of life, or individual existences, or groups of elements, have all totally vanished. This all systems of philosophy admit, i.e., that the Absolute is a negation of the Phenomenal." *The Conception of Buddhist Nirvāṇa,* p. 198; also see pp. 10, 195–96.

267 In his studies on the *Yuktiṣaṣṭika* in *Master of Wisdom,* p. 259, Lindtner argues: "Reality is beyond all ontological and epistemological dualities *(dvaya),* while the empirical world of origination, destruction, and so forth is illusory—due merely to ignorance *(avidya).*"

268 "Of constructive imagination are born attachment, aversion and infatuation, depending (respectively) on our good, evil and stupid attitudes. Entities which depend on these are not anything by themselves." See *The Mādhyamika Dialectic and the Philosophy of Nāgārjuna,* p. xxvii.

269 *Klu sgrub dgongs rgyan,* p. 182: *mdor na rang cag tha mal pa rnams la snang zhing/ shing rta rnam bdun gyi rigs pas dum bo stong du bzhigs kyang ldog du med pa'i snang ba 'de kun shes sgrib kho rang gam kho yis nus pa zhig yin par snang/...snang pa'i rnam bzhag 'de kun rigs ngor yongs su rdzogs par zhig pa na nyon sgrib spangs pa dang/ snang ngor yongs su rdzog par zhig pa na shes sgrib spangs pa yin no zhes slo dpon lda ba drags pa ni sgrib gnyis zad pa'i sangs rgyas la de ltar med par snang ngo// cog rtse snying thag pa nas mthong pa nyon sgrib dang/ mig gis yod par mthong pa tsam shes sgrib ste//.*

270 See Helmut Tauscher, "Phya pa chos kyi senge ge as a Svātantrika," in Dreyfus and McClintock, eds. *The Svātantrika-Prāsaṅgika Distinction,* p. 235.

271 See Thupten Jinpa, "Delineating Reason's Scope for Negation: Tsongkhapa's Contribution to Madhyamaka's Dialectical Method," *Journal of Indian Philosophy* 26 (1998): 275–308, and Jeffrey Hopkins, *Emptiness Yoga: The Tibetan Middle Way* (Delhi: Motilal Banarsidass, 1995), pp. 123–47.

272 See Ruegg, "Indian and the Indic in Tibetan Cultural History, and Tson khapa's Achievement as a Scholar and Thinker: An Essay on the Concepts of Buddhism in Tibet and Tibetan Buddhism," *Journal of Indian Philosophy* 32 (2004): 333–40.

273 *Prasannapadā,* p. 416b: *don yang de yin la dam pa yang de yin pas na don dam pa'o/ de nyid bden pa yin pas don dam pa'i bden pa'o//.* Cabezón, *A Dose of Emptiness,* p. 360, offers another translation of this passage.

274 *Rtsa shes ṭīk chen,* p. 411: *don dang dam pa gyis ka don dam bden pa nyid la bzhed do//.*

275 See Cabezón, *A Dose of Emptiness,* p. 360, for Mkhas grub Rje's emphasis on this point.

276 *Rtsa shes ṭīk chen,* p. 411: *don dam bden pa'i bden tshul ni/ mi slu ba yin la de yang gnas tshul bzhan du gnas shing snang tshul gzhan du snang nas 'jig rten la mi slu ba'i phir//.*

277 AN 3:137. Thanissaro Bhikkhu, trans., *An Anthology of Selected Suttas from the Aṅguttara Nikāya,* http://www.accesstoinsight.org/canon/anguttara/index.html. I chose to use the term *regularity* instead of his term "steadfast," and *dukkha* instead of "stress."

278 SN 12:20. Thanissaro Bhikkhu, trans., *An Anthology of Selected Suttas from the Saṃyutta Nikāya,* http://www.accesstoinsight.org/canon/samyutta/index.html.

279 *Nges don rab gsal,* p. 377d: *phags pa'i ye shes dam pa'i spyod yul du gyur pa'i chos nyid ni rtogs par bya'am brtag par bya ba yin pas na don/ 'de las mchog tu gyur pa gzhan med pas na dam pa mi slu pas na bden ba zhes gzhi mthun gyis bldu ba ste//.*

280 Jayānanda, *Madhyamakāvatārasyabhāṣya*, p. 74a–b: *dam pa 'jig rten las 'das pa'i ye shes yin la/ don ni de'i yul yin pa'i phyir don dam pa yin la/ de yang bden pa nyid yin te/ mi slu ba'i phir ro/ yang na mchog tu gyur pa'i don ni don dam pa yin te/ de yang stong pa nyid do/ stong pa nyid las lhag pa'i dngos po mchog tu gyur pa med pas so//.*

281 *Lta ba ngan sel*, f. 714*: gnas skabs der rtogs bya dang rtogs byed dam yul yul can tha dad du med pa'i phir ro//.* Also see ff. 727–29.

282 Taktsang Lotsawa, *Grub mtha'i rnam bshad*, f. 305: *gnyis snang med pa'i ye shes yul med du bshad//.*

283 *Lta ba ngan sel*, f. 611: *de yang gzhi gcig nyid snang tshul gyis sgo nas so sor phye ba yin gyi yul gyi ngos nas so sor yod pa ni ma yin no//.*

284 *Lta ba ngan sel*, ff. 612–13: *don dam pa'i bden pa ni 'phags pa'i so so rang rig pa'i ye shes kyis gnyis snang nub ba'i tshul gyis myang bar bya ba yin gyi/ gnyis snang dang bcas na rnam mkhyen gyi bar gyi yul yang don dam bden pa ma yin//.*

285 *Grub mtha' mdzod*, f. 193: *paramārtha zhes pas/ nges par legs pa'i don du gnyer ba rnams kyi gnyer bya'i 'bras bu yin pas don dam pa/ de nyid blo ma 'khrul pa'i ngo bo rig pa'i shes pa'o/ de nyid gya nom pa mchog tu gyur pa yin pas kyang dam pa ste/ blo ma 'khrul ba de'i yul du bden pas na bden pa ste de zhin nyid do//.*

286 *Thub pa dgongs gsal*, p. 32b: *don dam pa la paramārtha ste/ parama ni mchog gam dam pa/ artha ni don te dam pa rnams kyis brtags na skyon med pa'i don yin pas na don dam pa zhes bsgyur//.* See also his *Gzung lugs legs bshad*, p. 72b.

287 *Don dam rnam bshad*, f. 185: *sangs rgyas kyi sas bsdus pa'i chos yin na/ kun rdzob kyi bden pa ma yin dgos te/ de yin na chos sku yin dgos la/ de yin na/ kun rdzob kyi bden pa ma yin pa dgos pa'i phir...//;* f. 186: *stong nyid mngon sum du rtogs pa'i slob pa'i mnyam bzhag ye shes rnams kyang don dam pa'i bden par thal ba ma yin nam snam na/de yang 'dir 'dod dgos pa yin te/ don dam pa dngos yin pa'i phir dang...//;* f. 187: *ye shes de chos can/ don dam pa'i bden pa yin te/ stong nyid dngos su rtogs pa'i mnyam bzhag ye shes kyi dngos kyi gzhal bya mtshan nyid pa yin pa'i phir/ rtags grub ste/ ye shes de so sor rang gis rig pa'i ye shes yin pa'i phir//.* In these statements, Shakya Chogden equates the status of the wisdom of meditative equipoise of āryas and ultimate truth. "Ultimate truth, after all, is the wisdom of the meditative equipoise. There is no ultimate truth apart from this wisdom. This wisdom itself serves as the apprehended object of the wisdom of the meditative equipoise." For this see f. 187: *stong pa nyid mngon sum du rtogs pa'i mnyam gzhag ye shes kyi gzhal bya dgos ni/ ye shes de nyid yin gyi/ stong pa nyid ces bya ba gzhan sel dang/ ldog pa med dgag gi gyur pa de nyid de'i dgnos kyi gzhal bya ma nyin no//.* Also see his *Theg pa chen po dbu ma rnam par nges pa'i bang mdzod lung rigs rgya mtsho las bden pa gnyis kyi rnam bzhag le'u bzhi pa* (hereafter, *Bde gnyis rnam gzhag*), *The Complete Works*, vol. 15 (Thimphu, Bhutan: Kunzang Tobgey, 1975), ff. 29–30, for more on this issue.

288 See Rongtön, *Dbu ma tsa ba'i rnam bshad zab mo'i di kho na nyid snang ba* (hereafter, *Dbu tsa'i rnam bshad*) (Sarnath: Sakya Students' Union, 1995), p. 287: *yul can ye shes kyang don dam pa ste/ don dam pa yul du yod pa'i phir/ yul skye ba med par bstan pa la sogs pa dang/ yul can stong pa nyid kyi don thos pa dang/ bsam pa dang/ sgom pa las byung pa'i shes rab dag kyang don dam pa zhes bya ste/ don dam rtogs pa'i thabs yin pa'i phir dang/ phyi ci ma log pa yin pa'i phir//.* Interestingly, he expressly equates the subjective consciousnesses of āryas and buddhas with the status of ultimate truth. In other words, instead of treating the verifying cognition of ultimate truth as conventional, he treats it as ultimate truth itself. Also see p. 287: *don dam*

pa nyid bden pa yin pas/ don dam pa'i bden pa ste/ rnam pa thams cad du de bzhin du gnas pa'i phir/ yul can ye shes kyang don dam pa ste/ don dam pa yul du yod pa'i phir/ yul skye ba med par bstan pa la sogs pa dang/ yul can stong pa nyid kyi don thos pa dang/ bsam pa dang/ sgom pa las byung pa'i shes rab dag kyang don dam pa zhes bya ste/ don dam rtogs pa'i thabs yin pa'i phir dang/ phyi ci ma log pa yin pa'i phir/ 'de ni rjes su mthun pa bstan no//.

289 *Dag brgyud grub pa'i shing rta,* f. 279: *'phags pa'i mnyam gzhag la ma ltos pa'am/ de las tha dad pa'i don du grub pa ni ma yin cing/ don dam pa'i bden pa las tha dad pa'i phags pa'i mnyam gzhag kyang yod pa ma yin no//.* Mikyö Dorje expressly equates ultimate truth with the wisdom of the meditative equipoise and denies any distinction between the two.

290 *Madhyamakāvatāra,* p. 155: *dngos kun yang dag brdzun pa mthong ba yis/ dngos rnyed ngo bo gyis ni 'dzin par 'gyur/ yang dag mthong yul gang de de nyid de/ mthong ba brdzun pa kun rdzob bden par gsungs/ 6:23/.* Also see Candrakīrti, *Madhayamkāvatārabhāṣya,* p. 98. I have largely adopted Newland's translation of this verse from *The Two Truths,* p. 95. Alternately, Huntington, in *The Emptiness of Emptiness,* p. 160, translates *yang dag mthong pa* as "correct perception" instead of "perceivers of falsities" and *mthong ba rdzun pa* as "incorrect perception" instead of "perceivers of reality."

291 Newland, *The Two Truths,* p. 96.

292 *Dgongs pa rab gsal,* p. 175: *kun rdzob bden pa 'jog byed brdzun pa mthong bas rnyed don...shes bya brdzun pa slu ba'i don 'jal ba'i tha snyad pa'i tsed mas rnyed pa'o//.* See Newland, *The Two Truths,* p. 95.

293 *Dgongs pa rab gsal,* p. 175: *yang dag pa'i don mthong ba ste 'jal pa'i rigs shes kyis rnyed pa'i yul gang yin pa de ni/ de nyid de don dam pa'i bden pa ste//.* Also see Tsongkhapa, *Rtsa shes ṭīk chen,* p. 406; and Newland, *The Two Truths,* p. 96.

294 Exterior phenomena include six spheres of senses, namely, form, sound, aroma, taste, tactility, and ideas, or concepts. Interior phenomena include six sense organs, namely, eyes, ears, nose, tongue, body, and mind, and six consciousnesses, namely, that of the eye, ear, tongue, body, and mind.

295 *Rtsa shes ṭīk chen,* p. 406: *phyi nang gi ngos po 'di rnams re re la yang don dam pa dang kun rdzob pa'i ngo bo gnyis gnyis yod de/ de yang myu gu lta bu gcig la mtson na/ shes bya yang dag pa de kho na'i don gzigs pa'i rigs shes kyis rnyed pa'i myu gu ngo bo'o/ shes bya rdzun pa slu ba'i don 'jal ba'i tha snyad pa'i shes pas rnyed pa'i myu gu'i ngo bo 'o/ de'i snga ma ni myu gu'i don dam bden pa'i ngo bo yin la phyin ma ni myu gu'i kun rdzob bden pa'i ngo bo'o//.*

296 *Madhyamakāvatārabhāṣya,* p. 98: *bden pa gnyis kyis rang gyi ngo bo phyin ci ma log pa mkhyen pa sangs rgyas bcom ldan das rnams kyis/ 'du byed dang myu gu la sogs pa nang dang phyi ro gyi dgos po thams cad kyi rang gyi ngo bo rnam pa gnyis nye bar bstan ste//.* Cited in Tsongkhapa, *Rtsa shes ṭīk chen,* p. 406.

297 *Dgongs pa rab gsal,* p. 173: *'dis ni myu gu lta bu gcig gi ngo bo la'ang phye na kun rdzob yin pa dang/ don dam yin pa'i ngo bo gnyis yod par ston gyi myu gu gcig nyid so skye and 'phags pa la ltos nas bden pa gnyis su bstan pa gtan min no//.*

298 Huntington, *The Emptiness of Emptiness,* p. 160.

299 *Lta ba ngan sel,* f. 603: *de ltar blo'i sgo nas ngo bo gnyis 'dzin pa'i mthong ba yang dag pa'i yul ni don dam bden pa yin la/ mthong ba brdzun pa'i yul ni kun rdzob bden pa'o//.*

300 *Lta ba ngan sel*, f. 603: *sangs rgyas bcom blden 'das kyis gdul bya la tha snyad pa'i sgo nas gnas lugs bstan pa'i tshe/ dngos po thams cad la kun rdzob dang don dam pa'i ngo bo gnyis bstan ste/ dngos po thams cad la 'phags pa'i mnyam bzhag ye shes kyis rang gi ngo bo stong nyid rnyed pa dang/ brdzun pa mthong ba'i so so'i skyes po'i blos rdzun pa'i stobs las rang gi ngo bo yod par rnyed pa la bden pa gnyis su bzhag pa yin.../.*

301 *Nges don rab gsal*, p. 375b*: brdzun pa mthong ba dang/ yang dag mthong ba gnyis sam/ 'khrul ma khrul gnyis/ rmongs ma rmongs gnyis/ phyin ci log ma log gnyis sam/ tshad ma yin min gnyis kyis mthong tshul gyi sgo nas kun rdzob den pa dang/ don dam bden pa gyis su phye ba ste//.* Also see p. 375b–d for his detailed defense of each of these assertions.

302 *Nges don rab gsal*, p. 384c: *bden pa gnyis yul can gyi blo rmongs ma rmongs sam brdzun pa mthong ba dang/ yang dag mthong ba'am/ 'khrul ma 'khrul gyi sgo nas 'jog dgos pas yul can gyi blo'i sgo nas 'jog pa pa ni rgya gar gyi thal rang thams cad mthun par snang la//.*

303 *Lta ba ngan sel*, f. 604: *gzhan yang myu gu ngo bo cig nyid la/ bden pa gnyis kyi ming gis btags pa'i btags don tha snyad du rnyed par thal/ myu gu'i ngo bo yin par gyur pa'i bden gnyis kyi ngo bo gnyis yod pa'i phyir/ yul can 'phags pa'i mnyam bzhag dis mthongs ba brdzun pas rnyed pa'i rnyed don de mthong par thal/ de mthong ba yang dag pas rnyed pa'i rnyed don la sgrub 'jug gang zhig yul de gnyis ngo bo gcig yin pa'i phir//.*

304 *Lta ba ngan sel*, f. 604: *myu gu'e ngo bor gyur pa'i kun rdzob kyi ngo bo de de'i ngo bor gyur pa'i don dam gyi ngo bor yin par thal/ di gnyis ngo bo gcig yin pa'i phir/ 'dod na/ mthong a brdzun pas rnyed pa'i ngo bo de mthong ba yang dag pas rnyed pa'i ngo bo yin par thal/ 'dod pa'i phir/ 'dod na/ mthong ba rdzun pas rnyed pa de mthong ba yang dag pas rnyed par thal/ 'dod pa de'i phir/ 'dod na/ de gnyis yul gyi ngo go rnyed tsul khyad par med par 'gyur ro//.*

305 *Nges don rab gsal*, p. 370a: *tshig gis rjod par bya ba ma yin zhing/ blos yul du bya ba ma yin pa'i phir te//.*

306 *Nges don rab gsal*, p. 370a: *don dam bden pa 'phags pa'i mnyam bzhag gis je ltar spros pa dang dral pa'i tshul kyis myong ba ltar mtshan nyid dang mtshan gzhi sogs gang gyis kyang bstan par mi nus te//.*

307 See Lindtner, notes on the *Yuktiṣaṣṭikā*, *Master of Wisdom*, p. 259.

308 It is no surprise that their definitions have some parallels. Both Tsongkhapa and Gorampa after all are glossing the same verse [6:23] of the *Madhyamakāvatāra* in the *Madhyamakāvatārabhāṣya*, p. 98: *dngos kun yang dag brdzun pa mthong ba yis/ dngos rnyed ngo bo gyis ni 'jin par 'gyur/ yang dag mthong yul gang de de nyid de/ mthong ba brdzun pa kun rdzob bden par gsungs//.*

309 *Madhyamakāvatārasyaṭīkā*, p. 70d: *yang dag mthong ba ste/ dngos po'i rang bzhin phyin ci ma log pa thogs su chud pa'i sangs rgyas bcom ldan ldas rnams so/ de rnams kye yul gang yin pa de ni de kho na nyid do/ de dag gi yul dang yul can gyi dngos po ni yul dang yul can mi dmigs pa gang yin pa'o/... mthog ba brdzun pa ni phyin ci ma log pa'i de kho na nyid ma rtogs pa dang ngos po rdzun pa rnams la mngon par zhen pas so de rnams kyi yul gang yin pa de ni kun rdzob yin no zhes pa'o//.*

310 See *The Master of Wisdom*, p. xx–xxi, for his introductory notes.

311 Jayānanda, *Madhyamakāvatārasyaṭīkā*, p. 71a: *gnyis mi dmigs pa'i sgo nas gang nyams su myong ba spros pa thams cad dang dral pa'i rang bzhin can yin.../.*

312 Jayānanda, *Madhyamakāvatārasyaṭīkā*, p. 71a: *don dam pa'i gnas skabs na ni yul dang yul can cung zad kyang yod pa ma yin no//.*

313 *Grub mtha'mdzod*, ff. 203–4: *kun rdzob kyi mtshan nyid gzung 'dzin spros pa dang bcas pa'i rnam par snang ba/ de'ang sgrib ba'i rnam par skyes pa ste//... don dam bden pa'i tshan nyid ni gzung 'dzin spros pa dang bral pa'i ngo bo//.*

314 *Gzhung lugs legs bshad*, p. 72b: *kun rdzob bden pa'i ngo bo ni snang ba yul dang yul can te/ gzung 'dzin gyis bsdus pa'i chos thams cad do/ de dag la ci'i phir kun rdzob kyi bden pa zhes bya zhe na/ kun ni shes bya'i gnas yin la/ rdzob ni sgrib ba ste// don dam bden pa'i ngo bo ni/ rigs pa yul dang bcas pa ste/ rigs pa ni sangs rgyas kyi ye shes dang byang chu sems dpa'i rnams kyis mnyam par gzhag pa'i shes pa dang/ so so skye bo'i gcig dang du bral la sogs pa/ spros pa gcod byed kyi rigs pa yin la/ rigs pa'i yul ni rigs pa des gtan la phab pa'am/ des rtogs pa'i chos rnams kyi chos nyid spros pa dang dral ba'o//.*

315 *Dbu 'jug rnam bshad*, p. 121: *'de la don dam pa ni 'phags pa rnams kyis yang dag pa'i ye shes kyi yul du bdag gi dngos po rnyed pa gang yin pa'o// kun rdzob ni so so skye po ma rig pa'i ling thog gyis blo gros kyi mig bsgrib pa rnams kyis rdzun pa thong pa ma rig stobs kyis bdag gi dngos po rnyed pa gang yin pa'o//.*

316 *Shes 'grel ke ta ka*, p. 3: *de la kun rdzob ni so skye sogs kyi rang bzhin med bzhin du der snang pa sgyu ma dang rmi lam skra shad lta bu'i snang tshul 'de yin la//.* Also in the *zla ba'i zhal lung*, ff. 80–81: *de la yang dag pa'i ye shes kyi mthong yul gang de de nyid de don dam yin la/ mthong ba brdzun pa ye yul ni kun rdzob bden par gsungs so//.* Not only does Mipham dichotomize the two truths on the basis of two conflicting experiences, he expressly reduces *kun rdzob bden* into *snang tshul*, which means the "modes of apprehensions" of ordinary folks. Also see Mipham, *Brgal lan nyin byed snang ba* (hereafter, *Brgal lan nyin byed*) (Sarnath: Nyingmapa Students' Welfare Committee, 1993), pp. 543–44: *nyon mongs can gyi ma rig pa'i dbang gis kun rdzob bden pa 'jog cing de mthong ba rdzun pa dang don dam pa ni mthong ba yang dang par gsungs//.*

317 See Shakya Chogden, *Bden pa gyis kyi gnas la 'jug pa nges don bdud rtsi'i thigs pa* (hereafter, *Bden gnyis gnas 'jug*), *The Complete Works*, vol. 5 (Thimpu, Bhutan: Kunzang Tobgey, 1975), f. 378: *'jig rten pa rnam kyi don dam pa'i bden pa 'jog 'byed ni/ lhan skyes pa'i ma rig pa'i sgri pa'o//; Dbu ma rtsa ba'i rnam bshad skal bzang 'jug ngogs* (hereafter, *Dbu rtsa'i rnam bshad*), *The Complete Works*, vol. 5 (Thimpu, Bhutan: Kunzang Tobgey, 1975), f. 220: *kun rdzob bden pa'i mtshan nyid ni/ yul can rdzun pa'i shes byar grub pa'o/ don dam bden pa'i mtshan nyid ni/ tha snyad kyi spros pa ma lus pa 'das pa'i de kho na nyid do//.*

318 *Grub mtha' kun shes*, f. 27: *mtshan nyid 'khrul ngor dang rig ngor rnyid//;* f. 28: *de 'phir kun rdzob nges byed 'khrul shes tsam//.* Also see its commentary, the *Grub mtha'i rnam bshad*, f. 220, for his critique of Tsongkhapa's definition of conventional truth, f. 221: *kun rdzob kyi bden pa ni gti mug gi ming can 'jig rten ngar 'dzin lhas skyes kyis 'jog la/ dag pa'i ye shes kyis ma gzigs par yang yang gsung pa'i phir ro//;* see also ff. 250–51. In the *Bdu ma chen po* section, ff. 263–64, in particular, while he focuses on the treatments of the truths, he offers perspective-based definitions: *bden gnyis kyi mtshan nyid ni/ rim pa bzhin ma phyad 'khrul pa'i shes ngor rnyed pa'i rnyed don dang/ ma 'khrul 'phags pa'i rig ngor rnyed pa'i rnyed don zhes bya ste//.*

319 *Dbu tsa'i rnam bshad*, p. 287: *kun rdzob ni chos can snang tshul las rnam par 'jog la/ don dam ni/ de'i gnas tshul stong pa nyid do//; Rigs tsogs dka' gnad*, f. 6: *kun rdzob kyi mtshan nyid ni gnas tshul la ma gzhug pa'i blo rnyed don/ don dam bden pa'i mtshan nyid gnas tshul la zhug pa'i blos rnyed don te//.* Also see f. 7: *bden pa gnyis po 'ang*

yul la chos gnyis yod pa'i dbang gis gzhag pa min gyi/ shes ngo gnyis la ltos nas gzhag pa ste//.

320 *Dag brgyud grub pa'i shing rta*, f. 275: *don dam pa ni 'phags pa yang dag pa gzig pa'i ye shes de ngor yul yang dag par 'jog go shes brjod par zad kyi/ rang gi bdag nyid du grub pa zhig blos rnyed bya yod pa ma yin no/ /kun rdzob ni so skye ma rig pa'i ling tog gis blo mig ma lus pa kebs pa rnams kyi blo ngor yul brdzun pa mthong pa yis blo'r jog go/ /blo dis mthong ba'i 'dzin stangs dang mthun par yul de ltar grub pa ni ma yin no/ /de na ngos po rnyed do cog thams cad don dam pa dang kun rdzob pa'i ngo bo gnyis ni 'dzin par 'gyur ro/ /de gnyis las 'phags pa yang dag pa mthong ba'i yul gang yin pa de ni de kho na nyid de don dam bden pa'o/ /mthong pa rdzun pa'i yul gang yin pa de ni kun rdzob bden par ston pas gsungs so//.* Also see ff. 280–81, 304–6.

321 *Klu sgrub dgongs rgyan*, p. 217: *mdor na bden gnyis bya ba de phal ba'i ngor bden pa zhig dang/ phags pa'i ngor bden pa zhig tu ma go bar/ phal pa'i gang bden pa de'i nang du phags pa'i gzigs tshul thams cad bsres pa na/ bsam gyis mi khyab pa'i gnas la yid ches chung zad tsam yong ba'i skal ba med la/ bsam gyis mi khyab pa'i ngas la ji srid sdo pa 'de srid du 'jig rten las cung zad kyang ma 'das par shes par bya'o//.* Also see pp. 220–21, 226, 237–38.

322 "*Saṃvṛtisatya* is truth so-called; truth as conventionally believed in common parlance... It is the object of the ignorant and immature. *Paramārthasatya* is unsignified by language and belongs to the realm of the unutterable, and is experienced by the wise in a very intimate way." See "Introduction," *Mādhyamika Dialectic and the Philosophy of Nāgārjuna*, ed. by Prof. Samdhong Rinpoche (Sarnath: CIHTS, 1985), p. xxv. In fact, he argues: "There is only one truth—the *paramārthasatya*, as there is only one real—the Absolute. The other—*saṃvṛtisatya*, is truth so-called in common parlance, it is totally false from the absolute standpoint."

323 "Phenomena viewed as relative, as governed by causes and conditions, constitute the world, and viewed as free of all conditions are the Absolute. The Absolute is always of uniform nature. Nirvāṇa or the Absolute is not something produced or achieved. Nirvāṇa only means the disappearance of the fabrications of discursive thought... Phenomena are appearances, and appearances point to their Reality. The veil gives a hint of that which is veiled." See "Introduction," *The Conception of Buddhist Nirvāṇa*, pp. 51–52. Ultimate truth in his sense is the only truth, "the Absolute as the essence of all being is neither born, nor does it cease to be...it is the reality of the appearances."

324 See "Madhyamaka" in *Mādhyamika Dialectic and the Philosophy of Nāgārjuna*, pp. 152–53, where he equates conventional dharmas with the daughter of a barren woman, and with the hairs that a monk with diseased eyes thinks he sees in his alms bowl, and argues "the object described, the description, and the person describing are all similarly nonexistent." Absolute truth, which, as he argues "is 'knowledge of Buddha,' is a 'not-knowledge';" it is like a man without diseased eyes who does not see hairs.

325 See Huntington's translation of the verse [6:23] of the *Madhyamakāvatāra* and compare it to his notes on the same verse in *The Emptiness of Emptiness*, p. 231–32n38. He defines ultimate truth as an object of wisdom, which is revealed through accurate perception. He argues that conventional truth is an object obtained "on the strength of false perceptions made by common people in whom

the eye of intelligence has been completely covered by the cataract of spiritual ignorance. This intrinsic nature is as well not established in itself, but is simply the object revealed through the perception of naïve people."

326 In *Mahāyāna Buddhism,* p. 71, Paul Williams argues that "all entities have two natures, because there is a correct perception and a delusory perception. The object of correct perception is reality *(tattva).* That of delusory perception is said to be conventional truth."

327 Huntington, *The Emptiness of Emptiness,* p. 92.

328 Williams, *Mahāyāna Buddhism,* p. 70.

329 Nāgārjuna, *Mūlamadhyamakakārika* 18:9, p. 45: *gzhan las shes min zhi ba dang/ /spros pa rnams ma spros pa/ /rnam rtog med don tha dad med/ /de ni de nyid mtshan nyid do/ /*. Also cited in Candrakīrti, the *Prasannapadā,* pp. 306–7.

330 *Rtsa shes tīk chen,* pp. 330–32: *gang zag gzhan gis stan pa stam las rtogs par bya ba min gyi rang gis zag pa med pa'i ye shes kyis rtogs par bya ba'o//...gnyis pa zhi ba ni rab rib med pas skra shad ma mthong pa ltar ngo bo nyid kyis yod par rang bzhin dang dral ba'o// de'i phyir don rnams spros par byed pa'i spros pa ngag gis ma spros pa ste ma brjod pa ni gsum pa'o// rnam rtog med pa ni sems kyi rgyu ba yin la/ de kho na nyid de mngon du gyur pa'i dus su ni de dang dral ba ste//...don tha dad med pa ni chos gcig don dam par ji lta bu yin pa der chos gzhan thams cad kyang mtshungs pas don dam par do so so ba med pa ste//.*

331 Gorampa, *Lta ba'i 'od zer,* p. 335b: *'phags pa'i mnyam gzhag so so rang gis rig pa'i ye shes kyis 'ga' yang mthong ba med pa'i tshul gis rig par bya ba yin gyi/ byis pa rnams kyis gzhan sgra dang/ gtan tshigs la sogs pa las ngo bo ji lta ba bzhin shes bar bya a ma yin pa dang/ gzod ma nas cir yang ma grub pas zhi ba dang/ ngag gi spros pa rnams kyis zhen nas brjod par bya ba a yin pas ma spros pa dang/ sems sems byung gyi spyod yul las 'das pas rnam par rtog pas 'gar yang brtag tu med pa dang/ mi 'dra ba'i byi drag med pas don tha dad min pa ste/ chos lnga po de ni don dam pa'i de kho na nyid kyi mtshan nyid do//.*

332 *Lta ba'i 'od zer,* p. 326a: *'on na dngos po rnams kyi rang bzhin de kho na'i rang bzhin ci lta bu zhig yin zhe na/ rang gi ngo bo ci lta ba bzhin bstan par mi nus mod/ gdul bya rnams kyis rtogs par bya ba'i phyir/ zag pa med pa'i ye shes kyi spyod yul chos rnams kyi de kho na'i rang bzhin dag gi mtshan nyid ni/ ngo bo rgyu rkyen gyis bcos pa min pa dang/ tha snyad rnam 'jog chos gzhan la ltos pa med pa dang/ gzhan du mi 'gyur ba ste/ chos gsum ldan yin la/ de'i mtshan gzhi ni spros dral gyi chos nyid yin te//.*

333 *Itivuttaka* 43. See Thanissaro Bhikkhu, trans., *An Anthology of Selected Suttas from the Khuddaka Nikāya,* http://www.accesstoinsight.org/canon/khuddaka/index.html.

334 AN 10.81. See Thanissaro Bhikkhu, trans., *An Anthology of Selected Suttas from the Aṅguttara Nikāya,* http://www.accesstoinsight.org/canon/anguttara/index.html.

335 *Nāgārjuna,* p. 272.

336 SN 35.116. See Thanissaro Bhikkhu, trans., *An Anthology of Selected Suttas from the Saṃyutta Nikāya,* http://www.accesstoinsight.org/canon/samyutta/index.html.

337 *Mūlamadhyamakakārika* 18:10, in the *Rtsa ba phyogs bsdus* (Varanasi: Sakya Students' Welfare Committee, 1996), p. 45: *gang la brten te gang 'byung ba/ /de ni re zhig de nyid min/ /de las gzhan pa'ang ma yin phyir/ /de phyir chad min rtag ma yin/*18:10/. Cited in Candrakīrti, *Prasannapadā,* p. 310.

338 *Rtsas she ṭik chen,* p. 332.
339 *Lta ba'i 'od zer,* p. 335b.
340 Murti, *The Central Philosophy of Buddhism,* p. 244.
341 Nāgārjuna, *Mūlamadhyamakakārikā* 24:10, p. 64: *tha snyad la ni ma brten par/ /dam pa'i don ni bstan mi nus/ /dam pa'i don ni ma rtogs par/ /mya ngan 'das pa thob mi 'gyur//.*
342 Nāgārjuna, *Yuktiṣaṣṭika* 6, in the *Rtsa ba phyogs bsdus,* p. 86: *srid pa dang ni mya ngan 'das/ /gnyis po 'di ni yod ma yin/ /srid pa yongs su shes pa nyid/ /mya ngan 'das zhes bya bar brjod//.*
343 Candrakīrti, *Madhyamakāvatāra* 6:29, p. 156: *rab rib mthu yis skra shad la sogs pa'i/ /ngo bo log pa gang zhig rnam brtags pa/ /de nyid bdag nyid gang du mig dag pas/ /mthong de de nyid de bzhin 'dir shes kyis//.* Cited in Candrakīrti, *Madhyamakāvatārabhāṣya,* p. 104.
344 *Dgongs pa rab gsal,* pp. 198–200.
345 *Lta ba ngan sel,* ff. 612–13.
346 *Lta ba ngan sel,* ff. 612–13: *don dam pa'i bden pa ni 'phags pa'i so sor rang rig pa'i ye shes kyis gnyis snang nub pa'i tshul gyis myang bar bya ba yin gyi/ gnyis snang dang bcas na rnam mkhyen gyi bar gyi yul yang don dam bden pa ma yin pa dang/ don dam bden pa rang gi ngo bo ji lta ba zhin gdul bya la bstan mi nus kyi/ gdul bya la tha snyad kyis bstan pa na sgra rtog gi yul thams cad rnams grangs pa'i don dam zhes bya pa kun rdzob bden pa yin par bstan no//.*
347 AN 4:175. Cited in Nyanaponika Thera's "Sāriputta: The Marshal of the Dhamma," in Nyanaponika Thera and Hellmut Hecker, *Great Disciples of the Buddha: Their Lives, Their Works, Their Legacy* (Boston: Wisdom Publication, 1997), p. 62. The word *diffuseness* here is also sometimes rendered as "elaboration" or "proliferation." It refers to the manifold nature of the phenomenal world and, in the verbal sphere, of language.
348 *Lta ba'i 'od zer,* p. 335b: *byes pa rnams kyis gzhan sgra dang/ gtan tshigs la sogs pa las ngo bo ji tla ba bzhin shes par bya ba ma nyin pa dang//.*
349 *Lta ba'i 'od zer,* p. 335b: *ngag gi spros pa rnams kyis zhen nas brjod par bya ba ma nyin pas ma spros pa dang/ sems sems byung gi spyod yul las 'das pas rnam par rtog pas 'gar yang rtag tu med pa dang//.*
350 "Would the True Prāsaṅgika Please Stand?" in Dreyfus and McClintock, eds., *The Svātantrika-Prāsaṅgika Distinction,* p. 335.
351 Gorampa, *Lta ba'i shan 'byed theg mchog gnad gyi zla zer* (hereafter, *Lta ba'i shan 'byed*) (Sarnath: Sakya Students Union, 1994), p. 127: *mdor na gnas lugs la dpyod par byed pa'i blo ni sgra don 'dres 'dzin gyi rtog pa las ma 'das pas/*. Cabezón and Dargyay render this passage as "The thought that engages in the analysis of reality is nothing but a conceptual thought that mixes up words and their meanings." *Freedom from Extremes,* p. 215.
352 *Lta ba'i shan 'byed,* p. 127: *mtha' bzhi'i spros pa gang rung du bzung bas bzhi po cig char du bkag pa mi srid. . .//.*
353 *Recognizing Reality,* p. 455.
354 *Recognizing Reality,* p. 459.
355 Shakya Chogden, *Dbu ma 'jug pa'i dka' ba'i gnad rnam par bshad pa ku mud phren mrdzes* (hereafter, *'Jug pa'i dka' gnad*), *The Complete Works,* vol. 5 (Thimpu, Bhutan:

Kunzang Tobgey, 1975), f. 460: *don dam pa 'jug 'byed kyi tshad ma la mtshan nyid ni... rjes dpag dang dpe nyer 'jal dang lung tshad ma gsum ni yod pa ma yin te/ tshad ma de gsum gyi 'jug mtshams ni yul de dang de la rtog par song pa'i cha nas 'jog la/ yul gang la rtog par song ba'i cha nas don dam bden pa 'jal byed kyi tshad mar song ba mi srid pa'i phyir/ de bas na mngon sum gcig po'o//.* Among the four means of knowledge *(pramāṇas),* his epistemology clearly discounts inferential knowledge *(rjes dpad, anumāna),* analogy *(dpe nyer 'jal, upamāna),* and verbal testimony *(lung, śabda)* as means of knowing ultimate truth. For him they are only means of knowing conventional truth, for they are all conceptual. He considers direct perception *(mngon sum, pratyakṣa)* alone as the means of knowing ultimate truth. For more details, see *'Jug pa'i dka' gnad,* ff. 460–65, 466–70, 475.

356 His analysis of the epistemic practices within the Prāsaṅgika excludes the use of logical inference as a means of knowing ultimate truth. See *Grub mtha'i rnam bshad,* ff. 273–74: *kun rdzob tsam mam bden pa gang yin yang rung nges byed kyi blo ni 'khrul shes tsam du nges te/ 'jig rten pa'i tshad ma'am bdu ma pa'i tshad min yin kyang rung ste gte mug kho na 'jog cing nges par byed pas so//.* Also see ff. 269–72. He expressly argues that the notion of *pramāṇa,* "valid" knowledge, is inappropriate in the Madhyamaka tradition. See ff. 222–23: *tshad ma bzhi po de 'jig rten gyi 'dod pa bkod pa yin gyi rang lugs bzhag pa ma yin pa'i phir te... dbu ma rang lugs la tshad ma dang tshad min kun rdzob gzhir byas la med par 'dod par bya'o//.*

357 *Shes 'grel ke ta ka,* p. 9: *chos nyid spros pa thams cad las 'das pa na de ni blos dmigs pa byar med pa yin te/ gang yul dang yul can du ma gyur cing mtshan ma gang du 'ang ma grub pa de la yang dag par ji ltar shes bya zhes rjord de//.* In commenting on the sixth chapter of Śāntideva's *Bodhicaryāvatāra,* Mipham categorically rules out the possibility of knowing ultimate truth by conceptual mind. This claim is reinforced in his response (*Shes 'grel ke ta ka,* pp. 9–10) to his critics. Mipham's claim, however, should not be taken too far. For he not only accepts ultimate truth as an object of knowledge by the nonconceptual mind or by direct personal realization (*Nges shes rin po che' sgron me* [hereafter, *Nges shes sgron me*], *The Collected Writings,* vol. 8 [Gangtok: Sonam Topgyal Kazi, 1976], ff. 82–87, 96), but he also argues that the conceptual-linguistic device offers us "mere understanding that all conventional realities are utterly false." See Mipham, *Dbu ma rtsa ba'i mchan 'grel gnas lugs rab gsal* (hereafter, *Dbu rtsa'i mchan 'grel*), *The Collected Writings,* vol. 1 (Gangtok: Sonam Topgyal Kazi, 1979), f. 217*: 'jig rten tha snyad kyi rjes su 'drang nas de'i mtshan nyid brjod cig ci na/ rtags dpe sogs bzhan gis bstan pas ji bzhin shes mi nus te rab rib can la de med par bstan pas rab rib med par lta ltar ngo bo ma mthong pa'i tshul kyis rtogs bya ji lta ba rtogs mi nus kyang/ 'de phyin ci log go bya ba tsam gzhig rtog go//.*

358 *Klu sgrub dgongs rgyan,* p. 211: *ji srid 'jig rten gyi rigs pa la snying thag pa nas yid ches yod pa de srid du 'jig rten las 'das pa'i do la yid ches yod pa nam yang mi srid de... 'jig rten gyi rigs pa la yid ches dgos na lam bsgom pa don med par 'gyur ba'i rgyu mtshan du bcom ldan 'das kyis mig dang rna ba sogs nas 'phags pa'i lam bya ba'i dbang po bzhan zhig yod par gsungs... //.* In this polemic Gendün Chöpel unleashes severe criticisms against the philosophy of Tsongkhapa. Gendün Chöpel renders the reasoning consciousness as utterly useless in terms of understanding ultimate reality. At the heart of his rejection of *pramāṇa* lies his equation of perception with the conception of true existence. See *Klu sgrub dgongs rgyan,* pp. 211–13.

359 Mkhan po Kun bzang dpal ldan. His commentary to Śāntideva's *Bodhicaryāvatāra* reveals his deep commitment to the concept of ineffability and inconceivability *(smra bsam bjod med)* of ultimate truth. See his *Byang chub sems pa'i dpyod pa la 'jug pa'i tshig 'grel 'jam dbyangs bla ma'i zhal lung bdud tsi'i thig pa* (hereafter, *Dpyod 'jug tshig 'grel*) (Sarnath: Nyingmapa Students' Welfare Committee, 1993), p. 440: *chos nyid spros pa thams cad las 'das pas na/ ni blos 'dmigs par byar med pas yin te/ gang yul dang yul can du ma gyur cing mtshan ma gang du'ang ma grub pa yang dag par na ji ltar shes bya shes brjod//.* For details see pp. 438–40.

360 "Ordinary beings," he says, "by means of following the inferential reasoning consciousness, ascertain [ultimate reality]." See *Grub mtha' mdzod,* f. 196: *don dam bden pa nges par byed pa'i tshad ma ni dpyad bzod mthar thug dpyod pa'i rig pa'i bzhal bya nges par byed pa'i tshad ma pa thob nas so so rang gi rig pa'i rnam par mi rtog pa'i ye shes kyis rtogs na'ang/ so so skye bo de dag gyis gtan tshigs kyi rjes su 'brang ba'i rigs shes rjes dpag gi nges par byed do//.*

361 Logical reasoning, as far as he is concerned, is an indispensable device for the direct realization of ultimate reality. In sharp contrast with most of his followers, such as Gorampa and Shakya Chogden, Sakya Paṇḍita holds that even ordinary beings possess the reasoning consciousness that could conceptually access ultimate reality. See *Gzung lugs legs bshad,* p. 72b: *don dam bden pa'i ngo bo ni/ rigs pa yul dang bcas pa ste/ rigs pa ni sangs rgyas kyi ye shes dang/ byang chub sems dpa' rnams kyis mnyam par bzhag pa'i shes pa dang/ so so skye bo'i gcig dang du dral la sogs pa'i spros pa gcod byed kyi rigs pa yin la/ rig pa'i yul ni rigs pa des gtan las phap pa'am/ des rtogs pa'i chos rnams kyis chos nyid spros pa dang dral ba'o//.*

362 Closely following in the footsteps of Sakya Paṇḍita, in *Rigs tsogs dka' gnad,* f. 22, Rongtön also differentiates between the reasoning consciousness analyzing conventional truth and that analyzing ultimate truth. And he argues that the "knowledge generated from the contemplation has the same continuum as the meditation, because the meaning *(don)* established by the means of analytical process is itself further processed through the meditative equipoise." See *Rigs tsogs dka' gnad,* f. 105: *bsam byung dang sgom byung yang rtogs pa'i rigs rgyun gcig ste/ bsam byung gis gtan la phabs pa'i don de nyid la sgom byung gis kyang mnyam par 'jog ba'i phyir ro/ de la bsam byung ni rta'i dkyus bstan pa ltar yin la/ sgom byung ni de las brten nas rta thogs med du rgyug pa bzhin yin no//.* Rongtön, however, admits the limits of inference and maintains that it is mistaken insofar as the inferential cognition mistakes the universal of selflessness as selflessness itself. However, inference, he argues, paves the way for an eventual eradication of the conception of self. In the *Rigs tsogs dka' gnad,* f. 105, he says: *gal te rjes dpag ni log shes yin pas des rtogs pa'i rigs rgyun goms pas phyin ci ma log pa'i rtogs pa skye ba ji ltar 'gyur zhe na/ bdag med pa'i don spyi la spyi'i bdag med du zhen pa'i cha nas 'khrul pa'i phyir de'i 'dzin stangs kyi cha nas goms par byed pa ma yin las/ 'on kyang yul bdag med du gnas pa ltar rjes dpag kyang bdag med pa'i rnam ba can du skye ba'i 'dzin stangs kyi cha nas phyin cin ma log pa dang rjes su mthun pa'i phyir de'i 'dzin stangs kyi cha nas goms par byas pas bdag 'dzin log nas bdag med mngon du rtogs pa'i rtogs pa skye ba'i phyir nges ba ga las yod//.* Moreover Rongtön criticizes the view that denies the role of inference as the epistemic means by which ultimate reality can be eventually accessed directly *(Rigs tsogs dka' gnad,* f. 39: *rjes dpag la rigs shes su mi 'dod na rigs pa la rten nas sgro 'dog gcod byed kyi blo min par*

'gyur ro//). He equates inference and the reasoning consciousness, and argues that the denial of the epistemic role of inference would be tantamount to denying analytical cognitions altogether. For him this would amount to denying the meditative equipoise that is a direct result of logical analysis. Therefore he writes in the *Rigs tsogs dka' gnad,* f. 40: *spros pa gcod pa'i rjes dpag la yul gyi snang ba mi mnga' bas mnyam bzhag snang med yin pa'i gnad kyang de yin te/ rigs shes kyi rnyed don de nyid las mnyam par 'jog pa'i phyir zhes 'dod do//.*

363 *Nges don rab gsal,* p. 370a: *don dam bden pa 'phags pa'i mnyam gzhag gis ji ltar spros pa dang dral pa'i tshul kyis myong ba ltar mtshan nyid dang mtshan gzhi sogs gang gis kyang bstan par mi nus te/ tshig gis brjod par bya ba ma yin zhing/ blos yul du bya ba ma yin pa'i phyir te//.*

364 *Dgongs pa rab gsal,* p. 198: *rab rib med pas mthong ba 'dra ba'i skra shad med pa mi rtogs pa gsungs pas/ nyan pa pos de ltar ma rtogs kyang skra shad med pa me rtogs pa min no//.*

365 *Dgongs pa rab gsal,* p. 199: *don dam bden pa ni zab mo'i don can gyi nges don gyi lung dang/ de ltar ston pa'i ngag gis brjod me nus pa…min te//.*

366 *Dgongs pa rab gsal,* p. 198–99: *dper byas nas de kno na nyid stan pa na ma rig pa'i rab rib kyi bslad pa dang dral bas mthong ba 'dra ba zhig mi rtogs kyang/ spyir de kho na nyid mi rtogs pa min par bzhed pas na/ don dam bden pa ni zab mo'i don can gyi nges don gyi lung dang/ de ltar ston pa'i ngag gis brtod mi nus pa dang/ de'i rjes su 'brang ba'i blos kyang rtogs mi nus pa min te/ de kho na nyid kyi don shes brjod kyi yul min par gsungs pa thams cad la yang de bzhin du shes par bya'o//.*

367 *Nges don rab gsal,* p. 384d: *don dam bden pa'i yul can ma 'khrul pa ni 'phags pa'i mnyam gzhag kho na la byas nas/ de'i ngor mi slu ba don dam bden pa yin no//.*

368 *Nges don rab gsal,* p. 384d: *so so skye bo'i rigs shes kyis rnam par dpyad nas gtan la 'bebs pa yin pa na mtshan nyid 'jog pa'i tshe yul can ma 'khrul ba ni 'phags pa'i mnyam gzhag kho nar rlom yang/ rigs shes tshad ma ni de'i khongs su gtogs pa'o//.*

369 Dreyfus, *Recognizing Reality,* p. 456.

370 Dreyfus, *Recognizing Reality,* p. 456.

371 Dreyfus, *Recognizing Reality,* p. 456.

372 Nāgārjuna, *Mūlamadhyamakakārikā* 18:7, p. 45: *brjod par bya ba ldog pa ste/ sems kyi spyod yul ldog pas so/ ma skyes pa dang ma 'gags pa/ chos nyid mnya ngan ldas dang mtshungs//.* Also cited in Candrakīrti, *Prasannapadā,* p. 299b–300a.

373 Candrakīrti, *Prasannapadā,* p. 300: *'dir 'brjod par bya ba 'ga' zhig yod na ni/ de ston par 'gyur ba zhig na/ gang gi tshe brjod par bya ba ldog cing/ tshig dag gi yul yod pa ma yin pa de'i tshe sangs rgyas rnams kyis cung zad kyang ma bstan to/ yang ci'i phyir brjod par bya ba med ce na/ sems kyi spyod yul ldog pas so// zhes gsungs te/ sems kyi spyod yul ni sems kyi spyod yul lo/ spyod yul ni yul te/ dmigs pa zhes bya ba'i tha tshigs go/ gal te sems kyi spyod yul 'ga' zhig yod par gyur na ni der rgyu mtshan 'ga' zhig sgro btags nas tshig dag 'jug par 'gyur na/ gang gi tshe sems kyi spyod yul nyid mi 'thad pa de'i tshe/ rgyu mtshan sgro btags nas tshig gar 'jug par 'gyur/yang ci'i phyir sems kyi spyod yul med ce na/ bstan pa'i phyir/ ma skyes pa dang ma 'gag pa/ chos nyid nya ngan 'das dang mtshungs/ zhes gsungs te/ gang gi phyir ma skyes pa dang ma 'gags pa chos nyid te chos kyi ngo bo dang chos skyi rang bzhin nya ngan las 'das pa dang tshung par bzhag pa de'i phyir de las sems mi 'jug go/ sems mi 'jug na rgyu mtshan sgro 'dogs par ga la 'gyur*

la/ de med pa'i phyir tshig dag 'jug pa ga la 'gyur te/ de'i phyir sangs rgyas rnams kyis cung zad kyang ma bstan to zhes bya bar gnas so//.

374 Candrakīrti, *Madhyamakāvatārabhāṣya*, p. 104: *de ni brjod du med pa'i phir dang/ shes pa'i yul ma yin pa nyid kyi phir dngos su bstan par mi nus pas/.*

375 *Rtsa she ṭīk chen*, p. 327: *don dam par brjod par bya yod na de ston par 'gyur na'ang don dam par brjod par bya ba ldog pa ste yod pa min pa*. . .//.

376 *Rtsa she ṭīk chen*, p. 327: *de'i rgyu mtshan ni don dam par sems kyi spyod yul gyi dmigs pa ldog pas so//.*

377 *Rtsa she ṭīk chen*, p. 327: *de'i rgyu mtshan yang chos thams cad don dam par ma skyes shing ma 'gags pa'i chos nyid nya ngan las 'das pa dang mtshungs pa ste//.*

378 *Rtsa she ṭīk chen*, p. 327: *de'i tshe sangs rgyas rnams kyis cung zad kyang ma bstan no//.*

379 *Nges don rab gsal*, p. 372d: *stong nyid rtogs nas goms pa mthar phyin pa'i tshe glo bur gyi dri ma zad nas blo nyid zag med kyi dbyings su gyur pa ni/ spangs rtogs phun sum tsogs pa don dam pa'i sangs rgyas yin la*. . ./.

380 *Lta ba ngan sel*, f. 728: *ye shes de'i ngor ji lta ba dang/ ji snyed pa dang/ yul can ye shes gsum po ngo bo tha dag me snang la*. . ./.

381 *Nges don rab gsal*, p. 371a–b: *'der spros pa zhes bya ba bden pa'i dngos po'am ma yin dgag kho na ma yin gyi gang la blo 'jug cing 'phro ba dgag sgrub ky chos kyi mtshan ma thams cad yin te*. . .*spros pa ni dngos po'i rgyu mtshan can yin la de bzhin gzhigs pa dngos po med pa la/ spros pa rnams 'jug pa ga la yod de/ de'i phyir de bzhin gshigs pa spros pa las 'das pa yin no//.*

382 *Nges don rab gsal*, p. 371a–b: *spros pa ni dngos po'i rgyu mtshan can yin la de bzhin gzhigs pa dngos po med pa la/ spros pa rnams 'jug pa ga la yod de/ de'i phyir de bzhin gshigs pa spros pa las 'das pa yin no//.*

383 *Nges don rab gsal*, p. 371a: *kun rdzob kyi bden pa ni*. . .*ci ltar so so'i skye bo rnams kyis dngos po yod pa dang med pa la sogs par brtags pa yin gyi/ de lta bu'i rang bzhin ni med pa yin te/ yod pa dang med pa la sogs pa rigs pas mi thad ba'i phir ro//.*

384 *Nges don rab gsal*, p. 370b: *gal te sems kyi spyod yul 'ga' zhig yod par gyur na ni der rgyu msthan 'ga' zhig sgro btags nas tshig dag 'jug par 'gyur na/ gang gyi tshe sems kyi spyod yul nyid mi 'thad pa de'i tshe rgyu msthan sgro btags nas tshig gar 'jug par 'gyur//.* Also see *Lta ba'i 'od zer*, p. 335a.

385 *Lta ba'i 'od zer*, p. 335a: *ci'i phir sems kyi spyod yul ldog ce na chos rnams kyi chos nyid de bzhin nyid gdod ma nas ma skyes pa dang/ ma 'gags pas blo bur gyi dri ma dang dral ba'i mnya ngan las 'das pa dang mtshungs pas/ gnyis snang dang bcas pa'i blo la rnam pa 'char rgyu med pa'i phyir ro//.*

386 *Nges don rab gsal*, p. 370b: *ci'i phyir sems kyi spyod yul med ce na/* . . .*gang gi phyir ma skyes pa dang ma 'gag pa'i chos nyid de chos kyi ngo bo dang/ chos kyi rang bzhin mnya ngan las 'das pa dang mtshungs par bzhag pa de'i phir de sems mi 'jug go//.*

387 *Nges don rab gsal*, p. 370b: *sems mi 'jug na rgyu mtshan sgro 'dogs par ga la 'gyur la de med pa'i phyir tshig dag 'jug par ga la 'gyur te/ de'i phyir sangs rgyas rnams kyis cung zad kyang ma bstan to zhes bya bar gnas so//.*

388 *Lta ba'i 'od zer*, p. 334d–335a: *brjod par bya ba'i chos 'ga' zhig yod na ston par 'gyur ba zhig na de kho na nyid la ni sgras zhen nas brjod par bya ba ldog pas 'ga' yang ma bstan to//.*

389 *Nges don rab gsal*, p. 335b: *don dam pa'i de kho na nyid rang gi ngo bo'i sgo nas bstan par mi nus kyang kun rdzob du sgro brtags nas bstan pa ltar mtshan nyid kyang sgro brtag nas bstan dgos//.*

390 Pettit, *Mipham's Beacon of Certainty*, p. 138.

391 See Mipham, *Dbu ma rtsa ba'i mchan 'grel gnas lugs rab gsal* (hereafter, *Dbu rtsa'i mchan 'grel*), *The Collected Works*, vol. 1 (Gangtok: Sonam Topgyal Kazi, 1979), p. 217: *'on na rtogs bya'i de kho na nyid ci lta bu zhe na/ de bsam brjod las 'das par bstan zin to/ /'on kyang 'jig rten tha snyad kyi rjes su 'brang nas de'i mtshan nyid brjod.../ /.*

392 *Dbu rtsa'i rnam bshad*, f. 175: *de kho na nyid sgras brjod pa'am rtog pas shes par nus sam zhes na/ sangs rgyas kyis de kho na nyid ston pa'is dbang du mdzad nas yongs bcod du ci yang bstan pa med de/ de kho na nyid ni sgras brjod par bya ba ldog pa ste/ brjod du med pa'i phyir te/ sems kyi rnan par rtog pa'i spyod yul du dmigs pa ste der 'dzin pa ldog pas so/ /de'i rgyu mtshan ni/ don dam par/ ma skyes pa dang ma 'gags pa'i chos nyid ni mya ngan las 'das pa dang tshungs par sgra rtog gi di lta ba bzhin bzhung du med pa'i phir ro/ /.*

393 Jaideva Singh, *The Conception of Buddhist Nirvāṇa*, pp. 15–18, endorses the same view, see esp. p. 39. "From the standpoint of the Absolute, *śūnyatā* means *prapañcair aprapañcitam,* that which is devoid of, completely free of thought-construction, *anānārthām,* that which is devoid of plurality. In other words, (a) in-expressible in human language, (b) that 'is,' 'not is,' 'both is and not is,' 'neither is nor not is'—no thought category or predicate can be applied to it. It is transcendence of thought."

394 We should not, however, take the similarity between Gorampa and his modern counterparts too far. The (nontraditional) reading of Nāgārjuna, in my view, is a consequence of equating Nāgārjuna's ultimate reality with either the Kantian absolute or the Upaniṣadic Brahman as *neti, neti.* For example, Murti, *The Central Philosophy of Buddhism,* p. 38, writes: "The similarity of the *avyākṛta* to the celebrated antinomies of Kant and the *catuṣkoṭi* of the Mādhyamikas cannot fail to strike us." Moreover he says, p. 48: "A close parallel...is the Upaniṣadic way of defining 'neti, neti,' as what cannot be grasped by speech, thought or senses." Similarly, Harsha Narain, "The nature of Mādhyamika thought," in S. Rinpoche, ed., *The Mādhyamika Dialectic and the Philosophy of Nāgārjuna* (Sarnath: CIHTS, 1985), p. 239, sees Mādhyamikas as Kantians insofar as they share the notion of "innate incapacity of human reason to reach the Absolute." Jaideva Singh, in the introduction to Theodore Stcherbatsky, *The Conception of Buddhist Nirvāṇa* (Delhi: Motilal Banarasidass, 1989), pp. 48, 72, however, focuses on the connections between the Brahmā and Īśvara of Vedanta and the *dharmadhātu* and *dharmakāya* of the Madhyamaka. Stcherbatsky, p. 26, also draws parallels emphasizing the transcendent character of *advaita-brahman,* particularly the connection between the Buddha's silence on the metaphysical question and Śaṅkara's silence on the issue about the essence of Brahman. I partly agree that there are parallels in the explanatory mode of the Madhyamaka's ultimate reality, the Kantian absolute, and the Upaniṣadic Brahman, specifically the incapacity of logical mind to grasp these. However, I also partly disagree. Except for the dialectical parallels, there is minimal intersection between the Madhyamaka's

ultimate reality (especially Tsongkhapa's) with either the Kantian absolute or Upaniṣadic Brahman.

395 Murti, *Mādhyamika Dialectic and the Philosophy of Nāgārjuna*, p. xi.

396 Narain, "The Nature of Mādhyamika," in S. Rinpoche, ed., *The Mādhyamika Dialectic and the Philosophy of Nāgārjuna*, p. 239.

397 Narain, "The Nature of Mādhyamika," in S. Rinpoche, ed., *The Mādhyamika Dialectic and the Philosophy of Nāgārjuna*, p. 236.

398 DN 22. See S. Rinpoche, ed., *Ten Suttas from Dīgha Nikāya: Long Discourses of the Buddha* (Sarnath: CIHTS, 1987); and for the translation of the entire Digha Nikāya, see Maurice Walshe, trans., *The Long Discourses of the Buddha: A Translation of the Dīgha Nikāya* (Boston: Wisdom Publication, 1995).

399 See Thanissaro Bhikkhu, trans., *An Anthology of Selected Suttas from the Majjhima Nikāya*, http://www.accesstoinsight.org/canon/majjhima/index/html. For an excellent translation of the entire Nikāya, see Bhikkhu Ñāṇamoli and Bhikkhu Bodhi., trans., *The Middle Length Discourses of the Buddha: A Translation of the Majjhima Nikāya* (Boston: Wisdom Publication, 1995).

400 Bhikkhu Bodhi, *The Noble Eightfold Path: The Way to the End of Suffering* (Kandy, Sri Lanka: Buddhist Publication Society, 1994), p. 5.

401 AN 10.121. See Bhikkhu Ñanamoli, trans., and Bhikkhu Bodhi, ed. and revised, *The Discourse on Right View: The Sammādiṭṭhi Sutta and Its Commentary* (Kandy, Sri Lanka: Buddhist Publication Society, 1994), p. 1.

402 AN 10.121. See Ñanamoli and Bodhi, *The Discourse on Right View: The Sammādiṭṭhi Sutta and Its Commentary*, p. 1.

403 MN 117. See Thanissaro Bhikkhu, trans., *An Anthology of Selected Suttas from the Majjhima Nikāya*, http://www.accesstoinsight.org/canon/majjhima/index/html.

404 MN 9. The first is physical food as nutriment, gross or subtle; contact via any of the six senses is the second; volition is the third; and consciousness of any kind is the fourth.

405 Ignorance, formations, consciousness, mentality-materiality, the sixfold base, contact, feeling, craving, clinging, being, birth, and aging and death.

406 Pettit, *Mipham's Beacon of Certainty*, p. 138.

407 See Bhikkhu Bodhi's introduction in *The Discourse on Right View: The Sammādiṭṭhi Sutta and Its Commentary*, p. 2.

408 Tsongkhapa, *Byang chub lam gyi rim pa chen mo* (hereafter, *Lam rim chen mo*) (Sarnath: Gelugpa Students' Welfare Committee, 1993), p. 789: *de ni rtog pa yin yang ye shes dang shin tu rjes su mthun pa'i rgyu yin te.../.*

409 *Lam rim chen mo*, p. 791: *so sor rtog pa'i shes rab kyi dpyad pa sngon du song ba'i mi rtog pa dgos kyi mi rtog pa tsam gis chog pa ma yin no//.*

410 *Lam rim chen mo*, p. 789: *de lta yin na lam zag bcas las zad med kyi lam 'byung ba yang mi srid pas so so skye bos 'phags pa thob pa med par 'gyur te...//.*

411 *Lam rim chen mo*, p. 789: *de bzhin du sa bon skya bo las myu gu sngon po skye ba dang/ me las du ba skye ba dang/ bud med las skyes pa sogs rnams pa mi 'dra ba'i rgyu 'bras mtha' yas pa zhig snang ngo//.*

412 *Lam rim chen mo*, p. 789: *'phags pa'i rnam par mi rtog pa'i ye shes ni bdag gnyis su 'dzin pa'i yul gis stong pa'i bdag med pa'i don mngon sum du rtogs pa yin la/ de skye ba la da lta nas bdag du 'dzin pa'i yul la so sor dpyad nas de med par rtogs pa'i sgo nas sgom dgos...//.*

413 See AN 1.16.2, SN 12.15, DN 1.
414 Bhikkhu Bodhi, *The Noble Eightfold Path: The Way to the End of Suffering*, p. 5.
415 Nāgārjuna, *Mūlamadhyamakakārikā* 27:30, p. 81: *gang gis thugs brtse nyer bzung nas/ /lta ba thams cad spang pa'i phyir/ /dam pa'i chos ni ston mdzad pa/ go tam de la phyag 'tshal lo//.*
416 For his detailed treatment of this issue, see *Legs bshad snying po*, pp. 248–50, 252–54; and *Rtsa she ṭīk chen*, pp. 258–59, 462–84.
417 Garfield, *Empty Words*, p. 47.
418 Garfield, *Empty Words*, p. 48.
419 Garfield, *Empty Words*, p. 48.
420 *Lta ba'i 'od zer*, p. 307a: *lta ba smad pa ni ma rig pa'i rab rib kyis blo'is mig myams pa'i blo chung gang dag phyi nang gi dngos po kun rdzob pa rnams las yang dag par yod pa nyid dang/ de bkag pa'i med pa nyid du lta ba'i gang zag de yis ni lta bar bya ba don dam par rang bzhin gis mya ngan las 'das pa spros pa thams cad nyi bar zhi ba dang/ zhi ba mthar mthog pa mi mthong ste/ dgag bya spros pa'i mtha la bltas pas spros dral lta ba'i mig dang mi ldan pa'i phyir/ dmus long bzhin no//.*
421 For a detailed analysis, see *Lta ba'i shan 'byed*, pp. 41–64, 66–76, for his critiques of Tsongkhapa's view, and pp. 116–54 for his own account.
422 *Nges don rab gsal*, p. 394d: *dbu ma rang nyid la zhe 'dod kyi khas len cung zad kyang med pa'r phyir//.*
423 *Nges don rab gsal*, p. 395a: *rang la zhe 'dod kyi dam bca' khas len med pa de sgrub pa'i rang rgyud gyi rtags shes bya la mi 'thad pa yin no/ /des na thal 'gyur gyi byed pas kyang pha rol po'i log par rtog pa'i dam bca' 'gog pa tsam yin gyi/ rang gi 'dod pa sgrub pa ni ma yin te//...des na dbu ma pa la rang 'dod pa'i bsgrub bya med pas dang/ chos can la mthun snang med pas rang rgyud kyi rtags mi 'thad cing gzhan gyi 'dod pa 'gog pa ni pha rol po nyid kyis khas blangs pa'i rtags las de dang brgyud nas 'gal ba'i pha rol po'i 'dod pa 'gog pa thal 'gyur ba'i lugs 'de nyid rigs pa yin no//.* Also see pp. 396a–400a.
424 Kalupahana, *Nāgārjuna*, p. 12.
425 *Lam rim chen mo*, p. 792: *bden par bzung nas gnas su mi rung ba yang sngar bshad pa ltar/ de dag bden par med par rtogs pa la rag las pas/ de 'dra ba'i mi gnas pa dang mi rtog par gsungs pa thams cad yul rnams rang bzhin gis grub pa'am bden par 'gog pa' yang dag pa'i so sor rtog po sngon du 'gro ba kho na la gsungs pa yin par shes par gis shig//.*
426 Narain, "The Nature of Mādhyamika Thought," in *The Mādhyamika Dialectic and the Philosophy of Nāgārjuna*, p. 238.
427 Narain, "The Nature of Mādhyamika Thought," in *The Mādhyamika Dialectic and the Philosophy of Nāgārjuna*, pp. 238–39.
428 For example, Longchen Rabjam, *Grub mtha' mdzod*, ff. 196, 294; Sakya Paṇḍita, *Gzung lugs legs bshad*, p. 72b; Rendawa, *Dbu 'jug rnam bshad*, p. 325; Mipham Rinpoche, *Shes 'grel ke ta ka*, p. 10; Rongtön Shakya Gyaltsen, *Rigs tsogs dka' gnad*, ff. 58–59; Taktsang Lotsawa, *Grub mtha'i rnam bshad*, f. 255; Shakya Chogden, *Dbu rtsa'i rnam bshad*, f. 117; Mikyö Dorje, *Dag brgyud grub pa'i shing rta*, f. 279; and Khenpo Künzang Palden, *Dpyod 'jug tshig 'grel*, p. 440.
429 *Mahāratnakūṭa Sūtra* 1. Chang, *Mahāyāna Sūtras*, p. 14.
430 Candrakīrti, *Madhyamakāvatārabhāṣya* 104: *nyan par 'dod pa rnams la rang gis myong ba nyid du de'i rang bzhin gsal par bya ba'i phir dpe bshad pa//.*

431 Candrakīrti, *Prasannapadā*, p. 307: *'de la bzhan las shes pa yod pa ma yin pas na gzhan las shes min te/ gzhan gyis bstan pa rtogs par bya ba ma yin gyi/ rang nyid kyis rtog par bya ba yin no zhes bya ba'i don to//.*

432 Candrakīrti, *Prasannapadā*, p. 307: *de'i tshe de kho na nyid ma rtogs pa'i tshul gyis rang nyid kyis rtogs par 'gyur te/ de ltar na dngos po rnams kyi rang gi ngo bo gzhan las shes ba ma yin pa...de ni de kho na nyid do//.*

433 *Madhyamakāvatārabhāṣya*, p. 105: *gal te rnam pa de lta bu'i rang bzhin ni mthong ba med pa nyid ma yin nam de'i phyir ji ltar de dag gis gzigs she na/ bden mod kyi 'on kyang ma gzigs pa'i tshul gyis gzigs so zhes brjod do//.*

434 See Mahāsi Sayadaw and Nyanaponika Thera, trans., *The Progress of Insight (Visuddhiñana-katha): A Modern Treatise on Buddhist Satipaṭṭhāna Meditation* (Kandy, Sri Lanka: Buddhist Publication Society, 1994), p. 6.

435 It is as Bodhidharma describes: "The dharmakāya is formless. Therefore, one sees it by no-seeing. Dharma is soundless. Therefore, one hears it by no-hearing. Insight does not have knowledge. Therefore, one knows by no-knowing." Broughton, *The Bodhidharma Anthology*, p. 15.

436 *Dgongs pa rab gsal*, p. 202: *de kho na nyid kyi gzig ngor gnyis snang nub pas gnyis kyi tshul gyis mi gzigs pa ni bden mod kyi/ 'on kyang ma gzigs pa'i tshul gyis de dag gis gzigs so zhes brjod do//.*

437 *Dgongs pa rab gsal*, p. 200: *don dam pa'i shes bya thams cad mkhyen tshul...phung po la sogs pa kun rdzob pa'i snang ba rnams ma gzigs pa'i tshul gyis/ de rnams kyi de kho na nyid mkhyen pa'o//.*

438 *Dgongs pa rab gsal*, p. 202: *sangs rgyas kyi don dam mkhyen pa'i ye shes kyis chos can la ma rig par chos nyid 'ba' zhig thugs su chud par gsungs te//.*

439 *Nges don rab gsal*, p. 446: *gnyis snang dang bcas ba'i snang ba ni med de/ 'khrul ba'i bags chags ma lus pa spangs pa'i phyir ro//.* By "predisposition without any trace" Gorampa means that ultimate wisdom is free from any reifying tendencies of defilements.

440 Cited in *Dgongs pa rab gsal*, p. 202: *mthong ba med pa ni mthong ba dam pa'o//.* Also cited in *Rtsa she ṭīk-chen*, p. 275.

441 *Dgongs pa rab gsal*, p. 202: *ci yang mi mthong ba mthong bar mi bzhed kyi//.* Also see *Rtsa she ṭīk chen*, p. 275–76.

442 *Dgongs pa rab gsal*, p. 202: *spros pa ma mthong ba ni spros dral mthong bar 'jog pas/ mthong ma mthong gzhi gcig la byed pa min no//.* Also see *Rtsa she ṭīk chen*, pp. 275–76: *mthong ba med pa ni mthong ba dam pa'i zhes gsungs pa'i don yang ci yang mi mthong ba mthong bar mi bzhed kyi/ sngar bshad pa ltar spros pa ma mthong ba ni spros dral mthong par 'jog pas mthong ma mthong gzhi gcig la byed pa min no//.*

443 *Lta ba'i shan 'byed*, p. 128b: *ma mthong ba'i tshul gyis mthong/ ma gzigs pa'i tshul gyis gzigs//.*

444 *Prapañca* in Buddhist philosophical discourse always carries a negative connotation. It usually means a tendency of thoughts to proliferate based on a false sense of self. It is therefore frequently used in analyses of the discord between things as we perceive them and things as they are, as the Buddha himself does in such discourses as the *Sakka-pañha Sutta* (DN 21), the *Madhupiṇḍika Sutta* (MN 18), and the *Kalaha-vivāda Sutta* (SN 4.11). Although this term is variously translated as "self-reflexive thinking," "reification," "falsification," "distortion," "elaboration,"

or "exaggeration," I opted for "conceptual elaboration" to emphasize the role of conception in *prapañca*.

445 See www.accesstoinsight.org/canon/majjhima/index.html for Thanissaro Bhikku's notes on *Madhupiṇḍika Sutta* [MN 18]. See also his mapping of the causal chain that gives rise to prapañca and that eventually leads to conflict. The presentation is somewhat linear, but the reality is much more complex and "provides plenty of room for feedback loops." It prevents, however, the explanation of causation as random, coincidental, accidental, or divine.

446 Ibid.

447 Ibid.

448 Ibid.

449 *Rtsa she ṭīk chen*, pp. 322–23: *'o na gang zad pas las nyon zad par 'gyur snyam na/ 'khor bar skye ba'i las nyon ni nyon mongs las skye la nyon mongs kyang sdug mi sdug dang phyin ci log gi tshul min yid byed kyi rnam rtog las 'byung gi ngo bo nyid kyis yod pa min no// tshul min yid byed kyi rnam rtog de dag ni shes pa dang shes bya dang rjod bya dang rjod byed dang bum snam dang skyes pa dang bud med dang/ rnyed ma rnyed la sogs pa la bden par zhen pa'i spros pa sna tshogs pa thog med nas goms pa las skyes'o/ bden 'dzin gyi spros pa ni yul de rnams stong pa nyid du lta ba goms pas 'gags par 'gyur ro//.* Also see pp. 327, 453.

450 *Rtsa she ṭīk chen*, pp. 420–21: *de la spros pa ni 'jir rtags kyi dgag bya'i spros pa tsam ma yin gyi snang ba'i spros pa yang yin no//.*

451 *Nges don rab gsal*, p. 371a: *'dir spros pa zhes pa bden pa'i dngos po'am ma yin dgag kho na ma yin gyi gang gang la blo 'jug cing sphro dgag sgrub kyi chos kyi mtshan ma thams cad yin te//.*

452 Dreyfus, *Recognizing Reality*, p. 459.

453 *Mahāratnakūṭa Sūtra* 2. Chang, *Mahāyāna Sūtras*, p. 32.

454 *Rtsa she ṭīk chen*, p. 421: *snang ba'i spros pa med pa med pa la mi bya ste.../*/.

455 *Rtsa she ṭīk chen*, p. 421: *de las 'das pa'i tshul ni de kho na nyid mngon sum du gzigs pa'i ngor gnyis snang gi spros pa thams cad nub pa la bya'i...//.*

456 *Nges don rab gsal*, p. 371a–b: *spros pa ni dngos po'i rgyu mtshan can yin la de bzhin gzhigs pa dngos po med pa la/ spros pa rnams 'jug pa ga la yod de/ de'i phyir de bzhin gshigs pa spros pa las 'das pa yin no//.*

457 *Dbu 'jug rnam bshad*, p. 127.

458 *Dbu rtsa'i rnam bshad*, pp. 216–21.

459 *Dbu rtsa'i rnam bshad*, ff. 223–24.

460 *Dag brgyud grub pa'i shing rta*, f. 279.

461 *Dbu rtsa'i mchan 'grel*, ff. 209–12.

462 *Klu sgrub dgongs rgyan*, pp. 149–52.

463 *Nges don rab gsal*, p. 371b: *spros pa'i ngos 'dzin bzhi tsam byung ba rnams ni mtha' bzhi char spros pa las ma 'das kyang skabs thob kyi spros pa ngos 'dzin pa'i dbang du byas pa'o/ de dang dral ba'i don yang 'khrul ngo'i yod med sogs kyi spros pa 'de dag gdod ma nas rang gyi ngo bos stong pa yin la...//.*

464 *Nges don rab gsal*, p. 371a–b: *'der spros pa zhes bya ba bden pa'i dngos po'am ma yin dgag kho na ma yin gyi gang la blo 'jug cing 'phro ba dgag sgrub ky chos kyi mtshan ma thams cad yin te...spros pa ni dngos po'i rgyu mtshan can yin la de bzhin gzhigs pa dngos po med pa la/ spros pa rnams 'jug pa ga la yod de/ de'i phyir de bzhin gshigs pa spros pa las 'das pa yin no//.*

465 *Rtsa she ṭīk chen,* p. 421: *gzhan du na chos nyid dang chos can snang ba'i spros pa gnyis ya mi dral bas don dam bden pa mi srid pa'r 'gyur ba'i phyir ro//.*

466 Bhikkhu Bodhi, *Transcendental Dependent Arising: A Translation and Exposition of the Upanisa Sutta* (Kandy, Sri Lanka: Buddhist Publication Society, 1980), p. 10; he adds that "with the attainment of dispassion, consciousness passes clear beyond the mundane level, and for a fleeting moment realises as its object the unconditioned state, *nibbāna.*"

467 Bhikkhu Bodhi, *Transcendental Dependent Arising,* p. 10.

468 Nāgārjuna, *Yuktiṣaṣṭikā* 6, p. 87: *srid pa dang ni mya ngan ldas/ /gnyis po 'di ni yod ma nyin/ /srid pa yongs su shes pa nyid/ /mya ngan 'das zhes bya bar brjod//.*

469 *Rtsa shes ṭīk chen,* pp. 25–26: *rten 'byung gi de kho na nyid gnas tshul bzhin 'phags pas gzhigs pa'i don bjord bya rjord byed dang mtshan mtshon la sogs pa'i spros pa thams cad ldog pa'i phyir rten 'byung gi de nyid la spros pa nger zhi zhes bya ba'i//.*

470 Bhikkhu Bodhi, *Transcendental Dependent Arising,* p. 10.

471 *Nges don rab gsal,* p. 371c–d: *ngos po rnams kyi rang bzhin mthar thug pa…ni de bzhin gshegs pa rrnams byung yang rung ma byung yang rung/ chos rnams kyi chos nyid ni gnas pa pa'o// zhes ba'i tshul gyis gsungs las sogs pa'i chos thams cad la dus thams cad du me'i tsha ba dang/ bu ram gyi mngar ba ltar cir yang ma grub pa'i stong nyid des khyab pa dang/ rigs pa yang dag gis mtha' gang du grub tsal ba na gang du yang ma grub par nges pa dang/ de la ji skad shad pa'i rang bzhin gyi chos gsum 'thad pa nyid phyir na dgos po rnams kyi rang bzhin mthar mthug pa'o//.*

472 *Rtsa she ṭīk chen,* p. 421: *de las 'das pa'i tshul ni de kho na nyid mngon sum du gzhigs pa'i ngor gnyis snang gyi spros pa thams cad nub pa la bya'i…//.*

473 *Mahāratnakūṭa Sūtra* 2. Chang, *Mahāyāna Sūtras,* p. 32.

474 *Rta she ṭīk chen,* p. 417: *des ji snyed pa'i don rnam mngon sum du 'jal ba ma yin te/ 'jal na ni shugs la rtogs pa mi rung bas dgnos su rtogs dgos shing de yang rnam pa med par 'jal ba 'de pa'i lugs min pas gsugs sgra la sogs pa'i rnam pa dngos su shar ba'i blo la yul yul can gnyis su snang ba med par byar mi rung ba'i phyir ro//.*

475 Metaphorically speaking, "it is like seeing the continuous successive vanishing of a summer mirage moment by moment; or it is like the quick and continuous bursting of bubbles produced in a heavy shower by thick raindrops falling on a water surface; or it is like the quick, successive extinction of oil lamps or candles, blown out by the wind, as these lights are being offered at a shrine by devotees." Sayadaw and Thera, *The Progress of Insight,* p. 6.

476 *Nges don rab gsal,* p. 372d: *stong nyid rtogs nas goms pa mthar phyin pa'i tshe glo bur gyi dri ma zad nas blo nyid zag med kyi dbyings su gyur pa ni/ spangs rtogs phun sum tshogs pa don dam pa'i sangs rgyas yin la…/.*

477 *Lta ba ngan sel,* f. 728: *ye shes de'i ngor ji lta ba dang/ ji snyed pa dang/ yul can ye shes gsum po ngo bo tha dag me snang la…/.*

478 *Lta ba'i shan 'byed,* p. 128: *mtha' bzhi'i spros pa cig char du 'gags nas rtog bya'i chos nyid dang rtogs byed kyi blo gnyis so sor mi snang//.*

479 *Lta ba'i shan 'byed,* p. 128: *blo de nyid spros dral dang dbyer med par mngon du gyur pa'i yul de nyid la/ don dam bden pa zhes pa'i tha snyad btags pa yin gyi/ de'i tshe yang don dam bden pa 'di'o zhes cung zad kyang bzung bar bya ba med do//.*

480 *Don dam rnam bshad,* ff. 187: *stong nyid mngon sum du rtogs pa'i mnyam bzhag ye shes kyi gzhal bya dngos ni/ ye shes de nyid yin gyi/.*

481 *Don dam rnam bshad,* ff. 187–88: *ye shes de chos can/ don dam pa'i bden pa yin te/ stong nyid dngos sum du rtogs pa'i mnyam bzhag ye shes kyi dngos kyi gzhal bya mtshan nyid pa yin pa'i phyir/ rtags grub ste/ ye shes de so sor rang gis rig pa'i ye shes yin pa'i phyir.../ /.* The following statement appears in between the above Tibetan citation: *stong pa nyid ces bya ba gzhan sel dang ldog pa med dgag gi char gyur ba de nyid de'i dngos kyi gzhal bya ma yin te/ dngos med dgnos su 'jal ba'i mngon sum ni phyogs glang yob sras kyis mi bzhed pa ltar/ zla ba'i zhabs kyis kyang me bzhed pa'i phyir ro/ /.* Shakya Chogden denies emptiness as being the object of the transcendent wisdom. "So-called emptiness—which eliminates other [entities] *(gzhan sel, anyāpoha)* and bears the nonaffirming negative aspect—is not its actual cognitive sphere. Just as Dīgnāga and his son [Dharmakīrti] deny the direct perception that supposedly directly perceives entitilessness *(dngos med),* so does Candrakīrti," he writes.

482 *Dag brgyud grub pa'i shing rta,* f. 279: *'phags chen rnams kyi mnyam gzhag rnam par mi rtog pa'i ye shes kyis spros pa dang mtshan ma thams cad 'ga' yang mthong ba med pa'i tshul du so so rang gis rig pa'i ye shes kyis gzhigs pa la ni gzugs nas rnam mkhyen gyi bar gyi don dam pa'i bden pa dang/ de bzhin nyid ces tha snyad btags par zad kyi/ 'phags pa'i mnyam gzhag la ma ltos pa'am/ de las tha dad pa'i don du grub ba ni ma yin cing/ don dam pa'i bden pa las tha dad pa'i phags pa'i mnyam gzhag kyang yod pa ma yin no/ /.* Only the last two sentences are translated here in the text.

483 *Dbud ma 'jug pa'i 'grel pa zla ba'i zhal lung dri med shel phreng* (hereafter, *Zla ba'i zhal lung*) (Sarnath: Nyingma Students' Welfare Committee, 1977), ff. 159–60: *mthar ni phyi don med de bags chags kyi snang ba tsam yin par dgnos stobs kyis 'grub ste.../ / phyi don yod yod lta bur bsgrub pa'i gzhung thams cad re zhig snang ngo'i dbang du byas te yod par bzhag/ /.*

484 *Zla ba'i zhal lung,* ff. 159–60: *pa rmi lam rang ngo'i rta glang bzhin no/ /dpyad cing dpyad na nang gi bag chags kyi rten 'byung la thar thug pa ni nang pa sangs rgyas pa'i grub mtha'i phug ste/ /.*

485 *Lta ba ngan sel,* f. 728: *de nas bzung ste ye shes de'i ngor dus snga phyi dbye ba yang med pa'i phyir te skye 'gag mi snang ba'i phyir ro/ /.*

486 For Gorampa's detailed treatment of *ālayavijñāna,* "the foundational consciousness," and how he imposes this doctrine on the Prāsaṅgika Madhyamaka, see *Nges don rab gsal,* pp. 402d–403b. Also see his criticisms directed toward Tsongkhapa's view for the latter's refusal to impose the conception of the "foundational consciousness" on the Prāsaṅgika system, see *Lta ba'i shan 'byed,* pp. 91–94. Also see *Lta ba ngan sel,* ff. 634–40. Introductions to the Yogācāra or Vijñānavāda school can be found in Paul Williams, *Mahāyāna Buddhism: The Doctrinal Foundations* (London: Routledge, 1989), pp. 77–117; A.K. Warder, *Indian Buddhism* (Delhi: Motilal Banarsidass, 1970), pp. 423–62; Ashok Kumar Chatterjee, *Yogācāra Idealism,* BHU Darsana Series no. 3 (Benares: Benares Hindu University, 1999); and Peter Harvey, *An Introduction to Buddhism: Teachings, History and Practices* (Cambridge: Cambridge University Press, 2000), pp. 104–20. On the term *vijñaptimātra,* see B.C. Hall, "The Meaning of Vijñapti in Vasubandu's Concept of Mind," *Journal of the International Association of Buddhist Studies* 9, no. 1 (1986): 7–24.

487 On this topic, see L. Schmithausen, *Ālayavijñāna: On the Origin and Early Development of a Central Concept of Yogācāra Philosophy*, Parts I and II, Studia Philologica Buddhica, Monograph Series IVab (Tokyo: International Institute for Buddhist Studies, 1989); and William S. Waldron, *The Buddhist Unconscious: The Ālaya-vijñāna in the Context of Indian Buddhist Thought* (London: RoutledgeCurzon, 2003).

488 *The Tibetan Book of Living and Dying* (Sydney: Random House Australia, 1992), p. 47.

489 *The Tibetan Book of Living and Dying,* p. 47

490 See Lindtner, "Studies on the Yuktiṣaṣṭikā," in the *Master of Wisdom: Writings of the Buddhist Master Nāgārjuna,* p. 259.

491 *Nges don rab gsal,* p. 373c?d: *spros dral don dam pa'i mtshan gzhir bsnyad pa'i tshul ni de ltar cir yang ma grub pa nyid yin yang ma grub pa nyid gdul byas rtogs pa'i don do mtshan gzhir sgro btags nas bsnyad pa yin gyi.../.*

492 *Nges don rab gsal,* p. 373d: *mtshan nyid bstan pa'i gzhir gyur ba'i mtshan gzhi ni mi srid do//.*

493 *Nges don rab gsal,* p. 373d: *des mtshon pa'i don yang mtshan nyid dang/ mtshon bya dang/ mtshan gzhi gsum du sgro btags pa'i tha snyad gsum gyi sgo nas don dam pa'i bden pa zhes kun rdzob kyi bden pa'i lda bor bsnyad pa yin te...//.*

494 *Nges don rab gsal,* p. 373b–c: *'on na sngar spros dral ngos gzung ba'i skabs su bjord bya rjord byed dang/ yul yul can dang/ dgag sgrub kyi mtshan ma thams cad dang dral bar brjod nas 'dir de lta bu'i che ba nam mkha' mi tok gi yon tan brjod pa ltar shes par mi nus so zhes na de lta mod kyi 'dir yang de rtog pa'i shes pa dang myong bas yul du byas pa'am 'ga' zhig gi byed rgyur bstan pa ma yin te/...'phags pa'i mi rtog pa'i shes rab kyis spros pa mtha' dag khegs pa nyid las stong nyid rtogs zhes dang/ bden pa mthong zhes bsnyad pa tsam yin gi rtog pa dang myong bas yul du byas na don spyi dang dngos po las ma 'das so//.*

495 Verse 9. Thurman, *The Holy Teaching of Vimalakīrti,* p. 73.

496 *Grub mtha'i rnam bshad,* f. 260: *phags pa'i mnyam bzhag ye shes la ni mtshan ma'i gnyis snang lta zhog snang ba'i snang tsam yang med par dbyings so so zhi ba cig dgos te/ rtogs bya dang rtogs byed yul and yul can du snang ba yod na byang chub ni med par phags pa klu sgrub zhabs kyis...gsungs pa'i phyir ro//.*

497 *Klu sgrub dgongs rgyan,* p. 186: *mnyam gzhag gi skabs su ci yang med pa de/ rjes thob kyi snang ba dang 'drel tshe mnyam gzhag gi skabs cir yang med pa dang/ rjes thob tu ci yang snang pa gnyis zung du 'drel ba'i don yin la/.*

498 *Klu sgrub dgongs rgyan,* p. 186: *de ni don dam par cir yang ma grub pa dang/ tha snyad du cir yang grub pa'i don do shes par bya'o//.*

499 *Lam rim chen mo,* pp. 773–83.

500 See Cabezón, *A Dose of Emptiness,* pp. 112–17, the section on "A Critique of Quietism."

501 *Grub mtha'i rnam bshad,* pp. 878–89.

502 See *Thub pa dgongs gsal,* pp. 24d–25c; his criticisms are directed toward Hva Shang's view and are not specifically targeted to Gorampa, but as Gorampa is committed to a similar view as Hva Shang's, particularly in equating *seeing nothingness* as *seeing emptiness,* Sakya Paṇḍita's criticisms may be extrapolated to apply to Gorampa's view.

503 *Dbu tsa'i rnam bshad,* f. 121: *gang dag ci yang yid la me byed pa tsam mnyam gzhag du 'dod par ltar na mnyam gzhag gis sgrib pa'i bag la nyal ba 'joms par me nus te/ stong nyid rtogs pa'i lhag mthong dang dral ba'i phyir/ 'dus shes med pa'i snyoms 'jug zhin//.*

504 *Dbu tsa'i rnam bshad,* ff. 121–22: *gal te ci yang yed la med byed pa tsam gyis spong ngo zhes na/ gnyid dang brgyal ba la sogs pas kyang spong bar 'gyur te/ yid la mi byed pa tsam 'de la yang yod pa'i phyir ro//.*

505 See Cabezón, *A Dose of Emptiness,* p. 400n31 for his brief analysis of the Chinese monk Hva Shang as a historical and philosophical figure. Sakya Paṇḍita, *Thub pa dgongs gsal,* pp. 24d–25c, in a brief historical account of the origin of Hva Shang's view in Tibet, argues that this view prevailed during the reign of the Tibetan king Trisong Deutsan (790–845 C.E.); Hva Shang Mahāyāna was held responsible for propagating this view in Tibet. Eventually he was defeated by the Indian pandita Kamalaśīla in the great Samye debate and was forced to return to China. His controversial doctrine, sometimes referred to as *quietism,* emphasizes stilling thought and speculative analysis in order to attain tranquillity. It is also said that this doctrine dismisses the moral aspects of spiritual practice.

506 *Nges shes sgron me,* f. 83: *kha cig cir yang mi dzin zer/ cir yang mi dzhin zer ba'i don/...dran med hwa shang lugs/ ma dpyad tse ner bzhag ba yes/ lhag mthong gsal ba'i cha med par/ mtsho gting rdo bzhin tha mal gnas...//.*

507 *Nges shes sgron me,* ff. 84, 87: *ma mthong stong par rtogs shes na/ chos tshul shin tu zab pa ste/ sems ni gzugs can ma yin pas/ /sus kyang mdog sogs mthong mi srid/ /ma mthong tsam las stong pa nyid/ /ngo 'phrod snyam na shin tu gol/ /len brgyar rtag kyang mi yi mgor/ /phyugs kyi rwa mthong mi srid/ /de ma mthong bas de stong par/ rtogs su zhes na sus kyang sla//...cir yang mi dzin lta ngan la/ /dngos po cir yang ma grub pa'i/ /nges shes skye ba ga la yod/ des na sgrib pa spong mi nus/ de phyir 'di gnyis khyad par yang/ du ba'i rtags la mi bzhin du/ spang rtogs bog skyed tshul las shes//.* Also see ff. 121–28, 174.

508 *Nges shes sgron me,* p. 446c: *skyes 'gag la sogs pa gdul bya las bstan ba'i ya gyal gyi kun rdzob bden pa'i snang ba med kyang dbyings rig dbyer med kyi don dam pa snang ba'i snang ba yod dgos te gzhan du chos dbyings goms pa mthar mthog pa'i tshe chos dbyings mi snang na/ chos dbying snang ba'i ye shes mthar mthog med par thal ba'i phyir ro//.*

509 *An Introduction to Buddhism,* p. 112.

510 *Mahāratnakūṭa Sūtra* 20. Chang, *Mahāyāna Sūtras,* p. 395.

511 See Candrakīrti, *Catuḥśatakaṭīkā* (Varanasi: Kargyud Students' Welfare Committee, 1996), f. 389: *rten cing 'brel bar 'byung ba ni ji lta ba bzhin mthong ba na sgyu ma byas pa lta bur 'gyur gyi/ mo gsham gyi bu lta bu ni ma yin no/ /gal te rnam par dpyad pa 'dis skye ba rnam pa thams cad du bkag pa las/ 'dus byas skye ba med pa bstan par 'dod na ni de'i tshe de sgyu ma lta bu nyid du mi 'gyur gyi/ mo gsham gyi bu la sogs pa dag gis nye bar gzhal bar 'gyur ba zhig na/ rten cing 'drel bar 'byung ba med pa thal bar 'gyur ba'i 'jigs pas de dag dang bstun par mi byed kyi/ de dang mi 'gal ba sgyu ma la sogs pa dag dang ni byed do//.* Also cited in Tsongkhapa's *Lam rim chen mo,* p. 743.

512 *Catuḥśatakaṭīkā,* f. 389: *rten cing 'brel bar 'byung ba ni ji lta ba bzhin mthong ba na sgyu ma byas pa lta bur 'gyur gyi/ mo gsham gyi bu lta bu ni ma yin no/.*

513 *Catuḥśatakaṭīkā,* f. 389: *rten cing 'drel bar 'byung ba med pa thal bar 'gyur ba'i 'jigs pas de dag dang bstun par mi byed kyi/ de dang mi 'gal ba sgyu ma la sogs pa dag dang ni byed do//.*

514 *Catuḥśatakaṭīkā,* f. 397: *di'i phyir de ltar yongs su dpyad pa na/ dngos po rnams kyi rang bzhin 'grub pa mi 'gyur bas so so nas dngos po rnams la sgyu ma lta bu de nyid lhag mar lus par 'gyur ro//.* Cited in Tsongkhapa, *Lam rim chen mo,* p. 744.

515 Tsongkhapa, *Lam rim chen mo,* p. 743–44: *rigs pa des rnam pa dpyad nas rang bzhin khegs pa'i shul du ngos po rnams la sgyu ma tsam gyi don nyid yod par 'dzin pa ni nges par skye dgos pas skyon min te//.*

516 Candrakīrti, *Catuḥśatakaṭīkā,* p. 743: *rang bzhin yod med 'tshol ba'i rigs shes kyis sgyu ma tsam gyi don yod par gzung na'ang skyon yin gyi...//*

517 Dreyfus, "Would the True Prāsaṅgika Please Stand?" p. 322.

518 See Pettit, *Mipham's Beacon of Certainty,* p. 136. Cf. Pettit, notes 483–85n.

519 *Rtsa she tīk chen,* p. 417: *des ji snyed pa ma gzhal na chos can dang chos nyid ya dral du thal bar mi gyur te/ de kho na nyid rtogs pa'i rigs shes kyi ngo na chos can dang chos nyid kyi 'drel pa mi 'jog pa'i phyir dang.../.*

520 Pettit, *Mipham's Beacon of Certainty,* p. 143.

521 *Rtsa she tīk chen,* p. 417: *sngon po rtogs pa'i tha snyad pa'i tshad ma'i ngo na don dam bden pa med pas de gnyis 'brel mi dgos pa dang 'dra ba'i phyir ro//.*

522 *Dgongs pa rab gsal,* p. 203: *don dam pa gzigs pa'i ngor don dam bden pa de/ phung sogs lus kyi dang ngag gi spyod yul dang/ yid kyi yul du 'gyur ba ltar du 'gyur na ni/ de kho na nyid mngon sum du gzigs pa'i ngor spros pa dang ma dral bas don dam bden par mi 'gyur gyi kun rdzob kyi spros par 'gyur ro zhes pa ste/ de ltar byas na ma gzigs pa'i tshul gyis gzigs pa'i shes byed du 'gro'o//.*

523 *Rtsa shes tīk chen,* p. 204: *de kho na nyid mngon sum du gzigs pa'i ye shes de don dam shes pa dang/ don dam bden pa de'i shes byar 'jog kyang.../.*

524 *Rtsa shes tīk chen,* p. 204: *ye shes de'i ngor bya byed de gnyis dang bral ba mi 'gal ba ni/ bya byed gnyis ni tha snyad pa'i blo kho na'i ngor 'jog pa'i phyir te//.*

525 *Rtsa shes tīk chen,* p. 204: *bya byed gnyis ni tha snyad pa'i blo kho na'i ngor 'jog pa'i phir...//.*

526 Ud I.10. Cited in Thanissaro Bhikkhu, *The Mind Like Fire Unbound: An Image in the Early Buddhist Discourses* (Barre, MA: Dhamma Dana Publications, 1999), p. 10.

527 *Rtsa shes tīk chen,* p. 204: *dper na rigs shes rjes dpag yul can dang/ don dam bden pa yul du 'jog nus kyang/ yul yul can gyi bya byed gnyis rigs ngor mi 'jog pa bzhin no//.*

528 Chang, *Mahāyāna Sūtras,* p. 395–96.

529 *Mahāratnakūṭa Sūtra* 20. Chang, *Mahāyāna Sūtras,* pp. 395–96.

530 Ibid.

531 Cited in *Dgongs pa rab gsal,* pp. 202–3; *Rtsa she ṭīk chen,* p. 276.

532 *Rtsa shes ṭīk chen,* p. 417: *de kho na nyid mngon sum du rtogs pa'i ye shes kyi ngor ni rang gi yul dang yul can gyi bar na gnyis su snang ba phra mo yang med par chu la chu bzhag pa bzhin du mnyam par zhugs pa yin la.../.*

533 *Mahāratnakūṭa Sūtra* 2. Chang, *Mahāyāna Sūtras,* p. 27.

534 *Mahāratnakūṭa Sūtra* 6:2. Chang, *Mahāyāna Sūtras,* pp. 110–11.

535 *Madhyamakāvatāra* 11:11, p. 205: *ji ltar snod kyi dbye bas mkha' la dbye ba med de ltar/ /dngos byas dbye ba 'ga' yang de nyid la med de yi phyir/ /ro mnyam nyid du yang dag thugs su chud par mdzad gyur na/ /mkhyen bzang khyed kyis skad cid gis ni shes bya thugs su chud//.* Cited in Candrakīrti, *Madhyamakāvatārabhāṣya,* p. 333. See Huntington, *The Emptiness of Emptiness,* p. 190, for a slightly different translation.

536 For Tsongkhapa, see *Dgongs pa rab gsal,* p. 455: *ji ltar dper na bum pa dang 'khar gzhong la sogs pa'i snod kyi mi 'dra ba'i dbye ba du ma yod kyang/ mi 'dra ba'i dbye ba*

de yis snod de dag tu gtogs pa ste der khyab pa'i nam mkha' la ni/ sgrib pa thams cad bkab tsam du mtshungs pa'i phyir/ de las gzhan pa'i dbye ba med.../ /. For Gorampa, see *Lta ba'i ngan sel,* f. 728: *gnyis snang nub pa'i lung ni ji ltar snod kyi dbye ba zhes sogs rtsa 'grel yin la/ gzhan yang shes bya'i yul skye ba med pa la yul can gyi blo yang skye ba med par ldan par gsungs pa rnams kyis stan to/ /.*

537 AN 8.19. Thanissaro Bhikkhu, trans., *An Anthology of Selected Suttas from the Aṅguttara Nikāya,* http://www.accesstoinsight.org/canon/anguttara/index.html.

538 *Samādhirājasūtra (Ting nge 'dzin rgyal po'i mdo)* 7:5. *A Complete Catalogue of Tohoku University Collection of Tibetan Works on Buddhism* (hereafter, Toh) (Sendai, Japan: Prof. Yensho Kanakura), 1934, 1953 no. 127, *Mdo sde Da,* f. 20b: *gcig gis thams cad shes gyur zhing/ /gcig gis thams cad mthong bar 'gyur/ /ji snyad mang po brjod byas kyang/ /de la dregs pa skye mi 'gyur/ /bdag gi 'du shes shes pa ltar/ de bzhin kun la blo sbyor bya/ chos kun de yi rang bzhin te/ /rnam par dag pa nam mkha' ngo bo yin/ /.* Cited in Candrakīrti, *Catuḥśatakaṭīkā,* f. 218; Gyaltsab Jé (Rgyal tshab Rje), *Yogic Deeds of Bodhisattvas: Gyeltsab on Āryadeva's Four Hundred,* Commentary by Geshe Sonam Rinchen, trans. and ed. by Ruth Sonam (Ithaca, NY: Snow Lion Publications, 1994), pp. 194, 356n16; also see Cabezón, *A Dose of Emptiness,* p. 166, for Khedrub Jé. Cabezón offers a slightly different translation.

539 *Samādhirājasūtra* 7:5. Toh. no. 127: *bdag gi 'du shes shes pa ltar/ de bzhin kun la blo sbyor bya/ chos kun de yi rang bzhin te/ /rnam par dag pa nam mkha' ngo bo yin/ /.*

540 *Nam mkha'i mdzod kyi ting nge 'dzin.* This citation is taken from Candrakīrti, *Catuḥśatakaṭīkā,* f. 218: *gang gis chos gcig sgom nas chos rnam kun/ /sgyu ma smig rgyu 'dra zhing gzung med la/ /gsob brdzun ther zug min par shes pa de/ /ring por mi thogs byang chub snying por 'gro/ /.* See Cabezón, *A Dose of Emptiness,* p. 166, for Khedrub Jé, and Ruth Sonam and Geshe Sonam Rinchen, *The Yogic Deeds of Bodhisattvas,* pp. 194, 356n17, for Gyaltsab Jé.

541 *Catuḥśataka* 8:191, in the *Rtsa ba phyogs bsdus* (Varanasi: Sakya Students' Welfare Committee, 1996), p. 268: *dngos po gcig gi lta po gang/ /de ni kun gyi ta por bshad/ /gcig gi stong nyid gang yin pa/ /de ni kun gyi stong pa nyid/ /.* Also cited in Candrakīrti, *Catuḥśatakaṭīkā,* f. 217.

542 Candrakīrti, *Catuḥśatakaṭīkā,* ff. 217–18: *gsugs kyi rang bzhin stong nyid gang yin pa de nyid tshor ba la sogs pa phong po rnams kyi rang bzhin stong pa nyid do/ /de bzhin du mig gi skye mched gyi rang bzhin stong pa nyid gang yin pa de nyid skye mched bcu gnyis char gyi yang yin no/ /de bzhin du mig gi khams kyi rang bzhin stong pa nyid gang yin pa de nyid khams bco brgyad char gyi yang yin no/ /de bzhin du dngos po dang yul dang dus dang rten gyi dbye bas tha dad cing rab tu dbye ba mtha' yas pa rnams las dngos pa gcig gi rang bzhin stong pa nyid gang yin pa de nyid dngos po thams cad kyi rang bzhin stong pa nyid do/ /bum pa dang 'khar bzhong la sogs pa tha dad kyang nam mkha' tha dad med pa bzhin no/ /gzugs la sogs pa'i dngos po tha dad kyang gzugs la sogs pa rnams kyi rang bzhin ma skyes pa la tha dad pa med pa'i phyir chos gcig kho na'i rang zhin gyis ma skyes pa yongs su shes na chos thams cad kyi rang bzhin gyis ma shes pa yongs su shes par 'gyur te/ /.*

543 *Dgongs pa rab gsal,* p. 455: *gzungs dang tshor ba la sogs pa la dngos po ste rang gi rgyu rkyen gyis byas pa'i dbye ba mi 'dra ba du ma yod kyang/ de dag tu gtogs pa de rang bzhin gyis grub pa'i skye ba med pa'i de kho na nyid dngos po byas pa'i dbye ba 'ga' yang med pa de'i phyir de kho na nyid ni ro mnyam pa ste ro gcig kho nar shes par bya'o/ /.*

544 Kalupahana, *Nāgārjuna,* p. 272.

545 In the *Cūḷa-viyūha Sutta*, Sn 4.12, the Buddha states: "The truth is one, there is no second about which a person who knows it would argue with one who knows. Contemplatives promote their various personal truths, that's why they do not say one thing and the same. But why do they say various truths, those who say they are skilled? Have they learned various truths or do they follow conjecture? Apart from their perception there are not many various constant truths in the world. Preconceiving conjecture with regard to views, they speak of a pair: true and false."

546 *Rten 'brel stod pa*, p. 38: *kyod kyis ji snyad bka' stsal pa/ /rten 'brel nyid las btsams te 'jug/ /de yang mya ngan 'da' phyir te/ /zhi gyur min mdzad kyod la med//.*

547 *Rten 'brel stod pa*, p. 37: *ston pa'i nang na rten 'grel ston pa dang/ /shes rab nang na rten 'brel shes pa gnyis/ /'jig rten dag na rgyal ba'i dbang po bzhin/ /phul byung legs par khyod mkhyen gzhan gyis min//.*

548 *Nges don rab gsal*, p. 381: *rang gi ngo bo nam mkha' ltar ro gcig pas rigs mi 'dra bas dbye ba med//.*

549 *Dgongs pa rab gsal*, p. 455: *ro mnyam de yang mkhyen yang mkhyen pa'i skad cig gcig kho nas yang dag par thugs su chud par mdzad par gyur pas na/ mkhyen pa bzang po can khyod kyis skad gcig gis ni shes bya thams cad thugs su chud pa'i ye shes brnyes so//.* Also see Candrakīrti, *Madhyamakāvatārabhāṣya*, p. 333: *de yang mkhyen pa'i skad cig gcig kho nas thugs su chud pas bcom ldan ldas kyis mkhyen pa'i skad cid gcig kho nas thams cad mkhyen pa'i ye shes brnyes so//.*

550 *Lta ba ngan sel*, f. 728: *skad gcig ma gcig la ye shes skad cig ma gcig gis chos thams cad chos kyi dbyings su ro gcig par rtogs pa'i tshe ye shes de'i ngor ji lta ba dang/ ji snyed pa dang/ yul can yes hes gsum po ngo bo that dad du me snang la//.*

551 *Lta ba ngan sel*, f. 728: *de'i rjes su mnyam bzhag de las langs pa yang mi srid de/ thugs mnyam par ma gzhag pa mi mnga' ba sangs rgyas kyi mthun mong ma yin pa'i yon tan du gsungs pa'i phyir dang//.*

552 *Lta ba ngan sel*, f. 728: *de nas bzung ste ye shes de'i ngor dus snga phyi'i dbye ba yang med pa'i phyir ste skye 'gag me snang ba'i phyir ro//.*

553 *Lta ba ngan sel*, f. 727: *'phags pa 'od ma gsum gyi mnyam rjes kyis yul rtogs tshul ma shes na sangs rgyas kyis ye shes kyis shes bya rtogs tshul gyi rnam gzhag khyad par du phyags pa mi shes pas thog mar de bshad na.../.*

554 *Lta ba ngan sel*, f. 727: *'on kyang bden par 'dzin par ni mi 'gyur te/ bden pa'i skyi med mngon sum du rtogs pa'i phyir ro//.*

555 See Gorampa, *Lta ba ngan sel*, f. 727, and Tsongkhapa, *Dgongs pa rab gsal*, p. 459.

556 Sn 3.12. See Thanissaro Bhikkhu, trans., *An Anthology of Selected Suttas from the Sutta Nipāta*, http://www.accesstoinsight.org/canon/khuddaka/suttanipata/index.html.

557 *Lta ba ngan sel*, f. 727: *de'i rjes la thob pa'i ye shes la ni chos can ji snyed pa skye 'gag dang bcas par snang ste/ gnyis snang gi bag chags ma spangs pas so//.*

558 *Lta ba ngan sel*, f. 727: *mnyam bzhag tu skye 'gag tsam yang mi snang bas ji ta ba rtogs.../.*

559 *Lta ba ngan sel*, f. 727: *rtogs pa gnyis res 'jog tu 'byung ba ni chos thams cad kyi dbyings su ro gcig tu rtogs pa'i rtogs pa mthar mthog pa'i gnad kyis so//.*

560 *Dgongs pa rab gsal*, p. 458: *sangs rgyas ma thob bar du blo gcig gis skad cig ma gcig la chos can so sor snang ba dang/ chos nyid gnyis ka dngos su mkhyen pa mi 'ong bas.../ de gnyis mkhyen pa res 'jog tu 'ong ngo//.*

561 *Lta ba ngan sel*, f. 728.

562 *Nges don rab gsal*, p. 446b: *zhes pa'i skabs nas bstan pa'i kun rdzob bden pa ni med de/ yul can mthong ba brdzun pa med pa/ de'i yul med pa'i phyir ro//.*

563 *Nges don rab gsal*, p. 446c: *skye 'gag la sogs pa gdul bya la bstan pa'i ya gyal gyi kun rdzob bden pa'i snang ba med kyang dbyings rig dbyer med kyi don dam pa snang ba's snang ba yod dgos ste.../*; also p. 447c: *mdor na rtsa ba shes rab kyi mchod brjod kyi skabs kyi skye 'gag las sogs pa brgyad dang/ rab byed nyi shu rtsa bdun gyis dpyad par bya ba'i rkyen nas lta ba'i bar nyi shu rtsa bdun dang/ des mtshon nas kun rdzob tha snyad kyi rnam bzhag thams cad spros pa yin pas de dag sangs rgyas kyi sar chos kyi dbyings su ro gcig par ye shes skad cig ma gcig gis mngon du gyur ba'i tshe spros pa de dag mi snang yang de dag rtogs zhes pa'i tha snyad ni mi 'gal te...//.*

564 Jayānanda, *Madhyamakāvatāsyaṭīkā*, p. 74c: *ci ltar rab rib can la snang ba'i skra shad la sogs pa'i de kho na nyid mig dag pas mthong pa yin las de bzhin du 'jig rten pa la snang ba'i kun rdzob kyi bden pa de spyan dag pas sangs rgyas bcom ldan 'das rnams kyis bdag nyid gang gis gzigs pa de kho na nyid yin no zhes pa'i don to//.* Also see pp. 75a–c, 161b–67a.

565 *Dbu 'jug rnam bshad*, p. 127: *snang ba med pa'i spyod yul can gyi sangs rgyas bcom ldan das rnams la ni thams cad du snang ba ma yin te/ chos thams cad rnam par thams cad du spros pa'i mtshan ma nyi bar zhi ba'i chos kyi dbying kyi ngo bor mngon par rdzogs par byang chub pa'i phyir/ sems dang sems byung las byung ba'i rgyu ba gtan log par 'dod par yin no//.*

566 *Dbu 'jug rnam bshad*, f. 335: *ji srid rab rib ma bsal ba de srid skra shad kyi snang ba mi ldog pa de bzhin du/ ji srid ma rig pa'i bag chags ma spangs pa de srid du kun rdzob kyi snang ba char la/ rab rib bsal na skra shad kyi snang ba ldog pa de bzhin du/ ma rig pa'i bag chags spangs pa'i sang rgyas kyi gzigs ngor kun rdzob sna tshogs kyi snang ba 'de mi char bar bzhed pa yin no//.* Also see ff. 328–36; *'Jug pa'i dka' gnad*, ff. 475–76; and *Don dam rnam bshad*, ff. 1185–88.

567 *Grub mtha'i rnam bshad*, f. 306: *sangs rgyas kyi gzugs sku dang 'phrin las bsam yas brjod kyis mi lang ba rnams/...rtog pa med par ma zad/ sems bskyed pa tsam mi dgos par sngon gyi smon lam dang 'dul bya'i las bzang po'i dbang gis gdul bya de dang de'i gzhan snang gi rnam rol kho na yin par bzhed de//.*

568 *Dag brgyud grub pa'i shing rta*, f. 318: *sangs rgyas rnams la ni kun rdzob pa'i chos thams cad rnam pa thams cad du snang ba ma yin te/ chos thams cad rnam pa thams cad du mngon par rdzogs par byang chub pa'i phyir sems sems las byung ba'i rgyu ba gtan log pa yin no//.* Also see ff. 320, 324.

569 *Dam chos dogs sel*, pp. 606: *skal ba du mar goms pa'i stobs kyis nyam bzhag ji brten ji rten dang kun rdzob 'khrul ba'i snang ba ji chung ji chung du song nas/ mthar rgyun mtha'i rdor ji gis gnyis snang 'khrul ba'i bag chags phra mo'ang ldog par gyur pa na/ chos kyi dbyings las slar ldang pa med par gnyis snang nub pa'i mnyam bzhag kho na de gnas pa'i tshe sangs rgyas su 'grub pa yin te//.*

570 *Klu sgrub dgongs rgyan*, p. 144: *'on kyang da ltar rang res gang mthong ba'i s rdo ri drag 'de dag sangs rgyas tshe da dung yang phra lam mer mthong rgyu yod snyam na shin tu nor//.* Also see pp. 147, 182, 191.

571 Kun mkhyen Pad ma dkar po, *Dbu ma'i gzhung gsum gsal byed* (hereafter, *Gzhung gsum gsal byed*) (Sarnath: Kargyud Students' Welfare Committee, n.d), p. 121: *ji srid sgrib pa'i lhag ma yod pa de srid du/ rjes thob pas snang ba'i sna tshogs 'de dag sgyu ma lta bu la sogs par snang la/ nam bag chags thams cad yongs su dag pa na rnam pa*

thams cad du kun rdzob kyi chos snang ma myong ba rang bzhin nyid la dus thams cad du mnyam par 'jog pa yin no//.

572 For a detailed treatment of how Gorampa imposes the ālayavijñāna on the Prāsaṅgika Madhyamaka, see his *Nges don rab gsal*, pp. 402d–403b. For his criticisms directed toward Tsongkhapa for the latter's refusal to impose the conception of the foundational consciousness on the Prāsaṅgika system, see *Lta ba'i shan 'byed*, pp. 91–94. Also see *Lta ba ngan sel*, ff. 634–40.

573 Gorampa treats the ālayavijñāna just like any other empirical truth. "All empirical truths are provisionally explained as vehicles to understand ultimate truth, and so is ālayavijñāna," he says, *Lta ba ngan sel*, ff. 632–39.

574 *Lta ba ngan sel*, f. 637: *dbu ma thal 'gyur bas tha snyad du kun bzhi khas len dgos te/ sangs rgyas bcom ldan 'das kyis mdo las gsungs shing/ de yang don dam bden pa rtogs pa'i thabs su gyur pa'i tha snyad bden pa yin par slo dpon 'di nyid kyis gsungs pa'i phyir te//.*

575 *Lta ba ngan sel*, f. 635: *tshogs drug las ngo bo tha dad yod pa ma yin gyi rnam par shes pa gsal tsam gyi ngo bo sems can nas sangs rgyas kyi sa'i bar du rgyun ma chad par yod pa 'de ni...kun gzhir 'jog//.*

576 *Lta ba'i 'od zer*, p. 322c: *skye 'gag mi snang bas/ 'dus byas dang mi rtag pa sogs med cing//.*

577 *Nges don rab gsal*, p. 447a: *'dus byas thams cad skad cig ma yin pas skye 'gag dang bcas par 'dod pa gnyis ka'ang mi 'thad de...//.*

578 *Nges don rab gsal*, p. 447a–447b: *'dus byas yin na 'rdzun pa bslu ba'i chos can yin dgos pa'i phyir dang/ skye 'gag snang na rten cing 'brel bar 'byung ba skye med kyi don du ma rgyur ba'i...phyir//.*

579 *Klu sgrub dgongs rgyan*, p. 191: *ji srid kun rdzob kyi snang ba ma 'gag pa de srid dang/ ji srid rnams kyi rten ma brje bar de srid du stong pa nyid mngon sum du rtogs kyang/ sngar gang khas blang ba de dbang med du khas len dgos//.*

580 *Lta ba ngan sel*, f. 730: *mi rtag pa dang/ 'dus byas dang/ brdzun pa dang/ bslu ba rnams don gcig par gsungs shing/ 'di 'phags pa 'og ma'i lam bden la yod cing/ sangs rgyas kyi ye shes la med pa cig dgos pa las//.*

581 *Lta ba ngan sel*, f. 730: *don dam par de dag med pa 'phags pa 'og ma'i lam bden la yang yod pa'i phyir ro//.*

582 *Nges don rab gsal*, p. 372d: *stong nyid stogs nas goms pa mthar phyin pa'i tshe glo bur gyi dri ma zad nas blo nyid zag med kyi dbyings su gyur pa ni spang stogs phun sum tshogs pa don dam pa'i sangs rgyas yin la//.*

583 *Nges don rab gsal*, p. 446d: *rdo rje lta bu'i ting ne 'dzin gis shes bya skye 'gag/ rtag chad la sogs pa'i bud shing bsrigs nas spros pa mtha' dag zhi ba'i chos dbyings dang/ sngar gyi rig pa'i rgyun de'ang skye 'gag la sogs pa'i spros a mtha' dag zhi nas de gnyis dbyer med du gyur pa la ye shes su 'jog pa'i phyir ro//.*

584 *Mahāratnakūṭa Sūtra* 6:2. Chang, *Mahāyāna Sūtras*, p. 105.

585 *Mahāratnakūṭa Sūtra* 6:2. Chang, *Mahāyāna Sūtras*, p. 105.

586 *Nges don rab gsal*, p. 446d: *sems sems 'byung ni khams gsum pa'i rnam pa can gyi gnyis snang dang bcas pa dang/ don gyi ngo bo dang khyad par mthong pa'i khyad par yod pa dang/ don gyi khyad par la'ang mi 'dra ba du ma mthong ba'i sgo nas gzhag par gsungs la//.*

587 *Nges don rab gsal*, pp. 446d–447a: *'dir shes bya skye 'gag la sogs pa'i spros pa mtha' dag dang dral ba'i shes pa dang dbyer med pa mngon du gyur pa'i tshe gnyis snang dang 'dzin stangs mi 'dra ba'i khyad par cung zad kyang med pa'i phyir ro//.*

588 *Lta ba ngan sel*, ff. 612–13: *gnyis snang dang bcas na rnam mkhyen gyi bar gyi yul yang don dam bden pa ma yin.../.*

589 *Lta ba ngan sel*, f. 729: *gal te de dag don dam par skye 'gag med pa'i don yin gyi tha snyad du ma yin no snyam na de ni ma nyin te/ tha snyad ni gdul bya'i ngor khas blangs pa tsam yin gyi sangs rgyas rangs snang la don dam pa dang tha snyad gnyis su dbyer med pa'i phyir//.*

590 *Klu sgrub dgongs rgyan*, p. 192: *sgyu ma mkhan gyis sgyu ma'i glang po sprul ba na/ ltad mo mkhan rnams kyis kyang glang po dngos su mthong/ sgyu ma mkhan gyis kyang glang po min pa zhig glang po dngos su mthong ba'i ched du sgyu ma stong pa yin pas/ ltad mo ba rnams kyis sgyu ma mkhan las 'de glang po dngos yin nam zhes dris tshe yin zhes brjod dgos pa de sgyu ma mkhan gyis glang chin gzhan ngor khas len pa yin//.*

591 *Lta ba ngan sel*, f. 734: *gzhan ngor ni don dam par skye ba dang tha snyad du skye ba gnyis ka yod do/ ma skye bar bshad pa rnams ni rang ngor te rang ngo rnams ni tha snyad dang don dam gang du yang skye ba med do//.*

592 *Lta ba'i 'od zer*, p. 322c: *sangs rgyas rang snang la...skye 'gag mi snang bas/ 'dus byas dang mi rtag pa sogs med cing/ gdul bya'i gzhan ngor ni dgi ba sky dang 'jig pas na...skye 'gag yod kyang//.*

593 *Lta ba'i 'od zer*, p. 322c: (contd.) *des sangs rgyas kyi ye shes la skye 'gag yod par mi grub ste/ gdul bya'i sems la snang tshul yin pa'i phir ro//.*

594 *Nges don rab gsal*, p. 447b: *gdul bya'i ngor skye 'gag tu snang ba ni gzhan snang yin gi rang snang ma yin te//.*

595 *Dam chos dogs sel*, p. 607: *rnam par mi rtog pa'i ye shes chos sku de'i byin rlab las/ gzhan ngor rtsol ba med par sku gnyis su 'char zhing/ phrin las kyi 'jug pa nam mkha'i ji srid du 'jug pa yin no//.*

596 *Grub mtha'i rnam bshad*, f. 306: *sangs rgyas kyi gzugs sku dang 'phrin las bsam yas brjod kyis mi lang ba rnams/ ...rtog pa med par ma zad/ sems bskyed pa tsam mi dgos par sngon gyi smon lam dang 'dul bya'i las bzang po'i dbang gis gdul bya de dang de'i gzhan snang gi rnam rol kho na yin par bzhed de//.* Also see ff. 206, 273, 305.

597 *Dag brgyud grub pa'i shing rta*, ff. 141–42: *tha snyad pa'i skye ba zhes bya ba de bzhin gshegs pas ma gzigs shing 'phags pa 'og ma rnams kyi mnyam bzhag gi gzigs don tha snyad du'ang yod pa ma yin la/ rigs pas dpyad na yang tha snyad du yod pa ma yin cing/ ...gzhan ngor tha snyad pa'i skye ba rnam par bzhag tshe...gzhan ngor khas len par byed...//.*

598 Rongtön Shakya Gyaltsen, *Rigs tsogs dka' gnad*, f. 127: *gal te gdul ba'i rgyud kyis bsdus pa yin no zhes na/ de dag tshogs gnyis yongs su rdzogs par mthar mthog pa 'thob par 'gyur te/ sangs rgyas kyi sku dang ye shes thams cad rang rgyud la rdzog par thob pa'i phyir//.*

599 *Lam rim chen mo*, p. 742: *de la snang ba yod par rigs shes kyi mi grub la/ rang bzhin gyis stongs par tha snyad pa'i tshad mas mi 'grub pas rang bzhin yod med 'tshol ba'i rigs pa'i shes pa dang gzhugs sogs yod par 'dzin pa'i tha snyad pa'i blo gnyis dgos pa'i rgyu mtshan ni de yin no//.*

600 *Dgongs pa rag gsal*, p. 201: *'khrul pa'i bag chags ma lus pa spangs pa na yeshe skad cig ma ri ri'i steng du yang ye shes gnyis ngo bo gcig tu skye ba rgyun mi 'chad pa…//.*

601 The meaning attributed to *subsequent attainment (rjes thob, pṛṣṭhalabdha)* by Tsongkhapa is radically different from that of most non-Gelug scholars. For others *rjes thob* means "aftermath of *mnyam gzhag*," which is translated as "postmeditation." For Tsongkhapa *rjes thob* means "subsequent attainment." It does not mean the aftermath of the meditative equipoise—in the sense of of occurring afterward; rather it means "an attainment due to the power of meditative equipoise, or what is being generated from it." See *Dgongs pa rab gsal*, p. 459: *rjes la thob pa zhes pa'i rjes kyi don ni/ mnyam gzhag las langs pa'i rjes zhes dus snga phyi'i rjes min gyi mnyam gzhag de'i stobs kyis thob pa'am byung ba'i don no//.* This is an important distinction for Tsongkhapa, for it allows him to argue that knowledge of both *rjes thob* and *mnyam gzhag* of an enlightened being have an equal status, whereas Gorampa and his counterparts argue that the *mnyam bzhag* of an enlightened being is superior to his *rjes thob*.

602 *Dgongs pa rab gsal*, p. 458: *bden 'dzin gyi bag chags ma lus pa zad de sangs rgyas pa nas dus rtag tu don dam bden pa mngon sum du rtogs pa'i mnyam gzhag las bzhugs pas/ de las bzhengs pa'i mnyam rjes res 'jog med pa'i phyir//.*

603 *Dgongs pa rab gsal*, pp. 458–59: *mnyam gzhag ye shes de las ngo bo tha dad pa'i ji snyad pa mkhyen pa'i rjes thob kyi ye shes med pa'i phyir na/ ye shes gcig gis bden pa gnyis kyis shes bya thams cad mkhyen par 'dod dgos so//.*

604 *Dgongs pa rab gsal*, p. 201: *dus gcig tu shes bya mngon gsum du 'jal mi 'jal gyi res 'jog mi dgos so//.*

605 *Dgongs pa rab gsal*, p. 461: *de bzhin du je lta ba mkhyen pa'i ye shes kyis rnyed cing yul de la je lta ba mkhyen pa'i ye shes su song ba dang/ je snyed pa mkhyen pa'i ye shes kyi rnyed cing yul de la je rnyed pa mkhyen par song ba'i sgo nas/ yul so so la ltos nas kun rdzob dang don dam mkhyen tshul yang shes par bya'o//.*

606 Pettit, *Mipham's Beacon of Certainty*, p. 143.

607 *Dgongs pa rab gsal*, p. 201: *ye shes gnyis ngo bo gcig yin kyang yul gnyis la ltos ba'i mkhyen tshul mi 'dra ba gnyis 'ong ba la 'gal ba cung zad kyang med pa ni/ sangs rgyas bcom ldan 'das nyag gcig kyi khyad chos su 'dug pa la…//.*

608 *Dgongs pa rab gsal*, pp. 458–59: *mnyam gzhag gi ye shes de las ngo bo tha dad pa'i je snyed pa mkhyen pa'i rjes thob kyi ye shes med pa'i phir na/ ye shes gcig gis bden pa gnyis kyi shes bya thams cad mkhyen par 'dod dgos so/ gang gi tshe chos nyid la ltos te ji lta ba mkhyen pa'i yeshe su song ba de'i tshe blo de'i ngor gnyis su snang ba thams cad nye bar zhe bas yi shes de chu la chu bzhag pa bzhin du ro gcig tu zhugs pa yin la/ gang gi tshe cho can la ltos te ji snyad pa mkhen par song ba de'i tshe/ yul yul can so sor snang ba'i gnyis snang yod kyang/ gnyis snang 'khrul pa'i bag chags drung phung pas snang yul la ma 'khrul pa'i gnyis snang yin gi 'khrul pa'i gnyis snang min te//.*

609 *Lam rim chen mo*, p. 742: *rigs pa'i shes pas chos can snang ba la skye 'gag sogs kyi rang bzhin rnam pa bcad pa tsam gyi stong pa la nam mkha la bu'i stong nyid//.*

610 SN 35.116. Thanissaro Bhikkhu, trans., *An Anthology of Selected Suttas from the Saṃyutta Nikāya*, http://www.accesstoinsight.org/canon/samyutta/index.html.

611 Ud 8.1. Thanissaro Bhikkhu trans., *An Anthology of Selected Suttas from the Udāna*, http://www.accesstoinsight.org/canon/khuddaka/udana/index.html.

612 *Lam rim chen mo*, p. 742: *de nas rang bzhin gyis stong yang rang bzhin du snang ba'i gzugs sogs kyi snang ba 'char ba la sgyu ma lta bu'i stong nyid ces sngon gyi mkhas pa rnams gsungs so//.*

613 For a detailed analysis on this subject see Khenzur Pema Gyaltsen (Mkhan zur Padma rgyal tshan), *Zab don gdams pa'i mig 'byed gser gyi thur ma* (hereafter, *Zab don mig 'byed*), vol. 3 (Mundgod: Drepung Loselling Printing Press, 1984), pp. 353–60. In particular note the following statement, p. 357: *gang gi tshe chos nyid la ltos te ji lta ba mkhyen pa'i ye shes su song ba de'i tshe blo de'i ngor gnyis su snang ba thams cad nye bar zhi bas ye shes de chu la chu bzhag ba bzhin du ro gcig tu zhugs pa yin la/ /gang gi tshe chos can la ltos te ji snyad pa mkhyen par song pa de'i tshe/ /yul can so sor snang ba'i gnyis snang yod kyang/ gnyis snang 'khrul ba'i bag chags drungs phyung bas snang yul las ma 'khrul ba'i snyis snang yin gyi/ /'khrul pa'i gnyis snang med te 'de.../ /.*

614 SN 12.20. Thanissaro Bhikkhu, trans., *An Anthology of Selected Suttas from the Saṃyutta Nikāya,* http://www.accesstoinsight.org/canon/samyutta/index.html.

615 *Lam rim chen mo*, p. 743: *de'i gnad shes na mnyam gzhag tu nam mkha' lta bu'i stong nyid sgoms pas de'i stobs kyis rjes thob tu sgyu ma lta bu'i stong nyid 'char ba'i tshul rnams legs pa shes par 'gyur ro//.*

616 For a detailed analysis on this issue see Gyaltsab Jé, *Bden gnyis kyi rnam gzhag dang lta ba'i 'khrid yid rin po che'i 'phrin ba*, in the *Dbu ma'i lta khrid phyogs bsdebs* (Sarnath: Gelukpa Students' Welfare Committee, 1985), pp. 138–40; see also Khenzur Pema Gyaltsen, *Zab don mig 'byed*, pp. 357–68; Jamyang Shepai Dorje, *Grub mtha' rnam bshad*, pp. 896–99; and Khedrub Jé (in Cabezón, *A Dose of Emptiness,* pp. 380–86).

617 *Rtsa she ṭīk chen*, p. 420: *ji lta ba dang ji snyed pa mkhyen pa'i ye shes kyang ngo bo tha mi dad pas sangs rgyas kyi ye shes gcig gis kyang shes bya kun la kyab par bshad pa dang yang mi 'gsal te//.*

618 See Melford E. Spiro, *Buddhism and Society: A Great Tradition and Its Burmese Vicissitudes* (Berkeley: University of California Press, 1982), p. 68.

619 MN 22:13–14. *The Middle Length Discourses of the Buddha,* p. 229.

620 Winston L. King, *In Hope of Nibbāna* (La Salle: Open Court, 1964), p. 67.

Glossary

English	Tibetan	Sanskrit
afflictive dharmas	*kun nas nyon mongs pa'i chos*	*sāmkleśikā dharmāḥ*
all aspects of phenomenal world	*ji snyed pa*	*yāvat, yaḥkāścana*
analogy, paradigm	*dpe nyer 'jal*	*upamāna*
appearing object: appearing object of thought	*snang yul/ rtog pa'i snang yul*	*pratibhāsa viṣya*
as it is, as they are	*ji lta ba*	*yathā*
childish, ordinary being	*byis pa, so skye*	*bāla, pṛthagjana*
conceived object: a referent object of the conception of self, etc.	*zhen yul*	*adhyavaṣāya*
conceptual	*rtog bcas*	*vikalpa*
conceptual elaboration; verbal elaboration	*spros pa*	*prapañca* (*Pāli*) *papañca*
conditioned or contingent phenomena	*'dus byas*	*saṃskṛta*
conditioned, fabricated	*bcos ma*	*kṛtrima*
definitive meaning	*nges don*	*nītārtha*
deluded ignorance, deluded concealer	*nyon mongs can gyi ma rig pa*	*kleṣṭāvaraṇa*
dependent arising	*rten cing 'brel bar 'byung ba*	*pratītyasamutpāda*

dependently arisen phenomena	*rten cing 'brel bar byung ba'i chos*	*pratītyasamutpanna-dharma*
different conceptual identities	*ldog pa tha dad*	*vyāvṛtti*
dualistic appearance	*gnyis snang*	*dvayābhatā/ ubhayābhāsa*
eighteen cognitive spheres	*khams bco brgyad*	*aṣṭadaya dhātu*
empirical truth/ empirical reality	*tha snyad bden pa*	*vyāvahārikasatya*
essence, characteristic, nature	*rang bzhin/ rang gi ngo bo*	*svabhāva*
established through self-defining characteristic	*rang gi mtshan nyid kyis grub pa*	*svalakṣaṇa siddhi*
existence by way of self-defining characteristic	*rang gi mtshan yid kyi yod pa*	*svalakṣaṇa bhāva*
false conventional	*log pa'i kun rdzob*	*mithya saṃvṛti*
five psychophysical aggregates	*phung po lnga*	*pañca skandhāḥ*
free from verbal elaboration, free from conceptual elaboration	*spros bral*	*aprapañca (Pāli) apapañca*
ignorance	*ma rig pa*	*avidyā*
ineffable, inexpressible	*brjod du med pa*	*avyākṛta, avācyate, avaktavyatva*
inferential knowledge	*rjes dpag*	*anumāna*
knowable, object of knowledge	*shes bya*	*jñeya*
meditative equipoise	*nmyam gzhag*	*samāhita*
mere conventionality	*kun rdzob tsam*	*saṃvṛtimātram*
nature/principal	*rang gzhin/ gtso bo*	*prakṛti/ pradhāna*
nonconceptual	*rtog med*	*nirvikalpa*
nondeluded ignorance, nondeluded concealer	*nyon mongs can ma yin pa'i ma rig pa*	*jñeyāvaraṇa*

nondiscerning meditative absorption	*'dus shes med pa'i snyoms 'jug*	*asaṃjñatāsamāpatti*
object	*yul*	*viṣaya*
objects, characterized object	*chos can*	*dharmin*
ordinary beings	*so so skye bo*	*pṛthagjana*
penetrating insight, special insight	*lhag mthong*	*vipaśyanā, (Pāli) vipassanā*
perceivers of falsity	*rdzun pa mthong ba*	——
perceptual knowledge, direct knowledge, direct awareness	*mngon sum*	*pratyakṣa*
predisposition, latency	*bags chags*	*vāsnā*
project, fabricate, impute, reify	*brtags pa*	*vijñapti*
provisional meaning	*drang don*	*neyārtha*
reality, as it is	*de bzhin nyid*	*tathatā, thatātva, tattva*
reality, true nature, things as they are	*chos nyid*	*dharmatā*
self-defining characteristic	*rang gi mtshan nyid*	*svalakṣaṇa*
single ontological identity	*ngo bo gcig eka*	*svābhava*
six sense powers	*dbang po drug*	*ṣaḍ indriyāṇ*
sphere of ultimate reality	*chos dbyings*	*dharmadhātu*
subject	*yul can*	*viṣayin*
subsequent attainment, postmeditative state	*rjes thob*	*pṛṣṭhalabdha*
subsequently attained wisdom, the wisdom of postmeditative equipoise	*rjes thob ye shes*	*pṛṣṭhalabdha jñāna*
subtle predisposition of misconception of dualistic appearance	*gnyis snang 'phrul ba'i bags chags*	——

superimposition, fabrication, reification	*sgro brtags pa*	*samāropa*
transcendent wisdom	*'jig rten las 'das pa'i ye shes*	*lokottara jñāna*
transworldly, transcendent	*'jig rten las 'das pa*	*lokottara*
true conventionality	*yang dag kun rdzob*	*tathya saṃvṛti*
truly existent, substantially existent	*bden grub*	*satya siddhi*
truth-for-concealer/ conventional truth	*kun rdzob bden pa*	*saṃvṛtisatya*
twelve sources of perception	*skye mched bcu gnyis*	*dvādaya āyatanāni*
ultimate truth	*don dam bden pa*	*paramārthasatya*
unworldly	*'jig rten ma yin pa*	*alaukika*
unworldly conventionality/ false conventionality	*ig rten ma yin pa'i kun rdzob/ log pa'i kun rdzob*	*aloka saṃvṛti/ mithya saṃvṛti*
valid verbal testimony	*lung/ sgra*	*śabda, śruti, āptavacana*
view of substantial 'I' and 'Mine' principle	*jig tshog la lta ba*	*satkāya dṛṣṭi*
wisdom arisen from conceptual analysis	*bsam byung shes rab*	*cintamayīprajñā*
wisdom arisen from hearing	*thos byung shes rab ś*	*śrutamayīprajñā*
wisdom arisen from meditational practices	*sgom byung gyi shes rab*	*bhāvanāmayīprajñā (Pāli) paṭivedha*
wisdom of meditative equipoise	*mnyam gzhag ye shes*	*samāhita jñāna*
wisdom realizing conventional phenomena, knowledge of conventional phenomena	*kun rdzob mkhyen pa'i ye shes*	——
wisdom realizing empirical phenomena as they are	*ji snyed pa mkhyen pa'i ye shes*	——
wisdom realizing reality as it is	*ji lta ba mkhyen pa'i ye shes*	——

wisdom realizing ultimate truth, knowledge of ultimate truth	*don dam mkhyen pa'i ye shes*	——
world, mundane	*'jig rten*	*loka*
worldly being	*'jig rten pa*	*laukika, lokataḥ*
worldly consciousness	*'jig rten pa'i shes pa*	*luakika jñāna*
worldly consensus	*'jig rten grags pa*	*lokaprasiddha*
worldly conventionality	*'jig rten kun rdzob dag kun*	*lokasaṃvṛti*
true conventionality	*rdzob*	*tathyasaṃvṛti*
worldly conventions	*'jig rten gyi tha snyad*	*lokavyavahāra*

Bibliography

Indian Sources

Śāntideva. *Bodhicāryāvatāra*. In *Rgyal tsap's Spyod 'jug rnam bshad rgyal sras 'jug ngogs*. Sarnath: Gelukpa Students' Welfare Committee, 1993.

A Complete Catalogue of Tohoku University Collection of Tibetan Works on Buddhism. Sendai, Japan: Prof. Yensho Kanakura, 1934 and 1953.

Atīśa. *'Drom ston rgyal ba'i byung gnas kyi kyes rabs bka' gdams bu chos*. Ziling: Mtsho ngon mi rigs dpe skrun khang, 1993.

———. *Bodhipathapradīpaṃpunjika (byang chub lam gyi sgron me'i dkha' 'grel)*. Dharamsala: Tibetan Government in Exile, 1993.

Candrakīrti. *Mūlamadhyamakavṛttiprasannapadā*. Rajpur: Sakya College, 1993.

———. *Madhyamakāvatārabhāṣya*. Varanasi: Sakya Students' Welfare Committee, 1994.

———. *Catuḥśatakaṭīkā*. Varanasi: Kargyud Students' Welfare Committee, 1996.

———. *Madhyamakāvatāra*. In the *Rtsa ba phyogs bsdus*. Varanasi: Sakya Students' Welfare Committee, 1996.

———. *Śūnyatāsaptativṛtti, Dbu ma* vol. *ya pa*, 533a-672g of Sde dge edition of the Bstan 'gur. Dharamsala: Paljor Press, 1997–98.

———. *Yuktiṣaṣṭikāvṛtti, Dbu ma*, vol. *ya pa*, 2a–6 of Sde dge edition of the Bstan 'gur. Dharamsala: Paljor Press, 1997–98.

Āryadeva. *Catuḥśataka*. In the *Rtsa ba phyogs bsdus*. Varanasi: Sakya Students' Welfare Committee, 1996.

Jayānanda. *Madhyamakāvatārasyaṭīkā*. Tokyo: University of Tokyo, 1978.

Nāgārjuna. *Dharmasaṃgrahah*. In the *'Phags pa klu grub kyis mdzad pa'i chos yang dag par bsdus pa*, translated and edited by Ācārya Gyaltsen Namdol. Bibliotheca Indo-Tibetan Series XV. Sarnath: Central Institute of Higher Tibetan Studies [CIHTS], 1988.

———. *Bodhicittavivaraṇa*. In the *Bodhicitta-Vivaraṇa of Ācārya Nāgārjuna and Bodhicitta-Bhāvanā of Ācārya Kamalaśīla*, translated and edited by Ācārya Gyaltsen Namdol. Bibliotheca Indo-Tibetan Series XXII. Sarnath: CIHTS, 1991.

———. *Śūnyatāsaptati*. In the *Rtsa ba phyogs bsdus*. Varanasi: Sakya Students' Welfare Committee, 1996.

———. *Mūlamadhyamakakārikā*. In the *Rtsa ba phyogs bsdus*. Varanasi: Sakya Students' Welfare Committee, 1996.

———. *Vigrahvyāvartanī*. In the *Rtsa ba phyogs bsdus*. Varanasi: Sakya Students' Welfare Committee, 1996.

———. *Yuktiṣaṣṭīka*. In the *Rtsa ba phyogs bsdus*. Varanasi: Sakya Students' Welfare Committee, 1996. Sde dge edition of the Bstan 'gyur. Dharamsala: Paljor Press, 1997–98.

The Nyingma Edition of the Sde dge Bka' 'gyur and Bstan 'gyur. Berkeley CA: Dharma Publishing, 1981.

Tibetan Tripiṭaka, Tokyo-Kyoto: Tibetan Tripiṭaka Research Foundation, 1959.

Tibetan Sources

Bstan pa'i mnga' bdag dpal lda sa skya pa'i lta grub theg pa'i rnam dbye kun dga'i bstan pa mdzes pa'i rgyan yid bzhin dbang gi rgyal po'i do shal. Gang can rig 'gya'i sgo 'byed lde mig, vol. 14. Peking: Mi rigs dpe skrun khang, 1989.

Changkya Rölpai Dorje (Lcang skya Rol pa'i rdo rje). *Grub mtha' thub stan lhun po'i mdzes rgyan*. Xiling: Mtsho sngon mi rigs par khang, 1989.

Don rdor and Bstan 'zin chos grags. *Gang ljongs lo rgyus thog gi grags can mi sna*. Lhasa: Bod ljongs mi dmangs par khang, 1993.

Gendün Chöpel (Dge 'dun chos 'phel). *Dbu ma'i zab gnad snying por dril ba'i legs bshad klu sgrub dgongs rgyan*. Lhasa: Bod ljongs bod yid dbe rnying khang, 1990.

Gorampa Sonam Sengé (Go rams pa Bsod nams seng ge). *Dbu ma spyi don nges don rab gsal. The Complete Works of the Sakya Scholars*, vol. 12. Tokyo: The Toyo Bunko, 1969.

———. *Lta ba ngan sel. The Complete Works of the Sakya Scholars*, vol. 13. Tokyo: The Toyo Bunko, 1969.

———. *Lta ba'i shen 'byed theg mchog gnad kyi zla zer*. Sarnath: Sakya Students' Union, 1994. See also the critical edition and translation on facing pages in Cabezón and Dargyay, *Freedom from Extremes*.

———. *Phung khams skye mched kyi rnam gzhag ji snyad shes bya'i sgo 'byed. The Complete Works of Go rams Bsod nams seng ge,* vol. 12. Tokyo: The Toyo Bunko, 1969.

———. *Rten 'brel gyi rnam par bzhag pa 'khor 'das rab gsal. The Complete Works of Go rams Bsod nams seng ge,* vol. 14. Tokyo: The Toyo Bunko, 1969.

———. *Yang dag lta ba'i 'od zer. The Complete Works of the Sakya Scholars*, vol. 12. Tokyo: The Toyo Bunko, 1969.

Gyaltsab Jé (Rgyal tshab Rje). Geshe Sonam Rinchen and Ruth Sonam, ed. and trans. *Yogic Deeds of Bodhisattvas: Gyeltsab on Āryadeva's Four Hundred.* Ithaca, NY: Snow Lion Publications, 1994.

———. *Bden gnyis kyi rnam gzhag dang lta ba'i 'khrid yid rin po che'i 'phrin ba*. In the *Dbu ma'i lta khrid phyogs bsdebs*. Sarnath: Gelugpa Students' Welfare Committee, 1985.

———. *Rtsa ba shes rab kyi dka' gnad chen po brgyad kyi bshad pa*. New Delhi: Lama Guru Deva, 1980.

Gyaltsen Namdol (Rgyal tshan rnam grol) and Geshe Ngawang Samten (Dge shes Ngag dbang bsam gtan), ed. and trans. *Rje tsong kha pa chen pos mdzad pa'i rten 'brel stod pa legs bshad snying po*. Sarnath: CIHTS, 1994.

———. *Ācārya Nāgārjuna's Bodhicittavivaraṇa and Ācārya Kamalaśīla's Bodhicittabhāvanā*. Bibliotheca Indo-Tibetan Series 23. Sarnath: CIHTS, 1991.

———. *Bhāvanākramaḥ of Ācārya Kamalaśīla*. Bibliotheca Indo-Tibetica Series 9. Sarnath: CIHTS, 1997.

Gyalwang Chöjé (Rgyal dbang Chos rje). *'Jam mgon chos kyi rgyal po tsong kha pa chen po'i rnam thar*. Sarnath: Gelugpa Students' Welfare Committee, 2000.

Jamyang Shepai Dorje ('Jam dbyangs bzhad ba'i Rdo rje). *Grub mtha'i rnam bshad kun bzang zhing gi nyi ma*. Tsho sngon: Kan su'i mi rigs par khang, 1992.

Karmapa Mikyö Dorje (Kar ma pa Mi skyod rdo rje). *Dbu ma la 'jug pa'i rnam bshad dpal ldan lus gsum mkhyen pa'i zhal lung dag rgyud grub pa'i shing rta*. Blockprint, n.d.

Khedrub Jé (Mkhas grub Rje). *Dbu ma'i stong thun skal bzang mig 'byed*. Dharamsala: Sherig Press, n.d.

Khenpo Künzang Palden (Mkhan po Kun bzang dpal ldan). *Byang chub sems pa'i dpyod pa la 'jug pa'i tshig 'grel 'jam dbyangs bla ma'i zhal lung bdud tsi'i thig pa*. Sarnath: Nyingmapa Students' Welfare Committee, 1993.

Khenzur Pema Gyaltsen (Mkhen zur Pad ma rgyal tshan). *Zab don gdams pa'i mig 'byed gser gyi thur ma*, vol. 3. Mundgod: Drepung Loseling Printing Press, 1984.

Khenzur Tenpa Tenzin (Mkhan zur Bstan pa bstan 'dzin). *Lta ba'i mnyams mgyur thun mongs ma yin pa a ma ngo shes kyi bsdus don gnad kyi drung thig dang de'i rnam bshad grub bzhi'i snying nor*. Mundgod: Drepung Loseling Printing Press, 1983.

Khoru Tsenam (Khro ru tse nams). *Dpal mnyam med mar pa dka' brgyud kyi grub pa'i mtha' rnam par nges par byed pa mdor bsdus su brjod pa dwags brgyud grub pa'i mi long*. Gang can rig 'gya'i sgo 'byed lde mig, vol. XIII. Peking: Mi rigs dpe skrun khang, 1989.

———. *Gang ljongs rgyal bstan yongs rtogs kyi phyi mo snga 'gyur rnying ma'i lugs kyi lta sgom spyod gsum gyi rnam gzhag mdo tsam brjod pa tshes pa'i lda ba*. Gang can rig 'gya'i sgo 'byed lde mig, vol. XII. Peking: Mi rigs dpe skrun khang, 1989.

Kunkhyen Pema Karpo (Kun mkhyen Pad ma dkar po). *Dbu ma'i gzhung gsum gsal byed*. Sarnath: Kargyud Students' Welfare Committee, n.d.

Legs par bshad pa bka' gdams rin po che'i gsungs gi gces btus nor bu'i bang mdzod. Ziling: Mtsho sngon mi rigs pde skrun khang, 1995.

Lobsang Palden (Blo bzang dpal ldan). *Dpal mnyam med ri bo dge ldan pa'i grub mtha' rnam gzhag mdo tsam brjod pa 'jam mgon bstan pa'i mdzes rgyan*. Gangs can rig 'brgya'i sgo 'byed lde mig, vol. X. Peking: Mi rigs dpe skrun khang, 1988.

Longchen Rabjam (Klong chen Rab 'byams). *Grub mtha' rin chen mdzod*, vol. 6. Gangtok, Sikkim: Khyentse Labrang, 1983.

Maja Jangchub Tsöndü (Sma ja Byang chub rtson grus). *Dbu ma rtsa ba shes rab kyi 'grel ba 'thad pa'i rgyan*. Delhi: XVI Karmapa, 1974.

Mipham Rinpoche (Mi pham Rin po che). *Don rnam par nges pa'i shes rab ral gri*. *The Collected Writings*, vol. 3. Gangtok: Sonam Topgyal Kazi, 1976.

———. *Nges shes rin po che' sgron me*. *The Collected Writings*, vol. 8. Gangtok: Sonam Topgyal Kazi, 1976.

———. *Dbud ma la 'jug pa'i 'grel pa zla ba'i zhal lung dri med shel phreng*. Sarnath: Nyingmapa Students' Welfare Committee, 1977.

———. *Dbu ma rtsa ba'i mchan 'grel gnas lugs rab gsal*. *The Collected Writings*, vol. 1. Gangtok: Sonam Topgyal Kazi, 1979.

———. *Brgal lan nyin byed snang ba.* Sarnath: Nyingmapa Students' Welfare Committee, 1993.
———. *Dam chos dogs sel.* Sarnath: Nyingmapa Students' Welfare Committee, 1993.
———. *Gzhan gyis brtsad pa'i lan mdor bsdus pa rigs lam rab gsal de nyid snang byed.* Sarnath: Nyingmapa Students' Welfare Committee, 1993.
———. *Shes rab kyi le'u 'grel pa nor bu ke ta ka.* Sarnath: Nyingmapa Students' Welfare Committee, 1993.
Palman Könchok Gyaltsen (Dpal man Dkon mchog rgyal mtshan). *Bden gtam snying rje'i rol mtsho las zur du phyung ba sa rnying bka' brgyud sogs kyi khyad par mgo smos tsam mu to'i rgyangs 'bod kyi tshul du bya gtong snyan sgron bdud rtsi'i bsang gtor. The Collected Works of Dpal man Dkon mchog rgyal mtshan,* vol. 6. Delhi: Gyaltan Gelek Namgyal, 1974.
———. *Gyi na ba zhig gi gzu bo'i sprin rum las 'ong ba'i bden gtam bdud rtsir 'khyil ba'i snying rje'i rol mtsho. The Collected Works of Dpal man Dkon mchog rgyal mtshan,* vol. 6. Delhi: Gyaltan Gelek Namgyal, 1974.
Rendawa (Red mda ba). Pema Tenzin (Padma Bstan 'dzin), ed. and trans. *Bshes pa'i spring yin yig gi 'grel pa don gsal.* Sarnath: CIHTS, 1996.
———. *Dbu ma bzhi brgya ba'i 'grel pa.* Sarnath: Sakya Students' Union, 1987.
———. *Dbu ma 'jug pa'i rnam bshad de kno na nyid gsal ba'i sgron ma.* Sarnath: Sakyapa Students' Union, 1995.
Rongtön Shakya Gyaltsen (Rong ston Śākya rgyal mtshan). *Dbu ma rigs pa'i tsogs kyi dka' ba'i gnad stan pa rigs lam kun gsal.* Blockprint, n.d.
———. *Dbu ma'i lta khrid kyi bsdus don snying po'e gsal byed.* Blockprint, n.d.
———. *Shes rab snying po'i rnam bshad yum don rab gsal.* Blockprint, n.d.
———. *Dbu ma tsa ba'i rnam bshad zab mo'i di kho na nyid snang ba.* Sarnath: Sakya Students' Union, 1995.
Rtsa ba phyogs bsdus. Sarnath: Sakya Students' Union, 1996.
Sakya Paṇḍita (Sa skya Paṇḍita). *Gzhung lugs legs par bshad pa. The Sakya 'Bka' 'bum,* vol. 5. Tokyo: The Toyo Bunko, 1968.
———. *Thub pa'i dgongs pa rab tu gsal ba. The Sakya 'Bka'' bum,* vol. 5. Tokyo: The Toyo Bunko, 1968.
———. *Sgom gsum rab tu dbye ba'i stan bcos.* Delhi: Sherig Parkhang, Sonam Tsering, n.d.
Sera Jetsün Chökyi Gyaltsen (Se ra Rje tsun Chos kyi rgyal mtshan). *Zab mo stong pa nyid kyi lta ba la log rtog 'gog par byed pa'i bstan bcos lta ba ngan pa'i mun sel zhes bya ba bshes gnyen chen po śākya mchog ldan pa la gdams pa.* New Delhi: Tibet House, 1969.
Shakya Chogden (Śākya Mchog ldan). *Bden pa gyis kyi gnas la 'jug pa nges don bdud rtsi'i thigs pa. The Complete Works,* vol. 5. Thimpu, Bhutan: Kunzang Tobgey, 1975.
———. *Dbu ma 'jug pa'i dka' ba'i gnad rnam par bshad pa ku mud phren mrdzes. The Complete Works,* vol. 5. Thimpu, Bhutan: Kunzang Tobgey, 1975.
———. *Dbu ma 'jug pa'i rnam bshad nges don gnad kyi ṭīkā. The Complete Works,* vol. 5. Thimpu, Bhutan: Kunzang Tobgey, 1975.
———. *Dbu ma chen po'i sgom rim 'khrul spong dbyangs kyi rnga sgra. The Complete Works,* vol. 5. Thimpu, Bhutan: Kunzang Tobgey, 1975.
———. *Dbu ma rtsa ba'i rnam bshad skal bzang 'jug ngogs. The Complete Works,* vol. 5. Thimpu, Bhutan: Kunzang Tobgey, 1975.

———. *Dbu ma'i byung tshul rnam par bshad pa'i gtam yid bzhin lhun po. The Complete Works,* vol. 5. Thimpu, Bhutan: Kunzang Tobgey, 1975.
———. *Stong thun chung ba dbang po'i rdu rje blo gsal mgu byed. The Complete Works,* vol. 5. Thimpu, Bhutan: Kunzang Tobgey, 1975.
———. *Theg pa chen po dbu ma rnam par nges pa'i bang mdzod lung rigs rgya mtsho las bden pa gnyis kyi rnam bzhag le'u bzhi pa. The Complete Works,* vol. 15. Thimphu, Bhutan: Kunzang Tobgey, 1975.
———. *Theg pa chen po dbu ma rnam par nges pa'i bang mdzod lung rigs rgya mtsho las kun rdzob bden pa'i rnam bshad le'u lnga pa. The Complete Works,* vol. 15. Thimphu, Bhutan: Kunzang Tobgey, 1975.
———. *Theg pa chen po dbu ma rnam par nges pa'i bang mdzod lung rigs rgya mtsho las don dam rnam bshad le'u drug pa. The Complete Works,* vol. 15. Thimphu, Bhutan: Kunzang Tobgey, 1975.
———. *Theg pa chen po dbu ma rnam par nges pa'i bang mdzod lung rigs rgya mtsho las gang zag bdag med le'u bdun pa. The Complete Works,* vol. 15. Thimphu, Bhutan: Kunzang Tobgey, 1975.
———. *Theg pa chen po dbu ma rnam par nges pa'i bang mdzod lung rigs rgya mtsho las bdag med sgrub rigs le'u brgyad pa. The Complete Works,* vol. 15. Thimphu, Bhutan: Kunzang Tobgey, 1975.
———. *Theg pa chen po dbu ma rnam par nges pa'i bang mdzod lung rigs rgya mtsho las lta ba'i gnas le'u dgu pa. The Complete Works,* vol. 15. Thimphu, Bhutan: Kunzang Tobgey, 1975.
———. *Theg pa chen po dbu ma rnam par nges pa'i bang mdzod lung rigs rgya mtsho las thabs shes bzung 'jug le'u bcu pa. The Complete Works,* vol. 15. Thimphu, Bhutan: Kunzang Tobgey, 1975.
———. *Theg pa chen po dbu ma rnam par nges pa'i bang mdzod lung rigs rgya mtsho las 'bras bu sku gnyis zung 'jug le'u bcu gcig pa dang dbu ma'i phan yon bstan pa'i le'u bcu gnyis pa. The Complete Works,* vol. 15. Thimphu, Bhutan: Kunzang Tobgey, 1975.
———. *Zab mo spros bral gyi bshad pa stong nyid bdud rtsi'i lam po che. The Complete Works,* vol. 5. Thimpu, Bhutan: Kunzang Tobgey, 1975.
Sun, Tang-yi. *Bod rgya tshig mdzod chen mo.* Peking: Mi Rigs Press, 1993.
Taktsang Lotsawa (Stag tsang Lo tsā ba). *Grub mtha' kun shes nas mtha' bral sgrub pa zhes bya ba'i stan cos rnam par bshad pa legs bshad rgya mtsho.* Blockprint, n.d.
———. *Grub mtha' kun shes nas mtha' bral sgrub pa zhes bya ba'i bstan cos.* Blockprint, n.d.
Tenzin Chödak (Bstan 'dzin chos grags). *Gang ljongs lo rgyus thog gi grags can mi sna.* Tibet: Bod ljongs Mi rigs Press, 1993.
Thupten Chödak (Thub stan chos grags). *Spyod 'jug gi 'grel bshad rgyal sras yon tan bum bzang.* Tsho sngon: Mi rigs Press, 1990.
Tsongkhapa Lobsang Dragpa (Tsong kha pa Blo bzang grags pa). *Rtsa ba shes rab kyi dka' gnas chen po brgyad kyi bshad pa.* Sarnath: Pleasure of Elegant Sayings Press, 1970.
———. *Dbu ma dgongs pa rab gsal.* Sarnath: Gelugpa Students' Welfare Committee, 1984.
———. *Lam gtso rnam gsum gyi rtsa ba.* In the *Dbu ma'i lta khrid phyogs bsdebs.* Sarnath: Gelugpa Students' Welfare Committee, 1985.
———. *Rtsa shes ṭīk chen rigs pa'i mrgya mtso.* Sarnath: Gelugpa Students' Welfare Committee, 1992.

———. *Byang chub lam gyi rim pa chen mo.* Sarnath: Gelugpa Students' Welfare Committee, 1993.

———. *Rten 'brel stod pa legs bshad snying po.* In Ācārya Gyaltsen Namdol and Ācārya Ngawang Samten, trans. and ed. *Pratītyasamutpādastutisubhāṣitahṛdayam of Ācārya Tsongkhapa.* Dalai Lama's Tibeto-Indological Series, vol. 3. Sarnath: CIHTS, 1994.

———. *Lam gtso rnam gsum.* In the *Zhal 'don phyogs bsdebs.* Sarnath: Gelugpa Students' Welfare Committee, 1995.

———. *Drang nges legs bshad snying po.* In Geshe Yeshé Tabkhé's *Shar tsong kha pa'i drang ba dang nges pa'i don rnam par byed pa'i bstan bcos legs bshad snying po.* Sarnath: CIHTS, 1997.

Tuken Chökyi Nyima (Thu'u bkwan Chos kyi nyi ma). *Thu'u bkwan grub mtha.* Kan su: Kansu'i mi rig dpe skrun khang, 1985.

Yeshé Tabkhé, Geshe (Dge shes Ye shes thabs mkhas). *Shar tsong kha pa'i drang ba dang nges pa'i don rnam par 'byed pa'i bstan bcos legs bshad snying po.* Sarnath: CIHTS, 1997.

Yönten Zangpo (Yon bstan bzang po). *Rgyu 'bras theg pa mchog gi gnas lugs zab mo'i don rnam par nges pa rje jo nang pa'i chen po'i ring lugs 'jigs med gdongs lnga'i nga ro.* Gang can rig 'gya'i sgo 'byed lde mig, vol. XV. Peking: Mi rigs dpe skrun khang, 1990.

English-language Sources

Akira, Hirakawa. *A History of Indian Buddhism: From Śākyamuni to Early Mahāyāna.* Delhi: Motilal Banarsidass, 1998.

Bodhi, Bhikkhu. *Transcendental Dependent Arising: A Translation and Exposition of the Upanisa Sutta.* Kandy, Sri Lanka: Buddhist Publication Society, 1980.

———. "A Look At the Kālāma Sutta." Kandy, Sri Lanka: Buddhist Publication Society, 1988.

———. *Nourishing the Roots: Essays on Buddhist Ethics.* Kandy, Sri Lanka: Buddhist Publication Society, 1990.

———. "A Buddhist Response to Contemporary Dilemmas of Human Existence." Kandy, Sri Lanka: Buddhist Publication Society, 1993.

———. "From Views to Vision." Kandy, Sri Lanka: Buddhist Publication Society, 1994.

———. *The Noble Eightfold Path: The Way to the End of Suffering.* Kandy, Sri Lanka: Buddhist Publication Society, 1994.

———. "Dhamma and Nonduality." Kandy, Sri Lanka: The Buddhist Publication Society, 1995.

———. "Towards a Threshold of Understanding." Kandy, Sri Lanka: Buddhist Publication Society, 1995.

———, trans. *The Connected Discourses of the Buddha: A New Translation of the Saṃyutta Nikāya.* Boston: Wisdom Publications, 2000.

Broughton, J.L., trans. *The Bodhidharma Anthology: The Earliest Records of Zen.* Berkeley: University of California Press, n.d.

Buddhaghosa, Ācārya. *The Path of Purification: A Translation of Visuddhimagga by Bhadanācariya Buddhaghosa.* Bhikkhu Ñāṇamoli, trans. Taipei, Taiwan: The Corporate Body of the Buddha Educational Foundation, 2001.

Buddharakkhita, Ācharya, trans. *The Dhammapada: The Buddha's Path of Wisdom.* Kandy, Sri Lanka: Buddhist Publication Society, 1995.

———. *Metta: The Philosophy and Practice of Universal Love.* Kandy, Sri Lanka: Buddhist Publication Society, 1995.

Cabezón, José I., "Two Views on the Svātantrika-Prāsaṅgika Distinction in Fourteenth-Century Tibet." In Dreyfus and McClintock, eds., *The Svātantrika-Prāsaṅgika Distinction.* Boston: Wisdom Publications, 2003.

———. "The Canonization of Philosophy and the Rhetoric of Siddhānta in Indo-Tibetan Buddhism." In J. Timm, ed., *Texts in Context: Traditional Hermeneutics in South Asia.* Albany: State University of New York Press, 1991.

———. *A Dose of Emptiness: An Annotated Translation of the sTong thun chen mo of mKhas grub dGe legs dpal bzang.* Albany: State University of New York Press, 1992.

Cabezon, José and Lobsang Dargyay. *Freedom from Extremes: Gorampa's "Distinguishing the Views" and the Polemics of Emptiness.* Boston: Wisdom Publications, 2007.

Carr, Brian, and Indra Mahalingam. *Companion Encyclopedia of Asian Philosophy.* New York: Routledge, 2001.

Chang, Garma C.C., trans. *A Treasury of Mahāyāna Sūtras: Sections from the Mahāratnakūṭa Sūtra.* Delhi: Motilal Banarsidass, 2002.

Chatterjee, A.K. *The Yogācāra Idealism.* BHU Darsana Series no. 3. Benares: Benares Hindu University, 1999.

Chimpa, Lama, and Debiprasad Chattopadhyaya, trans. *Tāranātha's History of Buddhism in India.* Delhi: Motilal Banarsidass, 1990.

Cozort, Daniel. *Unique Tenets of the Middle Way Consequence School.* Ithaca, NY: Snow Lion Publications, 1998.

De Barry, W. M. Theodore. *Sources of Indian Tradition,* vol. 1. New York: Columbia University Press, 1958.

Döl-bo-ba Shay-rap-gyel-tsen [Dol po pa Shes rab rgyal mtshan]. *Mountain Doctrine: Tibet's Fundamental Treatise on Other-Emptiness and the Buddha-Matrix.* Trans. by Jeffrey Hopkins. Ed. by Kevin Vose. Ithaca, NY: Snow Lion Publications, 2006.

Dreyfus, Georges B.J. *Recognizing Reality: Dharmakīrti's Philosophy and Its Tibetan Interpretations.* Albany: State University of New York Press, 1997.

———. "Would the True Prāsaṅgika Please Stand? The Case and View of 'Ju Mi Pham." In Dreyfus and McClintock, eds., *The Svātantrika-Prāsaṅgika Distinction.* Boston: Wisdom Publications, 2003.

Dreyfus, Georges B.J., and Sara L. McClintock, eds. *The Svātantrika-Prāsaṅgika Distinction: What Difference Does a Difference Make?* Boston: Wisdom Publications, 2003.

Garfield, Jay L. *The Fundamental Wisdom of The Middle Way: Nāgārjuna's Mūlamadhyamkakārikā.* New York: Oxford University Press, 1995.

———. *Empty Words: Buddhist Philosophy and Cross-Cultural Interpretation.* New York: Oxford University Press, 2001.

Glasenapp, H.V. *Vedanta and Buddhism: A Comparative Study.* Sri Lanka: Buddhist Publication Society, 1995.

Hall, B.C. "The Meaning of Vijñapti in Vasubandu's Concept of Mind." *Journal of International Association of Buddhist Studies* 9, no. 1 (1986): 7–24.

Harvey, Peter. *An Introduction to Buddhism: Teachings, History and Practices.* Cambridge: Cambridge University Press, 2000.

———. *An Introduction to Buddhist Ethics: Foundations, Values and Issues.* Cambridge: Cambridge University Press, 2000.

Honderich, Ted. *The Oxford Companion to Philosophy.* New York: Oxford University Press, 1995.

Hopkins, Jeffrey. *Emptiness Yoga: The Tibetan Middle Way.* Delhi: Motilal Banarsidass, 1995.

———. *Meditation on Emptiness.* Boston: Wisdom Publications, 1996.

Horner, I.B., trans. *Milinda's Question,* vol. I. *Sacred Books of the Buddhists,* vol. XXII. Oxford: The Pali Text Society, 1996.

———. *Milinda's Question,* vol. II. *Sacred Books of the Buddhists,* vol. XXIII. Oxford: The Pali Text Society, 1999.

Huntington, C.W. "The System of Two Truths in the *Prasannapadā* and the *Madhyamakāvatāra:* A Study in Madhyamaka Soteriology." *Journal of Indian Philosophy* 11 (1983): 77–106.

———. *The Emptiness of Emptiness: An Introduction to Early Indian Mādhyamika.* Honolulu: University of Hawaii Press, 1994.

Jinpa, Thupten. "Delineating Reason's Scope for Negation: Tsongkhapa's Contribution to Madhyamaka's Dialectical Method." *Journal of Indian Philosophy* 26 (1998): 275–308.

———. *Self, Reality and Reason in Tibetan Philosophy: Tsongkhapa's Quest for the Middle Way.* New York: RoutledgeCurzon, 2002.

Jones, J.J., trans. *The Mahāvastu,* vol. II. *Sacred Books of the Buddhists,* vol. XVIII. London: The Pali Text Society, 1976.

———, trans. *The Mahāvastu,* vol. III. *Sacred Books of the Buddhists,* vol. XIX. London: The Pali Text Society, 1978.

———, trans. *The Mahāvastu,* vol. I. *Sacred Books of the Buddhists,* vol. XVI. London: The Pali Text Society, 1987.

Kalupahana, David J. *Mūlamadhyamakakārikā of Nāgārjuna: The Philosophy of the Middle Way.* Albany: State University of New York Press, 1986.

Kapstein, Mathew T. "Abhayākaragupta on the Two Truths." In his *Reason's Traces: Identity and Interpretation in Indian and Tibetan Buddhist Thought.* Boston: Wisdom Publications, 2001.

———. "From Kun-mkhyen Dol-po-pa to 'Ba'-mda' Dge-legs: Three Jo-nang-pa Masters on the Interpretation of the *Prajñāpāramitā.*" In his *Reason's Traces: Identity and Interpretation in Indian and Tibetan Buddhist Thought.* Boston: Wisdom Publications, 2001.

———. "The Trouble with Truth: Heidegger on *Alétheia,* Buddhist Thinkers on *Satya.*" In his *Reason's Traces: Identity and Interpretation in Indian and Tibetan Buddhist Thought.* Boston: Wisdom Publications, 2001.

Keown, Damien. *Contemporary Buddhist Ethics.* Richmond, Surrey: Curzon Press, 2000.

———. *The Nature of Buddhist Ethics.* New York: Palgrave Publishers, 2001.

Khema, Sister Ayya. "Meditation on No-Self." Kandy, Sri Lanka: Buddhist Publication Society, 1994.

King, Winston L. *In Hope of Nibbāna.* La Salle: Open Court, 1964.

Klein, Anne. *Knowing, Naming, and Negation: A Sourcebook on Tibetan Sautrāntika.* Ithaca, NY: Snow Lion Publications, 1991.

La Vallée Poussin, Louis de. "Madhyamaka." In Samdhong Rinpoche, ed., *Mādhyamika Dialectic and the Philosophy of Nāgārjuna.* Sarnath: CIHTS, 1985.

Lindtner, Christian. "Atiśa's Introduction to the Two Truths, and Its Sources." *Journal of Indian Philosophy* 9 (1981): 161–214.

———. *Nagarjuniana: Studies in the Writings and Philosophy of Nāgārjuna,* vol. II. Delhi: Motilal Banarsidass, 1982.

———. *Master of Wisdom: Writings of the Buddhist Master Nāgārjuna.* Oakland, CA: Dharma Press, 1986.

———. *Nagarjuniana: Studies in the Writings and Philosophy of Nāgārjuna.* New Delhi: Motilal Banarsidass, 1987.

Lodrö, Geshe Gendün. *Walking through Walls: A Presentation of Tibetan Meditation.* Jeffrey Hopkins, ed. and trans. Ithaca, NY: Snow Lion Publications, 1992.

Lopez, Donald S., Jr. *Elaborations on Emptiness: Uses of the Heart Sūtra.* Princeton: Princeton University Press, 1996.

———. *The Madman's Middle Way: Reflections on Reality of the Tibetan Monk Gendun Chopel.* Chicago: University of Chicago Press, 2006.

Mahāsi Sayadaw and Nyanaponika Thera, trans. *The Progress of Insight (Visuddhiñanakatha): A Modern Treatise on Buddhist Satipaṭṭhāna Meditation.* Kandy, Sri Lanka: Buddhist Publication Society, 1994.

Mitchell, Donald. W. *Buddhism: Introducing the Buddhist Experience.* New York: Oxford University Press, 2002.

Murti, T.R.V. *The Central Philosophy of Buddhism.* London: Allen & Unwin, 1955.

———. Preface to Samdhong Rinpoche, ed., *Mādhyamika Dialectic and the Philosophy of Nāgārjuna.* Sarnath: CIHTS, 1985.

Nagao, G.M. "An Interpretation of the Term *Saṃvṛti* (Convention) in Buddhism." *Silver Jubilee Volume of the Zinbun Kagaku Kenkyo,* pp. 550–61.

Nakamura, Hajime. *Indian Buddhism.* Hirakata City: Kansai University of Foreign Studies Press, 1980.

———. *Indian Buddhism: A Survey with Bibliographical Notes.* Delhi: Motilal Banarsidass, 1999.

Ñāṇamoli, Bhikkhu. *Three Cardinal Discourses of the Buddha.* Kandy, Sri Lanka: Buddhist Publication Society, 1995.

———. *The Life of the Buddha.* Colombo: The Buddhist Publication Society, 1998.

———, trans. *The Path of Purification: A Translation of Visuddhimagga by Bhadanācariya Buddhaghosa.* Taipei, Taiwan: The Corporate Body of the Buddha Educational Foundation, 2001.

Ñāṇamoli, Bhikkhu, trans., and Bhikkhu Bodhi, ed. and revised. *The Discourse on Right View: The Sammādiṭṭhi Sutta and Its Commentary.* Kandy, Sri Lanka: Buddhist Publication Society, 1994.

Ñāṇamoli, Bhikkhu, and Bhikkhu Bodhi, trans. *The Middle Length Discourses of the Buddha: A Translation of the Majjhima Nikāya.* Boston: Wisdom Publications, 1995.

Narada Mahāthera, adapted and trans. *Everyman's Ethics: Four Discourses of the Buddha.* Kandy, Sri Lanka: Buddhist Publication Society, 1995.

———. *Buddhism in a Nutshell.* Kandy, Sri Lanka: Buddhist Publication Society, 1995.

Narain, Harsha. "The Nature of Mādhyamika Thought." In Samdhong Rinpoche, ed., *The Mādhyamika Dialectic and the Philosophy of Nāgārjuna.* Sarnath: CIHTS, 1985.

Narasu, P. Lakshmi. *The Essence of Buddhism.* Taipei: The Corporate Body of the Buddha Educational Foundation, 1993.

Newland, Guy. *The Two Truths.* Ithaca, NY: Snow Lion Publications, 1992.

Nyanaponika Thera, and Hellmut Hecker. *Great Disciples of the Buddha: Their Lives, Their Works, Their Legacy.* Boston: Wisdom Publications, 1997.

Pabongka Rinpoche. *Liberation in the Palm of Your Hand: A Concise Discourse on the Path to Enlightenment.* Trijang Rinpoche, ed. Michael Richards, trans. Boston: Wisdom Publications, 1991.

Pettit, John W. *Mipham's Beacon of Certainty: Illuminating the View of Dzogchen, the Great Perfection.* Boston: Wisdom Publications, 1999.

Powers, John, trans. *Wisdom of Buddha: the Saṃdhinirmocana Sūtra.* Berkeley, CA: Dharma Publishing, 1995.

———. *An Introduction to Tibetan Buddhism.* Ithaca, NY: Snow Lion Publications, 1995.

Rahula, Walpola. *What the Buddha Taught.* New York: Grove Press, 1974.

Ramanan, K.V. *Nāgārjuna's Philosophy as Presented in the Mahā-Prajñāpāramitā-Śāstra.* Delhi: Motilal Banarsidass, 1987.

Ruegg, David S. *The Literature of the Madhyamaka School of Philosophy in India.* Wiesbaden: Otto Harrassowitz, 1981.

———. "Indian and the Indic in Tibetan Cultural History, and Tsoṅ khapa's Achievement as a Scholar and Thinker: An Essay on the Concepts of Buddhism in Tibet and Tibetan Buddhism." *Journal of Indian Philosophy* 32 (2004): 321–43.

Samdhong Rinpoche, ed. *Mādhyamika Dialectic and the Philosophy of Nāgārjuna.* Sarnath: CIHTS, 1985.

———, ed. *Ten Suttas from Dīgha Nikāya: Long Discourses of the Buddha.* Sarnath: CIHTS, 1987.

Śāntideva. *The Bodhicāryātāra.* Kate Crosby and Andrew Skilton, trans. New York: Oxford University Press, 1995.

Sharma, P. *Śāntideva's Bodhicaryāvatāra: Original Sanskrit Text with English Translation.* New Delhi: Aditya Prakashan, 1997.

Siderits, Mark. "Causation and Emptiness in Early Madhyamaka." *Journal of Indian Philosophy* 32 (2004): 393–419.

Sing, R.P.B. *Where the Buddha Walked: A Companion to the Buddhist Places in India.* Delhi: INDICA, 2003.

Singh, Jaideva. "Introduction" in Theodore Stcherbatsky's *The Conception of Buddhist Nirvāṇa.* Delhi: Motilal Banarasidass, 1989.

Sogyal Rinpoche. *The Tibetan Book of Living and Dying.* Sydney: Random House Australia, 1992.

Sonam Rinchen, Geshe. *The Yogic Deeds of Bodhisattvas: Gyeltsap on Āryadeva's Four Hundred.* Ruth Sonam, ed. and trans. Ithaca, NY: Snow Lion Publications, 1994.

Sopa, Geshe Lhundub, and Jeffrey Hopkins. *The Practice and Theory of Tibetan Buddhism.* Ithaca, NY: Snow Lion Publications, 1990.

Spiro, Melford E. *Buddhism and Society: A Great Tradition and Its Burmese Vicissitudes.* Berkeley: University of California Press, 1982.

Sprung, Mervyn. *Lucid Exposition of the Middle Way: The Essential Chapters from the Prasannapadā of Candrakīrti.* Boulder, CO: Prajñā Press, 1979.

———, ed. *The Problem of the Two Truths in Buddhism and Vedanta.* Dordrecht: Reidel, 1973.

Stcherbatsky, T. *The Conception of Buddhist Nirvāṇa.* Delhi: Motilal Banarasidass, 1998.

Stearns, Cyrus. *The Buddha from Dolpo: A Study of the Life and Thought of the Tibetan Master Dolpopa Sherab Gyaltsen.* Albany: State University of New York Press, 1999.

Streng, Frederick. "The Buddhist Doctrine of Two Truths." *Journal of Indian Philosophy* 1 (1971): 262–71.

Tāranātha. *Tāranātha's History of Buddhism in India.* Lama Chimpa and Debiprasad Chattopadhyaya, trans. and ed. Delhi: Motilal Banarsidass, 1990.

Tauscher, Helmut. "Phya pa chos kyi senge ge as a Svātantrika." In Dreyfus and McClintock, eds., *The Svātantrika-Prāsaṅgika Distinction.* Boston: Wisdom Publications, 2003.

Thakchoe, Sonam. "The Relationship between the Two Truths: A Comparative Analysis of Two Tibetan Accounts." *Contemporary Buddhism: An Interdisciplinary Journal* 5, no. 2 (2003): 111–26.

———."How Many Truths? Are There Two Truths or One in the Tibetan Prāsaṅgika Madhyamaka?" *Contemporary Buddhism: An Interdisciplinary Journal* 4, no 2. (2004): 121–41. 2004.

Thanissaro Bhikkhu, trans. and expl. *The Wings to Awakening: An Anthology from the Pali Canon.* Taipei: The Corporate Body of the Buddha Educational Foundation, 1996.

———. *Itivuttaka: This Was Said by the Buddha.* Barre, MA: Dhamma Dana Publications, 2001.

———. "Questions of Skill," 2001.
www.accesstoinsight.org/lib/authors/thanissaro/ questions.html.

———. *The Mind Like Fire Unbound: An Image in the Early Buddhist Discourses.* Barre, MA: Dhamma Dana Publication, 2001.

———. trans. *An Anthology of Selected Suttas from the Majjhima Nikāya.*
www.accessto insight.org/canon/majjhima/index.html.

———. *An Anthology of Selected Suttas from the Saṃyutta Nikāya.*
www.accesstoinsight.org/canon/samyutta/index.html.

———. *An Anthology of Selected Suttas from the Digha Nikāya.*
www.accesstoinsight.org /canon/digha/index.html.

———. *An Anthology of Selected Suttas from the Aṇguttara Nikāya.*
www.accesstoinsight.org/canon/anguttara/index.html.

———. *An Anthology of Selected Suttas from the Khuddaka Nikāya.*
www.accesstoinsight.org/canon/khuddaka/index.html.

———. *An Anthology of Selected Suttas from the Sutta Nipāta.*
www.accesstoinsight.org/ canon/khuddaka/suttanipata/index.html.

———. *An Anthology of Selected Suttas from the Udāna.*
www.accesstoinsight.org/ canon/khuddaka/udana/index.html.

———. "Nibbāna." www.accesstoinsight.org/lib/authors/thanissaro/nibbana. html.

Thomas, J. Edward. *The Life of Buddha: As Legend and History.* Delhi: Motilal Banarsidass, 1997.

Thurman, Robert A.F., trans. and ed. *Life and Teachings of Tsong Khapa.* Dharamsala: Library of Tibetan Works and Archives, 1982.

———. *Tsong Khapa's Speech of Gold in the Essence of True Eloquence.* Princeton: Princeton University Press, 1984.

———, trans. *The Holy Teaching of Vimalakīrti: A Mahāyāna Scripture.* Delhi: Motilal Banarsidass, 1991.

Tillemans, Tom J.E. "Two Tibetan Texts on the 'Neither One nor Many' Argument for Śūnyatā." *Journal of Indian Philosophy* 12, no. 4 (1984): 357–88.

———. *Materials for the Study of Āryadeva, Dharmapāla and Candrakīrti.* The *Catuḥśataka* of Āryadeva, chapters XII and XIII, with the commentaries of Dharmapāla and Candrakīrti: Introduction, translation, Sanskrit, Tibetan, and Chinese texts, notes. 2 vols. Wiener Studien zur Tibetologie und Buddhismuskunde 24.1 and 24.2. Vienna: Arbeitskreis für Tibetische und Buddhistische Studien, 1990.

———. "Metaphysics for Mādhyamikas." In Dreyfus and McClintock, eds. *The Svātantrika-Prāsaṅgika Distinction.* Boston: Wisdom Publications, 2003.

Tillemans, Tom J.E., and Donald S. Lopez. "What Can One Reasonably Say about Nonexistence? A Tibetan Work on the Problem of Āśrayāsiddha." *Journal of Indian Philosophy* 26 (1998): 99–129.

U Na. *Three Fundamental Concepts.* In Samdhong Rinpoche, ed., *Ten Suttas from Dīgha Nikāya.* Sarnath: CIHTS, 1987.

Upadhyaya, K.N. "God, the Self and the Buddha's Silence." In H. Samatani, ed., *Śramaṇa Vidyā.* Sarnath: CIHTS, 1987.

Walshe, Maurice, trans. *The Long Discourses of the Buddha: A Translation of the Dīgha Nikāya.* Boston: Wisdom Publications, 1995.

Williams, Paul, *Mahāyāna Buddhism: The Doctrinal Foundations.* London: Routledge, 1996.

———. *Altruism and Reality: Studies in the Philosophy of the Bodhicaryāvatāra.* Richmond: Curzon Press, 1998.

———. *The Reflexive Nature of Awareness: A Tibetan Madhyamaka Defence.* Richmond: Curzon Press, 1998.

Yoshimizu, C. "Tsong kha pa's Reevaluation of Candrakīrti's Criticism of Autonomous Inference." In Dreyfus and McClintock, eds. *The Svātantrika-Prāsaṅgika Distinction.* Boston: Wisdom Publications, 2003.

Dictionaries

Das, Sarat Candra. *Tibetan-English Dictionary.* Delhi: Motilal Banarsidass, 1991.

Rigzin, Tsepak. *Tibetan-English Dictionary of Buddhist Terminology.* Dharamsala: Library of Tibetan Works and Archives, 1986.

Sun, Tang Yi. *The Great Tibetan-Chinese Dictionary (Bod rgya tshig mdzod chen mo).* Peking: Mi rigs Par khang, 1993.

About Wisdom Publications

Wisdom Publications, a nonprofit publisher, is dedicated to making available authentic works relating to Buddhism for the benefit of all. We publish books by ancient and modern masters in all traditions of Buddhism, translations of important texts, and original scholarship. Additionally, we offer books that explore East-West themes unfolding as traditional Buddhism encounters our modern culture in all its aspects. Our titles are published with the appreciation of Buddhism as a living philosophy, and with the special commitment to preserve and transmit important works from Buddhism's many traditions.

To learn more about Wisdom, or to browse books online, visit our website at www.wisdompubs.org.

You may request a copy of our catalog online or by writing to this address:

Wisdom Publications
199 Elm Street
Somerville, Massachusetts 02144 USA
Telephone: 617-776-7416 • Fax: 617-776-7841
Email: info@wisdompubs.org • www.wisdompubs.org

The Wisdom Trust

As a nonprofit publisher, Wisdom is dedicated to the publication of Dharma books for the benefit of all sentient beings and dependent upon the kindness and generosity of sponsors in order to do so. If you would like to make a donation to Wisdom, you may do so through our website or our Somerville office. If you would like to help sponsor the publication of a book, please write or email us at the address above.

Thank you.

Wisdom is a nonprofit, charitable 501(c)(3) organization affiliated with the Foundation for the Preservation of the Mahayana Tradition (FPMT).

Practicing the Path
A Commentary on the Lamrim Chenmo
Yangsi Rinpoche
Foreword by Geshe Lhundub Sopa
Preface by Lama Zopa Rinpoche
576 pages, ISBN 0-86171-346-X, $24.95

A complete commentary on Lama Tsongkhapa's great exposition on the stages of the path, as rendered by a young, contemporary teacher especially known for his eloquence and clarity.

"Readable and to the point, it brings this great classical tradition 'into the very palms of our hands.'"—José Ignacio Cabezón, XIVth Dalai Lama Professor of Tibetan Buddhism and Cultural Studies, University of California, Santa Barbara

Tantric Ethics
An Explanation of the Precepts for Buddhist Vajrayana Practice
Tsongkhapa
Translated by Gareth Sparham
Foreword by Jeffrey Hopkins
224 pages, ISBN 0-86171-290-0, $16.95

"A masterpiece. *Tantric Ethics* offers a glimpse into one of the most important debates in Tibetan Buddhist thought, and provides fertile ground for reflection on ways to define a Buddhist morality."—*Buddhadharma: The Practitioner's Journal*

"This wonderful book is a must-read for practitioners and scholars alike."—*Mandala*

Freedom from Extremes
Gorampa's "Distinguishing the Views" and the Polemics of Emptiness
José Ignacio Cabezón and Geshe Lobsang Dargyay
448 pages, ISBN 0-86171-523-3, $32.95

"A major contribution to the library of alternative Tibetan views of Madhyamaka. The text translated here is a classic of Tibetan polemical literature in which the great Sakya master Gorampa Sonam Senge presented refutations of the Madhyamaka explanations of both Dolpopa and Tsongkhapa. A wide-ranging introduction sets the stage for the text's meticulously annotated translation."—*Buddhadharma: The Practitioner's Journal*

Meditation on Emptiness
Jeffrey Hopkins
992 pages, ISBN 0-86171-110-6, $29.95

"An essential book for anyone interested in Tibetan Buddhism or Madhyamika philosophy...and an inexhaustible resource for the study of the Dharma and a major contribution to Buddhist studies."—*Buddhist Studies Review*

"An important and invaluble work."—*Tibet Journal*